Risk and Resilience in Military and Veteran Families

Series Editor
Shelley MacDermid Wadsworth
Department of Human Development and Family Studies,
Military Family Research Institute,
Purdue University,
West Lafayette, IN, USA

For further volumes:
http://www.springer.com/series/11919

Shelley MacDermid Wadsworth • David S. Riggs
Editors

Military Deployment and its Consequences for Families

 Springer

Editors
Shelley MacDermid Wadsworth
Department of Human Development
  and Family Studies
Military Family Research Institute
Purdue University
West Lafayette, IN, USA

David S. Riggs
Department of Medical & Clinical
  Psychology
Uniformed Services University
  of the Health Sciences
Bethesda, MD, USA

ISBN 978-1-4614-8711-1   ISBN 978-1-4614-8712-8 (eBook)
DOI 10.1007/978-1-4614-8712-8
Springer New York Heidelberg Dordrecht London

Library of Congress Control Number: 2013953258

Printed on acid-free paper

Springer is part of Springer Science+Business Media (www.springer.com)

To military families everywhere and all who serve them

Acknowledgments

We are grateful to the National Military Family Association for its work on behalf of families; we are pleased that they will receive the proceeds from this book. Of course nothing would have been possible without the contributions of the conference speakers and participants, which in turn were greatly facilitated by the excellent logistical support provided by MFRI staff. We also wish to acknowledge with gratitude the assistance provided by the panel of reviewers who provided constructive feedback:

- Elizabeth Allen, Ph.D., Department of Psychology, University of Colorado at Denver
- Aaron Belkin, Ph.D., Director, Palm Center; Professor, Political Science Department, San Francisco State University
- Adrian Blow, Ph.D. Program Director Couple and Family Therapy Program, Department of Human Development and Family Studies, Michigan State University
- Anita Chandra, Dr.P.H., Senior Policy Researcher & Director, Behavioral and Policy Sciences Department, RAND Corporation
- LtCol. Molinda Chartrand, M.D., United States Air Force
- Sanela Dursun, Ph.D., Director Research—Personnel and Family Support, Canadian Institute for Military and Veteran Health Research, Canada
- Christopher Erbes, Ph.D., Staff Psychologist, Minneapolis VA Health Care System
- Tanja Frančišković, Ph.D., Department of Psychiatry, University of Rijeka, Croatia
- Steffany Fredman, Ph.D., Center for Anxiety & Traumatic Stress Disorders and Home Base Program, Department of Psychiatry, Massachusetts General Hospital and Harvard Medical School
- Briana Nelson Goff, Ph.D., LCMFT, Director, Institute for the Health and Security of Military Families, Professor, School of Family Studies and Human Services, Kansas State University
- Abbie Goldberg, Ph.D., Department of Psychology, Clark University

- Talya Greene, Ph.D., Departments of Social Work and Disaster and Emergency Management, Tel Aviv University, Israel
- Joan M. Griffin, Ph.D., Research Investigator, Center for Chronic Disease Outcomes Research, Minneapolis VA Health System and Associate Professor, Department of Medicine, University of Minnesota Medical School
- Ramon Hinojosa, Ph.D., Research Health Scientist, North Florida/South Georgia Veterans Health System, Department of Veterans Affairs
- Michelle Kees, Department of Child and Adolescent Psychiatry, University of Michigan Health System
- Michelle Kelley, Ph.D., Department of Psychology, Old Dominion University
- Leanne Knobloch, Ph.D., Department of Communication, University of Illinois
- Harold Kudler, M.D., Associate Director, VA Mid-Atlantic Mental Illness Research, Education and Clinical Center and Duke University
- James A. Martin, Ph.D., BCD, COL, USA-Ret, Professor, Graduate School of Social Work and Social Research, Bryn Mawr College
- Laura A. Meis, Ph.D., Center for Chronic Disease Outcomes Research, Department of Medicine, University of Minnesota
- Sarah A. Mustillo, Ph.D., Department of Sociology, Purdue University
- Penny F. Pierce, Ph.D., RN, FAAN, COL, USAFR (ret), Director and Chair, PhD in Nursing Science Program, Uniformed Services University of the Health Sciences
- David S. Riggs, Ph.D., Executive Director, Center for Deployment Psychology, Uniformed Services University of the Health Sciences
- Joyce Wessel Raezer, M.A., Executive Director, National Military Family Association
- Lyndon Riviere, Ph.D., Research Psychologist, Military Psychiatry Branch, Walter Reed Army Institute of Research
- William Saltzman, Ph.D., Associate Director, Nathanson Family Resilience Center, University of California, Los Angeles
- J. Jill Suitor, Ph.D., Department of Sociology, Purdue University
- Shawn D. Whiteman, Ph.D., Department of Human Development and Family Studies, Purdue University
- Steven R. Wilson, Ph.D., Interim Department Head, Brian Lamb School of Communication, Purdue University

Contents

Contributors

Ann-Renée Blais, Ph.D. Psychology Group, Individual Behavior and Performance Section, Defence Research & Development Canada – Toronto, Toronto, ON, Canada

Adrian Blow, Ph.D. Department of Human Development and Family Studies, Michigan State University, East Lansing, MI, USA

Denise V. Brown, M.S. Veterans Affairs Medical Center, Memphis, TN, USA

Emily Hagel Campbell Center for Chronic Disease Outcomes Research, Minneapolis, MN, USA

Kathleen F. Carlson, Ph.D. Department of Veterans Affairs, Portland Center for the Study of Chronic, Comorbid Mental and Physical Disorders, Portland Veterans Affairs Medical Center, Portland, OR, USA

Department of Public Health and Preventive Medicine, Oregon Health and Science University, Portland, OR, USA

Sherry Dyche Ceperich, Ph.D. Hunter Holmes McGuire Veterans Affairs Medical Center, Richmond, VA, USA

Department of Psychology, Virginia Commonwealth University School of Medicine, Richmond, VA, USA

Laurel Davis Department of Family Social Science, University of Minnesota, Minneapolis, MN, USA

Charles Edmund Degeneffe Department of Administration, Rehabilitation and Postsecondary Education, Interwork Institute, San Diego State University, San Diego, CA, USA

Christopher R. Erbes, Ph.D. Minneapolis VA Health Care System, One Veterans Drive, Minneapolis, MN, USA

Center for Chronic Disease Outcomes Research, Minneapolis, MN, USA

University of Minnesota Medical School, Minneapolis, Minneapolis, MN, USA

Hannah Fairman Center for Chronic Disease Outcomes Research, Minneapolis, MN, USA

Deniz Fikretoglu, Ph.D. Psychology Group, Individual Behavior and Performance Section, Defence Research and Development Canada – Toronto, Toronto, ON, Canada

Cathy A. Flynn, Ph.D. Office of Military Community and Family Policy, Office of the Secretary of Defense, Department of Defense, Defense Pentagon, Washington, DC, USA

Tanja Frančišković Department of Psychiatry and Psychological Medicine, School of Medicine, University of Rijeka, Rijeka, Croatia

Melissa M. Franks, Ph.D. Department of Human Development and Family Studies, Purdue University, West Lafayette, IN, USA

Greta Friedemann-Sánchez, Ph.D. Humphrey School of Public Affairs, University of Minnesota, Minneapolis, MN, USA

Abigail Gewirtz, Ph.D., L.P. Department of Family Social Science & Institute of Child Development, University of Minnesota, Minneapolis, MN, USA

Lisa Gorman, Ph.D. Michigan Public Health Institute, Okemos, MI, USA

Marshall J. Graney, Ph.D. Department of Preventive Medicine, University of Tennessee Health Science Center, Memphis, TN, USA

Veterans Affairs Medical Center, Memphis, TN, USA

Amy Gravely, M.A. Department of Veterans Affairs, Minneapolis Health Care System, Center for Chronic Disease Outcomes Research, One Veterans Drive, Minneapolis, MN, USA

Candice Grayton, M.P.H. The CDM Group, Inc., Bethesda, MD, USA

Joan M. Griffin, Ph.D. Department of Veterans Affairs, Minneapolis Health Care System, Center for Chronic Disease Outcomes Research, One Veterans Drive, Minneapolis, MN, USA

Department of Medicine, University of Minnesota Medical School, Minneapolis, MN, USA

Jenny M. Hoobler, Ph.D. Department of Managerial Studies, College of Business Administration, University of Illinois at Chicago, Chicago, IL, USA

Linda Hughes-Kirchubel Military Family Research Institute, Purdue University, West Lafayette, IN, USA

Chris Jarman Department of Human Development and Family Studies, Michigan State University, East Lansing, MI, USA

Agnes C. Jensen, B.S. Department of Veterans Affairs, Minneapolis Health Care System, Center for Chronic Disease Outcomes Research, One Veterans Drive, Minneapolis, MN, USA

Alexandria K. Johnson Center for Chronic Disease Outcomes Research, Minneapolis, MN, USA

Michelle Kees, Ph.D. Department of Child and Adolescent Psychiatry, University of Michigan, Ann Arbor, MI, USA

Miro Klarić, M.D., Ph.D. Department of Psychiatry, University Hospital Mostar, Mostar, Bosnia and Herzegovina

Meredith Kleykamp, Ph.D. Department of Sociology, University of Maryland, College Park, MD, USA

Leanne K. Knobloch, Ph.D. Department of Communication, University of Illinois, Urbana, IL, USA

Mark Kramer, Ph.D. Center for Chronic Disease Outcomes Research, Minneapolis, MN, USA

Mary Jo Larson, Ph.D., M.P.A. Heller School for Social Policy & Management, Brandeis University Waltham, MA, USA

Laura Lorenz, Ph.D., M.Ed. Heller School for Social Policy & Management, Brandeis University, Waltham, MA, USA

Jennifer Martindale-Adams, Ed.D. Department of Preventive Medicine, University of Tennessee Health Science Center, Memphis, TN, USA

Veterans Affairs Medical Center, Memphis, TN, USA

Donald R. McCreary, Ph.D. Psychology Group, Individual Behavior and Performance Section, Defence Research and Development Canada – Toronto, Toronto, ON, Canada

Patricia E. Miller, M.A., N.C.C. Department of Preventive Medicine, University of Tennessee Health Science Center, Memphis, TN, USA

Veterans Affairs Medical Center, Memphis, TN, USA

Beth A. Mohr, M.S. Heller School for Social Policy & Management, Brandeis University, Waltham, MA, USA

Sidra Montgomery Department of Sociology, University of Maryland, College Park, MD, USA

Grady F. Murphy Department of Human Development and Family Studies, Purdue University, West Lafayette, IN, USA

Linda Olivia Nichols, Ph.D. Veterans Affairs Medical Center, Memphis, TN, USA

Department of Preventive Medicine, University of Tennessee Health Science Center, Memphis, TN, USA

Department of Internal Medicine, University of Tennessee Health Science Center, Memphis, TN, USA

Ramona Faith Oswald, Ph.D. Department of Human and Community Development, University of Illinois at Urbana-Champaign, Urbana, IL, USA

Jennifer M. Peach, Ph.D. Department of National Defence, Director General Military Personnel Research & Analysis, Ottawa, ON, Canada

Sean M. Phelan, Ph.D., M.P.H. Division of Health Care Policy and Research, SW, Rochester, MN, USA

Melissa A. Polusny Minneapolis VA Health Care System, Minneapolis, MN, USA

Center for Chronic Disease Outcomes Research, Minneapolis, MN, USA

University of Minnesota Medical School, Minneapolis, MN, USA

David S. Riggs, Ph.D. Center for Deployment Psychology and Department of Medical and Clinical Psychology, Uniformed Services University of the Health Sciences, Bethesda, MD, USA

Amber J. Seidel, Ph.D. Department of Human Development and Family Studies, Penn State, New York, PA, USA

Jim Spira, Ph.D. Pacific Islands Division, US Department of Veterans Affairs, Honolulu, HI, USA

National Center for PTSD, Honolulu, HI, USA

VA Healthcare, Honolulu, HI, USA

Martina M. Sternberg Military Family Research Institute, Purdue University, West Lafayette, IN, USA

Aleksandra Stevanović Department of Psychiatry and Psychological Medicine, School of Medicine, University of Rijeka, Rijeka, Croatia

Brent C. Taylor, Ph.D. Department of Veterans Affairs, Minneapolis Health Care System, Center for Chronic Disease Outcomes Research, One Veterans Drive, Minneapolis, MN, USA

Department of Medicine, University of Minnesota Medical School, Minneapolis, MN, USA

Division of Epidemiology and Community Health, University of Minnesota School of Public Health, Minneapolis, MN, USA

Jennifer A. Theiss, Ph.D. Department of Communication, Rutgers University, New Brunswick, NJ, USA

Mark Tucker Department of Administration, Rehabilitation, and Postsecondary Education, Interwork Institute, San Diego State University, San Diego, CA, USA

Marcia Valenstein, M.D. Department of Veterans Affairs Health Services Research and Development, University of Michigan, Ann Arbor, MI, USA

Department of Psychiatry, University of Michigan, Ann Arbor, MI, USA

Courtney Harold Van Houtven, Ph.D. Center for Health Services Research in Primary Care, Durham VA Medical Center, Durham, NC, USA

Division of General Internal Medicine, Department of Medicine, Duke University Medical Center, Duke University, Durham, NC, USA

Shelley MacDermid Wadsworth, M.B.A., Ph.D. Department of Human Development and Family Studies, Military Family Research Institute, Purdue University, West Lafayette, IN, USA

Kathryn Wilder-Schaaf, Ph.D. Department of Veterans Affairs, Hunter Holmes McGuire Veterans Affairs Medical Center, Richmond, VA, USA

Department of Physical Medicine & Rehabilitation, Neuropsychology & Rehabilitation Psychology Service, Virginia Commonwealth University, Richmond, VA, USA

Thomas V. Williams, Ph.D., M.S. Director, Methods, Measures, and Analyses, Defense Health Cost Assessment and Program Evaluation, TRICARE Management Activity, Falls Church, VA, USA

Jeffrey Zuber, M.A. Department of Preventive Medicine, University of Tennessee Health Science Center, Memphis, TN, USA

Veterans Affairs Medical Center, Memphis, TN, USA

Chapter 1
Research and Training About Military Families: Where Are We?

Shelley MacDermid Wadsworth, Linda Hughes-Kirchubel, and David S. Riggs

Abstract The chapters in this volume are a result of the 2011 International Research Symposium on Military Families, a joint effort of the Military Family Research Institute (MFRI) at Purdue University and the Center for Deployment Psychology (CDP) at the Uniformed Services University of the Health Sciences. The symposium was organized into four half-day sessions, respectively focusing on marital and family functioning, parenting and child outcomes, single service members, and family sequelae of wounds and injuries. Each session comprised a series of scholarly presentations and an extended period of structured discussion during which working groups considered research and training priorities for the future. Following the discussions, symposium participants were asked to endorse what they saw as the highest priorities for future research and training. In this chapter, we review the key points presented during each session and present the results of each structured discussion.

Keywords Military • Deployment • Family • Children • Adjustment

S. MacDermid Wadsworth (✉)
Department of Human Development and Family Studies, Military Family Research Institute,
Purdue University, 1202 W. State Street, West Lafayette, IN 47907-2055, USA
e-mail: shelley@purdue.edu

L. Hughes-Kirchubel
Military Family Research Institute, Purdue University, 1202 W. State Street, West Lafayette,
IN 47907-2055, USA
e-mail: lhughesk@purdue.edu

D.S. Riggs
Center for Deployment Psychology and Department of Medical and Clinical Psychology,
Uniformed Services University of the Health Sciences, Bethesda, MD, USA
e-mail: driggs@deploymentpsych.org

S. MacDermid Wadsworth and D.S. Riggs (eds.), *Military Deployment and its Consequences for Families*, Risk and Resilience in Military and Veteran Families, DOI 10.1007/978-1-4614-8712-8_1, © Springer Science+Business Media New York 2014

Introduction

The chapters in this volume are a result of the 2011 International Research Symposium on Military Families, a joint effort of the Military Family Research Institute (MFRI) at Purdue University and the Center for Deployment Psychology (CDP) at the Uniformed Services University of the Health Sciences. MFRI conducts research and outreach to improve the lives of service members, veterans and their families in Indiana and around the world. CDP trains military and civilian behavioral health professionals to provide high-quality deployment related behavioral health services to military personnel and their families. The organizations also have partnered to create and implement the Star Behavioral Health Providers Network.

The third symposium of its kind, this event brought together more than 70 leading researchers, clinicians, and policy makers from the U.S. and other countries to share the results of cutting-edge research, discuss the state of science regarding military families, and to consider needs for research and training in the future. Symposium presenters were asked to focus explicitly on family-related issues, based on the premise that service members are part of systems of family members including spouses, children, parents, and others who represent potential sources of both support and challenge.

The symposium was organized into four half-day sessions, respectively focusing on marital and family functioning, parenting and child outcomes, single service members, and family sequelae of wounds and injuries. Each session comprised a series of scholarly presentations and an extended period of structured discussion during which working groups considered research and training priorities for the future. Following the discussions, symposium participants were asked to endorse what they saw as the highest priorities for future research and training. In this chapter, we review the key points presented during each session and present the results of each structured discussion.

Session I: Marital and Family Functioning

The chapters in this section focused on family dynamics during and following deployment, both from the perspective of families themselves and from the perspective of policy makers within DoD with the responsibility for designing, implementing, and evaluating programs, policies, and practices to support families as they perform military services.

Seidel, Franks, and MacDermid Wadsworth (Chap. 2) examine communication between partners during deployment. The advent of widespread broadband access and social media have made it possible for service members and their family members to contact each other frequently and instantly during deployment, giving rise to questions about whether service members' safety could be compromised by distractions from their military duties, or whether such frequent contact could threaten relationships by escalating conflict and worry in the family. The research documented in this chapter demonstrated that couple communication during deployment was not just frequent (i.e., once or more than once per day), but also occurred via multiple modes, both spontaneously and with prior planning, and was interwoven throughout daily activities. Most interactions involved exchanges of support, consistent with the possibility that couples were aware of the risks they could promote and tried to minimize them.

In their chapter, Knobloch and Theiss (Chap. 3), focus on reintegration following deployment, exploring how couples re-connect following reunion. Their perspective is based on 'relational turbulence' theory, which proposes that transitions are periods of instability or discontinuity in relationships, during which partners may be especially reactive to one another, in part because of feelings of uncertainty about themselves, their partner, or the relationship (Knobloch, 2007; Solomon, Weber, & Steuber, 2010). Partners may experience stronger emotions and react to one another in more extreme ways than usual. The authors summarize findings from their research program showing that military members and their partners experience more conflict and difficulty following deployment even though they also report valuing their relationship more than before the deployment. Other findings show that during periods of turbulence, partners feel less satisfied with their relationships, express less support for one another, and make it harder for one other to complete everyday activities by, for example, pushing each other to allocate time differently or by generating work for each other (Knobloch & Theiss, 2011, 2012; Theiss & Knobloch, in press). Examination of the elements of relational uncertainty revealed that partners' uncertainty about their OWN feelings, as well as interference from partners, were particularly tied to relationship satisfaction (Knobloch & Theiss, 2011). The authors suggest that couples be educated to understand the dynamics of relationship turbulence and learn to consciously work on facilitating rather than impeding their partners' daily goals.

Nichols and her colleagues (Chap. 4) also focus on the post-deployment period, designing and testing an intervention aimed at supporting spouses as their families navigated the reallocation of roles and responsibilities, re-establishment of marital intimacy, and re-learned to communicate following deployment. Because many spouses report that it is hard to travel for face-to-face meetings, and are reluctant at times to seek services, the authors chose to test the benefits of telephone-based support groups. A premise of the intervention was that spouses often serve as 'lynchpins' in families, coordinating family activities and responding to early warning signs of developing problems. The content, based on the Spouse Battlemind curriculum originally developed by Army experts (Riviere, Clark, Cox, Kendall-Robbins, & Castro, 2007), focused on helping spouses to acquire the information, skills and support they needed to manage the challenges specific to reintegration as well as challenges related to managing the day-to-day life of their family. Evaluation results indicated that in addition to valuing the program content, spouses appreciated both the convenience and the anonymity of the technology-based method. In particular, spouses appreciated being recognized in their own right, rather than as simply the 'supporting cast' for the service member. The authors note that the process of family reintegration was prolonged, lasting as much as 2 years.

Flynn (Chap. 5) traces the evolution of DoD responses to family-related needs over the course of the war, identifying three important themes. First, the advent of large scale deployments prompted rapid expansion of supports for families, such as the mobilization of Military Family Life Consultants to provide non-medical counseling. The urgency of families' needs at times prompted the launching of programs without waiting or diverting funds to gather baseline data or embed rigorous evaluation procedures. Second, as they expanded, family support programs required increasingly large financial allocations, raising levels of scrutiny regarding cost-effectiveness, particularly regarding their connection to successful completion of the military mission. The focus shifted beyond utilization and satisfaction as criteria of 'success.' Third, there are challenging issues regarding appropriate comparisons between civilian and military populations, some of them statistical and some philosophical. It is always important to consider differences in the composition of military and civilian populations when drawing statistical comparisons—for example, the military population is considerably younger than the civilian population, composed predominantly of males, and has been screened to exclude individuals with certain characteristics. Because of these differences, it is sometimes very difficult to make comparisons at all—for example, it is very challenging to compare divorce rates in the military and civilian populations. It is even more challenging, however, to determine the benchmarks against which military families should be compared. For example, should military family support programs aim to reduce unemployment among military spouses to the same levels as comparable civilian spouses, or should additional funds be expended to lower levels even further in order to retain service members? What levels of psychological distress or divorce should be considered 'normal' in military populations, requiring no special attention beyond typical programs? Finally, the challenges of studying military families are considered, which include difficulties retaining participants because high mobility, lags in record-keeping, heavy pre-existing burdens, and privacy concerns. There are exciting as-yet unexploited opportunities to mine administrative data, and also to partner with population studies initiated with civilian children such as the National Children's Study.

Discussion and Endorsements

Following the research presentations, working groups discussed specific research and training questions that had been prepared in advance: The first research question engaged the debate of how best to attend to relationship quality in the military: "Data are mixed regarding rates of marital dissolution in relation to deployment, but suggest that the relationship, if it exists, is smaller than many people have assumed. Marital quality and stability are not typically tracked as indicators of 'health of the force.' What are the three most important indicators of relationship quality among married service members that military leaders should pay attention to, and why? Or why not?"

In response to this question, participants recognized that there are many possible, but no single 'gold standard' indicators of relationship quality. The most popular nominations for key elements to focus on included role negotiation, conflict resolution, and work-family conflict. Participants also suggested that leaders should pay attention to rates of domestic violence and child maltreatment in the military as key indicators of relationship quality.

The second research-related question asked: "What are the three most important research questions that need to be addressed in the military in relation to these indicators?" The most-endorsed response urged researchers to perform clinical studies establishing evidence-based treatment models for military couples. The second encouraged the development of a standardized index of positive family functioning. The third indicated interest in developing a clear understanding of normal reactions to deployment challenges and more precise identification of the point at which these reactions become clinically significant.

Participants also discussed two questions related to training. In these questions, "military" providers included uniformed and civilian individuals working as chaplains, psychologists, social workers, and family support workers in military settings. "Civilian" providers included social workers, family life educators, marriage and family therapists, and psychologists in community settings. "Students" referred to college students training to enter helping professions.

In the first training question, participants considered the three most serious gaps in training of students, military providers, and civilian providers regarding marital and family relationships in military families. The group identified the most serious gaps in training as accurately understanding what difficulties are military-caused (such as frequent separations and the ambiguity surrounding them), versus those that are expectable features of normal human experiences (such as those tied to age, financial condition, educational level, etc.). Related to this gap is the need for better understanding of when normal transitory distress crosses into clinically significant symptoms. In addition, participants endorsed the need for better training regarding how best to match needs with proper resources (either military or civilian). Other responses stressed the importance of training gaps in "systemic thinking" that understands service members as part of family systems that experience military service AS systems. Thus, the effectiveness of interventions may be limited when they focus on only the service members.

The session's final training question, "What does each of group of helpers really need to know that they don't now know about marital and family functioning in military families?" yielded a most-endorsed response helpers need to know that the military is a complex culture, and one size does not fit all. The other endorsed response indicated that "training should reflect the importance of understanding the military culture as an overlay over individual qualities."

The chapters in this section emphasize the dynamic nature of family life, which changes in response to changing technologies and to evolving family challenges. Those tasked with minimizing the effects of family challenges face several difficulties not only related to measuring challenges, but also in designing responses that will be successful regardless of the diversity of family characteristics and experiences. Military leaders face the added difficulty of determining which aspects of family functioning are most important for the ability of the force to carry out its assigned mission and how best to promote those specific characteristics in effective and efficient ways—sometimes with great speed in response to sudden demands.

Session II: Parenting and Child Outcomes

Concern has been expressed from various quarters about the degree to which the healthy development children of military parents has been compromised by their exposure to their parents' deployments over the past decade. Although children 'serve too,' they usually have little say in this decision because they are usually born after their parent has already joined. The chapters in this section examine specific aspects of children's experiences, including not only their own outcomes, but also the circumstances around them that may promote or compromise their well-being.

Larson and colleagues (Chap. 6) focused on health care received by over 137,000 children of active component Army soldiers who had experienced deployment within the past 12 months. Finding showed that the use of health care specialists, primarily in psychiatric care, increased 11 % for children younger than 12 and 3.8 % for children 12 or older. There were also substantial increases in the number of younger children using antidepressants and the number of older children using anti-anxiety and sedative medications (29 and 19 percentage points relative to base rates, respectively for younger and older children). One implication of these findings is potential increases in challenges associated with coordinating systems of care. Since primary care for active component families is usually provided via military medical facilities but specialist care is usually provided through civilian providers, parents may now have to coordinate care across multiple systems at a time when one of the parents is unavailable to assist.

Another potential implication is the possibility of inappropriate prescribing for children, if medications for anxiety, depression, or sleep disruptions are administered as the first line of treatment. Further research would be needed to assess the appropriateness of medications prescribed for children given their individual circumstances and symptoms. The authors suggest that the military health system might find it useful to review protocols for use of psychotropic medications with children and how best to monitor outcomes, as well as how best to ensure good continuity of care between military and civilian providers.

Gewirz and Davis (Chap. 7) focus on parents' behavior toward children, based on existing evidence demonstrating the importance of at-home caregivers for children's well-being during deployments. The researchers developed and tested an intervention based on the premise that deployment challenges parents' ability to regulate their emotions, which can in turn decrease the quality of their parenting. Thus, their research offers a window into the intra-familial processes through which the effects of deployment reverberate through family systems, with the potential to ultimately compromise children's well-being. ADAPT is a group intervention for parents with both face-to-face and web-based components that aims to improve parents' emotion regulation, parenting practices, and children's adjustment. Data from 89 military and civilian parents of children aged 5–12 showed that parents experiencing deployment reported more difficulties in emotion regulation than other parents, and that emotion regulation explained a significant proportion of the variance in parenting practices. Thus, to the extent that parents can minimize difficulties in their emotion regulation difficulties, and the negative parenting practices that tend to result, such as inconsistency, punitiveness, or dismissiveness, they can minimize the negative consequences of deployment for their children. While gender was not a statistically significant factor in the results, deployed mothers reported more difficulties in emotion regulation and parenting than fathers or other mothers. The authors speculated that deployment environments may be less supportive for females than males.

Oswald and Sternberg (Chap. 8) consider contextual factors that affect children, specifically challenges posed by policies related to lesbian, gay, and bisexual (LGB) families, which are estimated to affect 16,000 families with children. The 'don't' ask, don't tell' policy has now been lifted, and Secretary of Defense Panetta (Briggs & Miklaszewski, 2013; Outserve/SLDN, 2013) recently extended ID cards, family readiness programs, and joint duty assignments to gay spouses and partners. Nonetheless, the Defense of Marriage Act still precludes the Department of Defense from offering health benefits, housing allowances, on-base housing, or death benefits to LGB partners. As a result, some children will continue to be constrained from access to some programs and benefits. For example, children of LGB parents cannot live with both their parents in on-base housing.

In addition to the normative stressors faced by military families including relocations, challenging duties, risk of harm, demands of 'total institution,' children in LGB families may face additional challenges related to the fact that LGB families may be disproportionately headed by women and members of ethnic minority or interracial groups. As members of families in potentially multiple stigmatized groups, children may face minority stress—prejudice, discrimination, bullying, and expectations of rejection. There is evidence in the civilian literature that the mental health status of LGB individuals is poorer when they live in states with less supportive climates (Hatzenbuehler, Keyes, & Hasin, 2009), but there is as yet no research yet documenting whether a similar relationship exists in the military. A challenge for the future is how best to support the children of LGB parents who serve in the military.

Discussion and Endorsements

As with the first session, the first question during the structured discussion following this session asked participants to consider current research needs, taking into account that a great deal is known about risk factors for civilian children and that several large studies of military families have been conducted since 2001.

By far, the most-endorsed recommendation was to conduct longitudinal studies of the impacts of deployment on the children of veterans. Participants thought it particularly important to understand the impact of deployment on children's developmental trajectories and milestones. Attendees also endorsed the importance of understanding ways in which military children are similar to and different from civilian children who experience similar challenges, such as relocations and separations. Finally, because most studies of military children to date have focused on youth, researchers underscored the importance of studying younger children.

Two questions during this discussion focused on training. The first asked participants to identify the three most serious gaps in the training of students, military providers, and civilian providers regarding parenting and child outcomes. The top training gap identified pertained to the needs of children aged zero to five, about whom there is considerable disagreement about how best to diagnose and treat. A second gap identified was the need to teach students how to help parents develop the ability to coach their children. Finally, participants emphasized the importance of balanced attention to risk and resilience and the need to remember that children or families who need support or assistance do not necessarily require clinical treatment.

The second training question asked participants to identify training needs for military parents. Most suggestions focused on the idea that families could benefit from improved parent education. Specifically, participants emphasized the importance of helping parents (and providers) to recognize differences between transitory and clinically significant distress in children. This echoes a theme in another chapter of this volume (McCreary, Peach, Blais, & Fikretoglu, Chap. 10), which cautions both researcher and practitioners to maintain attention to both the positive and negative aspects of military service and the strengths—not just the vulnerabilities—of families.

The presentations and discussions during this session of the conference emphasized the need to find the balance between recognizing children's real and serious difficulties with their parents' deployments and children's transitory distress that might merit some assistance but not clinical treatment. They also recognize the importance of policy decisions that have consequences for children, such as which children or parents are given access to particular programs, or how long the deployments to which children are exposed will last, or who may provide covered care to military children. In addition, they bolstered existing evidence suggesting that the effects of deployment on children are strongly mediated by the functioning of at-home parents.

Session III: Single Service Members

In the military, "family" most often refers to the spouses and children of service members. Single service members are not the target of most programs focused on families, although there certainly are exceptions (e.g., the Army Strong Bonds

Single Soldier program, **B**etter **O**pportunities for **S**ingle **S**oldiers, single Marine, Sailor, and Airman programs target never-married, single parents, and geographical bachelors). Service members' parents are not usually an explicit focus of military support programs, even though they provide considerable care and can experience risks for doing so. Therefore, it is important to understand the population of single service members and the implications of this family status. We learned in the last volume that this group is diverse, including pre- and post-married, and parents and nonparents, and that theme continues here.

In a somewhat unusual but welcome examination of the pre-deployment period, Polusny, Erbes, Campbell, Fairman, Kramer, and Johnson (Chap. 9) compared levels of well-being between single and partnered soldiers and then examined connections between well-being and family factors. The sample included 527 parents and their Army National Guard children studied between 2 and 6 months prior to deployment as part of the Readiness and Resilience in National Guard Soldiers study. Data were collected at 'Family Preparation Academies' offered by the Minnesota National Guard, which parents were invited to attend.

Existing literature makes it clear that having a spouse or partner is associated with better psychological well-being and greater willingness to seek assistance (Meis, Barry, Erbes, Kehle, & Polusny, 2010), raising questions about possible risks of single status. Recent literature also documents that relationships with parents remain important for adults, with rises in recent years (Fingerman, Cheng, Tighe, Birditt, & Zarit, 2012). The researchers hypothesized that single soldiers would show poorer well-being than those with partners, which was found to be partly true. Single soldiers reported more alcohol use and less social support, but partnered soldiers reported higher levels of PTSD and depression symptoms as well as more family stressors. Partnered soldiers also were more likely to have been deployed before, and less likely to have had a parent complete the survey. With regard to the implications of connections between parents and children, the results showed that children's well-being was positively related to exchanges of support and communication with their parents only when soldiers were single and parents expressed high levels of concern about the deployment. Under these conditions, children reported fewer symptoms of PTSD and depression, but there was no relationship with alcohol use. Thus parental support appeared to carry different implications for single and partnered soldiers, with the potential to be an important source of support for single soldiers.

McCreary, Peach, Blais, and Fikretoglu (Chap. 10) focused on the post-deployment period, building on their earlier work to construct and refine a measure of positive and negative features of post-deployment reintegration. Based on extensive pilot work, identified four main themes associated with post-deployment reintegration: (1) reintegrating back into one's work environment; (2) reintegrating back into one's family; (3) dealing personally with one's deployment experiences; and (4) reintegrating back into one's Western, privileged culture. This last theme was new, and often not recognized in other studies of reintegration. Ultimately it appeared to overlap statistically with the personal domain and was dropped.

Age, marital status and the presence of dependents accounted for significant variability in positive (2 %) and negative (6 %) aspects of work, and between 2 and

9 % of the positive (9 %) and negative (2 %) aspects of family, but did not account for significant variability in personal factors. Not surprisingly, it was the family domain where the perspectives of single service members tended to be distinctive. Service members who were unmarried or did not have children were significantly less likely than their counterparts who were married or had children to endorse positive family items (e.g., feeling closer, have become more involved in family relationships). Service members who were unmarried and had children were more likely to endorse negative family items (e.g., tension in family relationships, difficulty getting back 'into sync' with family life) than service members who were married (regardless of whether or not they had dependents), or unmarried service members without children. Thus, single service members in general were less likely to endorse positive family items, but more likely to endorse negative family items only if they had children.

Kleykamp and Montgomery (Chap. 11) delve into the troubling issue of unemployment among young veterans. Guided by a life course perspective, they consider the role of military service in the transition to adulthood, during which decisions about education, employment and marriage figure prominently in the lives of young adults. Many young veterans are now completing military service and entering the civilian labor force in the aftermath of a deep recession, raising questions about the degree to which they are experiencing disadvantages and whether these accrue from personal characteristics (e.g., gender), military experiences (e.g., combat experiences), or economic circumstances (e.g., sluggish recovery). Using data from the Current Population Survey about 18–30 year olds with high school but not college degrees, they find that both male and female veterans are less likely than nonveterans with similar characteristics to participate in the labor force or to be employed, but once employed, earn more than comparable civilians. Both married and single veterans display this pattern, but it is statistically significant only among those who are married. Because veterans possess characteristics positively associated with employment (e.g., educated, drug-tested), and these are not typically taken into account in media reports, veterans' disadvantages in finding employment are LARGER than what is typically reported. The disadvantage is particularly large for veterans who performed combat-oriented jobs in the military, who do not seem to appeal to employers as much as veterans who performed more obviously transferable tasks. On balance, the authors concluded that military service may prolong the transition to adulthood by delaying education, civilian jobs, or marriage but does not require service members to forego those goals. Employment difficulties may ensue when military members leave service, but when surmounted, service members earn more than their civilian counterparts.

Hoobler (Chap. 12) extends the focus on workplaces to document a line of civilian research examining the degree to which women's performance evaluations and access to advancement are colored by managers' gender bias. Stereotypes about women—including single women—are alive and well, as evidenced by comments in 2011 by Simon Murray, Chairman of Glencore:

Women are quite as intelligent as men, [but]...they have a tendency not to be so involved quite often and they're not so ambitious in business as men because they've better things to do. Quite often they like bringing up their children and all sorts of other things... Do you think that means that when I rush out, what I'm absolutely desperate to have is young women who are about to get married in my company, and that I really need them on board because I know they're going to get pregnant and they're going to go off for nine months?

Civilian research suggests that supervisors make judgments about employees' family circumstances based on gender rather than other employee characteristics. For example, Hoobler's earlier research showed that supervisors judged women as having more family-to-work conflict than men and were less likely to recommend them for advancement (Hoobler, Wayne, & Lemmon, 2009)—even though women's ACTUAL family-to-work conflict was LOWER than men's.

There is some evidence that these biases extend into the military. For example, substantial proportions of civilians and military trainees and cadets express uncertainty about whether women should serve as military commanders (Matthews, Ender, Laurence, & Rohall, 2009). There is also evidence that when units are too imbalanced by gender, male superiors underrate the performance of female officers (Pazy & Oron, 2001).

Discussion and Endorsements

The first research question discussed by participants was, "The recent conflicts have led to expanded definitions of 'family' in some military programs, practices, and policies. What family issues are most important for military leaders to understand regarding single service members?" By far, the most-endorsed response to the question had to do with adjusting, broadening or refining definitions of 'family.' A substantial number of endorsements were also given to the concept of understanding the impact of technological advances on communications, and offering tailored reintegration support for single service members (which might need to be different for males and females). Participants also noted that attention needs to be given to children of single service members, blended families, "newly" single (i.e., divorced), parents of single service members and gay service members who are in significant relationships.

The second research question asked, "What research questions need to be addressed?" The most-endorsed answer suggested that researchers learn more about how parents or siblings can be more involved and best supported during the reintegration process. Participants also suggested research examine the experiences of single service members, including their peer relationships and social support, factors contributing to their resilience and decisions about reenlistment, and the impact of deployment on dating relationships.

There were also three training discussion questions for this session, the first of which asked, "What are the three most serious gaps in the training of students, military providers, and civilian providers as related to single service members?"

The most-endorsed responses indicated that training needs to include information about educating parents of single service members, and interventions for single service members who are parents. The second training question asked, "What do service members themselves need to know about family issues?" In the most-endorsed response, participants suggested that service members need to know that resilience and growth occur during all phases of the deployment cycle. Sexual harassment was another endorsed topic.The third and final training question of this session asked, "What do enlisted leaders need to know?" The most-endorsed responses suggested enlisted leaders be trained on how to give service members resources to communicate with various family members, and that enlisted leaders be alerted to those service members who might at high risk due to lack of social support—who may disproportionately be single.

The presentations and discussions in this segment of the conference underscored the diversity of single service members and also the distinctive aspects of their 'ecological niche.' For example, parents represent potentially very important sources of support for these service members, but not all parents function in that capacity. Many single service members are already parents, and others are still making their way through the transition to adulthood. Women may face special challenges because of biases imposed by their supervisors regardless of their family circumstances.

Session IV: Family Sequelae of Wounds and Injuries

In this section, chapters focus on the aftermath of service members being wounded or injured during their military service. As rates of survival have risen, so too has the prominence of psychological injuries. In addition, the prevalence of bomb blast injuries during conflicts in Iraq and Afghanistan has resulted in large numbers of 'polytraumatic' injuries, where brain injuries are combined with other physical and psychological injuries. In all cases, life-altering wounds and injuries have the potential to affect family life in a variety of ways. These effects may persist long after the period of acute treatment, following service members back to their home communities.

In Chap. 13, Gorman and colleagues explore the adjustment of military couples in the early aftermath of deployments in which service members sustained physical injuries. Focusing on families reunited for 45–90 days following deployment, they contrasted husbands and wives in couples where the service member had or had not sustained a physical injury. They found significant differences between couples with and without injuries on depression and PTSD symptoms but not dyadic adjustment, parental stress, or alcohol abuse. They also found significant differences between husbands and wives, and significant interactions between injury and spousal role (i.e., service member, spouse) on parental stress, alcohol use, PTSD, and depression, consistent with significant relationships between injury and psychological adjustment for service members but not spouses. Patterns for depression and PTSD symptoms were more pronounced among service members who had sustained a physical injury, as well as elevated levels of parental stress among service members with physical injuries relative to their spouses. The researchers interpreted this as evidence that service members but not spouses are experiencing compromised psychological health associated with physical injuries. Although these results were not consistent with theories about secondary traumatization of spouses, the authors suggested that at this early stage of reintegration, difficulties had yet to emerge, perhaps because spouses' compassion for their partners was serving a protective function.

In Chap. 14, Frančišković and colleagues extend the understanding of secondary traumatization further by chronicling the knowledge they gained while treating service members and their families in Croatia in the aftermath of conflicts during the 1990s. They report initially underestimating the importance of spouses in the treatment of service members, but soon coming to understand that treatment seemed to promise much greater success when the psychological distress of spouses was taken into account. Almost a third of spouses displayed symptoms consistent with secondary stress disorder. The authors describe a challenging confluence of stressors for spouses, who were providing support for the service member while being unable to count on receiving spousal support in return. Spouses 'ran interference' between service members and children, trying to prevent each from causing distress in the other, and in so doing, inadvertently encouraged service members to 'underfunction' by avoiding interaction with family members, in turn further increasing burden on spouses. The research group's studies of children suggested that veterans' trauma compromised spouses' mental health, which in turn promoted internalizing symptoms among children. They did not find direct relationships between veterans' traumatic experiences and children's distress.

Griffin and colleagues (Chap. 15) documented the experiences of family members providing care for veterans with polytrauma, defined as the combination of traumatic brain injury with one or more other injuries. About 60 % of the caregivers were parents of the care recipient, and about one third of the care recipients had high intensity needs for care. In general, many years had passed since the veterans in the study were injured, but care needs were still high. Parents were very involved in providing care, and both parents and spouses had suddenly taken on new roles as caregiver. For parents this represented reverting to a previous role of caregiver for their child, but for spouses, this represented the double loss of their partner and their role as a wife, as well as the acquired role of caregiver. While parents provided care for veterans who were more severely injured, they also had more social resources than spouses. The only significant demographic difference by intensity of need was that those caring for care recipients with high intensity needs were significantly less likely to be working for pay than those caring for care recipients with moderate intensity needs, consistent with other data showing that caregiving presents a risk for early departure from the labor force.

DeGeneffe and Tucker (Chap. 16) focus on the community contexts of families dealing with traumatic brain injuries. Data came from leaders of state affiliates of the Brain Injury Association of America. Participants reported that many community-based programs are available, but are insufficient to meet families' needs. Often this was due simply to insufficient levels of available services, but sometimes there were gaps in the array of services offered. For example, more than two-thirds of respondents reported that no training regarding sexuality was available in their state at all. Caregivers frequently had to coordinate among a complex array of systems of community-based care, sometimes including providers with insufficient understanding of brain injuries. Between 79 and 99 % of respondents rated a range of family needs as important, but no more than 10 % of respondents rated those needs as fully met.

Discussion and Endorsements

The first research question participants discussed was, "What are the most important research questions to answer regarding recent veterans as they relate to *physical* injuries and family issues?" The most-endorsed responses focused on the need to track family functioning over time, and to conduct qualitative research that documents the perspectives of multiple family members. Another heavily-endorsed response urged greater understanding of "how it is that many wounded warriors thrive despite their injuries." Other highly-ranked topics included how injuries impact effective parenting, and how and why caregiving changes over time, with particular attention to its economic implications and changes in the quality of care provided.

The second research question asked participants to consider "the most important research questions regarding recent veterans as they relate to *psychological* injuries and family issues." The most-endorsed responses focused on understanding differences between visible and invisible injuries. In particular, researchers felt it was important to understand how injury type affected caregivers' perceptions of meaning and burden related to the injury. The second-most endorsed responses focused on secondary traumatization and the co-occurrence of PTSD in the family. For example, researchers wondered whether pre-existing PTSD among spouses can trigger symptoms among service members or create mutually-reinforcing symptoms; and when such circumstances occur, how best to treat them. The third group of endorsed answers focused on the long term, including prospects for improvements in the functioning of care recipients and implications of aging caregivers, such as how to replace them as they 'age out' of being able to provide care, and the potentially negative consequences of providing stipends to caregivers, specifically whether they could promote "staying sick" among veterans with treatable injuries or disorders.

When asked to identify the most serious gaps in the training of students, military providers and civilians, the most-endorsed answers focused on improving coordination of care, including engaging "family care teams" rather than simply individual caregivers for wounded warriors, and engaging individuals and organizations beyond the families of wounded warriors, including schools, employers, and communities. Other endorsed responses focused on expanding caregiver support, education and resources so as to reduce strain and prevent burnout.

The second group of popular responses focused on the future, trying to anticipate the challenges that care systems will confront in the future, and also anticipating the needs of aging caregivers. The third most-popular response was how best to adapt treatment interventions for comorbidity.

The chapters in this section demonstrate that while the effects of wounds and injuries on family members may take time to emerge, they can nonetheless be substantial and very prolonged. Furthermore, they affect not only spouses and children of service members, but to a substantial degree parents and other family members. At times the level of care required is intensive, and family members may be faced with trying to coordinate complex interactions of multiple systems of care, particularly in the case of polytraumatic injuries. While civilian communities have support systems in place, they are rarely seen as adequate to meet families' needs, and accessibility can be a challenge.

Conclusions

At the 2011 International Research Symposium, which was presented by MFRI in partnership with the Center for Deployment Psychology, researchers, scholars and clinicians discussed the latest findings in the study of military families. After hearing presentations related to marital and family functioning, parenting and child outcomes, single service members and family sequelae of wounds and injuries, those in attendance participated in structured discussions to identify the most pressing needs for future research and training.

In the area of marital and family functioning, symposium presentations examined some of the microprocesses of family life that guide communication during deployment, as well as processes through which families reconstruct their lives together following service members' returns. Discussions emphasized the need for measurement tools that would allow more consistent understanding of family functioning and reintegration difficulties, as well as studies that will help to create evidence-based prevention and treatment models for military couples. Participants also identified training gaps, including distinguishing between relationship challenges caused by military service and those that commonly occur in relationships independent of military status. In addition, participants urged more widespread training on systemic approaches to families and ways to maximize the match between needs and resources.

In the area of parenting and child outcomes, symposium participants presented findings demonstrating elevated use of behavioral health care and psychotropic medications among children exposed to recent deployments. They also bolstered findings showing that the effects of deployment are mediated through the functioning of at-home parents. Participants recommended that researchers conduct longitudinal studies of children of combat veterans to examine the impact of deployment on the developmental trajectory of children. Participants also recommended studies comparing military and civilian children in similar contexts, and investigations of the impact of deployment, separation and re-integration on children aged zero to five.

Particular areas of concern regarding training included caring for the needs of children aged zero to five, and training providers to help military parents 'coach' their children more effectively.

With regard to single service members, symposium presentations focused on the distinctive importance of parents for the mental health of single service members, as well as the unique features of reintegration for them. When they leave military service, young service members face special challenges in establishing civilian employment, and experiences in the workplace may be especially challenging for women. Participants recommended that researchers examine ways to better support parents and siblings of single service members, as well as studying ways to better involve parents and siblings in the reintegration process. They also recommended studying "isolated" single service members at and after reintegration. Participants suggested paying special attention to research questions that asked whether this population is more likely than others to experience problems with drugs, homelessness, and other issues, and endorsed research that tracks family functioning over time, especially for veterans who do not receive services from the VA.

With regard to training gaps, participants recognized that leaders need to be made aware that "optimal" communication patterns can vary widely during deployment, since family contact can serve as a positive support or a distraction. To this end, participants suggested that single-service members, their families, and noncommissioned officers receive training on such issues as conflict resolution and boundary negotiation. A second gap could be filled by offering psychoeducation for parents of single service members, or whomever is important in service members' lives, as well as providers who work with these parents (or others).

In the area of family sequelae of wounds and injuries, symposium presentations focused on the aftermath for families in both the short and long terms. While consequences for spouses may not emerge immediately, the long-term challenges for both spouses and parents of some injuries can be substantial. Once veterans complete the acute phases of their recovery and return to community-based settings, the challenges may continue given shortfalls in civilian care systems. Participants recommended that researchers examine the factors that distinguish wounded warriors who appear able to thrive despite their injuries. Other recommendations included conducting qualitative research from the perspectives of different family members, and examining the phenomenon of care erosion. With regard to training gaps, participants advocated providing training that focuses on coordination of care. Participants also urged attention to anticipating future needs to which care system will need to respond, especially with regard to aging caregivers.

In sum, the presentations and discussions at the third International Research Symposium on Military Families provided a rich source of new findings and insights about future needs for research and training. The presentations were sometimes provocative, and the discussions were always animated, but the participants always shared an enthusiastic commitment to ensuring that service members and veterans—and their families—receive support programs and services that fully recognize both their strengths and their vulnerabilities.

References

Briggs, B., & Miklaszewski, J. (2013, February 11). *Outgoing DoD boss Panetta extends some benefits to same-sex spouses, partners of gay troops.* Downloaded March 16, 2013, from http://usnews. nbcnews.com/_news/2013/02/11/16927063-outgoing-dod-boss-panetta-extends-some-benefits-to-same-sex-spouses-partners-of-gay-troops?lite

Fingerman, K. L., Cheng, Y. P., Tighe, L., Birditt, K. S., & Zarit, S. (2012). Relationships between young adults and their parents. In A. Booth, S. L. Brown, N. Landale, W. Manning, & S. M. McHale (Eds.), *Early adulthood in a family context* (pp. 59–85). New York: Springer Publishers.

Hatzenbuehler, M. L., Keyes, K. M., & Hasin, D. S. (2009). State-level policies and psychiatric morbidity in lesbian, gay, and bisexual populations. *American Journal of Public Health, 99,* 2275–2281.

Hoobler, J. M., Wayne, S. J., & Lemmon, G. (2009). Bosses' perceptions of family-work conflict and women's promotability: Glass ceiling effects. *Academy of Management Journal, 52*(5), 939–957.

Knobloch, L. K. (2007). Perceptions of turmoil within courtship: Associations with intimacy, relational uncertainty, and interference from partners. *Journal of Social and Personal Relationships, 24,* 363–384.

Knobloch, L. K., & Theiss, J. A. (2011). Depressive symptoms and mechanisms of relational turbulence as predictors of relationship satisfaction among returning service members. *Journal of Family Psychology, 25,* 470–478.

Knobloch, L. K., & Theiss, J. A. (2012). Experiences of U.S. military couples during the post-deployment transition: Applying the relational turbulence model. *Journal of Social and Personal Relationships, 29,* 423–450.

Matthews, M. D., Ender, M. G., Laurence, J. H., & Rohall, D. E. (2009). Role of group affiliation and gender on attitudes toward women in the military. *Military Psychology, 21,* 241–251.

Meis, L. A., Barry, R. A., Erbes, C. R., Kehle, S. M., & Polusny, M. A. (2010). Relationship adjustment, PTSD symptoms, and treatment utilization among coupled National Guard solliders deployed to Iraq. *Journal of Family Psychology, 24,* 560–567.

Outserve/SLDN. (2013). *Panetta extends benefits: Frequently asked questions.* Downloaded March 16, 2013, from http://www.sldn.org/content/pages/3677/

Pazy, A., & Oron, I. (2001). Sex proportion and performance evaluation among high ranking military officers. *Journal of Organizational Behavior, 22,* 689–702.

Riviere, L. A., Clark, J. C., Cox, A. L., Kendall-Robbins, A., & Castro, C. A. (2007, August). Spouse Battlemind training: Elements and strengths. In C. A. Castro (Chair), *The Battlemind training system: Supporting soldiers throughout the deployment cycle.* Symposium conducted at the meeting of the American Psychological Association. San Francisco, CA.

Solomon, D. H., Weber, K. M., & Steuber, K. R. (2010). Turbulence in relational transitions. In S. W. Smith & S. R. Wilson (Eds.), *New directions in interpersonal communication research* (pp. 115–134). Thousand Oaks, CA: Sage.

Theiss, J. A., & Knobloch, L. K. (in press). Extending the relational turbulence model to the post-deployment transition: Self, partner, and relationship focused turbulence. *Communication Research.*

Part I
Relationship Functioning

Chapter 2
Bridging the Distance: Illustrations of Real-Time Communication of Support Between Partners and Deployed Members of the National Guard

Amber J. Seidel, Melissa M. Franks, Grady F. Murphy, and Shelley MacDermid Wadsworth

Abstract Exchanges of support are fundamental elements of intimate relationships and deployment separation may challenge partners' ability to provide and receive support due in part to challenges in "staying connected". Two studies examined daily exchanges of support between deployed service members and their partners at home. Although partners were geographically separated from a deployed member of the National Guard, all reported communicating with their partners during the 7-day study period. Our findings suggest that military couples frequently use interactive forms of communication (e.g., phone, Skype, instant messaging) though families generally are not able to schedule their contacts with one another during military deployment. Further, all partners reported providing and receiving support during the study period. Notably, decisions and disagreements were reported infrequently. Our findings underscore that access to multiple modes of communication can facilitate providing supportive contact between deployed military members and their families at home.

Keywords Communication • Relationship support • National Guard

A.J. Seidel, Ph.D. (✉)
Department of Human Development and Family Studies, Penn State,
New York, PA, USA
e-mail: ajs49@psu.edu

M.M. Franks, Ph.D. • G.F. Murphy
Department of Human Development and Family Studies, Purdue University,
West Lafayette, IN USA
e-mail: mmfranks@purdue.edu; gradyfmurphy@gmail.com

S. MacDermid Wadsworth, M.B.A., Ph.D.
Department of Human Development and Family Studies, Military Family
Research Institute, Purdue University, 1202 W. State Street,
West Lafayette, IN 47907-2055, USA
e-mail: shelley@purdue.edu

S. MacDermid Wadsworth and D.S. Riggs (eds.), *Military Deployment and its
Consequences for Families*, Risk and Resilience in Military and Veteran Families,
DOI 10.1007/978-1-4614-8712-8_2, © Springer Science+Business Media New York 2014

Exchanges of support are fundamental elements of intimate relationships, and married partners signal support for one another in many ways including physical contact, listening, and tangible assistance (Bradbury & Karney, 2004; Cutrona, Shaffer, Wesner, & Gardner, 2007; Diamond, Hicks, & Otter-Henderson, 2008; Schmitt, Kliegel, & Shapiro, 2007). Marriages characterized by high levels of such support provide protective buffers against economic, emotional, relational and daily challenges that many couples may experience during challenging times of heightened stress (Conger, Rueter, & Elder, 1999; Ledermann, Bodenmann, Rudaz, & Bradbury, 2010). Importantly, partners' established patterns of communicating support with one another are challenged at times when they are geographically separated (e.g., schooling, business trips, military deployments; Merolla, 2010a). Thus, we examined communication between married service members who are deployed and their partners at home, particularly their daily exchanges of support.

Deployment separation often is a stressor for close relationships particularly when the deployment is to a combat zone (e.g., Aducci, Baptist, George, Barros, & Goff, 2011; Dimiceli, Steinhardt, & Smith, 2010; Schumm, Bell, & Gade, 2000). Moreover, specific supportive behaviors partners would typically use (e.g., physical touch, relief from responsibilities) are not available in response to daily stressors during deployment. Further, one of the most prevalent problems reported in the daily life of spouses of deployed military members in combat zones is difficulty sending or receiving communications with their deployed partner (SteelFisher, Zaslavsky, & Blendon, 2008; see review MacDermid Wadsworth, 2010). In addition, most National Guard families tend to face the deployment of their service member isolated from both the military community and the civilian community that does not have a service member deployed.

Throughout history, modes of communication have changed for partners of deployed military members to combat zones. During World Wars I and II, letters and packages were the primary source of communication. During the Korean War and Vietnam conflict, military members had limited access to two-way communication home through the Military Affiliate Radio System (MARS). Since Operation Desert Storm, access to facsimile (fax), email, videotapes, and teleconference has become available (Ender, 2005; Schumm, Bell, Ender, & Rice, 2004). Although new modes of communication continue to emerge (e.g., Facebook, Twitter, Skype), communication concerns remain for deployed military members in combat zones and their family members to "stay connected" in real time. Technological advances such as phone access and internet provide military families with a range of options for interactive communication during combat deployments (Hertlein, 2012; Schumm et al., 2004), yet little is known about whether or how often these modes are used to exchange support between partners. Moreover, although disruptions in communication may be anticipated, when access to these technologies is limited, or security concerns (e.g., lack of privacy, potential for breach of classified information) hinder what can be shared with families, exchanges of support may be further disrupted (Frisby, Byrnes, Mansson, Booth-Butterfield, & Birmingham, 2011;

Hinojosa, Hinojosa, & Högnäs, 2012; Sahlstein, Maguire, & Timmerman, 2009). For example, it is likely that a spouse may not realize his or her partner is attempting to provide support because of the constraints placed on communication by the separation (e.g., not being able to see the partner's non-verbal cues or hear them clearly).

In light of anticipated challenges to partners' supportive exchanges during deployment, we investigated frequency and context of daily communication using daily diary methods. Capturing partners' day-to-day contact may uncover patterns of communication between geographically separated spouses that are otherwise missed in studies examining intermittent or retrospective reports of partner communication. Notable advantages of daily diary methods include: (1) assessing actual "lived" events of partners; (2) gathering reports of partners closer in time to the events of interest; (3) allowing ample opportunity for partners to experience events of interest; and (4) providing data that reflect short-term (day-to-day) changes and variability in target events and outcomes (Bolger, Davis, & Rafaeli, 2003; Laurenceau & Bolger, 2005). We investigated the variety and frequency of multiple modes of communication reported by state-side partners of deployed military members to a combat zone. Additionally, we investigated partners' provision and receipt of support, decision making, and disagreements using data from the daily diary portion of a feasibility study examining the impact of deployment on National Guard service members and their families. Two studies examining real-time communication between military members and their partners during deployment are described: (1) an initial feasibility study and (2) data from a preliminary sample from a study of military families facing deployment to a combat zone.

Feasibility Study

Participants

Ten partners of deployed National Guard service members who participated in a prior study were contacted for participation in this feasibility study. To be eligible, partners had to be continuously married to a deployed National Guard member throughout the deployment. Of these 10 partners, two did not meet inclusion criteria because the relationship had terminated and one declined to participate. The seven remaining partners consented to participate and were all European American and wives that had been married to the service member for 9.5 years, on average (SD 8.8). The mean age for military members (as reported by their partner) was 39 years old (SD 6.6) and the mean age for wives was 37 years old (SD 7.1). The highest level of education was a bachelor's degree for most military members (n = 5) and some college for wives (n = 5). Military members had spent 15.5 years on average in the military (SD 6.4) and had experienced 2.2 military deployments on average (SD .75; range = 1–3) in the previous 5 years.

Measures

Spouses completed a web-based end-of-day daily record of communication with the deployed service member for 7 consecutive days. A link to a web-based daily diary was emailed to each participant each evening. Daily assessments recorded participants' experiences between awakening and retiring on a given day. Assessing experiences at the end of the day reduces bias due to errors in memory that can affect self-reports when long time intervals elapse between events and reporting. Compared to assessments occurring several times per day, end-of-day diaries can keep participants from feeling overly burdened when many repeated assessments are made (Stone & Shiffman, 2002). Of the seven participants, three provided data for all 7 days, with a total of 41of a possible 49 daily observations completed.

Modes of Communication

Participants reported on their daily use of phone, webcast, email, instant messaging, blog, letter, and package by mail to communicate with deployed partners. For each contact, participants reported who initiated the contact, time of contact in 3 h increments (e.g., 6:00 a.m. to 9:00 a.m.; 9:00 a.m. to noon), duration of contact, and whether the contact was scheduled. For each communication mode (e.g., emailing, instant messaging) with the exception of phone calls, all contacts within the same 3 h interval were counted as one session of contact.

Context of Communication

Participants reported the context of each contact with their deployed partner including: their location (e.g., home, office) and their deployed partners' location (on base, off base), their own mood during each contact (ranging from 0 = very bad to 10 = very good), and their children's participation in the communication (i.e., Were your children present? Did they participate?).

Support Exchanges

Participants reported provision of support to their deployed partners with four items (i.e., provide support, provide information, shared feelings, ask questions), and receipt of support with three items (i.e., received support, shared feelings, felt connected), each rated as "not at all", "some", or "a lot." Responses from these items were combined to create a dichotomous variable representing whether or not participants' provided (or received) support (i.e., endorsed at least one item as "some" or "a lot") during each contact with their deployed partners.

Participants reported their communication involving disagreements and decision making differently for temporally proximal and interactive modes (i.e., phone calls, email, instant messaging, webcasts) than for temporally distal, independent modes (i.e., letters, packages, blogs). For the proximal modes of communication, participants reported whether they resolved a disagreement on any topic, "Did you and your partner discuss a new or existing disagreement?" and whether they made a decision, "Did you and your partner make decisions?" (rated as "not at all", "some", or "a lot"). No specific guideline as to type of decision or disagreement was given. For the distal modes of communication, participants reported whether they *addressed* a disagreement or decision. Responses for each item were combined to create dichotomous variables reflecting whether or not disagreements were resolved (or addressed) and whether or not decisions were made (or addressed).

Patterns of Communication

On the last day, participants reported whether their own and their partner's initiation of contact with one another during the study period was more, about the same, or less than usual. Open-ended questions assessed reasons for atypical contact during the study period. Participants also reported their next scheduled contact with their partner.

Daily Communication

All seven wives reported having at least one contact with their deployed partners during the study period. Across all wives and all days of our feasibility study, contact with deployed partners included 14 phone calls, 11 email sessions, 3 instant messaging sessions, and 1 blog. No wife reported using webcasts, letters, or packages during the study period. Most wives reported one mode of contact each day; however, three wives used email or instant messaging on the same day as they had a phone call.

Phone

Most wives (n = 5) received a phone call from their deployed partners during the study period (with a range of 1–6 phone calls received). The duration of the phone calls ranged from 5 to 45 min. During most phone calls, wives reported being at home (10 of 14 phone calls). Children were present during nine of the 14 phone calls but actively participated in only three of these phone calls. Wives often rated their mood as "10" (very good) while talking with their deployed partner (9 of 14 phone calls). Only one participant reported that her phone call was scheduled (i.e., the participant knew when her deployed partner would be calling).

Email

Three wives reported initiating email contact with their deployed partners during the study period (10 of 11 email sessions), and one reported that her deployed partner initiated email contact with her. Most wives reported being at home during email sessions (9 of 11 email sessions). Children were not present during any of the email sessions. No wife rated her mood as "10" while communicating with her deployed partner through email (reports of mood ranged from 5 to 8). None of the email sessions were scheduled.

Instant Messaging

Instant messaging sessions were reported by two wives during the study period. Wives reported that their deployed partner most often initiated these sessions (2 of 3). For all instant messaging sessions, wives reported that they were at work or home. Children were not present during any of the instant messaging sessions. No wife rated her mood as "10" while instant messaging with her deployed partner (reports of mood ranged from 3 to 9). None of these sessions was scheduled.

Blog

Most wives reported that they did not keep blogs (n = 5). One wife who reported blogging was at home and her children were not present.

Support Exchanges During Daily Communication

Wives reported giving support (e.g., provide information, shared feelings, ask questions), to their deployed partners during each of the 14 phone calls and the one blog. Wives also reported providing support in nearly all email sessions (10 of 11 sessions) and instant messaging sessions (2 of 3 sessions). Wives likewise indicated receiving support (e.g., shared feelings, felt connected) from their deployed partners during each phone call and each instant messaging session. Similarly, most wives reported receiving support from their partner during email sessions (8 of 11 sessions). In contrast, few decisions were reported during phone calls (5 of 14 calls) or email sessions (2 of 11 sessions). No decisions were reported during instant messaging or the blog post. Only one wife reported resolving a disagreement with her deployed partner during a phone call, and no wife reported resolving a disagreement during email communication, instant messaging sessions, or in a blog (see Fig. 2.1).

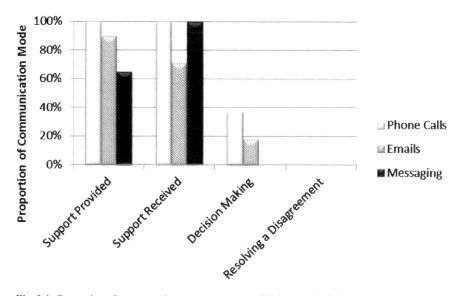

Fig. 2.1 Proportion of contacts where support was provided or received, decisions were made and disagreements resolved for each mode of communication in the feasibility study

Patterns of Daily Communication

Some wives (n = 3) reported that the amount of contact they had initiated with their deployed partners during the study period was typical (i.e., about the same as usual), whereas all others reported less contact than usual with their deployed partners ("he doesn't have access to a computer as easily as he did when he first arrived", "we haven't been getting along", "just keeping him updated on things at home"). Regarding contact initiated by deployed partners during the study period, three wives reported typical contact, two wives reported less contact than usual ("can't get to his computer as easily"), and two wives reported more contact than usual ("Needed to talk about some problems he was having, hear a friendly voice"; "Getting ready to return home"). Only one wife knew when the next contact would take place, and another two indicated that it would be whenever the deployed partner had time.

Findings from our feasibility study indicated that the method of using seven consecutive daily diaries was sufficient to capture a variety of communication modes involving support exchanges in real time. Given the success of recruiting partners who completed daily reports of their communication with deployed military members, we elected to include this method as part of an ongoing study with National Guard service members and their families. Notable revisions included addition of items assessing Facebook and Twitter to our daily diary. Moreover, two open ended questions were added requesting participants to sample topics partners discussed during their communications on any particular day, and other issues on their mind that they did not purposefully communicate with their partners on a particular day.

Family Journeys Study

Participants

Forty-five partners of deployed National Guard service members who participated in a prior wave of the Family Journeys Study were contacted for participation in a daily diary study of communication with their deployed partner. To be included in the daily diary portion of the study participants had to be in a committed relationship and live with the deployed National Guard member prior to deployment. To date, 39 partners have completed the initial daily diary component of the ongoing study. The majority of partners were married to the deployed military member (n = 32). Partners had been in a relationship with the service member for 7.2 years, on average (SD 5.9). The mean age for military members was 33-years-old (SD 8.5) and the mean age for partners was 31-years-old (SD 8.0). The highest level of education was some college for most military members (n = 16) and some college for partners (n = 15). Military members had spent 8.5 years on average in the military (SD 6.4) and had experienced 1 military deployment on average (SD .89; range = 0–3) in the previous 5 years. The majority of participants were female (n = 35) and Caucasian (n = 35). Most participants had at least one child living with them (n = 31) with a wide range in child age among participants (2–21 years-old). The mean child age was 9.44 (SD 5.42). A total of 181 of a possible 273 days of daily observations (39 participants × 7 days) were completed. Five participants provided data for all 7 days, with an average of 5 days of completed diaries across all participants.

Daily Communication

Across all days of our study, all partners reported communicating with deployed military members at least once during the study period. In addition, all modes of communication (except Twitter) were used by at least one couple. The modes of communication reported most frequently (by at least half of the participants) included Facebook (n = 26), Skyping (n = 25), instant messaging (n = 24), and phone calls (n = 22). Other forms of communication reported less frequently (i.e., by less than half of the participants) included email sessions, packages, letters, and blog posts. It is important to note that most partners reported one or two modes of

	Day 1	Day 2	Day 3	Day 4	Day 5	Day 6	Day 7
Partner 1	SK IM EM	IM EM	IM EM FB	IM EM	IM EM	IM EM SK PH	IM EM
Partner 2	PH SK IM EM	PH SK EM RB	PH SK EM	PH EM	PH SK EM	PH	PH
Partner 3	FB	PH FB	FB	FB	SK FB		FB
Partner 4	SK		FB EM	EM FB	SK		
Partner 5	PH	EM	PH EM SK	PH	PH	PH	PH EM

SK = Skype   PH = Phone   IM = Instant messenger   EM = Email   FB = Facebook

Fig. 2.2 Daily communication of partners who completed all seven days of the diary in the Family Journey's Study. *SK* Skype, *PH* Phone, *IM* Instant messenger, *EM* Email, *FB* Facebook

contact each day; however, many partners used multiple modes of communication or the same mode multiple times in a single day (see Fig. 2.2). Frequent modes of communication are detailed.

Facebook

Participants were asked to report whether they communicated on Facebook with their partner (For example, "post on your partner's wall, post something on your wall you intend on your partner seeing, etc."). They were also asked a similar question about their partners' communication with them on Facebook. Facebook posts were reported by 26 partners during the study period (with a range of 1–4 days of posting during the study period). Partners reported posting items or information on Facebook 60 times and that their deployed partners posted 48 times on Facebook. For Facebooking sessions, partners were most often at home while using Facebook (82 of 108 posts). Facebooking was primarily an adult interaction as children participated in only 4 of the Facebooking sessions to deployed partners. Almost half of participants rated their mood as "10" while posting to or reading posts from their deployed partners (reports of mood ranged from 3 to 10). Scheduling a post on Facebook almost never occurred (1 of 108 posts).

Skype

Participants were asked to report whether they "participated in a webcast/video conference/Skype". Many partners (n = 25) reported Skyping with their deployed partner during the study period (with a range of 1–4 Skype conversations during the study period) and 11 partners reported Skyping twice in 1 day. Couples varied in the amount of time they spent talking over Skype (range 10–180 min). During most Skype calls, partners reported being at home (59 of 64). Skyping included children during 32 of the 64 Skype calls and actively participating in 27 of these calls. Additionally, partners often rated their mood as "9" or "10" (very good) while talking with their deployed partner (39 of 64 call). Also, scheduling Skype occurred about one third of the time (28 of 64 calls).

Instant Messaging

Instant messaging sessions were reported by 24 partners during the study period (with a range of 1–7 days of messaging during the study period). Partners were often at home (61 of 80 sessions), and deployed partners initiated most sessions (59 of 80). Children were not often involved in instant messaging (participating in 10 of the 80 instant messaging sessions). Partners infrequently rated their mood as "10" while instant messaging with their deployed partners (4 of 24 partners). In addition, instant messaging was unlikely to be scheduled (4 of 80 sessions).

Phone

Many partners (n = 22) received a phone call from their deployed partners during the study period (with a range of 1–7 phone calls received). Couples varied in the length they talked on the phone (range 1–90 min). During most phone calls, partners reported being at home (49 of 65 phone calls). Although children were present during half of the phone calls (30 of the 65 phone calls), similar to Skyping, children actively participated in only 11 of these phone calls. Additionally, about one third of partners rated their mood as "10" (very good) while talking with their deployed partner (26 of 65 phone calls; mood ranged from 2 to 10). Phone calls were scheduled about one fifth of the time (13 of 65 phone calls).

Support Exchanges During Daily Communication

Partners reported giving support (e.g., providing information, sharing feelings, asking questions), to their deployed partners during each of the 53 Skype conversations and during each of the 65 phone calls. Partners also reported providing support during almost all instant messaging sessions (51 of 52 sessions) and Facebook posts (56 of 60 posts; see Fig. 2.3). Examples of providing support also was reported in the open ended question about the topics covered during each day. For instance, "I just emailed to say that I loved him and hoped he was safe." Another partner related, "I just let him know a quick cute incident that happened with the kids in the hopes it would bring a smile to his face and make him feel a little more connected."

In addition, partners indicated receiving support (e.g., providing information, sharing feelings, asking questions) from their deployed partners during all Skype conversations and instant messaging sessions. Partners also reported receiving support during most Facebook posts (43 of 48 posts received) and phone calls (64 of 65 calls) from deployed partners (see Fig. 2.3). Comments from partners also reflected support received from their deployed partner, "He sent me flowers for my upcoming birthday." Support may also be received during multiple communications throughout the day,

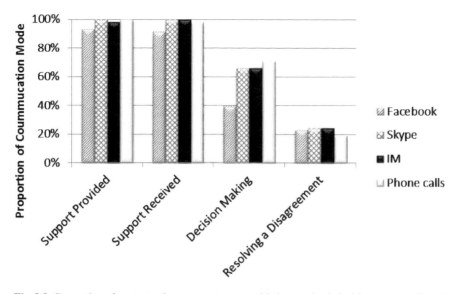

Fig. 2.3 Proportion of contacts where support was provided or received, decisions were made and disagreements resolved for each mode of communication in the Family Journey's Study

> Early on in the day he communicated with me about something he needs me to send him. Then he emailed me in the middle of the day just to encourage me and tell me how proud he was of me. When we talked I shared about some exciting things from my day and he asked me questions about that. At night instant messaging and emailing was about an issue with … that was frustrating me … so we discussed that and he backed me up and let me know he supported me because I was supporting him.

In contrast to the frequency of giving and receiving support, decision making was reported in just over half of the Skype conversations (35 of 53 calls) and instant messaging sessions (37 of 52 sessions). Furthermore, decision making was reported in about half of the phone conversations (34 of 65 phone calls) and infrequently in Facebook posts; (24 of 108 total posts see Fig. 2.3). An example of decision making included, "how much to pay our handy man for work he is doing for us." and, "finding a new place to live." Another partner reported, "I let him know the details from a meeting I had this morning … I've been trying to determine if I … and my husband disagrees with me. He took great care to voice his concern/opinion but not do it in a negative way."

Few partners reported discussing a disagreement during any mode of communication (14 of 108 total Facebook posts; 13 of 53 Skype conversations; 10 of 52 instant messaging sessions; and 9 of 65 phone calls) with deployed partners (see Fig. 2.3). Indications of disagreements include, "I asked my husband why he didn't say anything to me when he was online. I told him I leave my computer on. I let him know that it made me cry this morning to see he was on before I got on and no message." Another partner reported, "He hurt my feelings and must have caught on to the fact that he did. He was apologetic."

Patterns of Daily Communication

During the last day of the study, overall communication patterns during the week were assessed. Most partners (n = 21 of 29 reporting) indicated that the amount of contact they initiated with their deployed partners during the study period was typical (i.e., about the same as usual). Some reported initiating less contact (n = 5) with their deployed partners ("he only gets online when he gets a chance", "didn't get much feedback from his last time, thought maybe he wasn't interested in communicating", "he was on missions", "she was on a different base"). Others reported initiating more contact (n = 3) with their deployed partners ("I find myself getting lonely", "I wanted to hear his voice and see his face. I want him to know how much love he has waiting for him when he gets home"). Regarding contact initiated by deployed partners during the study period, 20 partners reported typical contact, five partners reported less contact than usual ("been on missions", "limited internet access on the base this week"), and four partners reported more contact than usual ("because of the holidays coming up"; "he said he missed me a lot and wanted to see me and hear my voice"). Further, about one half of partners (14 of 29) knew when the next contact with their deployed partner would take place.

Discussion

Our findings suggest that, despite challenges of geographic separation, partners are able to sustain communication that often includes supportive exchanges (Joseph & Afifi, 2012; Merolla, 2010a). Further, our findings suggest that military couples frequently use interactive forms of communication (e.g., Facebook, phone, Skype, instant messaging), consistent with earlier research indicating that phone calls, emails, instant messaging, and blogs are the most frequent modes of communication used by families during military deployment (Merolla, 2010b). We also found that families generally are not able to schedule their contacts with one another during military deployment (Sahlstein et al., 2009).

Notably, all wives reported providing and receiving support during the study period (see Figs. 2.1 and 2.3), and support exchanges were reported for each mode of communication used. As positive support exchanges (Bradbury & Karney, 2004) and marital communication (Ledermann et al., 2010) have been linked with higher marital quality and greater marital stability, if the patterns of support exchanges are disrupted through geographic separation, couples relationships may suffer. On the other hand, if partners are able to sustain patterns of support exchanges during geographic separation, their marriages may be resilient to the stresses associated with geographic separation. Further, our findings of infrequent reports of resolving disagreements during all modes of communication or making decisions echo earlier work where wives reported avoiding disagreements and trying to stick to everyday matters when communicating with their deployed partners (Sahlstein et al., 2009).

Moreover, sticking with everyday matters may also keep service members from being distracted and their performance being negatively affected by worries about home that are being communicated. Partners provided examples of communication that include, "happenings at home", "weather differences between here and there", "how we spent our days", "decorating for the holidays", "hair cut", "how the kids are doing".

By nature of the fact that children often live in the same house as their parents, they are sometimes present during their parents' support exchanges. Little research has been done to demonstrate the frequency or effect of children participating with parents in support communication. In our illustration, children were present during some of the communications, mostly listening in to the conversation. In previous research on wives' experiences during deployment, mothers reported the importance of their children talking with their deployed father on the phone as a way for them to gain authority and respect from their children (Sahlstein et al., 2009).

Findings from our feasibility study and the Family Journeys Study indicated that the method of using seven consecutive daily diaries was adequate to capture a variety of communication modes involving support exchanges in real time. However, improvements to our assessment strategy may increase participants' compliance with daily diary methods. For example, adding a single item at the beginning of each daily diary assessing whether communication with the deployed partner had occurred on that particular day may reduce missing diary days. It is possible that, on days when no communication with the deployed partner had taken place, participants elected not to complete the daily diary assuming they had nothing to report. Moreover, instructions for completing the daily diary should emphasize the importance of accessing and completing each diary each day of the study period. Although some information about support exchanges, decisions, and disagreements were elicited from the additional question asking about topics that were addressed, more information could be obtained by asking participants to describe a supportive exchange, decision or disagreement.

Despite the strength of our daily assessments focusing on modes of communication and support exchanges, limitations of our study should be noted. Our sample reported communication for only 1 week of deployment. A larger sample of families and multiple diary assessments throughout the deployment would afford greater opportunity to capture support communication over time. In addition, although children often were present some communications, reports about the communication between children and their deployed parents were limited. More research on children's exchanges of support with their deployed parents is needed (Sheppard, Malatras, & Israel, 2010).

Furthermore, this chapter is a descriptive representation of daily support exchanges between deployed service members and their partners. When more data are available, an in-depth look at daily support exchanges and partner well-being can be explored. In addition, work examining differences between the modes of communication can be conducted to determine if some modes are more conducive to communicating support during deployment. Importantly, future work should examine whether frequent daily support exchanges are associated with relationship outcomes such as relationship quality during deployment and relationship resiliency during reintegration.

Our study of daily support exchanges in military families provides an initial glimpse into the ways in which spouses interact and communicate support for one another while separated during deployment (Karney & Crown, 2007; for miscommunication or communication problems during deployment see Hinojosa et al., 2012). Our findings regarding daily support exchanges extend existing knowledge by revealing that partners used multiple modes of contact to exchange support with one another. Clinicians, practitioners, and others should be aware of the importance of providing multiple modes of communication for deployed partners to sustain supportive contact with families at home. More attention to support exchanges during deployment and resiliency of military families clearly is warranted.

Acknowledgment This research was supported in part by the Military Family Research Institute with funding from the Lilly Endowment.

References

Aducci, C. J., Baptist, J. A., George, J., Barros, P. M., & Goff, B. S. N. (2011). The recipe for being a good military wife: How military wives managed OIF/OEF deployment. *Journal of Feminist Family Theory, 23*, 231–249.

Bolger, N., Davis, A., & Rafaeli, E. (2003). Diary methods: Capturing life as it is lived. *Annual Review of Psychology, 54*, 579–616.

Bradbury, T. N., & Karney, B. R. (2004). Understanding the longitudinal course of marriage. *Journal of Marriage and Family, 66*, 862–879.

Conger, R. D., Rueter, M. A., & Elder, G. H., Jr. (1999). Couple resilience to economic pressure. *Journal of Personality and Social Psychology, 76*, 54–71.

Cutrona, C. E., Shaffer, P. A., Wesner, K. A., & Gardner, K. A. (2007). Optimally matching support and perceived spousal sensitivity. *Journal of Family, 21*, 754–758.

Diamond, L. M., Hicks, A. M., & Otter-Henderson, K. D. (2008). Every time you go away: changes in affect, behavior, and physiology associated with travel-related separations from romantic partners. *Journal of Personality and Social Psychology, 95*, 385–403.

Dimiceli, E. E., Steinhardt, A. M., & Smith, E. S. (2010). Stressful experiences, coping strategies, and predictors of health-related outcomes among wives of deployed military servicemen. *Armed Forces and Society, 36*(2), 351–373.

Ender, M. G. (2005). Military brats: Film representations of children from military families. *Armed Forces & Society, 32*, 24–43.

Frisby, B. N., Byrnes, K., Mansson, D. H., Booth-Butterfield, M., & Birmingham, M. K. (2011). Topic avoidance, everyday talk, and stress in romantic military and non-military couples. *Communication Studies, 62*, 241–257.

Hertlein, K. (2012). Digital dwelling: Technology in couple and family relationships. *Family Relations, 61*, 374–387.

Hinojosa, R., Hinojosa, M. S., & Högnäs, R. S. (2012). Problems with veteran-family communication during operation enduring freedom/operation Iraqi freedom military deployment. *Military Medicine, 177*(2), 191–197.

Joseph, A. L., & Afifi, T. D. (2012). Military wives; stressful disclosures to their deployed husbands: The role of protective buffering. *Journal of Applied Communication Research, 38,* 412–434.

Karney, B. R., & Crown, J. S. (2007). *Families under stress: An assessment of data, theory, and research on marriage and divorce in the military.* Santa Monica, CA: National Defense Research Institute, RAND Corporation.

Laurenceau, J. P., & Bolger, N. (2005). Using diary methods to study family processes. *Journal of Family Psychology, 19,* 86–97.

Ledermann, T., Bodenmann, G., Rudaz, M., & Bradbury, T. N. (2010). Stress, communication, and *marital quality in couples. Family Relations, 59,* 195–206. doi:10.1111/j.1741-3729. 2010.00595.x

MacDermid Wadsworth, S. (2010). Family risk and resilience in the context of war and terrorism. *Journal of Marriage and Family, 72,* 537–556.

Merolla, A. J. (2010a). Relational maintenance and noncopresence reconsidered: Conceptualizing geographic separation in close relationships. *Communication Theory, 20,* 169–193. doi:10.1111/j/1468-2885.210.01359.x

Merolla, A. J. (2010b). Relational maintenance during military deployment: Perspectives of wives of deployed U.S. soldiers. *Journal of Applied Communication Research, 38*(1), 4–26. doi:10.1080/00909880903483557

Sahlstein, E., Maguire, K. C., & Timmerman, L. (2009). Contradictions and praxis contextualized by wartime deployment: Wives' perspectives revealed through relational dialectics. *Communication Monographs, 76,* 421–442. doi:10.1080/03637750903300239

Schmitt, M., Kliegel, M., & Shapiro, A. (2007). Marital Interaction in middle and old age: A predictor of marital satisfaction? *The International Journal of Aging and Human Development, 65*(4), 283–300. doi:10.2190/AG.65.4.a

Schumm, W. R., Bell, D. B., Ender, M. G., & Rice, R. E. (2004). Expectations, use, and evaluations of communications media among deployed peacekeepers. *Armed Forces and Society, 30,* 649–662.

Schumm, W. R., Bell, D. B., & Gade, P. A. (2000). Effects of a military overseas peacekeeping deployment on marital quality, satisfaction, and stability. *Psychological Reports, 87,* 815–821.

Sheppard, S. C., Malatras, J. W., & Israel, A. C. (2010). The impact of deployment on U.S. military families. *American Psychologist, 65,* 599–609.

SteelFisher, G. K., Zaslavsky, A. M., & Blendon, R. J. (2008). Health-related impact of deployment extensions on spouses of active duty army personnel. *Military Medicine, 173*(3), 221–229.

Stone, A. A., & Shiffman, S. (2002). Capturing momentary, self-report data: A proposal for reporting guidelines. *Annals of Behavioral Medicine, 24,* 236–243.

Chapter 3
Relational Turbulence Within Military Couples During Reintegration Following Deployment

Leanne K. Knobloch and Jennifer A. Theiss

Abstract Reunion following deployment is a critical juncture for returning service members and their romantic partners. Studies suggest that reintegration can be an emotionally volatile period of heightened expectations, profound joys, and unexpected frustrations. We draw on the *relational turbulence model* to shed light on how military couples navigate the reentry period. The model argues that times of transition are turbulent within romantic relationships because people encounter relational uncertainty as well as interference from partners in their everyday routines. We devote this chapter to reviewing the model's assumptions, describing data from investigations involving recently-reunited romantic partners, proposing recommendations for practice, and delineating pathways for future research.

Keywords Interference from partners • Military deployment • Relational turbulence • Relational uncertainty • Transitions

> *After my husband returned from deployment,*
> *there was some difficulty in adjusting to living with each other*
> *again [...]*
> *the few months after his return were certainly the most trying*
> *time in our relationship.*
>
> – at-home National Guard wife, 28 years old

L.K. Knobloch, Ph.D. (✉)
Department of Communication, University of Illinois, 3001 Lincoln Hall,
702 South Wright Street, Urbana, IL 61801, USA
e-mail: knobl@illinois.edu

J.A. Theiss, Ph.D.
Department of Communication, Rutgers University, 4 Huntington Street,
New Brunswick, NJ 08901, USA
e-mail: jtheiss@rutgers.edu

S. MacDermid Wadsworth and D.S. Riggs (eds.), *Military Deployment and its Consequences for Families*, Risk and Resilience in Military and Veteran Families,
DOI 10.1007/978-1-4614-8712-8_3, © Springer Science+Business Media New York 2014

The cycle of deployment and reunion is emotionally charged for U.S. military personnel and their romantic partners. During a tour of duty, service members focus on accomplishing their mission and protecting the safety of those around them (Hosek, Kavanagh, & Miller, 2006), and at-home partners shoulder sole responsibility for running the household, managing finances, and caring for children (Merolla, 2010; Wood, Scarville, & Gravino, 1995). Although many military couples eagerly await reunion, sometimes with romanticized expectations of what the reintegration period will be like (Wood et al., 1995), the post-deployment transition presents new obstacles (Sahlstein, Maguire, & Timmerman, 2009; Wiens & Boss, 2006). Returning service members may have trouble acclimating to the changes that transpired while they were away (Bowling & Sherman, 2008), partners who managed the household autonomously during the deployment may find it difficult to cede their decision-making power (Gambardella, 2008), and both people may be unsure how to reestablish physical and emotional intimacy (Vormbrock, 1993).

The challenges posed by reunion have led some scholars to argue that reintegrating service members back into home life can be more difficult than deployment itself (Huebner, Mancini, Wilcox, Grass, & Grass, 2007; Mmari, Roche, Sudhinaraset, & Blum, 2009). In fact, military personnel and at-home partners can experience heightened levels of depression, anxiety, post-traumatic stress disorder, and dyadic distress during the 6 months following homecoming (McNulty, 2005; Nelson Goff, Crow, Reisbig, & Hamilton, 2007; Renshaw, Rodrigues, & Jones, 2008). Unfortunately, however, much remains unknown about the relationship characteristics that impede dyadic well-being upon reunion (Bowling & Sherman, 2008; Palmer, 2008; Sayers, 2011).

We have collaborated with colleagues over the past decade to construct a theory that may shed light on this topic. The *relational turbulence model* distinguishes the relationship parameters that foster upheaval during times of transition within romantic relationships (Knobloch & Theiss, 2010; Solomon & Knobloch, 2004; Solomon & Theiss, 2011). Our goal is to synthesize our scholarship on the model to illuminate how military couples negotiate the post-deployment transition. We allocate the bulk of this chapter to explaining the model's core premises and describing empirical tests conducted both inside and outside the context of military couples. We conclude by identifying implications for practice and directions for future inquiry.

Using the Relational Turbulence Model to Understand Reintegration

> *Things are much more intense, the good times are better, the sex is incredible, the fights are more intense as well.*
>
> – at-home Army wife, 37 years old

The relational turbulence model (depicted in Fig. 3.1) seeks to explain how romantic partners experience times of transition (Solomon & Knobloch, 2001, 2004). According to the model, *transitions* are periods of discontinuity within

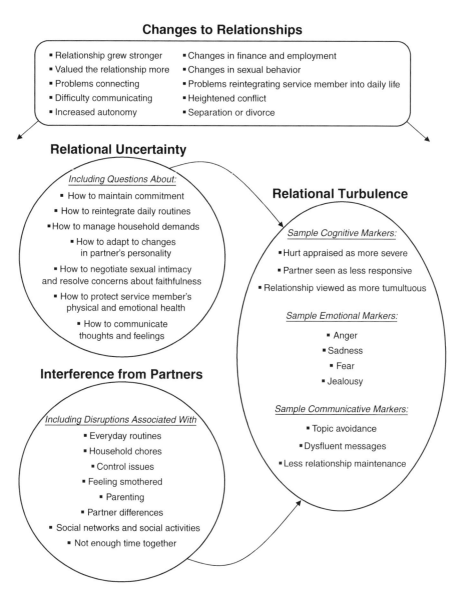

Fig. 3.1 The relational turbulence model in the context of reintegration following deployment

interpersonal relationships marked by changes in how people define their partnership and act toward each other (Knobloch, 2007). The model proposes that day-to-day events take on heightened significance during times of transition (Solomon, Weber, & Steuber, 2010). *Relational turbulence* is people's tendency to be cognitively, emotionally, and behaviorally reactive to relationship circumstances that otherwise would be relatively commonplace. The model argues that individuals draw extreme conclusions, feel intense emotions, and behave in polarizing ways during transitions. Both positively-valenced and negatively-valenced events may be more consequential to people when relationships are in flux (e.g., a small romantic gesture takes on added importance, a partner's mildly annoying habit becomes fodder for conflict, a constructive suggestion is interpreted as a critical jab).

Relational turbulence, the core outcome in the model, is an umbrella construct that encompasses a diversity of cognitive, emotional, and behavioral markers of upheaval (Solomon & Theiss, 2011). Examples include (a) cognitive appraisals of irritations, (b) feelings of anger, sadness, and hurt, and (c) behaviors such as avoiding communication about sensitive issues (Solomon et al., 2010). As these examples make clear, relational turbulence is not a proxy for people's perceptions of intimacy, closeness, commitment, or satisfaction (e.g., Theiss & Knobloch, in press). Rather, relational turbulence indexes the cognitive, emotional, and behavioral ways individuals are reactive to daily events that would be quite routine if partners were not in the midst of a transition (Solomon & Theiss, 2011; Solomon et al., 2010).

Scholars have employed the relational turbulence model to shed light on a variety of transitions within romantic relationships, including how dating partners negotiate the transition from casual dating to serious involvement, how romantic couples cope with infertility, and how spouses manage a breast cancer diagnosis (Solomon et al., 2010). More importantly for our purposes, a growing body of research implies that the model has utility for understanding how military couples navigate the transition from deployment to reintegration. The following subsections discuss our work on this front.

Changes to the Relationship

> We both experienced very different lives through the
> deployment, and it was an adjustment to become a
> married couple again.
>
> – at-home National Guard wife, 30 years old

A central assumption of the relational turbulence model is that romantic couples are inundated by changes to their relationship during times of transition (Solomon & Theiss, 2011; see Fig. 3.1). To test this claim in the context of reunion following deployment, Knobloch and Theiss (2012) asked 259 recently-reunited individuals (137 service members, 122 at-home partners) to answer the following question: "In what ways, if any, did your relationship change after deployment compared to before deployment?" Participants' responses were content analyzed and then coded into 10 categories by a team of independent judges (Krippendorff's α = .81). Ten changes were salient to military couples during reintegration: (a) their relationship grew stronger, (b) they valued their relationship more, (c) they had problems reconnecting, (d) they had difficulty communicating, (e) one or both partners grew more autonomous, (f) they encountered changes in finances and employment, (g) they experienced changes in sexual behavior, (h) they had problems reintegrating the service member into daily life, (i) their relationship contained more conflict, and (j) they contemplated separation or divorce. See Table 3.1 for exemplars in participants' own words.

These data are valuable for depicting the kinds of upheaval that may transpire upon reunion. They also imply a good news/bad news scenario for military couples facing reintegration. A cause for optimism is that 33 % of people's substantive comments noted that they grew stronger as a couple or that they appreciated their partner more. In contrast to work highlighting the destructive outcomes of deployment, these findings echo other results implying that separation during a tour of duty can be constructive for military couples (e.g., Hosek et al., 2006; Karney & Crown, 2011; Newby et al., 2005). Conversely, a cause for pessimism is that participants noted a host of ways that their relationship was harmed by deployment. The relational turbulence model recognizes that times of transition open the door for both dyadic growth and dyadic decline (Solomon & Theiss, 2011); the vital task is pinpointing the relationship characteristics that leave some military couples vulnerable to turbulence. We turn to that issue next.

Relational Uncertainty: An Intrapersonal Mechanism of Turbulence

> *How can we try to reconnect after such a long separation?*
>
> – deployed Army husband, 23 years old

The relational turbulence model delineates two processes to explain why transitions are filled with upheaval (see Fig. 3.1). The model's intrapersonal explanation for turbulence emphasizes the multitude of questions that materialize when romantic relationships are in flux. *Relational uncertainty* is the degree of confidence people have in their perceptions of involvement within interpersonal relationships (Knobloch, 2010; Knobloch & Solomon, 2002a). More colloquially, relational uncertainty is how sure or unsure individuals are about the dynamics of a relationship. Although relational uncertainty and relationship satisfaction tend to be negatively correlated (Knobloch, 2008a; Knobloch & Knobloch-Fedders, 2010), relational uncertainty is distinct because it indexes how definitive, conclusive, and decisive people are in their judgments about involvement (Knobloch & Theiss, 2011a; Theiss & Knobloch, in press).

Relational uncertainty arises from self, partner, and relationship sources (Berger & Bradac, 1982; Knobloch & Solomon, 2002a). *Self uncertainty* involves the questions people have about their own participation in a relationship. Sample items measuring self uncertainty include "How certain are you about your view of this relationship?" and "How certain are you about how important this relationship is to you?" (Knobloch & Solomon, 1999). *Partner uncertainty* indexes the questions individuals have about their partner's participation in a relationship. Sample items include "How certain are you about how your partner feels about your relationship?" and "How certain are you about your partner's goals for the future of your

Table 3.1 Relationship changes reported by recently-reunited individuals

1. *Relationship is Stronger* (18.0 % of the substantive comments)

After being apart for so long, [our relationship] is stronger than ever. We truly appreciate each other and realize the sacrifices we both make for us and our daughter.

  – at-home Army wife, 21 years old

We are more committed than ever.

  – at-home National Guard wife, 39 years old

Since I returned home, our marriage and relationship with each other has been much improved.

  – deployed Army husband, 35 years old

2. *Value the Relationship More* (14.7 %)

My husband appreciates me more.

  – at-home National Guard wife, 36 years old

I think we've become more appreciative of each other and are more caring towards one another.

  – deployed wife, part of a dual-deployed couple, branch not reported, 37 years old

I have a greater appreciation for my husband. I respect him for what he does. [...] No matter what the circumstances are, the longer we are together, the better our relationship becomes. Although deployments are hard, they allow us to see exactly what our relationship is made of.

  – at-home National Guard wife, 42 years old

3. *Problems Reconnecting* (11.8 %)

It was very hard to get used to him being back in the house, disciplining the children, making decisions.

  – at-home National Guard wife, 37 years old

It has been very difficult on our three girls because they don't understand why Daddy has changed.

  – deployed Army husband, 32 years old

Closer to wife, more separate from children. They have changed more than I have, I feel. [...] This was my third deployment, the second in two years [...] Pending a board [evaluation] due to twenty IED blasts in Iraq, so maybe I have changed and not them.

  – deployed National Guard husband, 44 years old

4. *Difficulty Communicating* (10.9 %)

The communication piece has been tougher due to PTSD.

  – at-home National Guard wife, 38 years old

By the time I got back home he was very excited and so was I, but we are having a few challenges with [...] communicating.

  – deployed Air Force wife, 39 years old

Communication was difficult.

  – deployed National Guard husband, 28 years old

5. *Increased Autonomy* (10.4 %)

My husband was a little withdrawn and [more] independent than before he left. He doesn't rely on me as much as he used to.

– at-home Army wife, 37 years old

My spouse became more independent and took on more responsibilities.

– deployed Marine husband, 31 years old

We are used to being on our own and now have our own patterns of doing things.

– at-home National Guard wife, 38 years old

6. *Changes in Finances and Employment* (9.5 %)

I am now out of work due to being laid off [...] there is much more stress than before.

– deployed National Guard husband, 47 years old

I still need his help with bills.

– at-home Navy wife, 22 years old

7. *Changes in Sexual Behavior* (7.6 %)

Intimacy initially decreased upon return.

– deployed Army husband, 35 years old

Things are much less romantic, more of a friendship than a romantic relationship.

– at-home Army wife, 41 years old

We are both more affectionate toward each other.

– at-home woman involved in a serious dating relationship with a National Guard member, 28 years old

8. *Problems Reintegrating the Service Member into Daily Life* (5.7 %)

I was used to being the only one taking care of three children and the household. I had a hard time adjusting to him being here again and he had a hard time not taking control.

– at-home National Guard wife, 41 years old

I functioned as a single parent and handled the kids and household on my own. I found he returned to "my" home instead of "our" home.

– at-home Army wife, 47 years old

(continued)

Table 3.1 (continued)

9. *Heightened Conflict* (5.7 %)

He is more angry.

– at-home National Guard wife, 39 years old

I have a shorter temper to put up with the daily B.S.

– deployed National Guard husband, 36 years old

A little more conflict.

– at-home National Guard wife, age not reported

10. *Separation or Divorce* (5.7 %)

We grew apart and ended up filing for legal separation.

– deployed National Guard husband, 45 years old

There was an issue that arose because of the deployment that almost brought us to a break up.

– deployed National Guard husband, 32 years old

Note. $N = 211$ substantive comments in response to the item: "In what ways, if any, did your relationship change after deployment compared to before deployment?" (Knobloch & Theiss, 2012)

relationship?" *Relationship uncertainty* encompasses the questions people have about the nature of the relationship itself apart from self or partner concerns. Sample items include "How certain are you about the current status of your relationship?" and "How certain are you about the future of your relationship?" The three sources of ambiguity together comprise relational uncertainty.

If the model's reasoning is correct, then military couples are likely to encounter a diversity of questions about their relationship upon reunion. Scholars have speculated that individuals navigating reentry may face questions about how to cultivate closeness, how much their partner values their relationship, how to reconnect emotionally and physically, how to broach sensitive topics, and how much to reveal about their experiences during the separation (Bowling & Sherman, 2008; Faber, Willerton, Clymer, MacDermid, & Weiss, 2008; Sahlstein et al., 2009). We conducted an explicit investigation of this issue by asking returning service members and at-home partners to list issues of relational uncertainty, if any, they experienced during reunion following deployment (Knobloch & Theiss, 2012). Outside observers coded the data into seven themes: (a) how to maintain commitment, (b) how to reintegrate daily routines, (c) how to manage household demands, (d) how to adapt to changes in their partner's personality, (e) how to renegotiate sexual intimacy and address concerns about faithfulness, (f) how to protect the service member's physical and emotional health, and (g) how to communicate their thoughts and feelings to each other (Krippendorff's $\alpha = .84$). Table 3.2 contains examples of how participants articulated each theme. The responses, viewed as a set, suggest that reentry is rife with relational uncertainty for military couples.

The relational turbulence model theorizes that relational uncertainty fosters turmoil because people are hampered in their ability to comprehend, interpret, and understand their relationship (Knobloch, 2007; Knobloch & Theiss, 2010; see also Knobloch, Miller, Bond, & Mannone, 2007). Accordingly, the model argues that individuals should be cognitively, emotionally, and behaviorally reactive under conditions of relational uncertainty (Solomon et al., 2010; Theiss, Knobloch, Checton, & Magsamen-Conrad, 2009). In other words, people experiencing questions about their relationship should experience upheaval.

Empirical evidence supports the model's premise that relational uncertainty predicts relational turbulence in various forms. For example, dating partners experiencing relational uncertainty judge unexpected episodes (Knobloch & Solomon, 2002b), hurtful events (Theiss et al., 2009), and irritating partner behavior (Solomon & Knobloch, 2004; Theiss & Knobloch, 2009; Theiss & Solomon, 2006b) to be more severe. They also feel more anger, sadness, fear, and jealousy (Knobloch, Miller, & Carpenter, 2007; Knobloch, Solomon, & Cruz, 2001; Theiss & Solomon, 2006a) and view their courtship as more tumultuous (Knobloch & Theiss, 2010; McLaren, Solomon, & Priem, 2011). In fact, when individuals are unsure about their dating partner's commitment, their courtship is more likely to dissolve (Arriaga, Reed, Goodfriend, & Agnew, 2006). Moreover, spouses experiencing relational uncertainty report more negative reactions to sexual activity (Theiss & Nagy, 2010). Although these studies were conducted outside of the deployment context, they suggest that relational uncertainty may generate turbulence.

Table 3.2 Relational uncertainty reported by recently-reunited individuals

1. *How to Maintain Commitment* (19.1 % of the substantive comments)

Were we going to stay married?
– deployed Army husband, 35 years old

I worry that our relationship is not the "idealized" one he focused on while he was gone.
– at-home National Guard wife, 33 years old

Not sure he would still want to be with me.
– at-home National Guard wife, 36 years old

2. *How to Reintegrate Daily Routines* (18.5 %)

How do we go back to doing things together when we got used to life apart?
– deployed National Guard husband, 45 years old

If I would ever get back into the swing of things, normal life, and a routine.
– deployed National Guard man, involved in a serious dating relationship, 28 years old

I had been used to being "single" and the breadwinner and the head of the household. I was curious and unsure about our re-adjustment being back together.
– at-home wife, branch not reported, 27 years old

3. *How to Manage Household Stressors* (15.9 %)

If we could make it on less money once I left active duty.
– deployed Army husband, 33 years old

Was my partner going to handle the kids ok? Was he going to handle everyday life that I had been dealing with for the last year?
– at-home National Guard wife, 27 years old

Will he get his job back? Can we afford to buy a house now?
– at-home National Guard wife, 39 years old

4. *How to Adapt to Personality Changes* (15.0 %)

Why do we feel like we must relearn the other person?
– deployed National Guard husband, 28 years old

Will I be the same as when I left?
– deployed and engaged National Guard male, 55 years old

I became extremely independent and self-sufficient while he was gone, would I be able to give back some of the responsibilities so that we'd be an interdependent couple again, or would I be too self-sufficient and not need him?
– at-home Army wife, 28 years old

5. *How to Renegotiate Sexual Behavior and Address Questions about Infidelity* (14.3 %)

You always see these dramatic, romantic welcome homes. But we did not have that; it was a peck on the lips and load up the bags. Even when we tried to do something romantic it was forced. My confidence in this relationship is gone and I am unsure of how to get it back.
  – deployed wife, branch not reported, 32 years old

She wasn't sure if I felt sexually attracted to her. I wasn't sure of our intimacy also.
  – deployed National Guard husband, 32 years old

Did he meet someone he would rather be sharing his life with?
  – at-home National Guard wife, 40 years old

6. *How to Protect the Service Member's Health* (11.8 %)

Will he have problems sleeping and/or readjusting?
  – at-home National Guard wife, 41 years old

Will my partner stay angry like he is now ever since he has gotten home?
  – at-home woman engaged to a National Guard member, 22 years old

Not sure if she will understand or look at me the same way after finding out I killed people.
  – deployed National Guard husband, 37 years old

7. *How to Communicate Effectively* (5.4 %)

Would we be able to talk about anything? We had lived very separate lives for several months.
  – at-home National Guard wife, 40 years old

Concerns about large amounts of silence, nothing to talk about.
  – deployed Marine male involved in a casual dating relationship, 21 years old

At first you don't know how to treat that person b/c they may not have told you "everything" that went on out there.
  – at-home National Guard wife, 27 years old

Note. N = 314 substantive comments in response to the item: "Please list and briefly describe issues of uncertainty you experienced when you/your partner returned from deployment (after you were reunited)." (Knobloch & Theiss, 2012)

Other tests of the model reveal that relational uncertainty may make communicating more challenging. Individuals experiencing relational uncertainty judge communication with their dating partner to be more difficult (Knobloch, Satterlee, & DiDomenico, 2010; Knobloch & Solomon, 2005; Knobloch & Theiss, 2011b), formulate requests that are less fluent (Knobloch, 2006), and engage in fewer relationship maintenance behaviors (Dainton, 2003). Spouses who are entertaining questions about their marriage appraise conversations with their partner to be more threatening to themselves and to their marriage (Knobloch, Miller, Bond, et al., 2007) and communicate indirectly about sexual intimacy (Theiss, 2011). Individuals who are grappling with relational uncertainty avoid talking about sensitive topics within sibling relationships (Bevan, Stetzenbach, Batson, & Bullo, 2006), parent–child relationships (Afifi & Schrodt, 2003), cross-sex friendships (Afifi & Burgoon, 1998), and dating relationships (Knobloch & Carpenter-Theune, 2004). All of these findings cohere with the theorizing of the relational turbulence model that relational uncertainty may escalate the difficulty of communicating with a partner.

Does relational uncertainty portend upheaval during the post-deployment transition as well? Two recent tests of the model imply that that military couples grappling with relational uncertainty during reunion are vulnerable to turbulence. In a first study, Knobloch and Theiss (2011a) surveyed 220 service members living in 27 states who had returned home from deployment within the past 6 months. Findings indicated that military personnel experiencing relational uncertainty were less satisfied with their romantic relationship. In a second study, Theiss and Knobloch (in press) collected online self-report data from 235 individuals (128 service members, 107 at-home partners) recently reunited following a tour of duty. Results demonstrated that returning service members and at-home partners who were experiencing relational uncertainty (a) reported doing less to maintain their relationship, (b) judged their partner to be less responsive to their needs, and (c) perceived their relationship to be more tumultuous. These results implicate relational uncertainty in the upheaval that military couples may face upon homecoming.

Interference from Partners: An Interpersonal Mechanism of Turbulence

The dynamics of the household are somewhat different. My wife knows so much about the kids, the bills, everything. I am attempting to find where I fit in.

– deployed Army husband, 31 years old

The relational turbulence model designates interference from partners as a second foundation of turmoil during times of transition (Solomon & Knobloch, 2001, 2004; see Fig. 3.1). *Interference from partners* occurs when a partner disrupts an individual's ability to accomplish a goal. Sample items measuring interference from partners include "My partner interferes with the things I need to do each day." and "My partner causes me to waste time." (Knobloch & Solomon, 2004). The model proposes that times of transition are tumultuous because shifts in everyday routines make romantic partners prone to interfering with each other's goals. During times of dyadic stability, individuals integrate their daily activities in ways that help them facilitate each other's goals, but when circumstances change, frequent disruptions are inevitable. The model posits that transitions are stressful until partners learn how to participate in each other's daily activities in ways that are facilitative rather than disruptive (Knobloch & Solomon, 2004; Solomon et al., 2010). Although interference from partners tends to correspond with relationship dissatisfaction, interference from partners is a different construct because it indexes disruptions to goal-directed behavior (Knobloch & Theiss, 2011a; Theiss & Knobloch, in press).

According to the model, military couples may be susceptible to interference from partners during reintegration. Both anecdotal evidence and empirical evidence suggest that reunion following deployment can be disruptive for everyone involved. Anecdotally, scholars have surmised that returning service members must rediscover their place in the family system and adjust to the household routines that evolved while they were away, and at-home partners must assimilate the newcomer and yield at least some control over domestic decisions (Bowling & Sherman, 2008; Faber et al., 2008; Gambardella, 2008; Wood et al., 1995). Empirically, we evaluated the model's claim by asking recently-reunited service members and at-home partners to report ways their mate has made it harder for them to complete their everyday activities upon reunion (Knobloch & Theiss, 2012). The data were content analyzed and then coded by independent judges (Krippendorff's α = .84). Results revealed disruptions tied to (a) everyday routines, (b) household chores, (c) control issues, (d) feeling smothered, (e) parenting, (f) partner differences, (g) social networks and social activities, and (h) not enough time together (see Table 3.3 for sample comments). These results imply that reintegration provides ample opportunities for romantic partners to interfere with each other's daily routines.

The relational turbulence model draws on Berscheid's (1991) premise to propose that people experience strong negative emotion when their romantic partner disrupts their everyday goals (e.g., Knobloch, Miller, & Carpenter, 2007). By extension, the model argues that interference from partners should spark turbulence because individuals are frustrated by the hindrance (e.g., Knobloch & Theiss, 2010; Solomon & Theiss, 2008; Theiss & Solomon, 2006a). The model's theorizing suggests that people are likely to be reactive when interference from partners is salient (e.g., Solomon et al., 2010).

Extant data support the model's prediction that interference from partners coincides with relational turbulence in myriad forms. Individuals experiencing disruptions from a dating partner report that their relationship contains more turmoil (Knobloch, 2007; Knobloch & Theiss, 2010; McLaren et al., 2011). Similarly, they feel more negative emotion, including anger, sadness, fear, and jealousy (Knobloch & Theiss, 2010; Theiss & Solomon, 2006a). Not only do they perceive their partner's irritating behavior to be more severe and more threatening to their relationship (Solomon & Knobloch, 2004; Theiss & Knobloch, 2009), but they also appraise

Table 3.3 Interference from partners reported by recently-reunited individuals

1. *Everyday Routines* (27.1 % of the substantive comments)

I got used to being able to watch the TV shows I wanted to after work. I got used to being able to wait until the weekends to take care of the finances and the usual chores around the house. I got used to having a bed to myself.

– at-home National Guard wife, 46 years old

I feel like the time it would take me to complete a task during the deployment was not an issue as long as I met the deadline […] after the deployment I feel like I am rushed a lot by my wife as it seems she doesn't think about how long something takes to accomplish.

– deployed National Guard husband, 32 years old

Well, our way of life for a year has been disrupted so it is just hard to get back into a new "normal" routine.

– at-home National Guard wife, 38 years old

2. *Household Chores* (19.6 %)

At times I felt I was making it harder for my wife when doing certain daily tasks, such as loading/unloading the dishwasher. […] I felt I was getting in her way sometimes.

– deployed National Guard husband, 35 years old

My husband didn't know what to do all day long and he always had to be doing something. He tried to be overly helpful around the house.

– at-home National Guard wife, 21 years old

Extra laundry. More cooking. Another person to clean up after.

– at-home National Guard wife, 40 years old

3. *Control Issues* (14.1 %)

He is a morning person and used to being in charge. I am a night person and used to being in charge. Trying to coordinate schedules and cooperate with each other has been difficult … often we have totally different ideas about what needs to get done each day.

– at-home National Guard wife, 40 years old

I was used to doing things on my own and without thought to others except for on a business level.

– deployed National Guard husband, 51 years old

He has made it more challenging by having to coordinate everything with him and make sure he is on board with it from chores to entertainment. It was easier just being the one who called the shots.

– at-home National Guard wife, 29 years old

4. *Feeling Smothered* (12.2 %)

Wanting to be around me all the time.

– deployed Air Force husband, 53 years old

I had an anxiety of leaving again. So I found myself smothering my family.

– deployed Army husband, 26 years old

My husband was very clingy at first.

– at-home National Guard wife, 21 years old

5. *Parenting* (9.0 %)

My partner has a set routine with the children and I have to reintegrate.
  – deployed National Guard husband, 40 years old

I think my wife is struggling with pushing back from the primary and sole parent role because it's been her routine for so long.
  – deployed National Guard husband, 33 years old

[He] wanted to stay out and not stay home with the family and help out with the kids.
  – at-home National Guard wife, 28 years old

6. *Partner Differences* (7.4 %)

During the short time he has been back he has been very moody.
  – at-home woman engaged to a National Guard member, 25 years old

It was harder for her to adjust than it was for me. It was a reversal of PTSD in a way. I noticed that she would be more agitated than I was at times.
  – deployed Army husband, 29 years old

His frustration level with the situation is much higher than mine – his tension is making me more tense.
  – at-home National Guard wife, 33 years old

7. *Social Networks and Social Activities* (6.3 %)

He doesn't understand that I want to spend time with my friends that I served with.
  – deployed National Guard wife, 43 years old

Time with family and friends is sometimes an issue.
  – deployed Army husband, 39 years old

I am used to being able to see my family and friends when it works for me and not have to check the schedule with anyone else.
  – at-home National Guard wife, 30 years old

8. *Not Enough Time Together* (4.3 %)

I want to spend time with him instead of my normal activities.
  – at-home National Guard wife, 38 years old

Always wanting to be together.
  – deployed husband, branch not reported, 24 years old

I would rather spend more time with him rather than accomplishing what I need to do.
  – at home woman involved in a serious dating relationship with an Army member, 19 years old

Note. $N = 255$ substantive comments in response to the item: "Please list and briefly describe ways in which your partner has made it harder for you to complete your everyday activities since you have been reunited after deployment." (Knobloch & Theiss, 2012)

their partner's hurtful behavior to be more intense, intentional, and damaging to their relationship (Theiss et al., 2009). Within the context of marriage, spouses who are grappling with interference from partners report more negative responses to sexual relations (Theiss & Nagy, 2010). These findings, although not tied to military couples directly, corroborate the theory's premise that interference from partners may prompt turbulence.

Two other investigations demonstrate that people may have difficulty communicating under conditions of interference from partners. In Knobloch and Schmelzer's (2008) study of message production within courtship, individuals contending with hindrance from their romantic partner formulated date request messages that were less fluent, and they also evaluated those messages to be more threatening to themselves and their relationship. Similarly, in Knobloch's (2008b) observational study of 125 married couples, spouses experiencing interference from partners (a) engaged in conversations that were less fluent and less synchronous, (b) judged the conversations to be less pleasant and less effective, (c) displayed less liking for their spouse and perceived less liking from their spouse, and (d) felt more anger and sadness during the conversations. These results imply that couples who frequently disrupt each other's everyday routines may have problems communicating effectively.

If the reasoning of the relational turbulence model is valid in the context of reunion following deployment, then military couples experiencing interference from partners during reintegration should encounter turbulence. Two studies support the model's premise linking interference from partners with upheaval among military couples. For example, Knobloch and Theiss (2011a) found that military personnel recently home after deployment were less satisfied with their romantic relationship under conditions of interference from partners. Similarly, Theiss and Knobloch (in press) observed that returning service members and at-home partners who were experiencing interference from partners (a) provided fewer assurances to their partner, (b) employed less constructive conflict management behaviors, (c) judged their partner to be less responsive to their needs, and (d) appraised their relationship as more tumultuous. The results of these two investigations bolster the model's claim that military couples grappling with interference from partners upon reunion may face turbulence.

Recommendations for Practice

> *The deployment has caused a well-oiled team before the mobilization to be disjointed. [This is surprising] because we both had plans to yield to the other to help reintegration. So there is no leader in our relationship at this point—only two followers trying to follow each other around.*
>
> – deployed Army husband, 39 years old

Our theorizing and our data, taken together, imply three guidelines for promoting dyadic well-being during reintegration. One suggestion is that military couples prepare for the possibility of turbulence. If military couples recognize that upheaval is a predictable part of reunion, they may be better equipped to address any issues that materialize. Related advice is to avoid being caught off-guard by a delayed onset of turbulence. Military couples may enjoy a honeymoon period of tranquility immediately after homecoming, but individuals are vulnerable to disappointment if the harmony is fleeting (Wood et al., 1995). Indeed, the reintegration period may grow more challenging after the initial excitement of reunion dissipates and everyday hassles emerge. Two of our recent cross-sectional investigations revealed that the length of time service members had been home was positively associated with the degree of relational uncertainty, interference from partners, and relationship dissatisfaction participants reported (Knobloch & Theiss, 2011a; Theiss & Knobloch, in press). Longitudinal evidence of a similar phenomenon was documented by Milliken, Auchterlonie, and Hoge (2007), who found that Army personnel reported a fourfold increase in interpersonal conflict 3 to 6 months into the reunion phase compared to immediately after homecoming. Although it may take time for upheaval to set in, military couples may be wise to embrace the old adage that forewarned is forearmed.

A second guideline is that military couples take steps to forestall relational uncertainty. This advice, however, is more complex than simply directing returning service members and romantic partners to communicate more openly across the deployment cycle. Several complicating factors are at work here. First, some military couples prefer to avoid talking about challenging issues during deployment to circumvent conflict and to keep the service member focused on the mission (e.g., McNulty, 2005; Merolla, 2010); this habit may be hard to break upon reunion. Second, individuals may feel too vulnerable to seek information directly under conditions of relational uncertainty due to fear of discovering bad news (e.g., Knobloch & Solomon, 2002a). Third, people who insist on communicating frankly about every topic may dwell needlessly on divisive issues (e.g., Knobloch, 2010). For all of these reasons, managing relational uncertainty is not a straightforward task (Knobloch & Satterlee, 2009). At the same time, we see value in encouraging military couples to develop shared expectations to mitigate the turmoil that relational uncertainty may foster upon reintegration. The family skills component of the Comprehensive Soldier Fitness Program (Gottman, Gottman, & Atkins, 2011), which includes communication-building exercises designed to help military couples create joint meaning, build trust, enhance supportiveness, and recognize when to seek professional help, may be promising for helping military couples communicate effectively to manage relational uncertainty.

A final suggestion is that military couples be mindful of ways to facilitate rather than hinder each other's daily goals. According to Berscheid (1991), people enact their everyday routines quite unconsciously until an unexpected event interrupts their behavioral sequence. Times of transition, of course, are rife with opportunities for individuals to inadvertently interject themselves into each other's taken-for-granted customs. But those interruptions can be constructive as well as destructive (Berscheid, 1991; Knobloch & Solomon, 2004). As Berscheid (1991) theorized, unexpected helpfulness in the form of facilitation from partners may spark positive emotion ("Thanks for picking up stamps at the post office—you saved me a trip!"), whereas unexpected hindrance in the form of interference from partners may trigger negative emotion ("You threw out my favorite sweatshirt?"). We suspect that military couples may fare better during the reintegration period if they work proactively to replace episodes of interference with episodes of facilitation (see also Algoe & Fredrickson, 2011). Our data on frequently-mentioned issues of interference from partners (see Table 3.3) may provide a starting point for troubleshooting aspects of daily routines that repeatedly ignite hindrance.

Directions for Future Research

> *We didn't follow orders, and we didn't respond the way the soldiers in his command did when he was on deployment. The difficulties of returning from that deployment lasted for three years until this last deployment. I was able to convince him to seek counseling with me, but that got interrupted when he got called up to go to Afghanistan.*

> – at-home National Guard wife, 37 years old

A pressing avenue for additional research is to follow military couples across the reintegration period. Longitudinal data are necessary for a definitive test of the claims the relational turbulence model makes about how romantic relationships progress over time. Several lingering questions about reunion merit over-time observation. For example, what is the timing of the onset of turbulence? What is the temporal pathway linking the mechanisms and outcomes of turbulence? In other words, is the model correct that relational uncertainty and interference from partners provoke turbulence, or does turbulence spawn questions about involvement and disruptions to everyday routines? How does the prospect of a subsequent deployment affect reunion? What circumstances mark the end of the reintegration period? All of these questions await longitudinal data.

A related task is to consider the full spectrum of transitions across the deployment cycle. At present, the relational turbulence model is silent about how the reunion experiences of military couples may be shaped by patterns established long before deployment orders were issued. Consequently, work that considers all of the transitions embedded in the deployment cycle is a key agenda item. For example, Morse (2006) proposed a 7-stage emotional cycle of deployment: (a) *anticipation of departure* (e.g., preparing for loss), (b) *detachment and withdrawal* (e.g., creating emotional distance), (c) *emotional disorganization* (e.g., adjusting to new responsibilities), (d) *recovery and stabilization* (e.g., cultivating resiliency), (e) *anticipation of return* (e.g., getting ready for arrival), (f) *return adjustment and renegotiation* (e.g., reestablishing roles), and (g) *reintegration and stabilization* (e.g., creating family stability). All of the transitions lodged in these stages carry the potential for turbulence, and the cycle becomes even more complex with the possibility of multiple deployments. Additional research would be valuable for illuminating crucial periods of upheaval as military couples connect, disconnect, and re-connect their lives across the trajectory of deployments.

A third direction for future work is to broaden the relational turbulence model beyond romantic couples to encompass military families as a whole. One question is whether military youth are susceptible to turbulence as well. Research demonstrates that children grapple with questions about family life (e.g., Huebner et al., 2007) and disruptions to their daily routines (e.g., Mmari et al., 2009) when a parent is deployed. These findings imply that the model may have relevance for understanding how military youth negotiate transitions across the deployment cycle. A related question is whether typically-nonresidential family members of returning service members (e.g., grandparents, parents, siblings) are vulnerable to reactivity (e.g., Park, 2011). An even broader question is how the dynamics of military families are situated in their surrounding social networks, their local communities, and their niche in military culture (e.g., Cacioppo, Reis, & Zautra, 2011; Huebner, Mancini, Bowen, & Orthner, 2009). Locating answers to these questions is important for determining the scope of turbulence in military families across the deployment cycle.

Conclusion

> *I was told that our relationship would be "different," so I*
> *wondered the whole deployment what "different" meant.*
>
> – at-home woman involved in a serious dating relationship
> with a National Guard member, 28 years old

U.S. service members and their romantic partners make substantial sacrifices to serve and safeguard their country, but the difficulties they face in sustaining healthy relationships have not garnered adequate research attention (American Psychological Association, 2007). We dedicated this chapter to discussing how military couples experience reintegration following deployment. We employed the relational turbulence model, a theory designed to explicate times of transition within romantic relationships (Knobloch & Theiss, 2010; Solomon & Knobloch, 2001, 2004), as a framework for understanding the dynamics of reunion. We presented evidence that recently-reunited individuals (a) experience significant changes to their relationship, (b) grapple with poignant issues of relational uncertainty, and (c) report substantial interference by their partner in everyday routines. Moreover, we reviewed findings demonstrating that relational uncertainty and interference from partners predict turmoil in diverse forms. If future research continues to verify the model's assumptions about how military couples navigate transitions across the deployment cycle, then an exciting next step would be to formulate an educational curriculum based on the model to help service members and their romantic partners sustain healthy relationships throughout the trajectory of deployment.

References

Afifi, T. D., & Schrodt, P. (2003). Uncertainty and the avoidance of the state of one's family in stepfamilies, post divorce single-parent families, and first-marriage families. *Human Communication Research, 29*, 516–532.

Afifi, W. A., & Burgoon, J. K. (1998). "We never talk about that": A comparison of cross-sex friendships and dating relationships on uncertainty and topic avoidance. *Personal Relationships, 5*, 255–272.

Algoe, S. B., & Fredrickson, B. L. (2011). Emotional fitness and the movement of affective science from lab to field. *American Psychologist, 66*, 35–42.

American Psychological Association. (2007). *The psychological needs of U.S. military service members and their families: A preliminary report*. Washington, DC: American Psychological Association.

Arriaga, X. B., Reed, J. T., Goodfriend, W., & Agnew, C. R. (2006). Relationship perceptions and persistence: Do fluctuations in perceived partner commitment undermine dating relationships? *Journal of Personality and Social Psychology, 91*, 1045–1065.

Berger, C. R., & Bradac, J. J. (1982). *Language and social knowledge: Uncertainty in interpersonal relationships*. London, UK: Edward Arnold.

Berscheid, E. (1991). The emotion-in-relationships model: Reflections and update. In W. Kessen, A. Ortony, & F. Craik (Eds.), *Memories, thoughts, and emotions: Essays in honor of George Mandler* (pp. 323–335). Hillsdale, NJ: Erlbaum.

Bevan, J. L., Stetzenbach, K. A., Batson, E., & Bullo, K. (2006). Factors associated with general partner uncertainty and relational uncertainty within early adulthood sibling relationships. *Communication Quarterly, 54*, 367–381.

Bowling, U. B., & Sherman, M. D. (2008). Welcoming them home: Supporting service members and their families in navigating the tasks of reintegration. *Professional Psychology: Research and Practice, 39*, 451–458.

Cacioppo, J. T., Reis, H. T., & Zautra, A. J. (2011). Social resilience: The value of social fitness with an application to the military. *American Psychologist, 66*, 43–51.

Dainton, M. (2003). Equity and uncertainty in relational maintenance. *Western Journal of Communication, 67*, 164–186.

Faber, A. J., Willerton, E., Clymer, S. R., MacDermid, S. M., & Weiss, H. M. (2008). Ambiguous absence, ambiguous presence: A qualitative study of military reserve families in wartime. *Journal of Family Psychology, 22*, 222–230.

Gambardella, L. C. (2008). Role-exit theory and marital discord following extended military deployment. *Perspectives in Psychiatric Care, 44*, 169–174.

Gottman, J. M., Gottman, J. S., & Atkins, C. L. (2011). The Comprehensive Soldier Fitness Program: Family skills component. *American Psychologist, 66*, 52–57.

Hosek, J., Kavanagh, J., & Miller, L. (2006). *How deployments affect service members*. Santa Monica, CA: RAND Corporation.

Huebner, A. J., Mancini, J. A., Bowen, G. L., & Orthner, D. K. (2009). Shadowed by war: Building community capacity to support military families. *Family Relations, 58*, 216–228.

Huebner, A. J., Mancini, J. A., Wilcox, R. M., Grass, S. R., & Grass, G. A. (2007). Parental deployment and youth in military families: Exploring uncertainty and ambiguous loss. *Family Relations, 56*, 112–122.

Karney, B. R., & Crown, J. S. (2011). Does deployment keep military marriages together or break them apart? Evidence from Afghanistan and Iraq. In S. MacDermid Wadsworth & D. Riggs (Eds.), *Risk and resilience in U.S. military families* (pp. 23–45). New York, NY: Springer.

Knobloch, L. K. (2006). Relational uncertainty and message production within courtship: Features of date request messages. *Human Communication Research, 32*, 244–273.

Knobloch, L. K. (2007). Perceptions of turmoil within courtship: Associations with intimacy, relational uncertainty, and interference from partners. *Journal of Social and Personal Relationships, 24*, 363–384.

Knobloch, L. K. (2008a). The content of relational uncertainty within marriage. *Journal of Social and Personal Relationships, 25*, 467–495.

Knobloch, L. K. (2008b). Extending the Emotion-in-Relationships Model to conversation. *Communication Research, 35*, 822–848.

Knobloch, L. K. (2010). Relational uncertainty and interpersonal communication. In S. W. Smith & S. R. Wilson (Eds.), *New directions in interpersonal communication research* (pp. 69–93). Thousand Oaks, CA: Sage.

Knobloch, L. K., & Carpenter-Theune, K. E. (2004). Topic avoidance in developing romantic relationships: Associations with intimacy and relational uncertainty. *Communication Research, 31*, 173–205.

Knobloch, L. K., & Knobloch-Fedders, L. M. (2010). The role of relational uncertainty in depressive symptoms and relationship quality: An actor-partner interdependence model. *Journal of Social and Personal Relationships, 27*, 137–159.

Knobloch, L. K., Miller, L. E., Bond, B. J., & Mannone, S. E. (2007). Relational uncertainty and message processing in marriage. *Communication Monographs, 74*, 154–180.

Knobloch, L. K., Miller, L. E., & Carpenter, K. E. (2007). Using the relational turbulence model to understand negative emotion within courtship. *Personal Relationships, 14*, 91–112.

Knobloch, L. K., & Satterlee, K. L. (2009). Relational uncertainty: Theory and application. In T. D. Afifi & W. A. Afifi (Eds.), *Uncertainty, information management, and disclosure decisions: Theories and applications* (pp. 106–127). New York, NY: Routledge.

Knobloch, L. K., Satterlee, K. L., & DiDomenico, S. M. (2010). Relational uncertainty predicting appraisals of face threat in courtship: Integrating uncertainty reduction theory and politeness theory. *Communication Research, 37*, 303–334.

Knobloch, L. K., & Schmelzer, B. (2008). Using the Emotion-in-Relationships Model to predict features of interpersonal influence attempts. *Communication Monographs, 75*, 219–247.

Knobloch, L. K., & Solomon, D. H. (1999). Measuring the sources and content of relational uncertainty. *Communication Studies, 50*, 261–278.

Knobloch, L. K., & Solomon, D. H. (2002a). Information seeking beyond initial interaction: Negotiating relational uncertainty within close relationships. *Human Communication Research, 28*, 243–257.

Knobloch, L. K., & Solomon, D. H. (2002b). Intimacy and the magnitude and experience of episodic relational uncertainty within romantic relationships. *Personal Relationships, 9*, 457–478.

Knobloch, L. K., & Solomon, D. H. (2004). Interference and facilitation from partners in the development of interdependence within romantic relationships. *Personal Relationships, 11*, 115–130.

Knobloch, L. K., & Solomon, D. H. (2005). Relational uncertainty and relational information processing: Questions without answers? *Communication Research, 32*, 349–388.

Knobloch, L. K., Solomon, D. H., & Cruz, M. G. (2001). The role of relationship development and attachment in the experience of romantic jealousy. *Personal Relationships, 8*, 205–224.

Knobloch, L. K., & Theiss, J. A. (2010). An actor-partner interdependence model of relational turbulence: Cognitions and emotions. *Journal of Social and Personal Relationships, 27*, 595–619.

Knobloch, L. K., & Theiss, J. A. (2011a). Depressive symptoms and mechanisms of relational turbulence as predictors of relationship satisfaction among returning service members. *Journal of Family Psychology, 25*, 470–478.

Knobloch, L. K., & Theiss, J. A. (2011b). Relational uncertainty and relationship talk within courtship: A longitudinal actor-partner interdependence model. *Communication Monographs, 78*, 3–26.

Knobloch, L. K., & Theiss, J. A. (2012). Experiences of U.S. military couples during the postdeployment transition: Applying the relational turbulence model. *Journal of Social and Personal Relationships, 29*, 423–450.

McLaren, R. M., Solomon, D. H., & Priem, J. S. (2011). Explaining variation in contemporaneous responses to hurt in premarital romantic relationships: A relational turbulence model perspective. *Communication Research, 38*, 543–564.

McNulty, P. A. F. (2005). Reported stressors and health care needs of active duty Navy personnel during three phases of deployment in support of the war in Iraq. *Military Medicine, 170*, 530–535.

Merolla, A. J. (2010). Relational maintenance during military deployment: Perspectives of wives of deployed U.S. soldiers. *Journal of Applied Communication Research, 38*, 4–26.

Milliken, C. S., Auchterlonie, J. L., & Hoge, C. W. (2007). Longitudinal assessment of mental health problems among active and reserve component soldiers returning from the Iraq war. *Journal of the American Medical Association, 298*, 2141–2148.

Mmari, K., Roche, K. M., Sudhinaraset, M., & Blum, R. (2009). When a parent goes to war: Exploring the issues faced by adolescents and their families. *Youth & Society, 40*, 455–475.

Morse, J. (2006). *The new emotional cycles of deployment*. Retrieved from http://www.hooah-4health.com/deployment/familymatters/emotionalcycle.htm

Nelson Goff, B. S., Crow, J. R., Reisbig, A. M. J., & Hamilton, S. (2007). The impact of individual trauma symptoms of deployed soldiers on relationship satisfaction. *Journal of Family Psychology, 21*, 344–353.

Newby, J. H., McCarroll, J. E., Ursano, R. J., Fan, Z., Shigemura, J., & Tucker-Harris, Y. (2005). Positive and negative consequences of a military deployment. *Military Medicine, 170*, 815–819.

Palmer, C. (2008). A theory of risk and resilience factors in military families. *Military Psychology, 20*, 205–217.

Park, N. (2011). Military children and families: Strengths and challenges during peace and war. *American Psychologist, 66*, 65–72.

Renshaw, K. D., Rodrigues, C. S., & Jones, D. H. (2008). Psychological symptoms and marital satisfaction in spouses of Operation Iraqi Freedom veterans: Relationships with spouses' perceptions of veterans' experiences and symptoms. *Journal of Family Psychology, 22*, 586–594.

Sahlstein, E., Maguire, K. C., & Timmerman, L. (2009). Contradictions and praxis contextualized by wartime deployment: Wives' perspectives revealed through relational dialectics. *Communication Monographs, 76*, 421–442.

Sayers, S. L. (2011). Family reintegration difficulties and couples therapy for military veterans and their spouses. *Cognitive and Behavioral Practice, 18*, 108–119.

Solomon, D. H., & Knobloch, L. K. (2001). Relationship uncertainty, partner interference, and intimacy within dating relationships. *Journal of Social and Personal Relationships, 18*, 804–820.

Solomon, D. H., & Knobloch, L. K. (2004). A model of relational turbulence: The role of intimacy, relational uncertainty, and interference from partners in appraisals of irritations. *Journal of Social and Personal Relationships, 21*, 795–816.

Solomon, D. H., & Theiss, J. A. (2008). A longitudinal test of the relational turbulence model of romantic relationship development. *Personal Relationships, 15*, 339–357.

Solomon, D. H., & Theiss, J. A. (2011). Relational turbulence: What doesn't kill us makes us stronger. In W. R. Cupach & B. H. Spitzberg (Eds.), *The dark side of close relationships II* (pp. 197–216). New York, NY: Routledge.

Solomon, D. H., Weber, K. M., & Steuber, K. R. (2010). Turbulence in relational transitions. In S. W. Smith & S. R. Wilson (Eds.), *New directions in interpersonal communication research* (pp. 115–134). Thousand Oaks, CA: Sage.

Theiss, J. A. (2011). Modeling dyadic effects in the associations between relational uncertainty, sexual communication, and sexual satisfaction for husbands and wives. *Communication Research, 38*, 565–584.

Theiss, J. A., & Knobloch, L. K. (2009). An actor-partner interdependence model of irritations in romantic relationships. *Communication Research, 36*, 510–537.

Theiss, J. A., & Knobloch, L. K. (in press). Relational turbulence and the post-deployment transition: Self, partner, and relationship focused turbulence. *Communication Research.*

Theiss, J. A., Knobloch, L. K., Checton, M. G., & Magsamen-Conrad, K. (2009). Relationship characteristics associated with the experience of hurt in romantic relationships: A test of the relational turbulence model. *Human Communication Research, 35*, 588–615.

Theiss, J. A., & Nagy, M. E. (2010). Actor-partner effects in the associations between relationship characteristics and reactions to marital sexual intimacy. *Journal of Social and Personal Relationships, 27*, 1089–1109.

Theiss, J. A., & Solomon, D. H. (2006a). Coupling longitudinal data and multilevel modeling to examine the antecedents and consequences of jealousy experiences in romantic relationships: A test of the relational turbulence model. *Human Communication Research, 32*, 469–503.

Theiss, J. A., & Solomon, D. H. (2006b). A relational turbulence model of communication about irritations in romantic relationships. *Communication Research, 33*, 391–418.

Vormbrock, J. K. (1993). Attachment theory as applied to wartime and job-related marital separation. *Psychological Bulletin, 144*, 122–144.

Wiens, T. W., & Boss, P. (2006). Maintaining family resiliency before, during, and after military separation. In C. A. Castro, A. B. Adler, & T. W. Britt (Eds.), *Military life: The psychology of serving in peace and combat* (Vol. 3, pp. 13–38). Westport, CT: Praeger.

Wood, S., Scarville, J., & Gravino, K. S. (1995). Waiting wives: Separation and reunion among Army wives. *Armed Forces & Society, 21*, 217–236.

Chapter 4
Feasibility of Telephone Support Groups for Spouses of Returning Iraq and Afghanistan Service Members

Linda Olivia Nichols, Jennifer Martindale-Adams, Marshall J. Graney, Jeffrey Zuber, Patricia E. Miller, and Denise V. Brown

Abstract Reintegration of the returning service member and the family can be difficult, especially for families that are not near military resources. We tested a telephone support group intervention targeted to spouses, providing them with information about combat consequences and reintegration concerns, skills to manage the tasks of reintegration such as role negotiation and to take care of themselves such as stress management, and support from other spouses. Our strategy was to focus on the spouse as the lynchpin of the family who would manage the transition and reintegration process and to provide the intervention using a low cost, established, and widely accessible technology. Telephone support groups proved feasible for this group of spouses, and they learned skills to help their families and themselves with reintegration tasks.

Keywords Spouses • Social support • Telephone support • Reintegration • Problem solving • Coping skills

L.O. Nichols, Ph.D. (✉)
Veterans Affairs Medical Center, 1030 Jefferson Avenue, Memphis, TN 38104, USA

Department of Preventive Medicine, University of Tennessee Health Science Center, Memphis, TN, USA

Department of Internal Medicine, University of Tennessee Health Science Center, Memphis, TN, USA
e-mail: linda.nichols@va.gov

J. Martindale-Adams, Ed.D. • M.J. Graney, Ph.D. • J. Zuber, M.A. • P.E. Miller, M.A.
Department of Preventive Medicine, University of Tennessee Health Science Center, Memphis, TN, USA

Veterans Affairs Medical Center, 1030 Jefferson Avenue, Memphis, TN 38104, USA
e-mail: Jennifer.Martindale-Adams@va.gov; mg914@bellsouth.net; Jeff.Zuber@va.gov; pat.miller@va.gov

D.V. Brown, M.S.
Veterans Affairs Medical Center, 1030 Jefferson Avenue, Memphis, TN 38104, USA
e-mail: Denise.Brown4@va.gov

S. MacDermid Wadsworth and D.S. Riggs (eds.), *Military Deployment and its Consequences for Families*, Risk and Resilience in Military and Veteran Families, DOI 10.1007/978-1-4614-8712-8_4, © Springer Science+Business Media New York 2014

Introduction

Spouses of Active Duty service members who have been deployed to Iraq and Afghanistan show mental health diagnoses of depression, anxiety, sleep disorders, acute stress reaction and adjustment disorders (Mansfield et al., 2010) with rates that are similar to those of service members (Eaton et al., 2008). National Guard spouses are also at risk, with 34 % of significant others, compared to 40 % of Guard members, screening positive for mental health problems (Gorman, Blow, Ames, & Reed, 2011).

Reunion and reintegration are often stressful for a variety of reasons (Blow et al., 2012; Knobloch & Theiss, 2011; Wood, Scarville, & Gravino, 1995). Post deployment, 22 % of spouses of soldiers who have returned from Iraq or Afghanistan report that reunion is "difficult" or "very difficult" (Booth, Wechsler Segal, & Bell, 2007). Certain types of families struggle with reintegration, including those who are younger, financially less secure, or are in a first deployment. Difficulties before deployment and major life transitions such as pregnancy during deployment are also indicators that the post deployment transition may be difficult (Booth et al., 2007; Faber, Willerton, Clymer, MacDermid, & Weiss, 2008).

However, for most families, the major sources of conflict and stress during reintegration are differences between deployment and home routines (Booth et al., 2007; Hosek, Kavanagh, & Miller, 2006) and re-negotiating role boundaries around responsibilities (Bell & Schumm, 2000; Blow et al., 2012; Drummet, Coleman, & Cable, 2003; Faber et al., 2008; Segal & Segal, 2003). Family members have difficulty resuming previous roles and responsibilities, negotiating new roles and responsibilities and interdependencies, and giving up roles taken on during deployment (Knobloch & Theiss, 2011; Sayers, Farrow, Ross, & Oslin, 2009). Changes in communication patterns between spouses during deployment, and the need to open communication channels after deployment contribute to these difficulties in managing reintegration tasks (Faber et al., 2008; Knobloch & Theiss, 2011; Slone & Friedman, 2008; Walsh, 2006).

Recommendations (Booth et al., 2007) to support military families with these reintegration tasks include: (1) providing longer-term support infrastructure post deployment for families; and (2) integrating research findings into training materials and workshops that cover advice and strategies on how to deal with deployments and reunions. Topics should include dealing with the culture shock of return, adjusting to changes in family members, identifying and dealing with psychological symptoms, positive outcomes of deployment, and available support resources.

These recommendations to assist military families with reintegration tasks translate into strategies that more specifically focus on education about the effects of combat and deployment on the service member and family, support from others who have been through the same experiences, and practical skills building, including problem solving skills, communication skills, stress reduction skills, and cognitive/mood management. These strategies are consistent with basic health-stress models in which the goal is to change the nature of specific stressors, the behavioral response to the stressors, and/or any individual's emotional or cognitive response to stressors

(Gottman, Gottman, & Atkins, 2011; Lazarus & Launier, 1978; Schulz et al., 2003). These strategies increase family members' resilience, their ability, singly and together, to cope with disruption and adapt to change (MacDermid Wadsworth, 2010). There are many successful Department of Defense (DoD) and Department of Veterans Affairs (VA) programs that teach these strategies through counseling sessions, online and face to face training, retreats, resource linking, and support groups, e.g., Comprehensive Soldier Fitness (CSF) (Gottman et al., 2011), FOCUS (Families OverComing Under Stress™) (Lester et al., 2011), Strong Bonds (Stanley, Allen, Markman, Rhoades, & Prentice 2010), Wounded Warrior Project (http://www.woundedwarriorproject.org/), Coaching into Care (http://www.mirecc. va.gov/coaching/), Operation Home Front (http://www.operationhomefront.net/), and Creative Healing Connections (http://www.creativehealingconnections.org/).

However, some of these programs are focused on the dyad of service member and spouse or the family and may depend on the participation of both parties. Many military families during and post deployment do not make use of resources that are available, perhaps because the resources are not in a form that families feel comfortable with, or that do not address the particular stressors that families are experiencing (Di Nola, 2008). Because they may live far from unit headquarters, Reserve and Guard families are less likely to have access to military resources, may not have other unit members in the same town, and may not have support from other military spouses (Blow et al., 2012; Burrell, Durand, & Fortado, 2003; Gorman et al., 2011; Gottman et al., 2011).

To meet the need for information, support and skills, and to overcome the obstacles of distance and access, we provided telephone support groups for spouses as the focal point that would provide support for the returning service member and manage the transition and reintegration process for the family. This pilot study was designed to determine the feasibility of providing post deployment telephone support groups that focused on reintegration tasks for spouses/significant others and to assess participants' satisfaction with these support groups. This chapter reports on the spouses' response to the support groups.

Telephone Support

The development of this telephone support group intervention was funded by the Defense Health Program (DHP), managed by the U.S. Army Medical Research and Materiel Command, through the Congressionally Directed Medical Research Program (CDMRP). Our goal was to develop a simple, low cost intervention using established technology that could be easily implemented, would be widely accessible to military spouses wherever their location and circumstances, and would provide ongoing assistance during post deployment. Ongoing assistance can be critical for service members and spouses who may be isolated and struggling to readjust to life together in the absence of a social network that understands how to support this transition.

Telephone groups were chosen because they circumvent resource obstacles such as lack of local services, access, and travel. Telephone-based triage and clinical care is a low cost, distance neutral intervention that uses established technology and has been used successfully in the Veterans Health Administration (VHA) system of the Department of Veterans Affairs. The telephone groups were designed to replicate face to face support groups, providing participants an opportunity to interact with others, gain factual/current information, ask difficult questions with relative anonymity, share expertise and experiences with others who can benefit from their exchanges, receive and give social support, learn and practice skills to reduce distress, and seek assistance in addressing problems specific to their own circumstances. In the community, telephone support groups have been used for many kinds of individuals and caregivers. In dementia caregiving telephone support groups participants from various ethnicities report good satisfaction and little difficulty in managing the technology (Bank, Argüelles, Rubert, Eisdorfer, & Czaja 2006; Martindale-Adams, Nichols, Burns, & Malone, 2002). Results have included improvements in mental health status, self-efficacy, and social support (Marziali & Garcia, 2011).

Telephone support groups may have a lack of interpersonal verbal and physical cues, technical problems such as static, distractions in the home that can potentially limit or interfere with participation, and support group leaders who are inadequately trained in directing groups that lack face to face interaction. However, these problems can be fairly easily overcome.

Intensive training for Group Leaders, monitoring sessions, and group rules are strategies we employed for overcoming potential problems associated with telephone interactions. Group rules encouraged group members to identify themselves and give clear feedback. Strategies by the Group Leader to engage individuals included use of prompts and open-ended questions to solicit information, use of rephrasing, reflection, and summarization, use of members' own language/descriptors, and assessment of members' understanding of the intervention by "checking in" and by asking questions. Group Leaders were trained to maintain group structure over the telephone through an appropriate level of assertiveness and use of empathetic responses while remaining on protocol.

Telephone Groups Content and Sessions

The intervention was designed as a preventive health model to allow spouses to identify potential difficulties in the family system and to intervene before these stressors become overwhelming. Groups were closed with membership the same and a trained mental health professional Group Leader. Based on face to face community support groups and those provided in the VA for veterans and family members, the groups met for an hour each month during 1 year. Although community and VA support groups are often ongoing, these groups were designed to cover the critical first year post deployment when reintegration difficulties and mental health problems typically increase (Hoge, Auchterlonie, & Milliken, 2006).

Table 4.1 Group session activities

Activity	Time[a]	Description
Welcome	5	Introduction and group format, review group rules, facilitate Signal Breath exercise to help segue into session
Check in/review of strategies from last call (treatment fidelity—enactment)	15	Check in with group members, initiate discussion on last session commitments (coping strategies tried) by each member, successes, failures and barriers, problem-solve difficulties
Didactic topic presentation (treatment fidelity—delivery)	10	Provide brief overview of topic, ask group members for brief comment on portion of topic most relevant to them, present topic, discuss service member, spouse, and family experience, and ways to meld, highlight "red flags"—areas of difficulty or potential distress for the group member, direct members to resources in Participant Workbook
Practice and discussion of ways to implement strategies from presentation (treatment fidelity—receipt)	20	Encourage discussion of topic, solicit strategies and activities to try from each group member, practice use of strategies through role play, walk-through, practice asking for help, experiential exercise, identification of role models, out-loud self-talk, process of perceived obstacles and barriers to implementing strategies, involvement of support, replay of something that went wrong, review of key points, questions and answers
Closure	5	Summarize what was accomplished, remind about next session, ask spouses to review workbook topic for next session, encourage use of signal breath and strategies identified, provide support and encouragement, request group members' commitments (identification of strategy they will implement), discuss use of commitment worksheet and expectation of self-report at next session

[a]Time measured in minutes

Because individuals in a supportive or caregiving role face multiple challenges, there is no one method that will be consistently effective (Schulz et al., 2003). Consequently, the intervention offered semi-structured education, training in coping skills and cognitive restructuring, and support, as shown in Table 4.1. The telephone groups were participant centered to incorporate participant input and direction of discussion. The groups focused on practical suggestions to help spouses "normalize" their experiences in a safe environment. Spouses were encouraged to practice skills during the session through role play, self talk, and modeling of appropriate behavior.

To personalize the intervention to the specific needs of each spouse, group members were encouraged to make a commitment at the end of each session to select and practice at least one strategy or skill between sessions (Najavits, 2002).

Taking Action sheets were available at the end of each section of the accompanying Spouse Workbook for the commitment to be written down, signed and dated by the spouse for her own use. At the beginning of the next telephone session during check-in, to determine enactment for treatment implementation, each spouse was queried about her commitment, whether she tried it, and whether it worked; barriers to implementation were problem solved by the entire group.

The intervention content was informed by the Spouse Battlemind concept (Riviere, Clark, Cox, Kendall-Robbins, & Castro, 2007) and was designed to reduce or eliminate reunion and reintegration difficulties and guide behavior to build family resilience and support. This practical model highlighted ways the returning service member, spouse and family may have changed during deployment, built on existing strengths and skills, and used experiences that are familiar to spouses.

Specific topics focused on resilience in reintegration tasks and skills (Black & Lobo, 2008) including problem solving, gaining social support, negotiating family roles and family dynamics, communication, anger management, conflict resolution and negotiation, reestablishing emotional intimacy, recognizing mental health needs, accessing resources, appreciation of family sacrifices, future planning, and stress reduction. The Spouse Workbook provided material related to each topic. In addition to the topic material, supplemental Red Flag topics in the Workbook referred to potentially dangerous or unsafe situations and a need for increased awareness of behaviors and/or situations that may be encountered post deployment. Red Flags included substance abuse and addictions, child abuse, depression, domestic violence, grief, stress and reintegration, suicide risk, and anger.

Recruitment

To be eligible, participants had to be married to or living as married with a service member who had deployed to Iraq or Afghanistan and was at least 1 month post deployment. Participants were recruited online by the study web site, through brochures, through e-mails, and through referrals from military family advocates, Veterans Health Administration clinicians, and the national Wounded Warrior Project (WWP) office. All interactions (screening, consent and data collection) were by telephone. Participants were compensated only for data collection. The study was overseen by the Memphis VA Institutional Review Board.

Assessment and Analysis

The intervention content focused on improving spouses' ability to manage basic reintegration tasks. These tasks were conceptualized by the Army as reintegration concerns for soldiers and spouses and were evaluated at the beginning of the groups and at their conclusion. Each potential concern was listed as a phrase rated on a scale of 1 (not very concerned) to 4 (seriously concerned). Phrases could target the spouse or the service member (SM) because either spouse or service member functioning may be perceived sources of concern.

There were six domains of potential reintegration difficulty: social life (e.g., I think SM and/or our family spend too little time together with our friends or our activities); home life (e.g., I think there are changes in my roles and/or responsibilities in the household since SM returned from deployment); couple (e.g., I think SM is less committed to our relationship); family (e.g., I think our family is having problems communicating with each other. For example, either we talk too little or we pretend everything is all right); service member (e.g., I think SM is more angry or irritable a lot of the time); and self (e.g., I think I have concerns about my future). Each domain of concern had from 3 to 9 questions (total of 44 questions) and a summary question for overall concern about each domain (e.g., How concerned are you about your family life overall?).

Because one of our objectives was to determine if the groups were a feasible strategy to meet spouses' needs, we collected information at the end of the groups on satisfaction with the intervention overall, with the logistics and structure of the group, and with the three foci of the groups: education/information, skills building, and support (all scored from 1—not at all satisfied to 5—extremely satisfied). Open ended questions addressed benefit, difficulties, what components of the study were useful and changes recommended (Martindale-Adams et al., 2002). The Group-Growth Evaluation (Pfeiffer & Jones, 1987) measured group climate and data flow to determine how each group had changed since its inception, focusing on closeness, accomplishment, trust, and willingness to share personal information. The 11 questions were rated on a five point scale with 5 as the highest rating. Participants were asked to rate how the group functioned initially and at its conclusion.

Each participant served as her own control. Data for all participants enrolled were analyzed. Data analysis used mixed-effects models on all Potential Reintegration measures to compare baseline and follow-up scores to estimate the fixed effect parameter of change over time. The model assumes that data were missing at random; there was nothing found in our data analysis to challenge this assumption. Because mixed-effects model analysis accommodates missing data without loss of subjects, no data imputation strategy was necessary for missing data. Means and standard deviations were calculated for all satisfaction questions. Group Growth Evaluation questions were analyzed using paired t-tests. Each measure was analyzed independently of the others. P values less than or equal to .05 were considered statistically significant, and those between .05 and .10 were considered to document trends that approached, but did not attain, statistical significance.

For statistically significant comparisons, an effect size (d) of at least 0.2 SD improvement was considered clinically significant (Cohen, 1988), consistent with effect sizes reported for psychosocial interventions, which are generally small to medium (Sörensen, Pinquart, & Duberstein, 2002). Effect sizes were estimated as mean change from baseline to 12 months relative to estimated population standard deviation (Cohen, 1988).

Participants

Of the 107 spouses screened, 86 enrolled. Although husbands were welcome, none were recruited. On average, spouses were 37 years old and had been married about 10 years with 1.5 children. They were predominantly white/Caucasian. More than half were employed, most had greater than a high school education, and household income was a little less than $5,000 a month. For their husbands, almost half were Guard or Reserve and most were noncommissioned officers. Approximately two-thirds were employed and about 60 % were receiving VA services. They had had, on average, slightly less than three deployments total with the last deployment lasting almost 1 year. The husbands had been back from deployment a little more than 2 years. Almost two thirds had been injured during deployment.

Telephone Support Groups' Role in Improving Spouse Skills

When summary questions for each potential reintegration concern domain were examined, spouses had significant improvement in all domains of concern except their functioning as a couple. Table 4.2 shows overall scores for each domain. In addition to statistical significance, clinical effects were between small and medium, as documented by the effect size d (Cohen, 1988). This is consistent with effect sizes reported for psychosocial interventions (Sörensen et al. 2002).

Spouses' monthly commitments generally were targeted to one of the areas of reintegration concerns: social life, home life, their relationship as a couple, the family, the service member, or themselves. Their success in these commitments suggests that the statistical and clinical improvements were results of behaviors and actions spouses were taking. Their commitments were examples of moving from dysfunctional behavior (e.g., being mad and frustrated at the service member) to functional behavior (e.g., making a plan to get back into marriage counseling), which is one parameter of clinical significance (Jacobson, Foilette, & Revenstorf, 1984).

Table 4.2 Potential reintegration concern summary questions over time (N = 86)

Variable[a]	Baseline M ± SD	6 Months M ± SD	12 Months M ± SD	p-value[b]	d[c]
Social life concern	1.95 ± 1.05	1.77 ± 0.90	1.65 ± 0.82	.02	.29
Home life concern	2.21 ± 1.03	1.93 ± 0.98	1.81 ± 0.94	.001	.39
Couple concern	2.09 ± 1.07	1.90 ± 1.00	1.87 ± 0.96	.10	.21
Family concern	2.22 ± 0.94	2.18 ± 1.07	1.88 ± 1.02	.001	.36
Concern with service member	2.73 ± 1.00	2.47 ± 1.03	2.29 ± 1.07	<.001	.44
Concern about self	2.06 ± 0.94	1.86 ± 0.98	1.72 ± 0.86	.002	.36

Note: [a]Scale for all variables is 1–4
[b]p-values for change over time from repeated measures mixed model analyses
[c]Mean change over time relative to estimated population standard deviation

Some areas of <u>social life</u> commitment included strategies to make friends in the area, attend church more, reach out to other military spouses in the same situations across the country, and socialize more. Their specific commitments reflected their plans: *"I am going on 'caregiver/veteran strike' today since the boys are out of school and we are going to see a children's movie. Tomorrow I may be on strike too as I want to see a different movie."* *"I am proactive in staying in touch with other wives who are going through this."*

One commitment from a spouse around <u>home life</u> showed the outcome of her renegotiation of the family jobs: *"We set up a list of chores so that everyone can help not just me."* Other spouses used commitments to make home life less stressful for everyone. *"Over the month, husband and I went through the chart of changes* [that may have affected the relationship], *and I'm working on my anger management. I may not be completely successful every time… but I am much more conscious of getting angry. So I am better able to stop the anger/frustration before it gets too far."*

As spouses worked on their relationships with their husbands as a <u>couple</u>, their commitments focused on finding happiness in marriage again, working on communication, putting respect back into the relationship, working on sex life with husbands who had suffered physical injuries, and showing appreciation for the husband and the relationship. Spouses were eager to share their successes with the group when things worked well. One spouse reported in an email to the Group Leader and to the other spouses during the session, *"My goal for last month was to have a date night with my hubby. Awesome news on that front - we had TWO dates!!"*

Family commitments frequently focused on children and their concerns, from the more serious realization that therapy for children regarding their issues might be needed, and a commitment to secure therapy, to a plan to create bonding activities for the family and help the service member's communication with the children. *"The school really helps us with her now."* *"We did get to the movies finally and it was really nice."* *"I was able to show appreciation by telling them, this is about family and this is what family is all about."* Spouses also saw their role in helping the extended family in the reintegration of the service member. *"I used the chart* [of changes that may have affected the relationship] *to help his parents understand that he isn't the same person as before."*

Spouses were aware of their important role in the family in reintegrating the service member back into civilian life and into the family, particularly when the service member had been injured. Their commitments often focused on their role in supporting the <u>service member</u> through finding resources, encouraging the service member to retry work, advocating for treatment, and setting up systems to help the service member to be more independent and less frustrated. *"I apologized for getting so mad and frustrated with him and we talked about a plan to get him evaluated for TBI therapy and for us to get back into marriage counseling as well as individual counseling."* *"We have made his alarm on his phone as a new tone, and we moved his phone into the kitchen where his med box is located and we have labeled everything to help him to remember to take his medication."*

In addition to their practice of stress management techniques, spouses used other strategies to take care of themselves and to find center and balance in their lives, such as learning to let go and relinquish control, working on their own life's focus, finding more "me time," and cultivating a more positive outlook. *"I'm submitting my name and letter of interest to the commander of my husband's unit by Wednesday this week for the FRG leader position." "We did the resilience questions together and talked about how we can do a lot that we didn't think we could."*

Telephone Support Groups Feasibility for Spouses

Spouse Satisfaction with Group Format

Overall, spouses were satisfied with the groups with a mean score of 4.5 ± 0.7 of a possible 5 points. Spouses were satisfied with the overall format of the telephone support group, with scores ranging from very to extremely satisfied as shown in Table 4.3, *"Easy to use… very accessible."* Although most spouses were very satisfied with the length of the calls, several spouses wanted the calls to be longer than one hour. We were initially concerned that the lack of visual cues would hamper spouses' ability to participate, and this was true for some spouses: *"Being on the phone it wasn't like face to face, no strong connection."* However, most spouses reported that they could talk to unseen group members and identify who was

Table 4.3 Spouse satisfaction with group participation (N = 66)

Variable[a]	M ± SD
Group format	
Call format	4.5 ± 0.7
Call length	4.1 ± 0.9
Ease of using telephone	4.7 ± 0.5
Talk to unseen group members	4.6 ± 0.9
Identify who was talking	4.2 ± 1.1
Overall satisfaction with sessions	4.5 ± 0.7
Education and information	
Written information	4.5 ± 0.8
Information learned from group	4.3 ± 0.9
Skills building	
Stress/relaxation helpful	4.1 ± 1.1
Enhance negotiation with service member	3.7 ± 1.2
Help solve family problems	3.4 ± 1.1
Improve family communication	3.5 ± 1.3
Improve coping skills	4.0 ± 1.2
Support	
Amount of support from leader	4.6 ± 0.7
Amount of support from members	4.2 ± 1.0
Amount of support spouse gave to members	4.0 ± 1.1

[a]Scale for all variables is 1–5

talking. As is often the case for telephone support groups, the anonymity of the groups was often beneficial. *"I like the anonymousness of it, not knowing anyone else…"* *"They couldn't see your face and you could say anything you want."*

Convenience was important. One spouse commented, *"You can be on the phone anywhere, even if you are away from home."* Many spouses participated in the groups from their work sites or using their cell phones. Spouses were across the country, even in the Pacific Islands, and many lived in rural locations. As one spouse said, *"Living in a rural community… it's nice to not have to drive an hour… that's too long it takes to get to our support. It's nice to sit at home and pick up the phone and talk to someone."* Others were not near a base or other military or VA resources. *"… my husband was individually mobilized … there were no military families in my community. It was a way to connect in that way."*

On the group climate questions from the Group Growth instrument, participants reported a significant increase in their estimation of the group's cooperation and their rewards from being a member of the group from their initial participation to study end (3.8 versus 4.4; p < .001). Participants also reported feeling more comfortable sharing personal information from their initial participation in the group to study end (3.6 versus 4.5; p < .001). *"I liked the ability to hear others talk, to voice my opinion; to give each other support. I liked the book, the coach, the freedom of having a girls' night out too."*

Spouse Perceptions of the Components of the Group

The three components the support groups focused on were education/information, skills building, and support, as shown in Table 4.3 above.

Education/Information

Spouses found the written information helpful. One spouse commented, *"I loved the workbook, loved the information, loved the leader…"* Spouses also reported high satisfaction with information from fellow group members and reported that the groups were: *"Easy to use… very accessible. The overall information given by the members and how they coped with situations."*

Skills Building

In general, spouses were eager to try skills and strategies from each session. One spouse reported that her favorite part of the sessions was *"the monthly commitment and the coaching."* Another said, *"The book was great but the telephone support helped put the concepts into every day practice."* Problem solving was an important component of the intervention and spouses' commitments were frequently about using the problem solving techniques. *"I broke the problem down into smaller pieces and saw that it was doable." "I was always trying to solve the big problems and got overwhelmed before."*

The stress reduction and relaxation skills were highly rated, with 89 % of spouses using these skills. Commitments showed that spouses were using the skills in practical situations. *"I had to use the breathing technique the other day because my kids weren't listening to me at all and I wanted to scream but I didn't...."*

Spouses also reported that the groups helped enhance negotiation, solve family problems, improve family communication, and improve general coping skills, although these areas were rated between moderately and very satisfied. As one spouse commented, *"Feel more confident in options you have...more resilient... never give up... being able to solve any problems you're facing." "I was able to get feedback and suggestions from the group leader and the other participants and an objective perspective on issues too difficult for me to handle by myself."*

Support

Spouses rated the amount of support from other group members and the group leader highly. The feeling of validation was important. A spouse commented, *"Being able to speak freely about things most civilians cannot relate to. Feeling validated." "She* [group leader] *was caring and showed empathy."* Normalization of spouses' concerns made them feel less isolated. *"Having other spouses I could relate to. Some made me think I'm not the only one going through this. It made me feel connected." "Being able to share your problems with others who knew what you were going through. Hearing about other people's difficulties and problems."*

Although spouses appreciated the support they received, their scores showed that they were slightly less convinced that they had provided good support for other group members. However, providing support was important for them. *"Talking it out. Realize we had a lot in common. Helping others through their difficulties."*

How Telephone Support Groups Could Better Meet Spouse Needs: Lessons Learned

The busy lives led by military spouses had been one of our initial impetuses for developing telephone support groups. Work, school, household duties, children, care for aging parents or a husband who may have been injured are all excellent reasons why spouses frequently cannot travel to a site for an intervention. However, although the telephone support groups were convenient and did not necessitate leaving home, these same reasons still affected spouses' ability to participate. Spouse attendance in the groups and continuation in the study varied. Half (50 %) of the participants attended at least 6 sessions. A little less than one quarter (22.1 %) of participants attended 9 or more sessions. About a fourth (25.6 %) of the participants attended 3 or fewer sessions. Seventeen spouses (19.8 %) either discontinued or were lost to follow-up.

Spouses' daily schedules changed with the seasons and with children's schedules, and another family or work commitment could take precedence. In general *"It was hard to work around everyone's schedules."* Marital changes could also be a factor. As one spouse reported, *"I split up with husband, had to get a job, have two kids…. I always had to work on the night we did our group."* One spouse summarized the frequent chaos that she and many of the spouses experienced: *"My personal schedule changes constantly."* Another put it even more succinctly: *"My busy, busy life."*

With monthly sessions, if spouses missed a session they had 2 months between group meetings. *"If something critical occurred last minute and I was unable to attend, then I felt I missed something which I was unable to regain (knowledge and support). I wished there was a way to dial in later with a code and listen to what was discussed."* In addition, spouses reported having a need to talk with the group more often than monthly. One spouse summed up her need, *"Thirty days is a long time… thirty days of hell for some people."*

For many spouses, hour-long calls were too short. They wanted more time to talk and share strategies related to the topic. Spouses suggested a variety of ways to make up sessions and to supplement the sessions, including repeat sessions of the same topic, online information, Facebook groups, and a special blog for questions and issues that arise between calls. In addition to their request that sessions occur more frequently than monthly, they also suggested a shorter time commitment than a year.

When the telephone support group intervention was initially proposed, the timeline for inclusion was at least 1 month post deployment. Because reintegration difficulties and mental health problems for service members increase during the first year post deployment (Hoge, Auchterlonie, & Milliken, 2006), our expectation was that spouses would need support during or shortly after the first year. Although the average time since deployment return for this group of spouses was more than 2 years, spouses reported a need for the information sooner. *"I also wish this information could have been presented to us 6 months earlier so we could watch for the signs." "Start it sooner (pre-deployment or during deployment) so you have the skills before and know where to go."*

Based on spouses' suggestions, we are currently testing two models of providing education, skills and support, telephone support groups and online webinars, to spouses of post deployment service members and spouses of deployed service members. These two randomized controlled trials are also funded by the Defense Health Program, managed by the U.S. Army Medical Research and Materiel Command. The interventions are 6 months long, meet twice monthly, and each session is repeated three times during 2 weeks so that participants have the option of a make-up session. The telephone support groups have a shorter didactic presentation and a longer time for spouse interaction.

Implementation into Practice

In May 2010, Public Law 111-163 Caregivers and Veterans Omnibus Health Services Act of 2010 was signed into law. The Act allowed VA to provide benefits to caregivers of veterans. As part of this initiative, VA implemented the Spouse

Telephone Support (STS) program, telephone support groups for spouses of Iraq and Afghanistan veterans. One of the initial impetuses for the STS program came from the testimony before Congress of a spouse who was participating in our telephone support groups. Based on the pilot study, STS is designed to improve spouse resilience and coping and ease the post deployment transition for Iraq and Afghanistan veterans. Staff from each VA Medical Center are trained and certified in delivering the intervention. Training, materials including Spouse Workbooks, and coaching are provided by the Veterans Health Administration's Caregiver Support Program through the Caregiver Center at the Memphis VA Medical Center.

Just as for the research studies, spouses' requests and suggestions have influenced the design of the groups and the sessions. The intervention is 6 months long; a recommended number of 6–10 spouses and a trained and certified Group Leader participate in 12-hour-long calls that include education, skills building, and support but with more time allocated for spouse participation. There are repeat sessions available. The Spouse Workbook and session topics target the same topics as the pilot study: problem solving and communication, relationships, mental health and psychological conditions, and building the spouse's resilience and strengths. However, per spouse request, there is increased emphasis on their needs in addition to their role as a support for the service member and the center of their families.

Research Implications

As this intervention is implemented in practice, evaluation of its effectiveness is being undertaken. Our support groups were telephone based with participants recruited nationally who generally did not know each other. VA clinicians who are presenting the support groups are implementing several different models, such as face to face groups and including participants from one local area who may have met each other. These and other models are being evaluated for effectiveness and accessibility. Participants had suggested many other ways to connect in addition to the telephone, such as through social media or online or videoconferencing and these models should be tested, also. Although social media provide a very accessible and popular way for people to connect, privacy and security concerns and the potential for unauthorized access to group information will also need to be addressed. Computer and smart phone applications, such as the Care4Caregivers app developed through the VA's Caregiver Support Program and the PTSD Family Coach app developed by the VA's National Center for PTSD, are another way to provide information and skills building to spouses and should be investigated for this population.

Clinical Implications

For clinicians, these telephone support groups and the comments made by the spouses suggest a need to remember the spouse's concerns when treating a service member or veteran. Spouses can have a dramatic effect on the reintegration of the family after deployment and can be a major support for the service member/veteran. Conversely, it is important to remember that military and veteran spouses are dealing with challenging and unique situations that civilian spouses do not routinely encounter. Spouses are more likely to report that stress or emotional problems impact their work or other activities than are service members (21.7 % vs. 6.2 %) and when they seek care for these concerns, it is generally from a primary care provider according to Hoge, Castro, and Eaton (2006). Military and veteran spouses may need special attention from their community primary care and mental health providers, particularly for Guard, Reserve and veteran spouses who are not near a military installation and do not have other military support.

Conclusion

Telephone support groups proved to be a feasible way to increase information, build skills, and provide support for spouses of Iraq and Afghanistan service members who were post deployment. Spouses reported an improvement in their concerns about the effects of reintegration on their social life, their home life, their family, their husband, and themselves. They were satisfied with the groups and found them easy to use. Logistically, the confidential and anonymous nature of the telephone support groups allowed spouses to speak freely about difficult and challenging topics, such as intimacy. The groups were scheduled to accommodate the spouses' busy and hectic lives, rather than around usual agency working hours.

Most of our participants entered the study after their husbands had been home from deployment more than 2 years, suggesting that they and their families were still struggling with reintegration. Providing early and ongoing education, support and practical strategies for spouses could help them support the service member, assist the family with the transition, and perhaps avoid negative mental health consequences. While face to face training with travel included could be cost prohibitive, telephone support groups could be provided at a much lower cost.

From literature, our study results, and particularly from the comments of spouses, there are critical factors that should be considered for any implementation of spouse telephone support groups. In addition to practical skills building, including problem solving skills, communication skills, stress reduction skills, and cognitive/mood management (Gottman et al., 2011; Schulz et al., 2003), we believe that the structure and design of the intervention and its logistics are critical to success.

Multicomponent interventions have been shown to be effective if they target several domains of risk, such as emotional and physical well-being and need for social support, that family members who are serving in a caregiving role encounter. Risks and coping strategies are individualized, and interventions that only address one area of risk may not be effective for all participants (Belle et al., 2006; Schulz et al., 2003; Sörensen et al. 2002). Interventions that incorporate practice in addition to information have been shown to have greater effectiveness (Belle et al., 2003; Czaja, Schulz, Lee, & Belle, 2003; Gitlin et al., 2003). Trained group leaders to guide discussion and practice have also been shown to improve outcomes

(Martindale-Adams et al., 2002; Toseland, Rossiter, & Labrecque, 1989). Standardized interventions are more easily translated and replicated by agencies and provide similar experiences for participants. However, including an element of targeting such as the commitments made by each spouse ensure that the intervention is germane to each participant (Schulz et al., 2003). The commitments allowed spouses to focus on practical strategies they could implement and to problem solve with the group to fine tune the strategies.

One strong concern of the spouses was to have more of an appreciation of them as individuals and less of a focus on their role as a support for the service member. Although they acknowledged that their support role is critical in their families, they did not always feel that their contributions were honored and respected. More importantly, they often felt that they receeded, or were perceived to have receeded, into the military spouse role and had lost some of their identity as a person separate from that role. By focusing on the spouse, the telephone support groups gave them back some sense of self and control. One spouse found solace within the group. *"I liked taking time for myself and being able to share my problems and accomplishments with women who understand."*

Acknowledgment This research was supported through the Defense Health Program (DHP), managed by the U.S. Army Medical Research and Materiel Command, through the Congressionally Directed Medical Research Program (CDMRP) and the Department of the Army Medical Research Acquisition Activity (W81XWH-08-2-0195). Our thanks to Dr. Katharine Nasseuer and COL Carl Castro, PhD for their support and encouragement. It was also supported in part by the Office of Research and Development, Department of Veterans Affairs, and the Memphis VA Medical Center.

We thank Robert Burns, M.D. for his insightful comments on the manuscript.

References

Bank, A. L., Argüelles, S., Rubert, R., Eisdorfer, C., & Czaja, S. J. (2006). The value of telephone support groups among ethnically diverse caregivers of persons with dementia. *The Gerontologist, 46*(1), 134–138.

Bell, D. B., & Schumm, W. R. (2000). Providing family support during military deployments. In J. A. Martin, L. N. Rosen, & L. R. Sparacino (Eds.), *The military family: A practice guide for human service providers*. Westport, CN: Praeger.

Belle, S. H., Burgio, L., Burns, R., Coon, D., Czaja, S. J., Gallagher-Thompson, D., et al. For the REACH II Investigators. (2006). Enhancing the quality of life of dementia caregivers from different ethnic or racial groups: A randomized, controlled trial. *Annals of Internal Medicine, 145*, 227–238.

Belle, S. H., Czaja, S. J., Schulz, R., Burgio, L., Gitlin, L. N., Jones, R., et al. For the REACH Investigators. (2003). Using a new taxonomy to combine the uncombinable: Integrating results across diverse interventions. *Psychology and Aging, 18*, 396–405.

Black, K., & Lobo, M. (2008). A conceptual review of family resilience factors. *Journal of Family Nursing, 1*, 33–55.

Blow, A., MacInnes, M., Hamel, J., Ames, B., Onaga, E., Holtrop, K., et al. (2012). National Guard service members returning home after deployment: The case for increased community support. *Administration and Policy in Mental Health and Mental Health Services Research, 39*(5), 383–393.

Booth, B., Wechsler Segal, M., & Bell, D. B. (2007). *What we know about army families: 2007 Update*. Alexandria, VA: Caliber Associates for the U.S. Army Family and Morale, Welfare and Recreation Command.

Burrell, L., Durand, D. B., & Fortado, J. (2003). Military community integration and its effect on well-being and retention. *Armed Forces & Society, 30*(1), 7–24.

Cohen, J. (1988). *Statistical power analysis for the behavioral sciences* (2nd ed.). Hillsdale, NJ: Lawrence Erlbaum Associates.

Czaja, S. J., Schulz, R., Lee, C. C., & Belle, S. H. For the REACH Investigators. (2003). A methodology for describing and decomposing complex psychosocial and behavioral interventions. *Psychology and Aging, 18*, 385–395.

Di Nola, G. M. (2008). Stressors afflicting families during military deployment. *Military Medicine, 173*(5), v–vii.

Drummet, A. R., Coleman, M., & Cable, S. (2003). Military families under stress: Implications for family life education. *Family Relations, 52*, 279–287.

Eaton, K. M., Hoge, C. W., Messer, S. C., Whitt, A. A., Cabrora, O. A., McGurk, D., et al. (2008). Prevalence of mental health problems, treatment need, and barriers to care among primary care-seeking spouses of military service members involved in Iraq and Afghanistan deployments. *Military Medicine, 173*(11), 1051–1056.

Faber, A. J., Willerton, E., Clymer, S. R., MacDermid, S. M., & Weiss, H. M. (2008). Ambiguous absence, ambiguous presence: A qualitative study of military reserve families in wartime. *Journal of Family Psychology, 22*(2), 222–230.

Gitlin, L. N., Burgio, L., Czaja, S., Mahoney, D., Burns, R., Zhang, S., et al. For the REACH Investigators. (2003). Effect of multi-component interventions on caregiver burden and depression: The REACH multi-site initiative at 6 month follow-up. *Psychology and Aging, 18*, 361–374.

Gorman, L. A., Blow, A. J., Ames, B. D., & Reed, P. L. (2011). National Guard families after combat: Mental health, use of mental health services, and perceived treatment brriers. *Psychiatric Services, 62*, 28–34.

Gottman, J. M., Gottman, J. S., & Atkins, C. L. (2011). The comprehensive soldier fitness program: Family skills component. *American Psychologist, 66*(1), 52–57.

Hoge, C. W., Auchterlonie, J. L., & Milliken, C. S. (2006). Mental health problems, use of mental health services, and attrition from military service after returning from deployment to Iraq or Afghanistan. *Journal of the American Medical Association, 295*, 1023–1032.

Hoge, C., Castro, C., & Eaton, K. (2006). Impact of combat duty in Iraq and Afghanistan on family functioning: Findings from the Walter Reed Army Institute of Research Land Combat Study. In *Human Factors and Medicine Panel Symposium (HFM-134) on human dimensions in military operations. Military leaders' strategies for addressing stress and psychological support*. Retrieved from http://www.socialwork.vcu.edu/pdfs/Impact_of_Combat_Duty.pdf

Hosek, J., Kavanagh, J., & Miller, L. (2006). *How deployments affect service members*. Santa Monica, CA: RAND.

Jacobson, N. S., Foilette, W. C., & Revenstorf, D. (1984). Psychotherapy outcome research: Methods for reporting variability and evaluating clinical significance. *Behavior Therapy, 15*, 336–352.

Knobloch, L. K., & Theiss, J. A. (2011). Depressive symptoms and mechanisms of relational turbulence as predictors of relationship satisfaction among returning service members. *Journal of Family Psychology, 25*, 470–478.

Lazarus, E. B., & Launier, R. (1978). Stress-related transactions between persons and environment. In L. Pervin & M. Lewis (Eds.), *Perspectives in international psychology* (pp. 287–325). New York: Plenum.

Lester, P., Mogil, C., Saltzman, W., Woodward, K., Nash, W., Leskin, G., et al. (2011). Families overcoming under stress: Implementing family-centered prevention for military families facing wartime deployments and combat operational stress. *Military Medicine, 176*(1), 19–25.

MacDermid Wadsworth, S. M. (2010). Family risk and resilience in the context of war and terrorism. *Journal of Marriage and Family, 72*, 537–556.

Mansfield, A. J., Kaufman, J. S., Marshall, S. W., Gaynes, B. N., Morrissey, J. P., & Engel, C. C. (2010). Deployment and the use of mental health services among U.S. Army wives. *The New England Journal of Medicine, 362*(2), 101–109.

Martindale-Adams, J., Nichols, L., Burns, R., & Malone, C. (2002). Telephone support groups: A lifeline for isolated Alzheimer's disease caregivers. *Alzheimer's Care Quarterly, 3*(2), 181–189.

Marziali, E., & Garcia, L. J. (2011). Dementia caregivers' responses to 2 internet-based intervention programs. *American Journal of Alzheimer's Disease and Other Dementias, 26*(1), 36–43.

Najavits, L. M. (2002). *Seeking safety: A treatment manual for PTSD and substance abuse.* New York, NY: Guilford.

Pfeiffer, J. W., & Jones, J. E. (Eds.). (1987). *A handbook of structured experiences for human relations training* (Vol. III). San Diego, CA: University Associates.

Riviere, L. A., Clark, J. C., Cox, A. L., Kendall-Robbins, A., & Castro, C. A. (2007, August). Spouse Battlemind training: Elements and strengths. In C. A. Castro (Chair), *The Battlemind training system: Supporting soldiers throughout the deployment cycle.* Symposium conducted at the meeting of the American Psychological Association. San Francisco, CA.

Sayers, S. L., Farrow, V. A., Ross, J., & Oslin, D. W. (2009). Family problems among recently returned military veterans referred for a mental health evaluation. *Journal of Clinical Psychiatry, 70*(2), 163–170.

Schulz, R., Burgio, L., Burns, R., Eisdorfer, C., Gallagher-Thompson, D., Gitlin, L. N., et al. (2003). Resources for enhancing Alzheimer's caregiver health (REACH): Overview, site-specific outcomes, and future directions. *The Gerontologist, 43*, 514–520.

Segal, M. W., & Segal, D. R. (2003). Implications for military families of changes in the Armed Forces of the United States. In Caforio (Ed.), *Handbook of the sociology of the military* (pp. 225–233). New York: Kluwer Academic/Plenum.

Slone, L. B., & Friedman, M. J. (2008). *After the war zone: A practical guide for returning troops and their families.* Philadelphia, PA: Da Capo Books.

Sörensen, S., Pinquart, M., & Duberstein, P. (2002). How effective are interventions with caregivers? An updated meta-analysis. *The Gerontologist, 42*(3), 356–372.

Stanley, S. M., Allen, E. S., Markman, H. J., Rhoades, G. K., & Prentice, D. (2010). Decreasing divorce in Army couples: Results from a randomized clinical trial of PREP for Strong Bonds. *Journal of Couple and Relationship Therapy, 9*, 149–160.

Toseland, R. W., Rossiter, C. M., & Labrecque, M. S. (1989). The effectiveness of peer-led and professionally led groups to support family caregivers. *The Gerontologist, 29*, 465–471.

Walsh, F. (2006). *Strengthening family resilience.* New York: Guilford.

Wood, S., Scarville, J., & Gravino, K. (1995). Waiting wives: Separation and reunion among Army wives. *Armed Forces and Society, 21*(2), 217–236.

Chapter 5
Evolution of a Research Agenda
for Military Families

Cathy A. Flynn

Abstract Military programs for families have evolved in the past decade to address changing demands in the context of increased deployments and ongoing relocations, and as this has occurred, the research agenda for family support has shifted. As the wars in Iraq and Afghanistan grew, the central research question in military family policy was "*What is the impact of deployments on service members and families?*" Later, the focus shifted to "*What is the impact of the programs on service members and families?*" For research to be influential in the military policy setting, it must address the military population and it must provide actionable findings. The recent shift in focus, which reflects a constricting budget climate, means that programs need concrete evidence that outcomes are linked to key military objectives, such as being ready to carry out the mission (readiness) and willingness to stay in the military (retention). Despite significant challenges, there are real opportunities to expand research and evaluation work, with the potential to tie changes in individual and group behavior to components of government social programs. The reintegration of military members into families and civilian life will require ongoing research on the long-term impacts of military service during sustained years of combat deployments.

The views expressed by this author are not necessarily the views of the Department of Defense or of the Federal Government.

C.A. Flynn, Ph.D. (✉)
Office of Military Community and Family Policy, Office of the Secretary of Defense,
Department of Defense, Defense Pentagon, Washington, DC, USA
e-mail: Cathy.Flynn@osd.mil

Military programs for families have evolved in the past decade to address changing demands in the context of increased deployments and ongoing relocations. While programs were being developed and enhanced to meet emerging needs, the research agenda for family support shifted.

As the wars in Iraq and Afghanistan continued, the central research question in military family policy was *"What is the impact of deployments on service members and families?"*[1] Policymakers, program development staff and advocates were all focused on what was needed to care for the warfighter and the family. This was not only a question of how to provide social support; it was also a business question. The nation relies on 1 % of the population to volunteer and fight for the country. The Department of Defense (DoD) needs those who volunteer to be ready to deploy, ready to be in combat, ready to return and be part of a family and community back home, and then return to combat. The strain on those who have dependents—to include 75,000 single parents in uniform—means that the family also has to be ready to manage for months if not years at a time without a key member.

In the years after 9/11, DoD and others were busy identifying the immediate needs of the service members and responding with programs that would enable them to be emotionally and mentally fit to fight—something they could not do if they were worried about financial or marital or parental concerns back home. Research during this period focused on the impact of deployments on marriage, on spouses, on children. Spouses of Active Duty members rated loneliness as the number one problem encountered with deployments (DMDC, 2009). In the middle of the decade of war, one in four service members identified communication with loved ones back home when asked what deployment issues impacted their desire to stay in the military (DMDC, 2009). To address the issues of loneliness and connection, the DoD leveraged new technologies, setting up the infrastructure downrange to enable service members to connect with loved ones back home. This meant that service members could now correspond in real time and in many cases, have ready access to the proliferation of communication resources that were not widely available in previous conflicts (for example e-mail, cell phones and video chat). These new technologies, however, also meant that service members and family members had to manage the unintended consequences of connecting someone in a war zone with the daily issues of family life.

As policymakers scrambled to understand what the new tempo of deployments meant for the needs of our warriors and families, the primary requirement for new programs was that they be designed to address the needs of service members and families. Large scale surveys were used as the primary means to identify and document needs and follow trends. Outcome evaluation data were rarely built in to the program design; in most cases program quality, utilization and satisfaction were the primary data that were collected to ensure that programs were reaching military families.

---

[1] It should be noted that given the history of frequent deployments as Sailors "go to sea", the Navy has been looking at the impact of deployments for some time. The question became relevant across the military services with increased combat deployments to the wars in Afghanistan and Iraq.

Recently the focus has shifted. No longer is the central question, "*What is the impact of deployments on service members and their families?*"[2] The central question has become "*What is the impact of the programs on service members and families?*" Until the tempo of deployment slowed in 2011, the reality of meeting immediate needs meant that programs for military members and their families were often stood up without the means to measure participant outcomes. At this time in order to continue to receive DoD funding, family programs need to be able to demonstrate effectiveness. Increased evaluation rigor is a result of resource constraints. With reduced resources, it is no longer enough to show a program is designed to meet a demonstrated need and is highly used by very satisfied participants—now programs are being asked "*Where are your measures of effectiveness?*" It is a paradox that when money was flowing, there was a decreased requirement for rigorous evaluation because programs did not have to compete for funding. The first decade of this century was an unprecedented opportunity to meet the needs of military members and their families—seemingly almost as fast as they could be identified and prioritized. In the current period of limited resources for programs or evaluation, programs for military members and their families must now demonstrate effectiveness to justify their existence.

This is however, not just a question of funding evaluation. Researchers and practitioners alike know how difficult it is to measure the impact of a social policy or program on aspects of well-being, how difficult it is to measure subtle changes in behavior and link that outcome to a specific program or initiative. Even more difficult is how to measure the impact of a social program on preventing an undesirable outcome such as divorce, abuse or suicide, issues of critical importance for leaders.

Policy Relevant Research: Challenges and Opportunities

For research to be influential in a military policy setting, it has to be meaningful, in that it has to address the military population and it has to provide actionable findings. Research on the military population begs the question "How does the data compare to the data in the civilian world?" Comparisons are often difficult because data was collected from non-comparable samples (the military population is skewed younger than the general adult population), or by significantly different methods. For example, military divorce statistics do not have a direct civilian comparison due to the way the DoD collects the data versus the way that the United States Census Bureau collects the national data. Similar issues exist for military child abuse and neglect data; incidents and reports bridge the military and civilian reporting systems. The inability to compare data across military and civilian populations is a challenge that is not insurmountable; building bridges across civilian and military researchers is a first step that is exemplified by the papers in this volume.

---

[2] This is not to say we know the full impact of deployments on service members or family members; much research is still needed to understand the long term consequences of the combat deployments of the last 10 years.

The research that has been utilized most readily by government recently has helped identify the problem as one unique to or exacerbated by military life—for example spouse employment trajectory disrupted by military moves. The vast majority (95 %) of civilian military spouses are women (DMDC, 2011). These spouses have long faced the challenge of trying to maintain a career trajectory while relocating on a regular basis for their military spouse's career. Researchers showed that military spouses were actually less likely to be employed than their civilian counterparts, providing hard evidence that the military lifestyle created a constraint for spouse employment (Harrell, Lim, Werber, & Golinelli, 2004). Recent DoD data shows that up to 26 % of military spouses who would like to be employed cannot find work, and analysis of 2010 Census data show that that there is a significant wage gap between military spouses and their married civilian women counterparts (Kniskern & Segal, 2010). The disruption of a move while trying to maintain employment, especially considering that installations in some cases are located in depressed local economies, means that it can take a military spouses many months to find employment again (DMDC, 2012). These findings, supported by years of political strategy and advocacy, resulted in DoD establishing the Military Spouse Education and Career Opportunities (SECO) program, which includes financial support for education and training as well as linkages to employers.[3]

The recent shift in focus, which reflects a constricting budget climate, means that programs need concrete evidence that outcomes are linked to key military objectives, such as being ready to carry out the mission (readiness) and willingness to stay in the military (retention). Again, demonstrating effectiveness was less critical when all energies were directed at increasing and improving service delivery. Evaluation was not the leadership's priority in the pulse of war—a time of a high needs with a relatively high resource environment. In fact, evaluations in such an environment could be seen as diverting energies from the important work of addressing the many emerging issues for families. But the current need to retrofit programs with evaluation components also poses a risk of over-focusing on evaluation and programs that can demonstrate measures of effectiveness. Balancing the current demands for program effectiveness data with the need to understand the short and long-term consequences of the experiences associated with deployments will prove a challenge for researchers and policymakers alike.

There are several known challenges in a resource constricted environment. First and foremost is the challenge of defending a program against funding cuts because it cannot be demonstrated to be effective (or ineffective, for that matter). Another challenge is producing outcome data when programs were not designed to collect any data—in at least one case in a conscious choice to enhance the program delivery. DoD's Military & Family Life Counselor Program, a non-medical counseling program that supports service members and families all over the world without collecting any identifying information, was designed in large part to address geographical dispersion and the stigma of seeking counseling as a warfighter or a

---

[3] A key component of the SECO program was an expansion of the Army Spouse Employment Program which links spouses with employers.

family member. Therefore, participant data cannot be linked to any database which would show that they have different outcomes than non-participants.

Another challenge is dealing with the turnover in the military population. Attrition in the military makes it difficult to do longitudinal research, key for determining the longer term effects of deployments and programs on families (i.e., more than 30 % of service members leave within the first 3 years of service). We need to understand how military families manage over time, as they transition to civilian life and become a potentially invisible population as civilian families who have served. This challenge could also be seen as an opportunity based on the current national focus on transitioning veterans; such attention could prompt interest in more research on the experiences of veteran families.

There are also many opportunities which demand ingenuity and collaboration. The DoD has a great deal of data. Large administrative data sets in some cases could be better mined to answer research questions. For example, child health records were used to look at whether children whose parents received domestic violence services had different health outcomes than children who do not have any record of domestic violence in the family (Department of Defense, 2011b). An important step is collaboration with investigators on population based studies. Adding questions which identify military members in a large data collection, something that is currently being developed with the National Institutes of Health National Children's Study, allows for us to better understand military families within the context of all families. Building networks across researchers, and where possible including identifiers of the military population within their data collection, means that military members could be better understood in the context of the entire population. A series of questions in the demographic section would allow military families to be identified in any research sample. While it is harder to match data sets using unique identifiers, it can be done—and has been done with Social Security wage data in the case of service members in the Reserve component (Martorell, Klerman, & Loughran, 2008).

None of this is easy. Important measures in place to protect privacy and identity sometimes mean that even de-identified data in existing data sets cannot be used for new research purposes. While it may seem that the institutional structure of the military would make it an easier place in which to conduct research than the civilian population, the multiple layers of leadership and diverse military service cultures often mean it is more difficult to conduct research with a military sample. Moreover, maneuvering within the federal bureaucracy is time consuming, measured sometimes in years rather than months.

And yet, given all of the challenges, there are real opportunities to expand research and evaluation work, with the potential to tie changes in individual and group behavior to components of government social programs. The reintegration of military members into families and civilian life will require ongoing research on the long-term impacts of military service during sustained years of combat deployments.

References

Defense Manpower Data Center. (2008, September). *April 2007 status of forces survey of active duty members: Retention, tempo, Military OneSource, financial health, and annual leave briefing* (DMDC Report No. 2008-030). Arlington, VA: Author.

Defense Manpower Data Center. (2009, July). *2008 Survey of military spouses: Impact of deployments on spouses and children*. Arlington, VA: Author.

Defense Manpower Data Center. (2011, May). *The 2010 Military Family Life Project briefing*. Arlington, VA: Author.

Defense Manpower Data Center. (2012, November). *2011 Military Family Life Project briefing*. Arlington, VA: Author.

Department of Defense. (2011a). *Plans for the Department of Defense for the support of military family readiness annual report to the congressional defense committees Pursuant to Section 1781b of Title 10, United States Code* (Fiscal Year 2011). Arlington, VA: Author.

Department of Defense. (2011b, October). *Report to congress on impact of domestic violence on military families*. Arlington, VA: Author.

Harrell, M. C., Lim, N., Werber, L., & Golinelli, D. (2004). *Working around the military: Challenges to military spouse employment and education* (RAND Corporation Monograph). Arlington, VA: RAND Corporation.

Kniskern, M. K., & Segal, D. R. (2010). *Mean wage differences between civilian and military wives*. College Park, MD: University of Maryland Center for Research on Military Organizations.

Martorell, P., Klerman, J. A., & Loughran, D. S. (2008). *How do earnings change when reservists are activated? A reconciliation of estimates derived from survey and administrative data* (RAND Corporation Technical Report). Arlington, VA: RAND Corporation.

Warner, J. T. (2012). The effect of the civilian economy on recruiting and retention. In *Eleventh Quadrennial Review of Military Compensation: Supporting Research Papers* (pp. 71–91). Downloaded April 12, 2013, from http://militarypay.defense.gov/REPORTS/QRMC/11th_QRMC_Supporting_Research_Papers_Files/SR05_Chapter_2.pdf

Part II
Parenting and Child Outcomes

Chapter 6
General and Specialist Health Care Utilization in Military Children of Army Service Members Who Are Deployed

Mary Jo Larson, Beth A. Mohr, Laura Lorenz, Candice Grayton, and Thomas V. Williams

Abstract This paper on children in Army families is the first to examine objective, non-self-report, measures of all health care utilization inclusive of prescription medications among children experiencing the deployment of a parent. It employs a quasi-experimental, pre–post, non-equivalent group design to compare changes in pediatric health care utilization. Multivariate difference-in-differences regression models isolate the effect of deployment on change in service usage comparing a period prior to deployment to a period starting with the parent's deployment. The proportion of children using any specialist office visits showed a net increase, while the proportion with any generalist office visits showed a net decline. Post-hoc analysis revealed that these pediatric specialist visits were predominantly, not exclusively, for psychiatric-type services. There also was, in users of antidepressants prescriptions, a 28 % relative increase in children under age 12 and 18 % relative increase in children age 12 years and older. Policy and procedures to support the increased care coordination

Author Note This paper was delivered at the 2011 International Research Symposium of the Military Family Research Institute. The opinions or assertions herein are those of the authors and do not necessarily reflect the view of the United States Department of Defense.

M.J. Larson, Ph.D., M.P.A. (✉) • B.A. Mohr, M.S. • L. Lorenz, Ph.D., M.Ed.
Heller School for Social Policy & Management, Brandeis University, 415 South Street, MS 035, Waltham, MA 02454, USA
e-mail: larson@brandeis.edu; mohr@brandeis.edu; llorenz@brandeis.edu

C. Grayton, M.P.H.
The CDM Group, Inc., 7500 Old Georgetown Rd. Suite 900, Bethesda, MD 20814, USA
e-mail: candice.grayton@cdmgroup.com

T.V. Williams, Ph.D., M.S.
Director, Methods, Measures, and Analyses, Defense Health Cost Assessment
and Program Evaluation, TRICARE Management Activity,
7700 Arlington Blvd, Suite 5101, Falls Church, VA 22042-5101, USA
e-mail: thomas.williams@tma.osd.mil

required of both primary care providers and parents of children who make use of psychiatric specialty services is important, especially since pediatric providers are often in the civilian, and not military, sector.

Keywords Health care utilization • Psychotropic medication • Deployment • Military children • Difference-in-difference analysis

Introduction

The Department of Defense (DoD) and the TRICARE Management Activity (TMA) have made concerted efforts to understand the military health care experiences of families through periodic surveys of military members and their dependents and also through commissioned studies. While the DoD has established a surveillance program associated with battlefield injuries and illnesses, and deployment-related assessments, there is no routine reporting on the health status of military families other than periodic surveys of spouses (Defense Manpower Data Center, 2009). Nevertheless, there is increasing recognition that the sacrifices made by families when a parent or spouse deploys may require additional attention (DeVoe & Ross, 2012; Lincoln, Swift, & Shorteno-Fraser, 2008; Paris, DeVoe, Ross, & Acker, 2010; The White House, 2012).

Careful analyses of dependent children's utilization of health care during deployment spells would provide useful information for DoD and civilian providers to implement effective responses. DoD maintains programs to reduce family problems that arise from deployment and arranges for non-medical counseling to mitigate family hardships that it can anticipate. Understanding emerging deployment-related problems may require large-scale population data to detect systematic effects that might not be easily quantified in survey studies. In survey data alone and small studies, it is difficult to disentangle deployment changes from confounding factors, such as children's stage of development or unique characteristics of specific locations. This chapter focuses specifically on objective measurement of health care utilization changes in a large sample of Army children at the time of a parent's recent deployment. The DoD defines deployment as an operation, location, command, or duty that is different from the military member's normal duty assignment (Department of Defense, 2008). In addition to combat, military forces are deployed for a variety of missions, including: military liaison and training support, joint and coalition force exercises, construction projects, humanitarian assistance, or health care and refugee relief.

Since 2003, deployments are the rule rather than the exception for the U.S. armed forces, and many have experienced long assignments and multiple deployments. More than two million U.S. children are estimated to have experienced one or more parental deployments to Iraq and Afghanistan (DeVoe & Ross, 2012). Of the more than 1.6 million service members deployed to Iraq and Afghanistan, the Army has sent the majority of troops and experienced the most combat deaths and troops wounded in action (Defense Manpower Data Center, 2011).

While there are informative studies on civilian children's use of health care services (Vingilis, Wade, & Seeley, 2006; Wertlieb, Weigel, & Feldstein, 1988), predictors of health care use among military children and adolescents have not been clearly delineated. Two recent population-based studies have identified an association of children's mental health diagnoses and parental military deployment. Gorman, Eide, and Hisle-Gorman (2010) studied children aged 3–8 years in all Armed Force branches in fiscal year (FY) 2006 and FY 2007. The study examined the incidence of children's outpatient visits for mental health diagnoses in association with months on and off of deployment of the military parent. They reported that in months a parent was deployed, visits with behavioral disorders increased 19 % and with anxiety disorders increased 18 % (Gorman et al., 2010). A second study of children with Army fathers ages 5–17 was conducted by Mansfield and colleagues (2011). Overall, 16.7 % of all children in the study had at least one mental health diagnosis during the 4-year study period with the most common diagnoses being acute stress and adjustment disorder (5.9 %), depression (5.6 %), and pediatric behavior disorders (4.8 %). Findings indicated an excess of 6,579 psychiatric diagnoses during the study period among children with parental deployed of more than 11 months compared to children without a deployed parent; psychiatric diagnoses associated with parental deployment were greater and increased for the group with more months of parental deployment.

Prior to these two studies, research had been conducted primarily on small samples, often Navy-only families, and sometimes of families stationed overseas; findings on the effect of deployment were inconsistent indicating they might not have provided reliable or generalizable estimates (Abbe, Naylor, Gavin, & Shannon, 1986; Keilberg, 2005; Levai, Kaplan, Ackerman, & Hammock, 1995; McNulty, 2003). Several recent review articles discuss the nature of children's stress and adjustment problems that may occur during deployments. Ambiguity surrounding deployment dates and lengths is identified as a stressor (Faber, Willerton, Clymer, MacDermid, & Weiss, 2008). Problems related to parental deployment may exhibit as poor academic performance, with boys appearing to suffer more effects than girls (Lincoln et al., 2008). There may be similarity to the mental and behavioral effects of school-aged children when separated from a parent because of divorce (Gorman & Braverman, 2008). Nevertheless, there appear to be unique stressors accompanying deployment events, such as the length of separation, repeated deployments, the impact on the parenting provided by military couples, and the risk of parental injury or death (DeVoe & Ross, 2012; White, de Burgh, Fear, & Iversen, 2011).

In sum, two recent studies which found increased mental health or behavioral disorders among children experiencing the most months of parent deployment provide evidence that children's mental health is vulnerable to periods of parental deployment. It is unknown to what extent this vulnerability spills over to an increased need for health care in general or to what extent it is specific to mental and behavioral services. Utilizing a large sample of Army children in two age groups (under age 12, 12 and older), the current study applies a quasi-experimental pre–post design to examine all pediatric health care utilization in the context of parent's deployment. Additionally, health care specialty services independent of diagnosis, and psychotropic medication receipt in young children and adolescents, are also

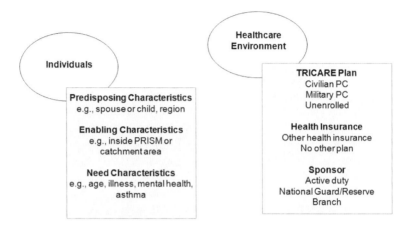

Fig. 6.1 Conceptual model of health care utilization. This figure illustrates the characteristics associated with individuals and the environment/organization

examined. To the best of our knowledge, this is the first national study to examine non-self-report, objective measures of all health care utilization inclusive of prescription medications among children experiencing the deployment of a parent.

Conceptual Framework

The current study used as a foundation a classic conceptual model of health care utilization that describes two levels of influence: those associated with the individual's characteristics, and those associated with the characteristics of the environment/organization (Andersen, 1995; Andersen & Aday, 1978; Andersen & Davidson, 2007). The individual and healthcare environment factors of interest are illustrated in Fig. 6.1.

The deployment of a spouse or parent to a war zone or peace-keeping mission can be a life-altering event for the children who remain at home. However, it is not clear what impact this change will have on health care utilization. Expanding on the foundational conceptual model, deployment represents a period when children may have additional health care *needs* associated with adjustment difficulties, or additional *coping* challenges associated with existing chronic conditions (e.g., depression), or challenges *maintaining* healthy lifestyles (e.g., increased risky drinking). Consistent with the prior literature, one would hypothesize that medical/mental health needs of dependents would increase during deployment (see Fig. 6.2). Alternatively, the deployment of a parent also represents a time of reduced adult availability to arrange for and transport to counseling and medical appointments. Competing demands and additional transportation problems may lead to lower attendance at socialization

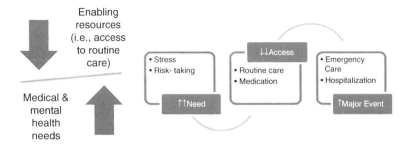

Fig. 6.2 Plausible effects of deployment. This figure illustrates the plausible decrease of enabling resources and increase in medical and mental health needs for family dependents with deployment

programs, or fewer preventive visits to generalist providers for minor problems associated with mild adjustment symptoms. Use of routine office visits and medications for chronic problems such as mild depression may decline. In some scenarios, the lack of routine care may lead to greater risk of hospitalization or more reliance on emergency departments as the source of care.

Thus, while many family dependents may be resilient and have successful coping strategies for periods of deployment, there still are necessary hardships associated with fewer transportation options, competing responsibilities, and perhaps a move to a new geographic area and lack of familiarity with new health care providers. On balance enabling resources would decline with deployment (see Fig. 6.2).

In sum, this study examines the cumulative influence of deployment on changes in overall health care patterns inclusive of medication usage; findings which have not been fully explored in prior research.

Methods

This paper addresses two primary research questions. First, do specific types of health care utilization change among children and adolescents during the deployment of their Army active duty parent, relative to a comparison group and compared to their own utilization prior to deployment? Second, does receipt of any medication and specifically psychotropic medications change among Army children and adolescents during a parent's deployment? We also provide post hoc analysis using FY2007 data to describe the type of care that comprises specialist and generalist office visits of military children and adolescents.

The project team performed this work in accordance with an approved Data Use Agreement and a submitted Security Assurance Questionnaire with the TRICARE Privacy Office and after review by the Brandeis University Institutional Review Board which found the project exempt from ongoing review.

Study Design

We employed a quasi-experimental, pre–post, non-equivalent group design to compare changes in health care utilization of children of deployed and comparison Army service members and to estimate the possible impact of deployment. Deployment was identified using military records of actual begin and end dates, and was defined in this study as mission assignments away from the service member's permanent station lasting 6 months or longer.

Setting: The Military Health System

The children included in this study were eligible as dependents of active duty service members for TRICARE health benefits. TRICARE is a health benefit program for the members of uniformed services, their spouses, and unmarried children, among others. TRICARE is a large health care delivery system for services delivered by military treatment facilities (MTF) and an insurance or payment program for health services of civilian providers used by dependents and others. As such, it shares some of the characteristics of the civilian insurance market. There are several TRICARE health plan options for dependents including: TRICARE Prime, a voluntary HMO-like option where the dependent is assigned or chooses a primary care provider (either in the military or a civilian provider) who provides or arranges for all care. TRICARE Prime Remote serves active duty family members in remote geographic areas accessing care through approved civilian providers. TRICARE Standard and TRICARE Extra are preferred provider-like options that do not require enrollment. Other special programs also exist.

TRICARE serves a substantial number of families and children and is an important health care program for children (Department of Defense, 2011). In 2010 more than 44 % of the 1.4 million active duty members were parents, and there were almost 1.25 million child dependent (Department of Defense, 2010).

Selection of Sample

The study sample was identified using the Defense Enrollment Eligibility Reporting System (DEERS) to first identify Army active duty service members (i.e., parents) that met study criteria and then selecting their child dependents identified in DEERS who met study criteria. The definition of child dependent reflects TRICARE participation definitions and includes the service member's stepchildren, foster children, and child 'wards'. Of note, the selection of child dependents associated with a service member could vary month by month as a result of birth, death, marriage, divorce, adoption, and child loss of eligibility due to aging out, disenrollment, or own military enlistment. Status as child dependent was based on the eligibility record the month prior to the service member's month of deployment (pseudo-deployment) so the first analytic step was to identify the analysis study-period specific to each service member.

Deployment-Window and Study-Period

The analysis data for each child dependent spans a 25-month deployment window based on the parent's deployment start date. The calendar month of deployment was not included in analysis. The deployment window consists of the pre-period: 12 calendar months before the deployment month, and the post-period: the 12 calendar months beginning after the deployment start month; for most Army members, they will be on deployment during the post-period but some have returned and are reintegrating with family and non-combat military work. In short, the deployment window represents different calendar months for each child. In this study the vast majority of deployment start months occurred in Federal fiscal year (FY) 2006 and FY2007. The median of the deployment start months was October, 2007; this date also was assigned as the 'pseudo' deployment month for each comparison group member. We selected those deployments that began with, ended in, or otherwise included, months of FY2007. The full analysis data set spanned from October, 2003 to September, 2008.

Study Inclusion and Exclusion Criteria

Children were selected who were dependents of an Army active duty parent during FY2007 and had 25 months of eligibility during the parent's deployment window. As the analysis required comparing equal months of data in the pre- and post-periods, children were excluded if they lacked enrollment one or more months any time during the window. Also excluded were children with other health insurance (OHI; 3 %) as this could lead to unobserved utilization for care paid by another insurer during the study period.

Data Sources

A TMA contractor prepared 37 separate data files covering FY2004–2008 and offered written and verbal file documentation to ensure the project team understood the conventions used in TRICARE data and typical analyses. Only encrypted person identification (ID) numbers were used. Dependents had their own encrypted ID and their records contained the encrypted ID of their military parent.

This study used data from two DoD administrative data files: the Defense Enrollment Eligibility Reporting System and the Contingency Tracking System.

For the former, we rolled up information to the person-level from monthly beneficiary records containing data on the parent's service branch and rank group; the child's beneficiary eligibility category, enrollment dates, primary care provider, age, gender, residence (3-digit zip code, region), military hospital catchment area and clinic area (PRISM). We used parent's race/ethnicity for the child as the child's characteristic was frequently missing.

From the Contingency Tracking System we constructed one deployment record per service member by identifying the first overseas mission with an end date in FY2007, and retaining the starting and ending months of this deployment (many stretching into FY2008) and the total number of mission deployments since September 11, 2001.

For health care utilization we analyzed direct care system (MTF) data captured in the CAPER file of ambulatory encounters and hospital stay data from the Standard Inpatient Data Record file. All purchased care services of civilian providers were captured in paid ambulatory claims of the TRICARE Encounter Data, Non-Institutional file and paid civilian sector inpatient and residential facility claims of the TRICARE Encounter Data, Institutional file. Finally, the Pharmacy Data Transaction Service file was analyzed for all prescription medication claims from direct care, MTF providers, mail order, and retail pharmacy sources.

Measures

Utilization Outcomes

We constructed a series of utilization measures (0 = not used, 1 = used) to encompass all health services independent of diagnosis used by children and adolescents in the sample. There was a measure for an overnight institutional stay, and three ambulatory care measures: emergency department visits, generalist office visits, specialist office visits. Following DoD convention, visits were defined as claims or encounters with at least one of several evaluation and management (E&M) Berenson-Eggers Type of Service codes (Department of Defense, 2009). There were five prescription medication measures: all prescription medications, any psychotropic prescription medications, any anxiety medications, any anti-depressant medications, and any stimulant medications. The prescription medication claims contained the American Hospital Formulary Services six-digit code and a therapeutic class name that was used to classify anti-depressants (28:16.04); anxiolytics, sedatives, hypnotics (28:24:XX); and stimulants (28:20:XX), and any psychotropic medication measure defined as any claim for these three classes or an anti-psychotic (28:16.08) or anti-manic (28:28:XX) medication (American Hospital Formulary Service, 2008). For each measure we first constructed indicator variables that were set to 1 if the child had utilization of the specified type during the period and 0 if the child did not have utilization. The dependent variable in our multivariate regression models was the change in the child's two indicator variables for the post- and pre-time periods for a measure.

Independent Variables

We included three different types of covariates in our analytic models: military parent covariates, health system covariates, and child status covariates, each derived from eligibility records 1 month prior to deployment. Service member covariates were characteristics for military rank (officer, warrant officer, enlisted) and race/ethnicity (Asian/Pacific Islander, Black non-Hispanic, white non-Hispanic, Hispanic, other) which served as a proxy for child race/ethnicity as that data value was frequently missing. Health system covariates were child's residence within a MTF service area (within 40 miles of inpatient MTF, within 20 miles of ambulatory clinic, within both inpatient and ambulatory clinic areas, outside both), and system of primary care provider (MTF/direct, civilian/purchased care, or not PRIME enrolled). Child characteristics were age, gender, residence region (north, south, west, Alaska/Hawaii/US territory), and a military health system-constructed indicator used for medical risk adjustment based on diagnoses reported on the previous year claims, the hierarchical condition category (HCC) score which was coded 1 if above the 90th percentile of children in the sample (Pope et al., 2004).

Difference-in-Differences Analysis

We used a multivariate difference-in-differences (DID) regression model to isolate the effect of deployment on changes in utilization from the pre- to post-periods (Ashenfelter & Card, 1985; Meyer, 1995). DID regression is commonly used to evaluate the effect of an event or policy change on outcomes. The unadjusted DID statistic is calculated by taking the difference in utilization from pre to post for the deployed and comparison groups, and then subtracting the two quantities, hence the term "difference-in-differences". In multivariate DID models, the coefficient for the deployment group indicator is the adjusted DID statistic and estimates the difference in average change in utilization of the two study groups (i.e. how much more the deployed group changed) after adjustment for other covariates.

The main benefit of DID analysis is that it simultaneously controls for pre-period utilization and factors affecting both groups. Since the child's pre-period utilization is adjusted for, each child serves to some extent as his/her own control. Also, because both children in the deployed and comparison groups could experience changes in utilization for reasons other than deployment (e.g. maturation, changes in social circumstances, policy changes), having both time periods and both groups in the DID model essentially adjusts the deployed group's change estimate for changes that would be expected for non-deployment reasons. Thus, the adjusted DID statistic is the net effect of deployment—net pre-period utilization and net non-deployment factors.

Change in use (described above) was regressed on the indicator for deployment group and on the covariates using ordinary least squares (OLS) regression (Singer & Willett, 2003; Wu et al., 1999). An OLS regression model with a categorical outcome is a linear probability model (LPM), and can be used to measure the association between explanatory variables on qualitative events (Wooldridge, 2005). In contrast to a logistic model, which models the odds of an event, an LPM models the probability of an event. We note that originally we intended to use hierarchical models to account for the correlation between the pre- and post-period utilization measures of the same person. Study samples were too large for the statistical software to estimate the models. However, the LPM can be specified to estimate the same DID effect as estimated by a hierarchical model (Wu et al., 1999).

In presenting results we report the adjusted DID statistic and the 95 % confidence interval (CI). CIs which do not overlap 0 indicate statistically significant results. We also report the *relative* percent change associated with deployment, which is calculated by dividing the adjusted DID (the numerator) by the unadjusted utilization percent of the deployed group during the pre-period (base rate). We interpret the relative percent change as suggestive of the importance of the deployment effect—as even a small change (i.e., small ADID) may be notable if the usage rate in the pre-year also is small. The findings and additional methods from the main study of spouses and children are reported in Larson et al. (2012).

In this chapter we also present two post-hoc analyses. Findings are based on subgroup analysis of two samples, younger children (under age 12) and older children (age 12 and older) based on age the month prior to deployment start. We also present descriptive analyses on the non-prescription health care services used in FY2007 by TRICARE children and adolescents to better understand what comprised the generalist and specialist visit categories, particularly examine use of psychiatric-related services and providers. Statistical analysis was performed using SAS/STAT software (version 9.2; SAS Institute Inc., Cary, NC).

Study Results

Sample Description

The initial data pass identified 302,607 Army active duty parents of whom 43 % were classified as deployed and 57 % were in the comparison group. For these military parents we found records for 440,236 children identified the month before the deployment (or pseudo-deployment) start date. After applying exclusion criteria (see methods above), there remained 137,602 children in the deployed group and 199,520 children in the comparison group. Twenty-one percent of eligible children were excluded because they lacked enrollment during one or several months of the 25-month study period (e.g., were born during the study period, aged out of TRICARE) and 3 % were excluded because of evidence of a second health insurance plan.

A detailed description of the sample was described previously and briefly summarized here (Larson et al., 2012). Half of the children in the study were female and the health of sample children was generally quite good, indicated by a low average "medical risk adjustment" score. Nearly three-quarters of the study's children

Table 6.1 Percent of study children in deployed group by age group with service utilization during the pre-deployment year[a]

	Children of deployed parents	
Utilization measure	Younger (<12 year) (N = 109,876)	Older (12+ year) (N = 27,726)
Any Emergency Department Visit	32 %	21 %
Any Generalist Office Visit	78.4 %	65.3 %
Any Specialist Office Visit	18.8 %	30.4 %
Any Hospital/Residential Stay[b]	2.4 %	2.7 %
Any Prescription	68.9 %	58.0 %
Any Psychotropic[c] Prescription	10.2 %	17.9 %
Any Anti-depressant Prescription	0.7 %	3.5 %
Any Anti-anxiety, Sleep-aid Prescription	2.5 %	2.1 %
Any Stimulant Prescription	3.8 %	5.1 %

[a]The pre-deployment year is the 12 calendar months before the deployment start month
[b]Non-hospital stay is residential care for cancer, mental health, and other chronic conditions provided in purchased care settings. Home health service excluded from these analyses
[c]Psychotropic medications defined using American Hospital Formulary Service codes; any psychotherapeutics and include antipsychotics and miscellaneous psychotherapeutic agents in addition to the classes separately analyzed (anti-depressant, anti-anxiety, stimulants)

received care delivered by or organized by a military-based primary care provider. One difference was observed between deployment and comparison group children; the median age was younger in the deployment group. This difference corresponds to a slight excess of enlisted-rank service members in the deployed group. Utilization measures were nearly equivalent for the children in the deployed and comparison groups: In each group about three-quarters of children had one or more visits with a generalist procedure code, and less than one-quarter had one or more visits classified as specialist care. More than a quarter had a visit to the ED. Regarding prescription medication utilization, 7.2 % of children in the deployed group and 7.6 % of children in the comparison group received a prescription medication in the therapeutic groups classified as psychotropic (Larson et al., 2012).

Pre-deployment Service Utilization

Table 6.1 presents data on the utilization measures for the pre-deployment year of sample children by age group. The younger age group relative to the older group had higher utilization of emergency department (ED) visits and generalist office visits, as well as any anti-anxiety or sleep-aid prescription. The older age group relative to the younger group had higher utilization of specialist office visits, hospital/residential institutional stays, any psychotropic medication prescription, any anti-depressant prescription, and any stimulant prescription.

Table 6.2 Net effect of deployment: adjusted difference-in-difference estimates on service usage of study children

| | | Net effect of deployment | |
| | | Adjusted difference-in | |
Utilization measure	Children[a]	difference estimate[d]	p Value
Any Outpatient ED Visits	Younger	−0.06	0.79
	Older	0.69	0.07
Any Generalist Office Visits	Younger	−1.07	<0.01
	Older	−1.09	<0.01
Any Specialist Office Visits	Younger	2.07	<0.01
	Older	1.16	<0.01
Any Hospital/Residential Stay[b]	Younger	0.08	0.32
	Older	0.11	0.49
Any Prescription	Younger	−0.42	0.05
	Older	−0.53	0.17
Any Psychotropic Prescription[c]	Younger	0.44	<0.01
	Older	1.00	<0.01
Any Anti-depressant	Younger	0.21	<0.01
	Older	0.29	0.04
Any Anti-anxiety, Sleep-aid	Younger	0.20	0.01
	Older	0.39	0.01
Any Stimulant Prescription	Younger	0.12	0.05
	Older	0.10	0.42

[a]Younger children are aged under 12 year, n = 252,953; older children are aged 12 and older, n = 84,169

[b]Non-hospital stay is residential care for cancer, mental health, and other chronic conditions provided in purchased care settings. Home health service excluded from these analyses

[c]Psychotropic medications defined using American Hospital Formulary Service codes; any psychotherapeutic and includes antipsychotics and miscellaneous psychotherapeutic agents in addition to the classes separately analyzed (anti-depressant, anti-anxiety, stimulants)

[d]The adjusted difference-in-differences statistics are adjusted for age, gender, service member rank and race/ethnicity, residence region, residence in proximity to inpatient and ambulatory catchment areas, "medical risk adjustment" (HCC) score above/below 90th percentile, military versus civilian primary care provider (vs. unenrolled)

Difference-in-Difference Estimates

Table 6.2 presents the adjusted DID (ADID) estimates associated with deployment and 95 % confidence intervals (CIs) from the series of multivariate regression models on each utilization outcome. The ADID represents the net effect of deployment considering all covariates, the pre-deployment baseline, and the comparison group's experiences.

The proportion of children using specialist office visits showed a net increase during deployment, particularly among younger children. The proportion for generalist visits showed a net decline. Changes were not significant for ED and institutional services.

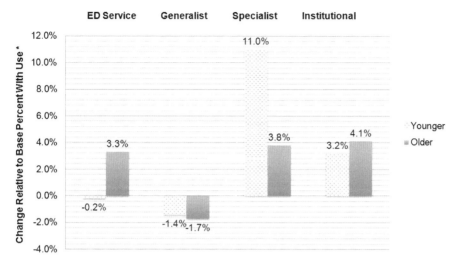

*Adjusted difference-in-difference (DID) estimates divided by percent utilization in base year;
P<0.01 except % change associated with deployment for ED service and institutional service.
ED = emergency department

Fig. 6.3 Relative percent change in any service use during deployment, by service category by age group. This figure shows the relative percent change in health care utilization for younger and older children associated with deployment

Deployment was associated with a significant net increase in all psychotropic medication utilization for both younger and older children, for antidepressants (younger children), and anxiolytics, sedatives, and hypnotics (older children) (Table 6.2).

Relative Percent Change in Utilization

Figure 6.3 presents the utilization findings for younger and older children from a "relative to baseline" perspective. These figures present the *relative* percent change in any utilization associated with deployment, for younger and older children, obtained by dividing the ADID (estimates on Table 6.2) by the pre-year utilization rate for the age group's deployed sample. While the ADID is the absolute magnitude of change, the same ADID value could equate to a small relative change in one age group (or one type of service) and a large relative change in a second age group (or a second service) if pre-year utilization levels were different.

The ADID for ED services and institutional services were not significant for either age group, and while the decline in generalist service utilization was significant, it was a small rate of change relative to the pre-year baseline (Fig. 6.3). The increase in specialist service utilization was moderate relative to baseline for younger children and small for the older children.

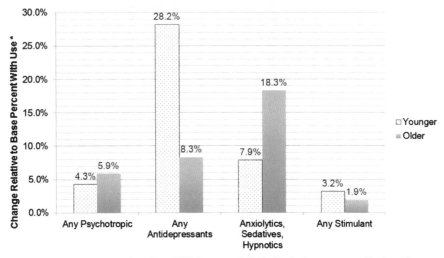

* Relative percent change is the adjusted DID (numerator) divided by the base percent utilization. All estimates significant at least p<0.05 except change value for any stimulant, older child (1.9%) which was not significant.

Fig. 6.4 Relative percent change in any psychotropic medication use during deployment, by therapeutic class and age group. This figure illustrates the relative percent change in psychotropic medication use, for four classes of medications, for younger and older children associated with deployment

The statistically significant increase in use of any psychotropic medication in association with parental deployment represented a moderate *relative* percent increase among both younger and older children (Fig. 6.4). There were large *relative* percent increases in antidepressant use among younger children and in use of anxiolytics/sedatives/hypnotics among older children, as well as statistically significant in all other classes for age subgroups except stimulants for older children.

Exploratory Results on Medical and Psychiatric (Non-prescription) Services

Figures 6.5, 6.6 and 6.7 present post-hoc analysis findings related to visits to health care providers, both specialists and generalists, in 2007 by children with Army parents. Service use is shown as the total number of annual visits for the provider type and as the sum of visits at an MTF (direct care) and civilian providers (purchased care).

Children's Visits to All Specialists

To further explore the finding on significant increases in use of specialists, we decomposed the distribution of specialist visits by type. The findings presented in Fig. 6.5 demonstrate that the vast majority of visits coded as specialist are for psychiatric type

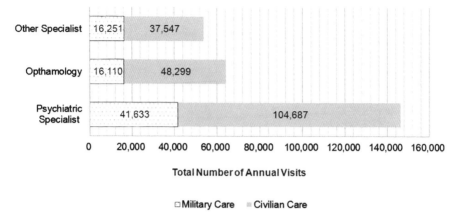

Fig. 6.5 Number of specialist visits by Army children, by specialty group and sector, FY2007. This figure shows the number of visits by younger and older Army children to health care specialists in three categories of specialty: other, opthamology, and psychiatry

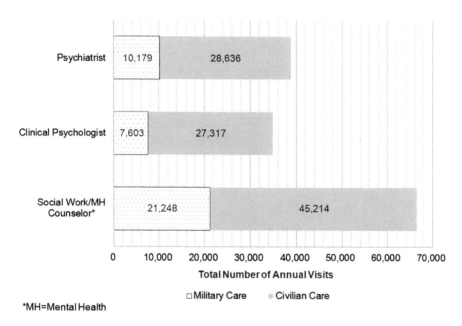

*MH=Mental Health

Fig. 6.6 Psychiatric-type visits of Army children, by type of provider seen and sector, FY2007. This figure illustrates visit by younger and older Army children to three types of psychiatric specialists: psychiatrist, clinical psychologist, and social worker or mental health counselor

of services, followed by opthamology, then other. For both the military sector (direct care) and civilian providers (purchased care), psychiatric-type visits exceeded the number of visits for other types of specialists combined. Further, psychiatric specialty visits to purchased care providers were more than twice as numerous as direct care services.

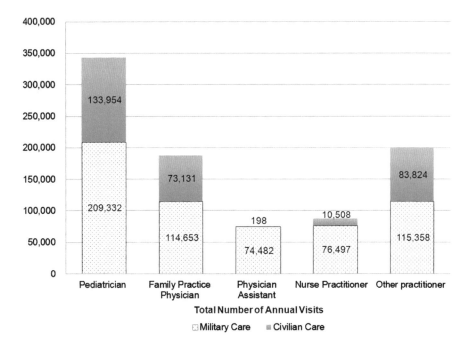

Fig. 6.7 Generalist visits of Army children, by provider type seen and sector, FY2007. This figure illustrates the number of visits made by Army children to generalist health care providers in MTFs and in the civilian sector

Children's Visits to Psychiatric Specialists

Figure 6.6 shows that among psychiatric specialists, social work/mental health counselors were visited more frequently than clinical psychologists or psychiatrists. Social work/mental health counselor was the largest provider of psychiatric specialists in direct care settings, while clinical psychologist was the largest provider of psychiatric services accessed through purchased care.

Children's Visits to Generalists

Figure 6.7 shows distribution of children's visits to generalists, a category of visits that declined in association with deployment. In contrast to use of specialists, the majority of visits children made to generalists was to MTFs, not to civilian providers. Visits to pediatricians exceeded visits to other types of providers, although a diverse group of providers was seen, including family practice physicians, physician assistants and nurse practitioners.

Discussion

This study presents findings of health care utilization changes that may reflect possible health effects on children and adolescents in military families that are associated with the start and first 12 months of mission deployment of their Army parent. To the best of our knowledge it is the first national study to examine non-self-report, objective measures of all health care utilization inclusive of prescription medications among children experiencing the deployment of a parent. The findings largely replicated for two age group subsamples, those under age 12 and those 12 and older, the main study findings (Larson et al., 2012). The study has a particularly strong quasi-experimental pre–post design that uses pre-year data from each child to control for historic utilization and compares changes for children with a deployed parent to changes for children in a comparison group. Our findings indicate that the overall magnitude of change (analyzed by difference-in-differences multiple regressions) in health care service usage in the deployment year ranges from small to large depending on service type with few services showing no change. While we report the statistical significance of the ADID estimates, we also interpret them using the relative percent change statistic; even small changes may be important if the pre-year usage rate is small. Most notable, we report large increases in association with deployment in specialist services for both age groups, and through ad hoc analysis we demonstrate that specialist services are predominantly composed of psychiatric type of care. In relative terms, the percent change in utilization was 11.0 % for younger children and 3.8 % for older children in association with deployment. In terms of our conceptual model, these findings provide support that some children are experiencing additional stress and increased behavioral and psychological symptoms in the immediate 12 months after an Army parent departs on deployment. These findings also imply that during this time of reduced family time resources, the at-home parent or guardian must organize appointments with additional providers for their children. Our post hoc analysis also showed that specialist care is primarily through purchased care, or civilian providers, while generalist services are primarily received through military treatment facilities. Thus, more parents or guardians are required to coordinate care across multiple systems and providers during the military parent's deployment. From this analysis it is unclear whether or not the use of civilian rather than military providers for pediatric specialty care is related to lack of availability or poor access within MTFs of services, although lack of access has been noted by others as a substantial problem (Defense Health Care, 2011; Department of Defense Task Force on Mental Health, 2007).

While access to up to five visits of psychiatric care may be arranged without approval by one's primary care provider in TRICARE, this finding also implies additional challenges for the pediatricians or primary care providers in their role as care coordinators during this stressful period. Our findings on increased use of specialists, primarily psychiatric care, is consistent with findings reported by Mansfield et al. (2011) of excess mental health visits among children 5–17 years old and of

Gorman et al. (2010) of increased behavioral disorders and anxiety disorders among children 3–8 years old. Our prior study of these Army children further disaggregated change in service utilization by sector of the military health system. We reported that for almost all service types, the utilization of services provided by providers at military treatment facilities declined in association with deployment, while the utilization of services provided through purchased care, or civilian providers, increased substantially. While we did not study this finding separately by age group, the implication again is that pediatricians and other primary care providers for children, typically located at a military treatment facility, have a more challenging task managing the care for children during times of deployment. Additionally, more parents are performing coordination of care for their children across two service sectors during deployment.

Also noteworthy were the large relative percent increases in usage of psychotropic medication in association with parental deployment. The number of antidepressant users increased 29 % (relative to base rate) in younger children and the number of users of anti-anxiety and sedative medications increased 19 % (relative to base rate) among older children. These findings are additional evidence that deployment of a parent can have immediate effects on children's well-being and in symptoms of stress and depression. Further exploration should consider whether users of psychotropic medications also received additional counseling services, or alternatively if the medications were 'substitutes' for counseling visits. If psychologists and counselors for children are in short supply in military treatment facilities, parents may feel more willing to accept pharmacological therapies for children with distress associated with deployment. Given more children are seeing psychiatric providers during times of deployment, it is not surprising that more children receive medication to treat their presenting problems. However, with the possible exception of attention deficit disorder, psychotropic medications are not considered the first line of treatment for children. Indeed, some anti-depressants have black box warnings when used with children, and many psychotropic medications have not been subjected to clinical trials with children as participants—thus their use represents 'off label' use (Larson, Miller, & Fleming, 2007), and may involve increased safety risks. We did not explore whether civilian or military providers were the predominant prescribers of these medications, nor the length of time these medications were prescribed. We also did not explore whether there were regional differences in use of psychotropic medications or whether or not the observed increased in use of psychotropic medications is partially or fully explained by children going to civilian, psychiatric specialist rather than using military treatment facility providers. These topics are important areas for future research.

We found a statistically significant decline in the number of users of generalist office services, however, the relative percent change was small for both age groups. Given more children were using specialists during this period, parents may be particularly challenged in making additional office visits and may neglect some of the routine care they otherwise would use. Considered together with the increased usage of specialists, the small decrease in usage of generalist care may reflect a substitution of the type of provider who is managing the child's care; once a specialist is involved, visits to the generalist office may be less necessary. For most children, however, it appears that primary care providers are challenged to manage use of more children with specialty services during deployment periods.

If the overall health of the population was poor and the supply of general medical care was too constrained during times of deployment, we would expect to see an increase in ED utilization. we did not witness changes in usage of ED services for either age group. We also did not observe an increase in the usage of hospital or residential (institutional) care. A shift to specialists versus generalists does imply possible increased symptom severity or disability among children, but the lack of increase in hospital/residential care appears to indicate the severity of problems could be managed with ambulatory services. While we examined separate age groups, we did not look separately at children with known vulnerabilities or special needs. These children may show additional signs of the impact of deployment compared to their healthy peer group.

Limitations

This study used observational data and can report association only; we cannot infer causal relationships between deployment and changes in psychotropic medication and services utilization, however the difference-in-difference study design does provide the best evidence short of a randomized trial. Further, 64 % of the comparison sample had parents who had at least one deployment in the past prior to their study window. It is possible that the observed deployment effects may be underestimated if we assume the comparison group children and their families may still be 'reacting' to a past deployment. Other limitations were that children of Army parents may have experiences that are different from children in other branches, and health care resources for families of active duty and National Guard/Reservists are not comparable. Findings may not generalize to short deployments or to dependents with other health insurance; both were excluded from the study. The number of dependents known to have other health insurance, however, was small among these active duty parents.

Our method of assigning pseudo-deployment dates to comparison children is another limitation. We assigned one date to the entire group after attempting to match a comparison group child to a deployed child. If successful, we would have assigned to each comparison group the deployment date and window of the matched deployed child. We had insufficient resources with this large sample to match on multiple variables and ensure the two children had TRICARE eligibility for the same period. The introduction of bias was mitigated by choosing children in the deployed group who had deployment start dates tightly clustered around FY2007.

On balance, the pre–post design and other quasi-experimental features of the study increase our confidence that the results are strong evidence that deployment has an immediate effect on the health and use of health services by Army children.

Implications

There are several policy implications derived from this study. First, military children might benefit if military and civilian health care providers (and schools) are made aware of when a military parent is about to deploy and that research findings show that children may have increased service needs during their parent's deployment. While plentiful information exists for providers on military websites, it is not clear the typical civilian health care provider is aware of this information or sees the relevancy in becoming culturally competent in the special issues that confront children with military parents. Second, all primary care providers of military children might benefit from training on best practice protocols to assist military families during these transitions, particularly on offering assistance to families who seek mental health services from civilian providers. While the DoD has provided some referral services through a website and telephone calls (see Military One Source), this service is not a substitute for assistance in coordinating care. Military treatment facilities would likely benefit from establishing standard procedures for primary care providers of children on coordinating care with specialty mental health providers, particularly with civilian providers, and including how to stay abreast of psychotropic medications that may have been prescribed. Knowledge of all medications given to children, their potential side effects, and their interactions with other medications possibly prescribed by the primary care provider, is essential for children's safety. Third, it could be useful for families to put in place during the pre-deployment period, care plans for times when the at-home parent is stressed and when a parent recognizes signs of stress in their child(ren). These plans could help families think through possible scenarios of care choices they might make, so decision-making does not occur at a time of crisis, and so that plans can be discussed with the support of the military parent about to deploy. This advanced planning would be especially important for families where a child has known vulnerabilities, either from young age, prior mental health or behavioral issues, or special health needs.

System-level policy implications include improving care coordination and integration between primary care and behavioral health services, especially across military and civilian sectors (American Psychological Association, 2007). Telephone or internet monitoring of mental health status and needs for behavioral health visits could facilitate access to care when needed. Primary care physicians (pediatricians) could be trained on addressing parent's stress when the child shows symptoms of stress. Finally, the military health system would benefit from reviewing its protocols for deciding when to prescribe psychotropic medications to children and how to monitor for side effects, Further, children's advocates in both the civilian and military systems could look for opportunities to provide education to civilian and military providers who see military children on the benefits and cautions of adding psychotropic medications when a parent is deployed.

Army active duty families are a self-selected group of predominantly young individuals, and many observers note that they have unusual abilities to cope with the transitions, uncertainties, and sacrifices associated with the typical deployment

(Huebner, Mancini, Bowen, & Orthner, 2009). This resilience is supported by additional non-medical support services offered on base (MHN Government Services, 2009), through the web (Department of Defense, 2009), and even through volunteer civilian services (Strategic Outreach to Families of All Reservists, 2005). Despite this resilience and existing support programs, our study provides evidence that the children of Army active duty parents have increased health care needs associated with deployment for which the military and concerned community providers can anticipate and plan. Given they are also seeking much of this care from civilian providers, it implies careful coordination and monitoring of the quality of these services during times of deployment. If parents are substituting civilian care for readily accessible services at military treatment facilities, the Army could review if services need to be strengthened for families while a service member is deployed.

Our study also has research implications, some previously described. A limitation of this study, we compared only two distinct years, is also a research opportunity. Military observers have identified five or more deployment phases that may each be associated with different stresses or challenges: pre-deployment (varies in time), deployment (1st month), sustainment (months 2–5), redeployment (last month), and post-deployment (3–6 months after return) (Pincus, House, Christenson, & Adler, 2001). Our study captures the time period primarily during a deployment. A study of changes in health status and health services utilization during reintegration of the deployed parent is also warranted, particularly given the high rate of symptoms and problems reported among service members upon return from deployment (Hoge et al., 2004, 2008; Institute of Medicine, 2010; Litz & Schlenger, 2009; Milliken, Auchterlonie, & Hoge, 2007). The military parent's problems, whether transitional or limited to an adjustment period or long-lasting, may directly affect family member health and be associated with increased child or spouse maltreatment, unstable behavior from excessive alcohol or drug use, unsafe weapon storage, and neglectful behavior from persistent suicidal ideation or depression (Bray et al., 2009; Jacobson et al., 2008; Milliken et al., 2007; Newby et al., 2005; Peebles-Kleiger & Kleiger, 1994; Rentz et al., 2007; Seal, Bertenthal, Miner, Sen, & Marmar, 2007). Survey responses consistently demonstrate the familial stress associated with long or repeat deployments including decreased marital satisfaction, increased intention to divorce, and increased spousal violence (Hoge, Castro, & Eaton, 2006). Future research could extend what is known to include the health consequences on children of soldiers returning under different conditions and with various re-integration experiences.

Acknowledgment This paper is based upon work supported by TRICARE Management Agency through a Program Support Center contract to The CDM Group, Inc. with subcontract to Brandeis University (Contract Number: HHSP23320045009XI, Task Order Number: HHSP233200800001T). We wish to acknowledge the contributions and able guidance of the Task Order Officer, Thomas Williams, PhD, and Ms. Pat Golson of HPA&E, and the invaluable assistance of Ms. Wendy Funk and Ms. Laura Hopkins of Kennell and Associates, and Jennifer MacLeod of Altarum Institute who prepared the project's data extracts. Finally, the project team benefited from the collaboration of other project staff, including Christopher Tompkins, PhD, Jennifer Perloff, PhD, Grant Ritter, PhD, and Galina Zolotusky at Brandeis University and Michael Keane, PhD and Robert O'Brien at The CDM Group, Inc.

References

Abbe, J. S., Naylor, G. S., Gavin, M., & Shannon, K. M. (1986). Temporary paternal absence and health care utilization: A cohort-controlled study. *Military Medicine, 151*(9), 469–472.

American Hospital Formulary Service. (2008). *AHFS pharmacologic-therapeutic classification system.* American Society of Health-Sytem Pharmacists (ASHP). Retrieved June 1, 2012, from http://www.ahfsdruginformation.com/class/index.aspx

American Psychological Association. (2007). *The psychological needs of U.S. military service members and their families: A preliminary report.* Washington, DC: American Psychological Association.

Andersen, R. (1995). Revisiting the behavioral model and access to medical care: Does it matter? *Journal of Health and Social Behavior, 36*(1), 1–10.

Andersen, R., & Aday, L. A. (1978). Access to medical care in the U.S.: Realized and potential. *Medical Care, 16*(7), 533–546.

Andersen, R., & Davidson, P. (2007). Improving access to care in America: Individual and contextual indicators. In R. M. Andersen, T. H. Rice, & G. F. Kominski (Eds.), *Changing the U.S. health care system: Key issues in health services policy and management* (3rd ed., pp. 3–31). San Francisco, CA: Jossey-Bass.

Ashenfelter, O., & Card, D. (1985). Using the longitudinal structure of earnings to estimate the effect of training programs. *The Review of Economics and Statistics, 67*(4), 648–660.

Bray, R. M., Pemberton, M. R., Hourani, L. L., Witt, M., Olmsted, K. L. R., Brown, J. M., et al. (2009). *2008 Department of Defense survey of health related behaviors among Active Duty Military Personnel.* Durham, NC: RTI International, Research Triangle Institute.

Defense Health Care. (2011, June 2). *Access to civilian providers under TRICARE standard and extra, GAO-11-500* (63 pages). Washington, DC: Highlights. http://www.gao.gov/highlights/d11500high.pdf

Defense Manpower Data Center. (2009, June 29). *Profile of service members ever deployed.* Arlington, VA: Author.

Defense Manpower Data Center. (2011). *Active duty military personnel strengths by regional area and by country* (309A). Arlington, VA: Author.

Department of Defense. (2008). *Deployment health clinical center.* Retrieved October 29, 2008, from http://www.pdhealth.mil/guidelines/annoC.asp

Department of Defense. (2009). *Evaluation of the TRICARE program FY2009 report to Congress.* Washington, DC: Office of the Assistant Secretary of Defense (Health Affairs).

Department of Defense. (2010). *Demographics 2010: Profile of the military community.* Washington, DC: Office of the Deputy Under Secretary of Defense (Military Community and Family Policy), Department of Defense.

Department of Defense. (2011). *Evaluation of the TRICARE Program FY2011 Report to Congress.* Washington, DC: Office of the Assistant Secretary of Defense (Health Affairs).

Department of Defense Task Force on Mental Health. (2007). *An achievable vision: Report of the Department of Defense task force on mental health.* Falls Church, VA: Author. Retrieved from www.health.mil/dhb/mhtf/MHTF-Report-Final.pdf

DeVoe, E. R., & Ross, A. (2012). The parenting cycle of deployment. *Military Medicine, 177*(2), 184–190.

Faber, A. J., Willerton, E., Clymer, S. R., MacDermid, S. M., & Weiss, H. M. (2008). Ambiguous absence, ambiguous presence: A qualitative study of military reserve families in wartime. *Journal of Family Psychology, 22*(2), 222–230. doi:10.1037/0893-3200.22.2.222

Gorman, B. K., & Braverman, J. (2008). Family structure differences in health care utilization among U.S. children. *Social Science & Medicine, 67*(11), 1766–1775. doi:10.1016/j.socscimed.2008.09.034

Gorman, G. H., Eide, M., & Hisle-Gorman, E. (2010). Wartime military deployment and increased pediatric mental and behavioral health complaints. *Pediatrics, 126*(6), 1058–1066. doi:10.1542/peds.2009-2856

Hoge, C. W., Castro, C. A., & Eaton, K. M. (2006). Impact of combat duty in Iraq and Afghanistan on family functioning: Findings from the Walter Reed Army Institute of Research Land Combat Study. In *Human dimensions in military operations – military leaders' strategies for addressing stress and psychological support* (pp. 5-1–5-6; Meeting Proceedings RTO-MP-HFM-134, Paper 5). Neuilly-sur-Seine, France: RTO.

Hoge, C. W., Castro, C. A., Messer, S. C., McGurk, D., Cotting, D. I., & Koffman, R. L. (2004). Combat duty in Iraq and Afghanistan, mental health problems, and barriers to care. *New England Journal of Medicine, 351*(1), 13–22. doi:10.1056/NEJMoa040603

Hoge, C. W., McGurk, D., Thomas, J. L., Cox, A. L., Engel, C. C., & Castro, C. A. (2008). Mild traumatic brain Injury in U.S. soldiers returning from Iraq. *New England Journal of Medicine, 358*(5), 453–463. doi:10.1056/NEJMoa072972

Huebner, A. J., Mancini, J. A., Bowen, G. L., & Orthner, D. K. (2009). Shadowed by war: Building community capacity to support military families. *Family Relations, 58*(2), 216–228. doi:10.1111/j.1741-3729.2008.00548.x

Institute of Medicine. (2010). *Returning home from Iraq and Afghanistan: Preliminary assessment of readjustment needs of military personnel, veterans, and their families.* Washington, DC: National Academy of Sciences.

Jacobson, I. G., Ryan, M. A. K., Hooper, T. I., Smith, T. C., Amoroso, P. J., Boyko, E. J., et al. (2008). Alcohol use and alcohol-related problems before and after military combat deployment. *Journal of the American Medical Association, 300*(6), 663.

Keilberg, P. L. (2005). *Deployments and the military family: Impact on levels of health care demand* (A949344). Bremerton, WA: Naval Hospital. Retrieved from http://handle.dtic.mil/100.2/ADA443949

Larson, M. J., Miller, K., & Fleming, K. J. (2007). Treatment with antidepressant medications in private health plans. *Administration and Policy in Mental Health, 34*(2), 116–126. doi:10.1007/s10488-006-0088-5

Larson, M. J., Mohr, B. A., Adams, R. S., Ritter, G., Perloff, J., Williams, T. V., et al. (2012). Association of military deployment of a parent or spouse and changes in dependent use of health care services. *Medical Care, 50*(9), 821–828.

Levai, M., Kaplan, S., Ackerman, R., & Hammock, M. (1995). The effect of father absence on the psychiatric hospitalization of Navy children. *Military Medicine, 160*(3), 104–106.

Lincoln, A., Swift, E., & Shorteno-Fraser, M. (2008). Psychological adjustment and treatment of children and families with parents deployed in military combat. *Journal of Clinical Psychology, 64*(8), 984–992. doi:10.1002/jclp.20520

Litz, B. T., & Schlenger, W. E. (2009). PTSD in service members and new veterans of the Iraq and Afghanistan wars: A bibliography and critique. *PTSD Research Quarterly, 20*(1), 1–7.

Mansfield, A. J., Kaufman, J. S., Engel, C. C., & Gaynes, B. N. (2011). Deployment and mental health diagnoses among children of US Army personnel. *Arch Pediatr Adolesc Med, 165*(11), 999–1005. doi:10.1001/archpediatrics.2011.123

McNulty, P. A. (2003). Does deployment impact the health care use of military families stationed in Okinawa, Japan? *Military Medicine, 168*(6), 465–470.

Meyer, B. D. (1995). Natural and quasi-experiments in economics. *Journal of Business & Economic Statistics, 13*(2), 151–161.

MHN Government Services. (2009). *Military family life consultants.* Retrieved July 22, 2009, from http://www.arfp.org/skins/ARFP/display.aspx?ModuleID=8cde2e88-3052-448c-893d-d0b4b14b31c4&Action=display_page&ObjectID=dc78097f-fbcc-49ee-b536-2935dad0f91e

Milliken, C. S., Auchterlonie, J. L., & Hoge, C. W. (2007). Longitudinal assessment of mental health problems among active and reserve component soldiers returning from the Iraq war. *Journal of American Medical Association, 298*(18), 2141–2148. doi:298/18/2141

Newby, J. H., Ursano, R. J., McCarroll, J. E., Liu, X., Fullerton, C. S., & Norwood, A. E. (2005). Postdeployment domestic violence by U.S. Army soldiers. *Military Medicine, 170*(8), 643–647.

Paris, R., DeVoe, E. R., Ross, A. M., & Acker, M. L. (2010). When a parent goes to war: Effects of parental deployment on very young children and implications for intervention. *American Journal of Orthopsychiatry, 80*(4), 610–618. doi:10.1111/j.1939-0025.2010.01066.x

Peebles-Kleiger, M. J., & Kleiger, J. H. (1994). Re-integration stress for Desert Storm families: Wartime deployments and family trauma. *Journal of Traumatic Stress, 7*(2), 173–194.

Pincus, S. H., House, R., Christenson, J., & Adler, L. E. (2001). The emotional cycle of deployment: A military family perspective. *U.S. Army Medical Department Journal, Apr–June*, 15–23.

Pope, G. C., Kautter, J., Ellis, R. P., Ash, A. S., Ayanian, J. Z., Iezzoni, L. I., et al. (2004). Risk adjustment of medicare capitation payments using the CMS-HCC model. *Health Care Financing Review, 25*(4), 119–141.

Rentz, E. D., Marshall, S. W., Loomis, D., Casteel, C., Martin, S. L., & Gibbs, D. A. (2007). Effect of deployment on the occurrence of child maltreatment in military and nonmilitary families. *American Journal of Epidemiology, 165*(10), 1199–1206. doi:10.1093/aje/kwm008

Seal, K. H., Bertenthal, D., Miner, C. R., Sen, S., & Marmar, C. (2007). Bringing the war back home: Mental health disorders among 103,788 US veterans returning from Iraq and Afghanistan seen at Department of Veterans Affairs facilities. *Archives of Internal Medicine, 167*(5), 476–482. doi:10.1001/archinte.167.5.476

Singer, J. D., & Willett, J. B. (2003). *Applied longitudinal data analysis*. New York: Oxford University Press.

Strategic Outreach to Families of All Reservists. (2005). In D. E. Levin & C. I. Daynard (Eds.), *The "So Far" guide for helping children and youth cope with the deployment of a parent in the Military Reserves*. Needham, MA: The Psychoanalytic Couple and Family Institute of New England. http://www.sofarusa.org/downloads/sofar_children_pamphlet.pdf

The White House. (2012). Joining forces: Taking action to serve America's military families. Retrieved June 30, 2012, from http://www.whitehouse.gov/joiningforces

Vingilis, E., Wade, T., & Seeley, J. (2006). Predictors of adolescent health care utilization. *Journal of Adolescence, 30*, 773–800.

Wertlieb, D., Weigel, C., & Feldstein, M. (1988). The impact of stress and temperament on medical utilization by school-age children. *Journal of Pediatric Psychology, 13*(3), 409–421.

White, C. J., de Burgh, H. T., Fear, N. T., & Iversen, A. C. (2011). The impact of deployment to Iraq or Afghanistan on military children: A review of the literature [Review]. *International Review of Psychiatry, 23*(2), 210–217. doi:10.3109/09540261.2011.560143

Wooldridge, J. (2005). *Introductory econometrics: A modern approach* (3rd ed.). Mason, IA: Thomson South-Western.

Wu, P., Hoven, C. W., Bird, H. R., Moore, R. E., Cohen, P., Alegria, M., et al. (1999). Depressive and disruptive disorders and mental health service utilization in children and adolescents. *Journal of the American Academy of Child & Adolescent Psychiatry, 38*(9), 1081–1090. doi:10.1097/00004583-199909000-00010

Chapter 7
Parenting Practices and Emotion Regulation in National Guard and Reserve Families: Early Findings from the After Deployment Adaptive Parenting Tools/ADAPT Study

Abigail Gewirtz and Laurel Davis

Abstract While a caregiver's military status per se is not a risk factor for children's adjustment, deployment is a significant family stressor, which places children at risk for behavior and emotional problems. We hypothesize that deployment (i.e. separation from spouse and child(ren), exposure to combat, reintegration, and further deployment) may impair parenting by influencing parents' emotion regulation capacities. We report baseline data from the After Deployment: Adaptive Parenting Tools study, an NIH-funded effectiveness study of a parenting program for Reserve component families. Data were gathered from N=89 military and civilian parents in families where a parent had deployed to the current conflicts. Parents completed self-report measures of emotion regulation, and parenting. On average, deployed individuals (N=52) reported more difficulties in emotion regulation than civilian parents. Across gender, mothers reported more difficulties than fathers with deployed mothers reporting the most difficulties. Emotion regulation explained a significant proportion of the variance in parenting practices, and associations of deployment to parenting and emotion regulation approached significance in a regression analysis. Results are discussed in the context of the challenges facing deployed parents—particularly mothers—and the potential for programs targeting parenting in military families experiencing deployment.

Keywords Parenting • Military families • Child adjustment • Emotion regulation • Prevention • Deployment • Parental adjustment • Intervention • ADAPT (After Deployment, Adaptive Parenting Tools)

A. Gewirtz, Ph.D., L.P. (✉)
Department of Family Social Science & Institute of Child Development,
University of Minnesota, 290 McNeal Hall, 1985 Buford Ave, St. Paul, MN, USA
e-mail: agewirtz@umn.edu

L. Davis, M.A.
Department of Family Social Science, University of Minnesota,
290 McNeal Hall, 1985 Buford Ave, St. Paul, MN, USA
e-mail: davis978@umn.edu

Introduction

Troop mobilization and deployments to the current conflicts in Afghanistan (Operation Enduring Freedom; OEF) and Iraq (Operation Iraqi Freedom; OIF; Operation New Dawn, OND) have been at their highest rates since the Vietnam War, with an unprecedented reliance on National Guard and Reserve (NG/R) troops. These Reserve Component civilian soldiers are on average older, and more likely to be married and parenting than regular active duty military personnel. Previously known as 'weekend warriors', NG/R personnel live in civilian communities, without the support, routine, or structure of the military base, and maintain civilian jobs and family lives. The reliance of the US Military on NG/R personnel brings into greater focus the need to understand and address the experiences, and the challenges associated with deployment and reintegration for these service members and their families.

Historically (prior to September 11, 2001) National Guard and Reserve personnel were rarely deployed to war, with those deployments limited to 6 months for each 5-years of regular drill. Over the past decade, deployment periods have increased nearly fourfold, to 24 months in a 6-year enlistment period (Committee on Armed Services, 2010). Average deployments to the current conflicts are 12–15 months, and on average, service members have served 2.2 deployments to the current conflicts (American Psychological Association Presidential Task Force on Military Deployment Services for Youth, 2007; Department of Defense Task Force on Mental Health, 2007).

Research that captures the impact of these large NG/R troop deployments on families is just emerging (e.g., Castaneda et al., 2008; Faber, Willerton, Clymer, MacDermid, & Weiss, 2008). However, extant data on military populations more generally, indicate the significant impact of extended separations and combat exposure on the deployed person, their partner, and children (Chandra et al., 2010; Huebner, Mancini, Wilcox, Grass, & Grass, 2007; Lester et al., 2010; Riggs & Riggs, 2011). While active duty military personnel and their families living on bases have routine access to deployment cycle supports and resources, NG/R families may find themselves isolated, living in communities with few other military service members to share their experiences, and fewer military-oriented supports and services.

Although research has yielded valuable data on the impact of deployment on service members, their spouses, and their children, relatively little research has examined parent–child relationships, and parenting in particular (Palmer, 2008). Parenting is a key buffer for children, particularly during times of adversity (e.g. Masten et al., 1999). Below, we review the extant research on parenting, deployment, and child adjustment. Using a family stress model framework (e.g., Conger et al., 2002), we propose that combat deployment and subsequent reintegration are family stressors, affecting children's adjustment via their effects on adults' parenting practices. Further, we suggest that parents' *emotion regulation* might be a key mechanism by which parenting practices are affected following deployment to combat zones, given data indicating associations between posttraumatic stress symptoms and emotion regulation difficulties (New et al., 2009; Tull, Barrett, McMillan, & Roemer, 2007).

Below, we review the literature on parenting, deployment to a combat zone, and child adjustment, and subsequently the putative mediating link of emotion regulation. We then report baseline data from a study of parenting in NG/R families to examine associations between parenting, deployment, and emotion regulation.

Deployment, Combat Stress, and Parenting in Military Families: The Link to Child Adjustment

The deployment process affects families in two primary ways: by the fact of the prolonged separation from the family and associated disruptions, and—following reintegration—via the effects of combat stress symptoms, injuries, and other influences of combat exposure on the returning service member (e.g., Cozza, Chun, & Polo, 2005; Pincus, House, Christensen, & Adler 2001). The significant separations inherent to the deployment process can be quite disruptive to family life (MacDermid, 2006). Deployments are unpredictable: although NG/R personnel now typically have many months advance notice of a deployment, neither the dates, nor the length of the deployment is within the individual's control. While deployed, the individual must leave his/her civilian job for what is likely to be an entirely different position and daily routine. The family at home also must adjust to the deployment and separation. Parents left at home are typically 'single parenting', and the added childcare and domestic burdens may be combined with family members' worries about the safety and health of the service member. Following reintegration, the family must readjust to the deployed individual's return; routines and family management tasks must be reassigned, and the deployed individual must reposition him/herself as partner and parent (Faber et al., 2008). Given the nature of multiple deployments in the recent conflicts, the reintegration period often includes preparation for the next deployment.

Two longitudinal qualitative studies of reserve and active duty OIF service members indicate that the process of reconciling family relationships during reintegration may be lengthier and more complex than previously documented (MacDermid, 2006). Service members reported physical, psychological and social challenges in transitioning from war to home, including emotional withdrawal, hyper-vigilance, hyper-stimulation, mood swings, substance use, and survivor guilt. Length of deployment, combat stress, and redeployment complicated and extended the adjustment process (MacDermid, 2006).

Not surprisingly, the deployment process is associated with difficulties both in parenting and in school-aged children's adjustment. Although growing up in a military family per se is not associated with children's adjustment difficulties (Jensen et al., 1995; Jensen, Xenakis, Wolf, & Bain, 1991) wartime deployment of parents is associated with child distress, behavior problems, and transitions for children (Chandra et al., 2010; Flake, Davis, Johnson, & Middleton, 2009; Jensen, Grogan,

Xenakis, & Bain, 1989; Jensen, Martin, & Watanabe, 1996; Levai, Kaplan, Ackermann, & Hammock, 1995). Moreover, child distress is positively associated with length of deployment (Chandra et al., 2010; Jensen et al., 1989). Studies indicate that children in NG/R families are at particular risk for emotional and behavioral difficulties (Jensen et al., 1996; Jensen & Shaw, 1996; Ursano & Norwood, 1996).

During the deployment process, parental stress may be associated both with child maladjustment (Flake et al., 2009), and with child maltreatment: in a study comparing Texas Child Maltreatment records among military and non-military populations from 2000 to 2003 (coinciding with increased troop mobilizations to OEF/OIF), child maltreatment rates rose by approximately 30 % for every increase of 1 % in operation-related deployment and reunion (Rentz et al., 2006).

Service members' combat-related symptoms provide an additional source of family stress and distress. NG/R military personnel appear to be particularly at risk for mental health and substance use problems following deployment. For example, self-reports of depression, PTSD, and relationship problems among NG/R troops in a broad screening of OIF returnees were more than double those of active duty service members (42.4 % compared with 20.3 %; Milliken, Auchterlonie, & Hoge, 2007). Moreover, PTSD rates appear to increase over the 6 months following return from deployment in NG/R soldiers, compared with active duty troops, with rates of positive screening for PTSD symptoms increasing from 12.7 % immediately following return from deployment to 24.5 % six months later. In contrast, over the same time period, the PTSD screening rate increased by just 4.9 % in active duty personnel (Milliken et al., 2007). On the same screening tool, NG/R soldiers also reported significantly more alcohol problems compared with active duty soldiers (15 % compared with 11.8 %). Jacobson et al. (2008), found increased risk of new-onset binge drinking, heavy weekly drinking, and alcohol-related problems among combat troops, and among NG/R soldiers compared with active duty personnel.

PTSD is a risk factor for family distress after deployment, and it is during and following the reintegration period that families may be particularly vulnerable to service members' combat-related mental health and substance use problems. Studies of male Vietnam veterans found PTSD to be associated with decreased parenting satisfaction (Samper, Taft, King, & King, 2004), poorer parenting skills (Glenn et al., 2002; Jordan et al., 1992), and family violence (Solomon et al., 1992). In addition, PTSD symptoms, combat exposure, and aggressive behavior were associated with child hostility and aggression (Glenn et al., 2002). Several other studies have described the association of PTSD with impairments in a range of parent–child and family relationship variables: effective problem-solving, interpersonal expressiveness, family cohesion, and conflict (Davidson & Mellor, 2001; Solomon, 1988; Solomon et al., 1992).

Just one study has examined associations between PTSD and parenting *practices* in the current conflicts, or among NG/R personnel. Among a sample of 468 male Army National Guard soldiers over the year after their return from deployment to Iraq, Gewirtz, Polusny, DeGarmo, Khalyis, and Erbes (2010) found that growth in PTSD over the year of reintegration predicted self-reported impairments in parenting practices 1-year following return. PTSD symptoms also were associated with impairments in couple functioning, but their effect on parenting was independent of their impact on couple adjustment.

The impact on children of parental PTSD, depression, and substance use, is well documented beyond military populations, with research demonstrating that parental stress and distress, and subsequent parenting impairments predict increases in child behavior and emotional problems (e.g., Beardslee, Bemporad, Keller, & Klerman, 1983; Patterson, Reid, & Dishion, 1998).

Given the associations of the deployment process with a range of transition-related stressors, mental health and substance use difficulties, and child and family challenges, it is not surprising that studies suggest that the negative impact of combat deployment on children is primarily mediated through its detrimental influence on *parenting practices* (Palmer, 2008). Indeed, evidence from studies of different populations have demonstrated robust associations between parental PTSD, substance abuse, other psychiatric illness, loss, and interpersonal conflict, and parenting difficulties and subsequent child emotional and behavioral problems (e.g. Beardslee et al., 1983; Patterson, 1982, 1986; Repetti, Taylor, & Seeman, 2002). In addition, both normative and severe family stressors and transitions (e.g., father absence, divorce, socioeconomic stress) have been shown to negatively affect parent and family functioning and lead to increased rates of coercive parent–child interactions, which in turn, impair child adjustment (e.g., Beardslee et al., 1983; Belsky, 1984; Capaldi, 1991; Conger et al., 2002; Dishion & Patterson, 2006; Patterson, DeBaryshe, & Ramsey, 1989).

Family Stressors, Emotion Regulation and Parenting

What mechanisms might account for difficulties in parenting practices associated with deployment? Emotion regulation—the experience, expression, and attempted management of emotions (Gross, 1998)—is key to individual functioning, and studies suggest that parents' expression, modeling, and responses to emotions in a family context (also known as emotion socialization) appear to be associated with child adjustment outcomes (Chaplin, Cole, & Zahn-Waxler, 2005; Eisenberg, Cumberland, & Spinrad, 1998). However, surprisingly little is known about the association of parents' emotion regulation capacities with their parenting practices (Teti & Cole, 2011).

Although we could find no research on the influence of parents' emotion socialization or regulation on parenting practices in military families, there is some broader developmental research to support the idea that parents' emotion regulation/socialization may be associated with parenting practices, as well as children's adjustment. For example, parents' avoidance and dismissing of children's emotional states contribute to the maintenance of anxiety problems in youth (Tiwari et al., 2008). Moreover, in a recent study of 144 low-income mothers of preschoolers, maternal experiential avoidance mediated the association between mothers' dysphoria and parenting stress (Shea & Coyne, 2011). Parenting stress, in turn, predicted inconsistent and punitive parenting practices.

The constructs of emotion regulation and socialization within the family context are particularly relevant for military families, because the stressors associated with deployment to a war zone (i.e., exposure to potentially traumatic events) may affect emotion regulation capacities, reinforcing the development of a coping approach that emphasizes emotional suppression, or experiential avoidance (Vujanovic, Niles, Pietrefesta, Schmertz, & Potter, 2011). Below, we briefly review an emerging body of research that has focused on associations between specific combat stress symptoms in military personnel and emotion regulation difficulties within the family context.

Deployment, PTSD, Emotion Regulation, and Parenting Practices

Military service to a combat zone requires individual service members to be extremely sensitive to danger, cope with extensive and consistent exposure to potentially traumatic events, and live in an environment that stresses immediate reactivity, and suppression of emotions. The return to civilian life may require a recalibration of emotional responding, but this may be complicated by the over-learned responses and heightened arousal that is needed on the battlefield, as well as traumatic memories, intrusive thoughts, and other potential combat stress symptoms (Ruscio, Weather, King, & King, 2002). Experiential avoidance—i.e. the attempted suppression or avoidance of distressing memories and affect (through alcohol use, distraction, or other strategies)—may result in increases in the frequency and intensity of negative thoughts and feelings. Similarly, hyper-arousal symptoms may result in extreme reactivity to emotionally distressing or arousing family events (possibly because the cues associated with these events function as trauma reminders). Avoidance of these situations results in reduced distress in the moment, reinforcing further avoidance, reactivity, and arousal, and increasing resistance to change.

Research cited earlier indicates that on the home front, family relationships in general, and parenting in particular, may be compromised for individuals suffering from combat-related posttraumatic stress disorder (PTSD) and associated problems (e.g., Riggs, Byrne, Weathers, & Litz, 1998), due to difficulties in emotion regulation. It appears that PTSD symptoms of avoidance or emotional numbing may result in parents withdrawing from family activities, monitoring of, and positive involvement with children. For example, Samper et al. (2004) found associations between emotional numbing symptoms of PTSD and parenting *satisfaction* in a nationally representative sample of 250 male Vietnam veterans. In stressful situations (e.g. conflict or discipline encounters), hyper-arousal symptoms may ignite volatile parent–child interactions (Gewirtz et al., 2010). Although no studies have examined associations of emotion dys-regulation in general, or symptoms of numbing/avoidance and anger/arousal in particular, with parenting practices, studies of couples have found that these symptoms are particularly related to impaired relationship satisfaction and interpersonal violence (see Galovski & Lyons, 2004, for a review).

We hypothesize that difficulties in emotion regulation, resulting from over-learned responses and heightened arousal needed on the battlefield, as well as posttraumatic stress symptoms of numbing/avoidance and anger/arousal, may generalize to the family context during reintegration. The family environment is often home to family members' most intense exchanges of emotions. Service members may react to intense family interactions (e.g. those involving discipline, conflict, or attention-getting) by withdrawing—becoming emotionally unavailable—or by overreacting with uncontrolled aggression and coercion. For example, reintegrating service members may respond in a harsh and punitive or volatile way to discipline interactions. Or, they may avoid them entirely, leading to further discipline challenges. They may dismiss children's emotion displays by minimizing, criticizing, or ignoring them—thus modeling the use of experiential avoidance as a tool to cope with negative emotions, and increasing children's risk for psychological problems.

These responses may result in similar reactions from children and spouse: coercive exchanges, withdrawal from the service member for fear of evoking strong reactions, facilitating the service member's withdrawal from family responsibilities, or insistent pleas for attention in response to unavailability and withdrawal. A 'dance' of family interaction may thus be created that interferes with effective parenting—particularly discipline and family communication—increasing the likelihood of adjustment difficulties across the family. These patterns may interfere with couple communication, parenting, and ultimately undermine social support as well as a normative return to family roles during reintegration.

Deployment, Emotion Regulation, and Parenting: Early Findings from the After Deployment, Adaptive Parenting Tools/ADAPT Study

Based on the literature reviewed above, we hypothesized that deployed military parents would demonstrate more difficulties in emotion regulation than civilian parents, that deployed military parents would report greater problems in parenting than civilian parents, and that difficulties in emotion regulation would mediate the association of deployment to parenting challenges. The hypothesized model is depicted in Fig. 7.1.

This study is part of a larger research study examining the effectiveness of a parenting program known as After Deployment, Adaptive Parenting Tools (ADAPT) for military families. The larger study tests whether providing a parent training program to military families following deployment will result in (i) improved parenting practices, (ii) improved parent emotion regulation, and (iii) improved child adjustment in intervention condition families, compared to treatment-as-usual control military families. Below, we provide an overview of the ADAPT effectiveness trial, and subsequently report baseline analyses from the early data, in order to test the hypotheses proposed in the paragraph above regarding parenting, emotion regulation, and deployment.

Fig. 7.1 Parent emotion regulation deficits are hypothesized to mediate the association between deployment and impaired parenting practices

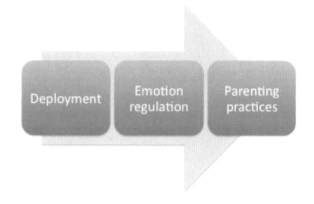

After Deployment, Adaptive Parenting Tools (ADAPT) is a mindfulness-infused parent training program tailored to the specific needs of military families. Based on the principles of Parent Management Training-Oregon Model (PMTO; Forgatch & Patterson, 2010), ADAPT targets improved parenting practices by training parents in five core PMTO skills: skill encouragement, family problem-solving, monitoring, positive involvement, and effective discipline. The hypothesized role of emotion regulation and socialization in effective parenting is targeted via the introduction of two additional core skills: mindfulness, and emotion coaching. ADAPT is delivered in group format over 14 weekly sessions each lasting 2 hours. Discrete parenting skills are taught each week using active teaching strategies (e.g. role play) and discussion. Parenting skills (e.g. encouragement, problem solving, monitoring) are taught as weekly topics, and skills in mindfulness and emotion coaching are infused into the curriculum at every session. In order to reach families juggling multiple competing demands, a web-enhancement resource is offered to all participating parents. The ADAPT website contains videos and other online resources to supplement the group sessions and provide resources for parents unable to attend the group on one or more occasions. The ADAPT groups are delivered by pairs of facilitators, trained in the PMTO model and in mindfulness. Fidelity of implementation is measured via an established fidelity system for PMTO that is observationally based (Knutson, Forgatch, Rains, & Sigmarsdottir, 2009). Each group session is videotaped, and PMTO expert coders rate sessions on fidelity.

A randomized controlled effectiveness trial funded by NIH (R01DA 030114) is currently underway to test the ADAPT program. Families in which a parent has deployed to OIF, OEF, or OND, and with a child ages 5–12 living in the Twin Cities Metropolitan area are eligible to participate. Four hundred families will be recruited; 240 to be randomly assigned to the intervention/ADAPT condition, and 160 to the services-as-usual condition. Parents enter the study via an online portal that provides consent information as well as baseline study questionnaires. Following that, in-home baseline assessments are conducted with parent(s) and target child. Multi-method and multi-informant measures assess parenting practices (via parent–child interactions), child adjustment (parent, teacher, and child report), and parent emotion regulation and coaching (self-report and physiological measures of arousal). Parents in families randomized to the intervention condition are invited to attend an ADAPT group. Groups are scheduled in twice-yearly cohorts in community locations (churches, community centers) close to where participants live. Groups are offered on weekday evenings from 6 to 8 p.m.; dinner and childcare is provided, and a small stipend given to participants to offset the cost of travel. Small incentives are provided for attendance and home practice completion.

Posttest follow up assessments will be gathered from all participants (intervention and services-as-usual conditions) at 6–8 months, 12 months, and 24 months post-baseline. Online questionnaires are completed by parents at all three time points; in-home and teacher assessments are scheduled for the two latter follow-up points. Below, we report baseline findings from the online assessments of the first cohort of 72 families recruited to the ADAPT study between July and October 2011.

Methods

Participants

Extensive outreach efforts were conducted in order to recruit parents for this study. Contacts were made with the Minnesota Army and Air National Guard, and subsequently, with local Reserve units. The ADAPT recruitment team were invited to all National Guard family events associated with deployment—including mandatory Family Preparation Academies for those about to deploy, Family Reintegration Academies for those returning from deployment, Family Picnics for individual military units or services (Air and Army Guard, Air, Army, Navy, Marine Reserves), and general community events by and for the Military (e.g. the Minnesota State Fair, ball games, etc). Minnesota has one of the largest National Guards in the USA, and has deployed over 15,000 troops since 2001. In addition, the Twin Cities Metro area houses a base for each of the services: Air Reserves, Army Reserves, Navy Reserves, and Marine Reserves. There are no active duty installations in Minnesota.

At events, eligible parents could sign up directly for the study (using available online tablets and laptop computers) or provide their names and contact information to be contacted by the study coordinator. Study outreach also extended to social media (a website, Facebook, and Twitter presence) and media (TV and newspaper articles about the study). As the study became known, increasing numbers of parents were recruited by word of mouth from other parents or military personnel. Of the 109 eligible families who provided contact information, 72 entered the study as of 10/15/11.

Each parent (up to two per family) entered the study through the ADAPT online portal, and completed a screener to ascertain eligibility. Inclusion criteria include: self and/or current or former spouse/partner deployed to OIF, OEF, or OND; living with (or having joint custody over) at least one child ages 5–12, and high-speed internet access in the home. In addition, parents had to indicate that they would be willing and able, if invited, to attend a weekly parenting group in the Twin Cities metro area. We did not limit the geographical area from which parents could apply to be in the study because there are variations in the distance people are willing to travel to a group. Parents who 'passed' the screener were invited to participate in the study and immediately taken to the webpage with the study consent form. After electronically signing the consent form, participants were taken directly to the base-line online self-report questionnaires. An auto-generated email was also sent to each participant's email account with a unique link to the survey for individuals needing to break and return to it.

The baseline survey included measures of demographics, parenting, adjustment, and emotion regulation, and took approximately 25 min to complete. Participants were reimbursed $25 for their time.

Measures

Emotion regulation: The Difficulties in Emotion Regulation Scale (DERS, Gratz & Roemer, 2004) is a 36-item questionnaire that assesses six domains of emotion dys-regulation in adults. The measure yields a total score which is the sum of scores on six subscales: non-acceptance/avoidance of emotional responses, difficulties in impulse control, and goal-directed behavior, lack of emotional clarity, and emo-tional awareness, and limited access to emotion regulation strategies. Sample items include: "When I'm upset, I have difficulty concentrating", "I have difficulty mak-ing sense out of my feelings", and "When I'm upset I believe that I'll end up feeling very depressed." Items are responded to on a 5-point Likert scale where 1 = almost never, to 5 = almost always. The total DERS score was used in this analysis (Cronbach's α = .94); items were reverse coded as necessary so that higher scores indicate perceptions of greater problems in emotion regulation. The possible range of scores is 36–180. There are no clinical cut-off scores published for the DERS. However, prior studies indicate mean scores for non-patient adults to be around 61–62 (Fox, Axelrod, Paliwal, Sleeper, & Sinha, 2007; Fox, Hong, & Sinha, 2008), with mean scores higher for clinical populations such as cocaine users (M = 86; Fox et al., 2007), drinkers (M = 74; Fox et al., 2008), and outpatients entering treatment for borderline personality disorder (M = 120–128; Gratz & Gunderson, 2006).

Inconsistent discipline was measured with the three items comprising the incon-sistent discipline scale from the short form of the Alabama Parenting Questionnaire (APQ), a brief self-report measure of parenting practices (Elgar, Waschbush, Dadds, & Sigvaldason, 2007). Items include "You threaten to punish your child and then do not actually punish him/her." Respondents rate their agreement with the statements on a five-point scale (1 = never, 2 = almost never, 3 = sometimes, 4 = often, 5 = always). Higher scores indicate greater perceived use of inconsistent discipline practices. Reliability for the inconsistent discipline scale is adequate (Cronbach's α = .37); the APQ-9 has demonstrated strong criterion validity as evidenced by moderate correla-tions with child symptoms (Elgar et al., 2007; α ranged from .64 to .90). This measure has been previously used with military samples, with adequate reliability ($\alpha = .65$; Gewirtz et al., 2010). Mean scores reported for the discipline subscale in the original validation study are: 7.15 for fathers, and 7.4 for mothers (Elgar et al., 2007).

Demographics

Participants reported their gender, and also responded to questions about military and deployment status: "Which branch of the military are you/were you associated with?", "Have you ever been in the National Guard or Reserves?", "Have you been deployed to OIF or OEF?", "How many times have you been deployed to OIF/OEF", and "How many times have you been deployed within the United States?"

Missing Data

In total, 108 parents (in 73 families) consented to participate in the study. Six were omitted from the present analysis because they had not completed the online surveys by the time of analysis (i.e. they had only completed the online study consent). An additional seven people were omitted because they did not provide information on the key constructs of interest in this study (parenting practices and difficulties in emotion regulation). Six of the parents in our sample are members of the military but have not been deployed. Because we are primarily interested in comparing deployed parents with civilian parents, we excluded these individuals from the analyses. In total, 89 individuals (in 59 families) were included in the regression analyses, which is 82.4 % of people who consented, and 87.3 % of people who provided any baseline data beyond the screening questionnaire.

Results

Demographics

Table 7.1 provides the demographic data for the 89 participants. Deployed men accounted for 44 % of our sample (39 individuals), with only 2 % civilian men (2 individuals); the sample included 15 % deployed women[1] (13 individuals), and 39 % civilian women (35 individuals). Eleven individuals were in the Air National

---

[1] Twenty-five percent of the deployed individuals in our sample are female (13 out of 52 deployed individuals); significantly higher than the proportion of women in the deployed military population as a whole (15 %).

Table 7.1 Sample
demographics

Sample demographics (N=89)	N	%
Gender		
Male	36	40.4
Female	53	59.6
Length of Deployment		
None (civilian)	37	41.6
6 months or less	5	5.6
7–12 months	22	24.7
13–18 months	8	9.0
19–24 months	6	6.7
25–30 months	4	4.5
31–36 month	6	6.7
37 months or more	1	1.1
Military Association		
None (civilian)	37	41.6
Air National Guard	11	12.4
Army National Guard	33	37.1
Army Reserves	4	4.5
Navy Reserves	3	3.4
Other	1	1.1
Race		
African-American/Black	2	2.25
Asian/Asian-American	2	2.25
Caucasian/White/Euro-American	83	93.26
Multiracial/Biracial	1	1.12
Native-American/Alaska Native	0	0.00
Native Hawaiian/Pacific Islander	0	0.00
Don't Know/Prefer Not to Answer	1	1.12
Ethnicity		
Hispanic/Latino	2	2.25
Non-Hispanic/Latino	84	94.38
Don't Know/Prefer Not to Answer	3	3.37
Education		
GED	1	1.12
High school diploma	6	6.74
Some college	23	25.84
Associates degree	11	12.36
4-Year college degree	39	43.82
Master's degree	7	7.87
Doctoral or professional degree	2	2.25
Occupational Status		
Full time employed	54	60.67
Part time employed	15	16.85
Homemaker	8	8.99
Student with additional employment	4	4.49
Student no additional employment	3	3.37
Unemployed	5	5.62

(continued)

Table 7.1 (continued)

Sample demographics (N = 89)	N	%
Marital Status		
Currently Married	74	83.15
Never married	4	4.49
Divorced	7	7.87
Separated	4	4.49
Number of Previous Marriages		
None	72	80.90
One	14	15.73
Two	2	2.25
Unknown	1	1.12
Household income ($)	76,705	37,485
Years married to current partner	9.08	4.77
Number of children in household	2.38	0.99

Guard, 33 in the Army National Guard, 4 in the Army Reserves, 3 in the Navy Reserves, and 1 were recently retired from active duty in the Navy. On average, service members were deployed overseas 1.85 times since 2001 (Range = 1 to 6). Five participants were deployed for 6 months or less, 26 were deployed for 7–12 months, 14 were deployed for 13–24 months, and 11 participants were deployed for 25 months or more. Twenty-two individuals were deployed to OEF (with 6 experiencing more than one deployment), 42 were deployed to OIF (with 9 experiencing more than one deployment), and 16 individuals were deployed to both conflicts. In addition to OIF and OEF deployments, 17 individuals also were deployed inside the US (natural disasters, peacekeeping, etc.).

Mean Scores for Variables of Interest

Table 7.2 shows means for each of the two measures of emotion regulation difficulties and ineffective parenting, for each gender, and for deployed and non-deployed parents. Deployed mothers and civilian mothers scored highest and lowest, respectively, on measures of inconsistent discipline and on difficulties in emotion regulation.

Mediation Analyses

To investigate whether the association between having been deployed to OEF or OIF and inconsistent discipline of children is mediated by deficits in emotion regulation abilities, we conducted regression analyses as outlined by Baron and Kenny (1986). Standardized beta weights and adjusted R^2 values are reported in Table 7.3.

Table 7.2 Descriptive statistics for parenting and emotion regulation measures

Means and standard deviations (N = 89)	N	M	SD
Inconsistent Discipline			
Deployed Males	39	7.15	0.36
Non-deployed Males	2	7.50	0.50
Deployed Females	13	8.38	0.69
Non-deployed Females	35	6.94	0.32
Difficulties in Emotion Regulation			
Deployed Males	39	70.03	3.08
Non-deployed Males	2	81.00	5.00
Deployed Females	13	82.46	7.22
Non-deployed Females	35	67.66	3.30

Table 7.3 Regression analysis examining associations of deployment status and gender with discipline and emotion regulation

Regression analyses (N = 89)	B	SE B	β	R^2
Difficulties in emotion regulation predicted by deployment status				0.01
Gender	8.25	6.02	0.20	
Deployment Status	10.50	6.09	0.25[†]	
Inconsistent discipline predicted by deployment status				0.02
Gender	0.94	0.63	0.22	
Deployment Status	1.14	0.63	0.26[†]	
Inconsistent discipline predicted by difficulties in emotion regulation				0.11
Gender	0.66	0.60	0.15	
Deployment Status	0.78	0.61	0.18	
DERS (Total score)	0.03	0.01	0.33**	

[†]$p < .1$, *$p < .05$, **$p < .01$

First, we regressed difficulties in emotion regulation on deployment status and gender. The resulting beta weight trended toward significance, $b = .25$, $t(86) = 1.72$, $p < .1$, in a model that accounted for 1 % of the variance in difficulties in emotion regulation. Next, we regressed inconsistent discipline on deployment status and gender. As in the previous model, the resulting beta weight trended toward significance, $b = .26$, $t(86) = 1.80$, $p < .1$, in a model that accounted for 2 % of the variance in use of inconsistent discipline. Finally, we regressed inconsistent discipline on deployment status, difficulties in emotion regulation, and gender. In this model, deployment status no longer trended toward significance, and difficulties in emotion regulation was highly significant, $b = .33$, $t(85) = 3.21$, $p < .01$ with this model accounting for 12 % of the variance in inconsistent discipline. Because the beta weight for difficulties in emotion regulation was significant, and the beta weight for deployment status dropped to a non-significant level, we concluded that difficulties in emotion regulation mediated the effect of deployment status on use of inconsistent discipline.

Discussion

In this small sample of deployed and civilian NG/R mothers and fathers, deployment status was marginally associated with difficulties in emotion regulation, and with parenting challenges. Our mediation analysis indicated that emotion regulation was a strong mediator of the link between deployment status and parenting, suggesting that the association of deployment with parenting challenges may largely be due to difficulties in deployed parents' emotion regulation. Our findings provide support for the notion that recalibrating emotional responding from the battlefront to the home front may be key to effectively reintegrating into the home environment for parents. Further, longitudinal research is needed to uncover how parenting practices and emotion regulation interact over time since deployment, and across the phases of the deployment process. Nonetheless, we have provided preliminary evidence that these constructs are relevant to families undergoing deployment.

While gender was not a significant contributor to the regression model (i.e. did not uniquely contribute variance to parenting challenges), these analyses masked the relatively large mean differences between deployed and civilian mothers on both emotion regulation and on parenting, and our small sample size (primarily the tiny number of civilian fathers) precluded the analysis of sample subgroups by gender and deployment status. Mean scores indicated that deployed mothers reported the most difficulties in emotion regulation, as well as the most difficulties in parenting, while civilian mothers demonstrated the fewest difficulties in both domains. These stark contrasts bring into relief the potential challenges facing mothers experiencing deployment to a combat zone, and the need for further research in this area. Little has been written about deployed mothers and we could find no published research findings on either parenting practices or emotion regulation in deployed mothers.

Kelley and colleagues' research has contributed most of what is known about deployed mothers. This group studied Navy mothers deployed prior to the current conflicts (1996–1998), finding that children of deployed mothers demonstrated more internalizing and externalizing symptoms than children of non-deployed Navy mothers, or civilian mothers, although symptoms did not reach clinical levels (Kelley et al., 2001). A later study (Kelley et al., 2002) found that deployed Navy mothers reported lower levels of depression and anxiety than single women, although length of most recent separation was associated with worse adjustment. In a study of Gulf War veterans, Vogt, Pless, King, and King (2005) found that deployed women reported receiving less social support during deployment, and that both social support and relationship/family disruptions had a stronger impact on deployed women's, compared with deployed men's mental health. Combined with our findings from the current study, these early findings indicate a need to learn far more about the stressors and the needs of deployed mothers, and particularly those in the NG/R.

Although our data should be considered preliminary, we speculate that the separation from children inherent to deployment may be more distressing to mothers—who still typically provide the bulk of the childcare in American families—than fathers (Yeung, Sandberg, Davis-Kean, & Hofferth, 2001). In addition, although we did not assess posttraumatic stress symptoms in this study, prior research has indicated that women may be more vulnerable to PTSD than men (e.g., Olff, Langeland, Draijer, & Gersons, 2007). We also did not measure social support, which is an important protective factor both for PTSD and for family relationships in general, but we speculate that women would find the male-oriented deployment environment to be less supportive to females. Much further research is needed to untangle and examine associations over time among parenting, emotion regulation and deployment—among both mothers and fathers.

Although our sample size was relatively small, deployed women constituted a greater proportion of the deployed study sample (25 %) than their numbers represent in the deployed population overall (just 15 %, and just 10 % in the National Guard). Our study outreach efforts did not target women specifically, although the topic of the study—parenting—could arguably be seen as particularly salient for mothers experiencing deployment. Our data also contribute to the relatively small body of knowledge on fathers' parenting. While most studies of military populations have naturally focused on men, the vast majority of parenting studies have focused on women. Our examination of military fathers' parenting has provided a preliminary look at issues that we plan to gather far more data on. We can make no conclusions about military, compared with civilian fathers—given that only 2 individuals in our sample were civilian fathers—but it is our hope that as we continue to gather data and reach 400 families we will be able to compare these groups.

While there is an increasing focus on relationships in military families, rather than the service member alone, the couple, or children, there exists very little data on parenting in military families, let alone in NG/R families (Gewirtz et al., 2010). Given the large numbers of deployed service members who are parenting, and the key role of parenting both for children, and for parents themselves, this area of research is critically important.

Still to be examined is whether—echoing findings from other populations—parenting practices mediate associations between the family stress of deployment, and children's adjustment. Additionally, although the associations of parenting challenges to family stress have been observed within and outside the military, the mechanisms underlying parenting challenges are yet to be investigated. In this early study, we demonstrated concurrent associations among emotion regulation, deployment status, and parenting challenges, with a small sample of military families. Our data has plenty of drawbacks: a very short measure of the outcome variable (parental discipline); sole reliance on parents as their own reporters, yielding the possibility of mono-informant bias; a small sample size, and non-independence of parents within families. Our small sample size prevents us from using statistical methods that could have controlled for the non-independence. The non-independence is somewhat mitigated by the nature of the measures that were focused on the individual adult's behavior, rather than perceptions of the couple, child(ren) or family. However, we recognize that deployment related stressors inexorably affect the entire family system, not solely the deployed parent. Further research with larger sample sizes will help to disentangle the pathways—direct and indirect—by which each spouse/partner, and child, is affected by deployment within a family. We are gathering multiple-method data—observational parenting data, as well as physiological data on arousal—which will greatly strengthen our ability to understand associations among emotion regulation, parenting, and deployment, as well as children's outcomes. Finally, outcome data from the larger prevention study will enable us to examine whether these variables are malleable—that is, whether the ADAPT program strengthens emotion regulation, and parenting among deployed families, ultimately improving children's adjustment.

This study has provided us with some important clues for further investigation. Longitudinal research with larger samples, using multiple methods, multiple informants, and longitudinal modeling, is needed to confirm these associations and determine whether parents' emotion regulation and their emotion socialization of their children is negatively impacted by deployment and combat stressors, and whether these factors impair parenting practices in general, and children's adjustment in particular. Our hope is that our larger randomized controlled trial of the ADAPT program will yield valuable data to address these questions.

Implications for Practice and Policy with Military Families

Our data provide preliminary clues about the challenges facing deployed parents in general, and deployed mothers in particular. Increasing attention is being paid to the toll that deployment can take on families, with more efforts to support families of service members, as well as service members themselves—across the branches of the US Military. Locally, the Minnesota National Guard/MNNG's Beyond the Yellow Ribbon Campaign provides an exemplary demonstration of what can be done to support NG/R families going through the deployment process (Minnesota National Guard, 2011). The MNNG provides mandatory full-day Family Preparation Academies for all individuals and their families prior to deployment. Upon return, military service members participate in 30-day, 60-day, and 90-day Reintegration Trainings, as well as a 1-year event; family members are invited to some of these events. These events provide workshop training for military personnel and their spouses on topics ranging from military benefits, and job-hunting, to smoking cessation, while children participate in their own activities. As a result of our collaboration with the MNNG on the ADAPT study, parenting workshops delivered by ADAPT outreach staff are now routinely provided at deployment events. Hundreds of parents have participated in our workshops and we have found that parents are hungry for information that will help their families through the deployment process. Parents bring profound questions and concerns, many of which cannot be answered in the course of a brief 50 min workshop. In response to these issues, we have developed a series of newsletters to support families undergoing deployment (http://www.cehd.umn.edu/fsos/projects/adapt/newsletters.asp).

Parenting is core to family life, and key to children's adjustment, particularly during times of family transition. Families undergoing deployment, and especially those who are more isolated—i.e. NG/R families—should have routine access to parenting supports specific to deployment (Gewirtz, Erbes, Polusny, Forgatch, & DeGarmo, 2011). Policies that address and facilitate parenting needs can promote resilience in service members, their partners, and their children.

Interventions to support emotion regulation in military populations are increasingly recognized as both therapeutic and useful in enhancing military fitness on the battlefield (e.g. Stanley & Jha, 2009). These interventions focus on mindfulness strategies to increase present moment awareness, and reduce experiential avoidance and hyper-reactivity. ADAPT incorporates these same strategies with parent training methods in order to promote parenting and strengthen the families—and the next generation—of our nation's warrior civilians.

Acknowledgements The research reported in this chapter was supported by grant # R01DA030114 from the Division of Epidemiology, Services, and Prevention Research at NIDA, to Abigail H. Gewirtz, Ph.D. We gratefully acknowledge the military families who have allowed us to learn from them by participating in the ADAPT study.

References

American Psychological Association Presidential Task Force on Military Deployment Services for Youth. (2007). *The psychological needs of U.S. military service members and their families: A preliminary report*. Washington, DC: American Psychological Association.

Baron, R. M., & Kenny, D. A. (1986). The moderator–mediator variable distinction in social psychological research: Conceptual, strategic, and statistical considerations. *Journal of Personality and Social Psychology, 51*, 1173–1182.

Beardslee, W. R., Bemporad, J., Keller, M., & Klerman, G. (1983). Children of parents with major affective disorder: A review. *American Journal of Psychiatry, 140*, 825–832.

Belsky, J. (1984). Determinants of parenting: A process model. *Child Development, 55*, 83–96.

Capaldi, D. M. (1991). Co-occurrence of conduct problems and depressive symptoms in early adolescent boys: Familial factors and general adjustment at grade 6. *Development and Psychopathology, 3*(3), 277–300.

Castaneda, L. W., Harrell, M. C., Varda, D. M., Hall, K. C., Beckett, M. K., & Stern, S. (2008). *Deployment experiences of guard and reserve families*. Santa Monica, CA: RAND.

Chandra, A., Lara-Cinisomo, S., Jaycox, L. H., Tanielian, T., Burns, R. M., Ruder, T., et al. (2010). Children on the homefront: The experience of children from military families. *Pediatrics, 125*, 13–22.

Chaplin, T. M., Cole, P. M., & Zahn-Waxler, C. (2005). Parental socialization of emotion expression: Gender differences and relations to child adjustment. *Emotion, 5*, 80–88.

Committee on Armed Services. (2010). Senate Hearing 111-701; Department of Defense Authorization for Appropriations for Fiscal Year 2011; Government Printing Office: Washington, DC. Retrieved Jan 20th, 2013 from http://www.gpo.gov/fdsys/pkg/CHRG-111shrg62159/html/.

Conger, R. D., Wallace, L. E., Sun, Y., Simons, R. L., McLoyd, V. C., & Brody, G. H. (2002). Economic pressure in African American families: A replication and extension of the family stress model. *Developmental Psychology, 38*, 179–193.

Cozza, S. J., Chun, R. S., & Polo, J. A. (2005). Military families and children during operation Iraqi freedom. *Psychiatric Quarterly, 76*(4), 371–378.

Davidson, A. C., & Mellor, D. J. (2001). The adjustment of children of Australian Vietnam veterans: Is there evidence for the transgenerational transmission of the effects of war-related trauma? *Australian and New Zealand Journal of Psychiatry, 35*, 345–351.

Department of Defense Task Force on Mental Health. (2007). *An achievable vision: Report of the document of defense task force on mental health.* Falls Church, VA: Defense Health Board.

Dishion, T. J., & Patterson, G. R. (2006). The development and ecology of antisocial behavior. In D. Cicchetti & D. Cohen (Eds.), *Developmental psychopathology* (Vol. 3: Risk, disorder, and adaptation, Revised ed., pp. 503–541). New York: Wiley.

Eisenberg, N., Cumberland, A., & Spinrad, T. L. (1998). Parental socialization of emotion. *Psychological Inquiry, 9*(4), 241–273.

Elgar, F. J., Waschbush, D. A., Dadds, M. R., & Sigvaldason, N. (2007). Development and validation of a short form of the Alabama Parenting Questionnaire. *Journal of Child and Family Studies, 16*, 243–259.

Faber, A. J., Willerton, E., Clymer, S. R., MacDermid, S. M., & Weiss, H. M. (2008). Ambiguous absence, ambiguous presence: A qualitative study of military reserve families in wartime. *Journal of Family Psychology, 22*(2), 222–230.

Flake, E. M., Davis, B. E., Johnson, P. L., & Middleton, L. S. (2009). The effects of deployment on military children. *Journal of Developmental & Behavioral Pediatrics, 30*, 271–278.

Forgatch, M., & Patterson, G. R. (2010). Parent management training-oregon model: An intervention for antisocial behavior in children and adolescents. In J. R. Weisz & A. E. Kazdin (Eds.), *Evidence-Based Psychotherapies for Children and Adolescents*: Guilford.

Fox, H., Axelrod, S., Paliwal, P., Sleeper, J., & Sinha, R. (2007). Difficulties in emotion regulation and impulse control during cocaine abstinence. *Drug and Alcohol Dependence, 18*, 298–307.

Fox, H., Hong, K., & Sinha, R. (2008). Difficulties in emotion regulation and impulse control in recently abstinent alcoholics compared with social drinkers. *Addictive Behaviors, 33*, 388–394.

Galovski, T., & Lyons, J. A. (2004). Psychological sequelae of combat violence: A review of the impact of PTSD on the veteran's family and possible interventions. *Aggression and Violent Behavior, 9*, 477–501.

Gewirtz, A. H., Erbes, C., Polusny, M. A., Forgatch, M. S., & DeGarmo, D. (2011). Supporting military families during and after deployment: The need for parenting interventions. *Professional Psychology: Research and Practice, 42*, 56–62. PCMID# 303635.

Gewirtz, A. H., Polusny, M., DeGarmo, D., Khalyis, A., & Erbes, C. (2010). Parenting, family relationships and posttraumatic distress symptoms among army National Guard members deployed to operation Iraqi freedom. *Journal of Consulting and Clinical Psychology, 78*, 599–610.

Glenn, D., Beckham, J. C., Feldman, M. E., Kirby, A. C., Hertzberg, M. A., & Moore, S. D. (2002). Violence and hostility among families of Vietnam veterans with combat-related posttraumatic stress disorder. *Violence and Victims, 17*, 473–489.

Gratz, K., & Gunderson, J. (2006). Preliminary data on an acceptance-based emotion regulation group intervention for deliberate self-harm among women with borderline personality disorder. *Behavior Therapy, 37*, 25–35.

Gratz, K., & Roemer, L. (2004). Multidimensional assessment of emotion regulation and dysregulation: Development, factor structure, and initial validation of the difficulties in emotion regulation scale. *Journal of Psychopathology and Behavioral Assessment, 26*, 41–54.

Gross, J. J. (1998). The emerging field of emotion regulation: An integrative review. *Review of General Psychology, 2*, 271–299.

Huebner, A. J., Mancini, J. A., Wilcox, R. M., Grass, S. R., & Grass, G. A. (2007). Parental deployment and youth in military families: Exploring uncertainty and ambiguous loss. *Family Relations, 56*, 112–122.

Jacobson, I. G., Ryan, M. A. K., Hooper, T. L., Smith, T. C., Amoroso, P. J., Boyko, E. J., et al. (2008). Alcohol use and alcohol-related problems before and after military combat deployment. *Journal of American Medical Association, 300*, 663–675.

Jensen, P. S., Grogan, D., Xenakis, S. N., & Bain, M. W. (1989). Father absence: Effects on child and maternal psychopathology. *Journal of the American Academy of Child & Adolescent Psychiatry, 28*(2), 171–175.

Jensen, P. S., Martin, D., & Watanabe, H. (1996). Children's response to parental separation during Operation Desert Storm. *Journal of the American Academy of Child & Adolescent Psychiatry, 35*(4), 433–441.

Jensen, P. S., & Shaw, J. A. (1996). *The effects of war and parental deployment upon children and adolescents*. Washington, DC: American Psychiatric Association.

Jensen, P. S., Watanabe, H. K., Richters, J. E., Cortes, R., Roper, M., & Liu, S. (1995). Prevalence of mental disorder in military children and adolescents: Findings from a two-stage community survey. *Journal of the American Academy of Child & Adolescent Psychiatry, 34*(11), 1514–1524.

Jensen, P. S., Xenakis, S. N., Wolf, P., & Bain, M. W. (1991). The "military family syndrome" revisited: "By the numbers". *Journal of Nervous and Mental Disease, 179*(2), 102–107.

Jordan, B., Marmar, C. R., Fairbank, J. A., Schlenger, W. E., Kulka, R. A., Hough, R. L., et al. (1992). Problems in families of male Vietnam veterans with posttraumatic stress disorder. *Journal of Consulting and Clinical Psychology, 60*(6), 916–926.

Kelley, M. L., Hock, E., Jarvis, M. S., Smith, K. M., Gaffney, M. A., & Bonney, J. F. (2002). Psychological adjustment of Navy mothers experiencing deployment. *Military Psychology, 14*, 199–216.

Kelley, M. L., Hock, E., Smith, K. M., Jarvis, M. S., Bonney, J. F., & Gaffney, M. A. (2001). Internalizing and externalizing behavior of children with enlisted Navy mothers experiencing military-induced separation. *Journal of the American Academy of Child & Adolescent Psychiatry, 40*, 464–471.

Knutson, N. M., Forgatch, M. S., Rains, L. A., & Sigmarsdottir. (2009). *Fidelity of Implementation Rating System (FIMP): The training manual for PMTO*. Eugene, OR: Oregon Social Learning Center.

Lester, P., Peterson, K., Reeves, J., Knauss, L., Glover, D., Mogil, C., et al. (2010). The long war and parental combat deployment: Effects on military children and at-home spouses. *Journal of American Academy of Child & Adolescent Psychiatry, 49*, 310–320.

Levai, M., Kaplan, S., Ackermann, R., & Hammock, M. (1995). The effect of father absence on the psychiatric hospitalization of Navy children. *Military Medicine, 160*(3), 104–106.

MacDermid, S. M. (2006). Multiple transitions of deployment and reunion of military families. Retrieved from http://www.cfs.purdue.edu/mfri/index.html

Masten, A. S., Hubbard, J. J., Gest, S. D., Tellegen, A., Garmezy, N., & Ramirez, M. (1999). Competence in the context of adversity: Pathways to resilience and maladaptation from childhood to late adolescence. *Developmental Psychopathology, 11*, 143–169.

Milliken, C. S., Auchterlonie, J. L., & Hoge, C. W. (2007). Longitudinal assessment of mental health problems among active and reserve component soldiers returning from the Iraq war. *JAMA: Journal of the American Medical Association, 298*, 2141–2148.

Minnesota National Guard. (2011) *Beyond the Yellow Ribbon Campaign.* Retrieved October 21, 2011, from http://www.minnesotanationalguard.org/btyr/

New, A. S., Fan, J., Murrough, J. W., Liu, X., Liebman, R. E., Guise, K. G., et al. (2009). A functional magnetic resonance imaging study of deliberate emotion regulation in resilience and posttraumatic stress disorder. *Biological Psychiatry, 66*, 656–664.

Olff, M., Langeland, W., Draijer, N., & Gersons, B. P. R. (2007). Gender differences in posttraumatic stress disorder. *Psychological Bulletin, 133*(2), 183–204.

Palmer, C. (2008). A theory of risk and resilience factors in military families. *Military Psychology, 20*(3), 205–217.

Patterson, G. R. (1982). *Coercive family process*. Eugene, OR: Castalia.

Patterson, G. R. (1986). Performance models for antisocial boys. *American Psychologist, 41*(4), 432–444.

Patterson, G. R., DeBaryshe, B. D., & Ramsey, E. (1989). A developmental perspective on antisocial behavior. *American Psychologist, 44*(2), 329–335.

Patterson, G. R., Reid, J. B., & Dishion, T. J. (1998). *Antisocial boys*. Malden, MA: Blackwell.

Pincus, S. H., House, R., Christenson, J., & Adler, L. E. (2001). The emotional cycle of deployment: A military family perspective. *U.S. Army Medical Department Journal, 2*, 21–29.

Rentz, E., Martin, S. L., Gibbs, D. A., Clinton-Sherrod, M., Hardison, J., & Marshall, S. W. (2006). Family violence in the military: A review of the literature. *Trauma, Violence, & Abuse, 7*(2), 93–108.

Repetti, R. L., Taylor, S. E., & Seeman, T. E. (2002). Risky families: Family social environments and the mental and physical health of offspring. *Psychological Bulletin, 128*(2), 330–366.

Riggs, D. S., Byrne, C. A., Weathers, F. W., & Litz, B. T. (1998). The quality of the intimate relationships of male Vietnam veterans: Problems associated with posttraumatic stress disorder. *Journal of Traumatic Stress, 11*(1), 87–101.

Riggs, S. A., & Riggs, D. S. (2011). Risk and resilience in military families experiencing deployment: The role of the family attachment network. *Journal of Family Psychology, 25*, 675–687.

Ruscio, A. M., Weather, F. W., King, L. A., & King, D. W. (2002). Male war-zone veterans' perceived relationships with their children: The importance of emotional numbing. *Journal of Traumatic Stress, 15*, 351–357.

Samper, R. E., Taft, C. T., King, D. W., & King, L. A. (2004). Posttraumatic stress disorder symptoms and parenting satisfaction among a national sample of male Vietnam veterans. *Journal of Traumatic Stress, 17*, 311–315.

Shea, S., & Coyne, L. W. (2011). Maternal dysphoric mood, stress and parenting practices in mothers of preschoolers: The role of experiential avoidance. *Journal of Child and Family Behavior Therapy, 33*, 231–247.

Solomon, Z. (1988). The effect of combat-related posttraumatic stress disorder on the family. *Psychiatry: Journal for the Study of Interpersonal Processes, 51*(3), 323–329.

Solomon, Z., Waysman, M., Levy, G., Fried, B., Mikulincer, M., Benbenishty, R., et al. (1992). From front line to home front: A study of secondary traumatization. *Family Process, 31*(3), 289–302.

Stanley, E. A., & Jha, A. P. (2009). Mind fitness: Increasing operational effectiveness and building warrior resilience. *Joint Force Quarterly, 55*, 144–151.

Teti, D. M., & Cole, P. M. (2011). Parenting at risk: New perspectives, new approaches. *Journal of Family Psychology, 25*, 625–634.

Tiwari, S., Podell, J., Martin, E., Mychailyszyn, M., Furr, J., & Kendall, P. C. (2008). Experiential avoidance in the parenting of anxious youth: Theory, research, and future directions. *Cognition and Emotion, 22*, 480–496.

Tull, M. T., Barrett, H. M., McMillan, E. S., & Roemer, L. (2007). A preliminary investigation of the relationship between emotion regulation difficulties and posttraumatic stress symptoms. *Behavior Therapy, 38*, 303–313.

Ursano, R. J., & Norwood, A. E. (1996). *Emotional aftermath of the Persian Gulf War: Veterans, families, communities, and nations*. Washington, DC: American Psychiatric Association.

Vogt, D. S., Pless, A. P., King, L. A., & King, D. W. (2005). Deployment stressors, gender, and mental health. *Journal of Traumatic Stress, 18*(2), 115–127.

Vujanovic, A. A., Niles, B., Pietrefesta, A., Schmertz, S. K., & Potter, C. M. (2011). Mindfulness in the treatment of posttraumatic stress disorder among military veterans. *Professional Psychology, Research and Practice, 42*, 24–31.

Yeung, W. J., Sandberg, J. F., Davis-Kean, P. E., & Hofferth, S. L. (2001). Children's time with fathers in intact families. *Journal of Marriage and Family, 63*(1), 136–154.

Chapter 8
Lesbian, Gay, and Bisexual Military Families: Visible But Legally Marginalized

Ramona Faith Oswald and Martina M. Sternberg

Abstract LGB military families will be increasingly visible now that Don't Ask/ Don't Tell has been repealed, and the military has stated that these servicemembers and their families are to be treated equally. Achieving equality in policy, practice, and attitudes will, however, take time and effort. Current Federal laws (e.g., the Defense of Marriage Act) prevent LGB servicemembers from being treated equally. Also, it is likely that anti-LGB attitudes held by some servicemembers did not simply end when DADT was repealed. Further, the military stance of neutrality is problematic given the need for LGB-affirming resources. These barriers to equal service are important to remedy because their existence may inhibit the strength of LGB military families, and the willingness of LGB adults to continue as enlisting as members of the U.S. armed forces.

Keywords Defense of Marriage Act • Don't Ask Don't Tell • Families • Lesbian/ Gay/Bisexual • Military • Minority Stress Theory • Sexual Orientation

On September 20, 2011, The United States (U.S.) became the 23rd of 26 NATO countries to allow LGB service members to openly serve in the military (Department of Defense, 2011). This historic step was achieved by repealing the 1993 "Don't Ask Don't Tell" (DADT) policy that had barred from military service any lesbian, gay, and bisexual (LGB) people who disclosed their identities to others. Not only

R.F. Oswald, Ph.D. (✉)
Department of Human and Community Development, University of Illinois at Urbana-Champaign, 263 Bevier Hall, MC-180, Urbana, IL 61801, USA
e-mail: roswald@illinois.edu

M.M. Sternberg, Ph.D.
Military Family Research Institute, Purdue University, 1202 W. State Street, West Lafayette, IN 47907-2055, USA
e-mail: msternbe@purdue.edu

S. MacDermid Wadsworth and D.S. Riggs (eds.), *Military Deployment and its Consequences for Families*, Risk and Resilience in Military and Veteran Families, DOI 10.1007/978-1-4614-8712-8_8, © Springer Science+Business Media New York 2014

did DADT ban openly LGB people from joining the military, but it was also used to investigate existing military personnel who were suspected of expressing an LGB orientation. These investigations led to the discharge of more than 14,000 service members (Servicemembers Legal Defense Network (SLDN), n.d. A).

Despite the DADT restriction on sexual minority military service, an estimated 71,000 LGB service members across all branches of the U.S. military were documented using Census data (Gates, 2010). Many of these LGB service members also have families who serve. In fact, an estimated 37 % of LGB active duty and 20 % of LGB guard and reserve members report living in a household with minor children (Gates, 2011, personal communication). This suggests that more than 16,000 LGB military families with children currently exist.

In addition to their sexual orientation minority status, LGB military families may, on average, be demographically distinct compared to heterosexual military families. First, LGB military families may be more commonly "mother-headed" than "father-headed". Although women are only 14 % of active duty personnel, more than 43 % of LGB servicemembers are female (Gates, 2010) and LB women are more likely to have children than are gay men (Gates & Ost, 2004). Further, LB military families may be more racially diverse, both in terms of servicemember race as well as the likelihood of interracial families among the LGB population. For example, Black women with female partners are almost four times as likely to report veteran status than Black women with male partners; Latinas with female partners are six times as likely to serve than those married to men (Cahill, 2009). Also, although Black female servicemembers represent only 1 % of military personnel, they were 3 % of those charged under DADT (Cahill, 2009). Same sex couples are more likely to be interracial than heterosexual married couples (Gates & Ost, 2004). Further LGB Blacks and Latino/as parent at higher rates than their White counterparts (Cahill, 2009), and White same-sex couples are more likely than heterosexual couples to adopt transracially (Goldberg, 2010).

The aim of this chapter is to summarize what is known about LGB military families. First we will describe the legacy of DADT and summarize the LGB-inclusive policy changes that have been made since its repeal. Then we will summarize the research on LGB parents and their children in general, and discuss the normative and minority stressors that may be faced by LGB military families specifically. The sources and effects of these stressors will be described. Furthermore we will discuss strategies for preventing and minimizing stressors, and identify specific changes that could be made in military policy and practice.

LGB Military Families Under DADT

Under the constraints of DADT, LGB service member families were completely invisible within the military. Having a same-sex partner was grounds for discharge so these relationships were hidden and heterosexual marriages were sometimes entered in to for "cover" (Balsam, Cochran, & Simpson, 2009). Furthermore, LGB service members with children were required to present themselves as single parents or in a heterosexual relationship, as any recognition of a second same-sex parent (for example by adopting a child together) was also grounds for discharge (SLDN, n.d. B).

The result of DADT-imposed invisibility was that LGB service member families under this policy were not eligible for any family benefits, a fact recognized by both LGB and heterosexual service members (RAND, 2010). Under DADT, LGB military couples were not eligible for joint duty assignments and did not have spousal privilege in the case of a court martial proceeding. In the case of LGB service members with non-military partners, those partners did not have access to military identification as a family member and thus had no access to base. Lack of access to base prevented them from obtaining base housing, commissary, child care, gas stations, and other entitlements. These partners were also not eligible for Tri-Care (the military health care program), free legal services, life insurance subsidized by the military, surviving spouse benefits, or any family support programs. LGB service members who were assigned overseas were not eligible to have their families relocate with them. The children of LGB service members were only eligible for family status and the resulting benefits through the LGB service member. In situations where this parent–child relationship was too risky to reveal, the children were not able to access the military-based supports and resources that are considered vital to the resilience of children in military families.

Anticipating the repeal of DADT, a RAND (2010) survey asked LGB service members if they would disclose their sexual orientation upon repeal. Fifteen percent would be completely open and 59 % would be "sometimes open, sometimes not." When asked how the repeal of DADT might impact LGB servicemembers overall, 87 % agreed that least some LGB servicemembers would bring partners to family events, 79 % expected same-sex partners and children to live in base/post housing; 76 % expected partners to play a spousal role in military ceremonies; and 77 % anticipated that LGB servicemembers would display photographs of family in their workspaces. It is clear LGB military families will become more visible. In the next section we describe benefits of this visibility, as well as remaining barriers to equality.

LGB Military Families Post-DADT

The repeal of DADT made it possible for LGB people to serve openly. Sexual orientation is no longer a barrier to military service, and former service members who were discharged under DADT may apply for re-entry. The military is striving to create a sexual orientation "neutral" environment and as such will not allow the creation of separate bathroom facilities or living quarters based upon sexual orientation. Nor will it release servicemembers from duty if they oppose serving with LGB individuals. As part of this neutrality stance, the military will not "request, collect or maintain information about the sexual orientation of servicemembers except when it is an essential part of an otherwise appropriate investigation or other official action" (Philpott, 2011).

The repeal has made some benefits available to LGB military families. For example, although LGB servicemembers were always eligible to enroll their legally-recognized children in military support programs, if doing so meant bringing attention to their sexual orientation or same-sex relationship then they might have chosen not to do so. Now that DADT has been repealed, LGB parents with legal parental rights can now provide military benefits to those children without fearing a military investigation and possible discharge. In addition, the Department of Defense is reviewing policies and regulations so that LGB servicemembers can obtain benefits on par with their heterosexual peers. Fourteen military benefits where servicemembers may designate beneficiaries including same-sex partners have been identified (Department of Defense, 2011, October 28); they are:

- All-volunteer Force Educational Assistant Program/Active Duty Death Benefit
- Casualty Notification
- Designation of Persons having Interest in Status of a Missing Member
- Escorts for Dependents of Deceased or Missing
- Final Settlement of Accounts
- Person Eligible to Receive Effects of Deceased Persons
- Post Vietnam-era Veterans Assistance Program
- Servicemember Group Life Insurance
- Survivor Benefit for Retirees
- Thrift Savings Plan
- Travel and Transportation Allowance/Attendance at Yellow Ribbon Reintegration Events
- Veteran's Group Life Insurance
- Wounded Warrior Designated Caregiver

It is notable that these policies provide benefits conferred upon disappearance, death, or injury, and not benefits related to daily living. The more expansive benefits related to daily living as military families are not fully available to LGB servicemembers due to the 1996 Federal Defense of Marriage Act [(DOMA); Public Law No. 104-199, 1996].

DOMA is a federal law that defines marriage as the legal union between one man and one woman and further defines a spouse as a person of the opposite sex who is a husband or wife. DOMA stipulates that if individual states allow and recognize same sex unions, other states do not have to recognize or allow same sex marriages. Furthermore, all federal policies and practices are to be in accordance with DOMA. Thus, as long as DOMA stands, military policies that use the terms "marriage" or "spouse" must be interpreted such that their benefits are only conferred upon heterosexually married spouses. All LGB servicemembers are thus legally single in the eyes of the military, even if they are partnered, and even if they are legally married to that same-sex partner in a given state (e.g., Vermont) or country (e.g., Canada).

Non-legal family members (e.g., same-sex partners, children to whom the servicemember does not have a legal tie) are not entitled to military medical and dental insurance or treatment in military facilities. Nor are they entitled to family support under the Morale Welfare and Recreation program offerings. Further, a same-sex spouse cannot be designated as "next of kin" and thus would not be the first person notified in the case of death or injury. A comprehensive review of military benefits that are and are not afforded to LGB servicemember and their families is beyond the scope of this chapter; readers are advised to consult the *Servicemembers Legal Defense Network* (n.d. B) (http://www.sldn.org/pages/family-benefits) for current information. Our point here is that, although now able to serve openly, LGB service-members and their families are treated unequally, largely as a result of DOMA.

LGB Parents and Their Children

The civilian research on LGB parents and their children has been deftly summarized by Goldberg (2010) and others (Stacey & Biblarz, 2001) as revolving around a debate of "no differences" versus uniqueness. In support of the no differences argument, LGB parents (the research has largely used lesbian mother samples) have been found to have parenting skills similar to their heterosexual counterparts, to live lives organized more by parenting than sexual orientation, and to seek environments that are supportive of their families. Furthermore, children with LGB parents have similar social and educational outcomes as their peers with heterosexual parents. Also, contrary to stereotypes, these children are not more likely to be LGB themselves.

Despite these similarities between heterosexual and LGB-headed families, researchers have identified unique strengths and stressors faced by sexual minori-ties (Goldberg, 2010). For example, unlike their heterosexual counterparts, LGB parents and their children may hide parental sexual orientation from others to avoid rejection, discrimination, or abuse. Further, they cannot take for granted support from extended family, friends, or others who may have anti-LGB attitudes and beliefs. LGB parents may be more likely to teach their children to respect diversity, and same-sex co-parenting couples have been found to share household and chil-drearing labor more equally than heterosexuals. It is perhaps not surprising that children with LGB parents may be more likely to explore their sexual orientation and to have personal identities and goals that are gender-flexible rather than gender-stereotyped.

Normative and Minority Stress for LGB Military Families

The similarities and differences between LGB and heterosexual families, both mili-tary and civilian, may be explained in part by minority stress theory (Meyer, 2003). According to this theory, LGB individuals (and their families) experience minority stress on top of normative stress.

Normative stressors for military families include chronic relocation, separation, reintegration, and fears of harm (Park, 2011). For example, military families move frequently, which requires adjustment to new peers, schools, and cultural contexts, and distance from familiar support networks. In addition to the challenges of whole-family relocation, military children with LGB parents and civilian partners of servicemembers may face extended separation from their deployed loved one. Perhaps even more challenging is the family readjustment that occurs when the servicemember returns from deployment and may suffer from PTSD, physical injury, or other problems. Throughout, family members face chronic uncertainty regarding current and future servicemember safety.

In addition to these features of military life, LGB servicemembers and their families face minority stress. Minority stress refers to stress that comes from being a member of a stigmatized minority group (Meyer, 2003). Processes that create minority stress can be distal or proximal. Distal stress processes include prejudice events, discrimination, and violence. For example, in a population-based survey of LGB adults (Herek, 2009), 49 % reported being verbally abused and 24.8 % reported that their person or property was criminally perpetrated against. Further, several studies of children with LGB parents have found that they reported being teased and bullied by peers (reviewed in Goldberg, 2010). Proximal stress processes include expectations of rejection, internalized homophobia, and identity concealment. For example, the majority of Herek's (2009) sample reported perceiving stigma in their residential communities (e.g., "most people where I live think less of a person who is LGBT"). Also, youth with LGB parents have been found to hide their parent's sexuality from peers in the hopes of preventing social rejection (Goldberg, 2010).

DADT-era surveys of veteran and active duty servicemembers document that minority stress processes beyond mandatory concealment of sexual orientation did occur in military contexts (Balsam et al., 2009; Office of the Inspector General, 2000; RAND, 2010). Although the surveys were not population based, it is notable that one-third to one-half of each sample reported experiencing or witnessing discrimination, harassment, or assault on the basis of the servicemember's perceived sexual orientation. Although there is no research on minority stressors in military contexts as experienced by the LGB servicemember's partner or children, it is reasonable to expect that they would be at least indirectly affected. The repeal of DADT is too recent for us to document an improvement or decline in minority stress processes within the military; these data provide an important baseline for future studies (Burks, 2011).

It is also important to recognize that so called "normative military stressors" also may be experienced as minority stressors by LGB military family members. For example, relocation could be devastating if it means leaving LGB-affirmation behind and facing the decisions about of having to disclose or hide all over again. In the case of same-sex partners without children, chronic relocation may be isolating for the civilian partner who has little access to military spouse support, and whose life may not be understood by nonmilitary LGB community members. The resources that both children and parents need during deployment and reintegration may be compromised if their family situation is not fully recognized and affirmed by potential sources of support (e.g., a school social worker). Also, if they are "over recognized" for their sexual orientation then their needs for military support may be overlooked because they are viewed as LGB rather than facing deployment (see Allen, 2007). Couple relationships can be severely stressed by separation (Knobloch & Theiss, 2012), and these stresses may be even higher for same-sex partners whose relationships may not be recognized by the law or valued by their families of origin. The risk of intimate partner violence rises upon re-integration (McCarroll et al., 2000), and this may be especially challenging for LGB military families given the widespread denial of same-sex abuse by both lay people and practitioners (Ristock, 2002). Throughout their service, chronic uncertainty regarding servicemember safety may compound fears already faced by LGB individuals and their loved ones regarding prejudice, discrimination, and violence.

Circumstances in the Environment

Minority stress processes flow from circumstances in the social environment that devalue the worth and legitimacy of (i.e., stigmatize) LGB people and their children (Meyer, 2003; Oswald & Holman, 2013). Tremendous gains have been made. For example, all state sodomy laws were overturned by the U.S. Supreme court ruling in *Lawrence et al. v. Texas* (2003). Also, same sex marriage is available in six states, the District of Columbia, and two Native American tribes; two states recognize same-sex marriages granted by other jurisdictions; and California recognizes same-sex marriages entered into before November 5, 2008. Further, President Obama recently issued two Executive Orders that extend recognition to LGB families. The first mandates hospital visitation rights for same-sex partners in any facility that receives Medicaid funding (Obama, 2010a). The second extends some federal benefits to the same-sex partners of federal employees (Obama, 2010b). In addition to these Executive Orders, the Obama administration has called DOMA unconstitutional and said that it will not defend DOMA in federal court. Indeed 2 days ago in response to *McLaughlin v. Panetta*, a lawsuit brought by LGB servicemembers who wish to obtain federal benefits for their same-sex spouses, U.S. Attorney General Eric Holder sent a letter to Congress declaring that DOMA is unconstitutional and that the military has not provided any justification in favor of it (Office of the Attorney General, 2012).

Despite this accelerating progress to end LGB stigma and discrimination, the problem remains significant. In a previous section we described the impact of DOMA on LGB servicemember access to military benefits. DOMA is a central component of the social environment that promotes minority stressors experienced by LGB military families. The repeal of DOMA would eliminate many of the inequities that they face. It would not however automatically change attitudes.

Research suggests that anti-LGB attitudes are held by some servicemembers. Although military policy forbids harassment (Department of Defense, 2011), these attitudes may still permeate some military contexts. For example, a recent survey of

3,057 civilian undergraduates, ROTC cadets, and military cadets found that military cadets had the least favorable attitudes towards LGB servicemembers, followed by ROTC cadets and then civilians (Ender, Rohall, Brennan, Matthews, & Smith, 2012). Cadet attitudes may change over time and with education in the post-DADT era; educational efforts should be evaluated to determine their effectiveness. Servicemembers who resist attitude change pose challenges for maintaining a military environment free of harassment or abuse. The experience of foreign militaries suggests that strong leadership is vital for maintaining a positive environment; regardless of their personal beliefs, leaders should publically state their support for integration of LGB servicemembers (RAND, 2010).

In addition to the within-military issues posed by DOMA and personal prejudices, LGB servicemembers and their families also face non-military barriers and prejudices. For example, it is legal in most U.S. locations to discriminate against LGB individuals in employment, housing, credit, and public accommodation (National Gay and Lesbian Task Force, 2012). Thus, for example, LGB servicemembers with a same-sex partner and/or children may be excluded from military housing and face housing discrimination off base. Furthermore, municipalities and states that offer sexual orientation protections against discrimination have religious exemptions that may be quite salient if local resources are offered through religious organizations. Thus in addition to being excluded from military family support programs, LGB military families may also be excluded (by policy or attitude) from civilian family support programs offered through churches, YMCAs and other religious organizations. Of the almost 200 U.S. religious denominations, only six officially respect LGB identities, and a minority (40 %) of U.S. religious adherents belongs to these denominations (Oswald, Cuthbertson, Lazarevic, & Goldberg, 2010). Thus the likelihood of finding military family support through religious organizations may be low.

Effects of Inequality and Minority Stress

The legal and policy inequalities faced by LGB servicemembers and their families may impact their health and well-being. The strongest empirical evidence for this claim comes from three longitudinal studies; supporting evidence can also be found in a body of cross-sectional research. The first longitudinal study (Hatzenbuehler, McLaughlin, Keyes, & Hasin, 2010) used two waves of the population-based National Epidemiologic Survey on Alcohol and Related Conditions to examine whether institutional discrimination led to increased psychiatric disorders among 577 LGB adults (parental status not specified); 34,076 heterosexual respondents were used as a comparison group. They found that in states that passed constitutional amendments banning same-sex marriage, the mood disorder symptoms of LGB respondents rose by more than 30 % from T1 (pre-election) to T2 (post-election), but decreased more than 20 % among LGB respondents living in states without such laws. Furthermore, generalized anxiety disorder increased more than

200 % among LGB respondents living in states that implemented amendments; no significant change was found for those living in states without amendments. Comorbidity (the co-occurrence of two or more disorders) also significantly increased for those living in amendment-states. Heterosexual respondents living in states with amendments did not have an increase in mood disorders; when heterosexuals living in these states did report an increase in a specific disorder (e.g., generalized anxiety) then the magnitude of change was much smaller than that evidenced by the LGB group (61 % versus 248 % respectively).

Rostosky, Riggle, Horne, and Miller (2009) also conducted a longitudinal study of this election. Despite the limitation of using a non-representative Internet-based convenience sample (N = 1,552), they also found increased depressive symptoms, stress, and negative affect among LGB adults after the election. A limitation of both of these studies is that neither examined minority stress processes as mediators linking the election to mental health symptoms. Further, these studies did not control for parental status. These weaknesses are improved upon in the third longitudinal study described below.

In a study that explicitly tested how legal context impacts LGB parents, Goldberg and Smith (2011) examined the effects of both stigma and social support on depression and anxiety symptoms among 52 lesbian and 38 gay couples over a 1-year transition to adoptive parenthood. Data were collected from each partner at three time points: pre-adoption (T1), several months' post-adoptive placement (T2), and 1 year post-placement (T3). The authors found that depression significantly increased from T1 to T3, and this change was predicted by an interaction between state legal climate and internalized homophobia. Specifically, lesbian and gay adoptive parents who reported low levels of internalized homophobia at T1 showed little change in their depressive symptoms regardless of their state's legal climate for adoption. Strikingly though, lesbian and gay adoptive parents who reported high levels of internalized homophobia at T1 showed a significant increase in depressive symptoms at T3 when they lived in a state with a negative legal climate, and a significant decrease from T1 to T3 when their state was more legally supportive. A similar pattern was found for anxiety: All participants reported an increase in anxiety over time, but the change was significant only among those with both high levels of internalized homophobia and a less supportive legal climate. This study suggests that living in a hostile legal context increases both depression and anxiety among LGB parents, especially if the parents struggle with internalized homophobia.

Complementing these longitudinal studies that show the negative effects of legal inequality, cross-sectional research (using geographically dispersed but predominately White, middle-class samples) has found that legal rights and protections are beneficial for LGB individuals, couples, and families. Specifically, LGB adults with a legally recognized same-sex relationship reported fewer depressive symptoms and stress, and higher well-being, compared to those in committed but non-legal relationships (Riggle, Rostosky, & Horne, 2010). In a qualitative study of married same-sex couples in Massachusetts, Shecter, Tracy, Page, and Luong (2008) found that marriage was described by participants as bringing increased couple commitment, acknowledgment of their relationship from family and colleagues, a sense of societal legitimacy, and a reduction of homophobia within self and others. Also, Canadian lesbian mothers (who were defined by the authors as living in a nonheterosexist legal context because they have full legal rights under Canadian law) were found to have significantly fewer stigma-related worries than their American counterparts (Shapiro, Peterson, & Stewart, 2009). Furthermore, the presence of nondiscrimination laws has been associated with higher levels of disclosure and social support, and lower levels of internalized homophobia, among LGB individuals (Riggle et al., 2010; see also Hatzenbuehler, Keyes, & Hasin, 2009).

Although the research just reviewed is based on civilian samples there is no reason to believe it does not extend to LGB servicemembers and their families. Regardless of civilian or military status, we argue that minority stress reduces well-being, while legal recognition and benefits can confer positive benefits to individuals and strengthen relationship quality.

Coping and Social Support as Protective Factors

Coping and social support moderate the impact of minority stress (Meyer, 2003). The military recognizes that providing social support for servicemember families is an effective way to promote military readiness and retention. However, an unintended consequence of the current "sexual orientation neutrality" stance may be that support designed to remedy minority stress is unavailable through military sources. This would be unfortunate, as minority-specific supports have been found to have positive effects. For example, children with lesbian mothers who were stigmatized by their peers had greater well-being when: their school had LGB curriculum content; they had contact with other children from LGB families; and/or their mothers had contact with other LB women (van Gelderen, Gartrell, Bos, & Hermanns, 2009). Furthermore, LGB individuals struggling with identity or social rejection issues may benefit from accessing LGB-specific supports. Military schools, social workers, and other providers may need to explore their options to provide more LGB-explicit resources to LGB military families.

It would be a mistake to assume that civilian LGB-identified services will provide what the military lacks. A master's thesis study of 19 community-based mental health services for lesbians found that they are not able to meet the needs of lesbian military families (Terp, 2011). This sample represented a majority (79 %) of the existing agencies specifically serving lesbian clients in the U.S. None target servicemembers or veterans as a category of clients. Furthermore, few reported employing staff with knowledge of military experience under DADT or the Veteran's Administration policies toward lesbian families. Few had staff with training on military family issues or mental health issues related to military service. None provided support groups for lesbian military families and none knew of actual resources to which they could refer these families. Most reported staff competency in treating substance abuse, depression, post-traumatic stress disorder, and intimate partner violence. However, staff competency was rare with regards to problems found more often in military than civilian populations (i.e., traumatic brain injury and military sexual assault). Although limited in scope, the results of this study strongly suggest that military-specific supports are needed for LGB servicemembers and their families.

Positive Identities as Protective Factors

Having a positive LGB identity, or access to contexts that affirm LGB dignity, can mitigate the negative effects of minority stress. For example, relationship satisfaction is higher among lesbian couples when their relationship is visible to, and accepted by, their families of origin; acceptance was operationalized as being able to show physical affection in front of family members (Caron & Ulin, 1997). Also, children with LGB parents report wanting safe spaces where they can talk about problems without fearing that their parents' sexuality will be blamed (Goldberg, 2007).

As discussed in the previous section, the military stance of sexual orientation neutrality may be problematic when affirmation is more effective than neutrality. Further, there is evidence that explicit support for LGB people and issues is central to the development of resilience among children with LGB parents. Specifically, it provides a narrative with which these children are able to construct positive identities and family relationships in the face of societal prejudice (Goldberg & Kuvalanka, 2012).

Summary

Like their civilian counterparts, LGB servicemembers and their families are impacted by their social environment, especially features that promote or mitigate minority stressors based upon sexual orientation stigma. Based upon the research reviewed in this chapter, it appears that the health and well-being of this population could be promoted by changing laws/policies that discriminate against LGB servicemembers, reducing the incidence of minority stress processes, strengthening LGB-affirming supports, and creating a safe environment for LGB servicemembers and family members to disclose their (or the servicemembers') sexual orientation. These will be developed in the next section.

Implications for Military Practice

The U.S. military recognizes the importance of the military family and the important role that servicemember families play in helping to create a strong military (Department of Defense, 2013). This value can be seen in the ongoing Department of Defense effort to revise policies and regulations so that LGB servicemembers can obtain benefits on par with their heterosexual peers.

The federal DOMA is in direct conflict with the Department of Defense effort to treat all servicemembers equally. As previously discussed, this law requires "marriage" and "spouse" to be interpreted as heterosexual only, and thus any military benefit that uses marital status as an eligibility requirement cannot be extended to same-sex partners even if they are married in a particular jurisdiction. For example, a same-sex partner cannot be identified as "next of kin" and thus cannot be the first person contacted in the event of servicemember injury, disappearance, or death. Although the repeal of DOMA is not a military decision, the Department of Defense could serve as a powerful advocate for its demise by pointing out the injustice it creates for people who commit their lives and their families to national service. Allied military leaders have advised the US to make policy changes quickly and decisively, as their experience suggest that this is the most effective way to promote equality (The Brookings Institution, 2010).

In addition to revising policies and advocating for the repeal of DOMA, the military could take steps to reduce both distal and proximal minority stressors. Unit commanders have a special role to play in these efforts. Because the military will not track sexual orientation as an equal opportunity class, claims of harassment, discrimination, or abuse (e.g., distal stressors) will be dealt with by commanders rather than through the military equal opportunity complaint process. Thus it falls to commanders to prevent mistreatment and to respond fairly and effectively when it occurs. If support referrals are made, providers should assess for minority stress in addition to other screening and diagnosis, and should have the competency to treat minority stress symptoms.

Commanders and providers should also be sensitive to proximal stressors such as negative self-evaluation and expectations of rejection. It would be helpful for commanders to convey a strong respect for all persons including those who are LGB, and to explicitly include same-sex partners and other loved ones as members of the military family. Service providers could include attention to sexual orientation when assessing clients for self-esteem or social adjustment.

Although closeting is considered a form of proximal minority stress (Meyer, 2003), and in the post-DADT military it is not required, the extent to which LGB servicemembers and their families wish to be recognized as such will vary. Thus, commanders and providers should not assume that a failure to disclose is problematic. It might be worth exploring with the person or family to see if there are perceived barriers to disclosure that could be remedied, but their preferred level of openness or privacy should be respected.

In this chapter we have presented the currently available research on LGB servicemembers and their families. The canon is small partly because research on LGB issues was impossible under DADT. The repeal of DADT has opened a door to increased understanding of, and improved supports for, LGB military families. Now is the time to target research funding towards understanding the needs and experiences of LGB military families.

Conclusion

LGB military families will be increasingly visible now that Don't Ask/Don't Tell has been repealed, and the military has stated that these servicemembers and their families are to be treated equally. Achieving equality will, however, take time and effort. Current Federal laws (e.g., the Defense of Marriage Act) prevent LGB servicemembers from being treated equally. Also, it is likely that anti-LGB attitudes held by servicemembers did not simply stop when DADT was repealed. Further, the military stance of neutrality is problematic given the need for LGB-affirming resources. These barriers to equal service are important to remedy because their existence may inhibit the strength of LGB military families, and the willingness of LGB adults to continue as enlisting as members of the U.S. armed forces.

References

Allen, K. R. (2007). Ambiguous loss after lesbian couples with children break up: A case for same-sex divorce. *Family Relations, 56*, 174–182.

Balsam, K., Cochran, B., & Simpson, T. (2009). Summary of the results of research with GLB veterans. In *Report of the American Psychological Association's Joint Divisional Task Force on Sexual Orientation and Military Service* (Appendix H). Retrieved February 9, 2012, from http://www.apa.org/pi/lgbt/resources/19-44-taskforce-report.pdf

Burks, D. J. (2011). Lesbian, gay, and bisexual victimization in the military. *American Psychologist, 66*, 604–613.

Cahill, S. (2009). The disproportionate impact of antigay family policies on Black and Latino same-sex couple households. *Journal of African American Studies, 13*, 219–250.

Caron, S. L., & Ulin, M. (1997). Closeting and the quality of lesbian relationships. *Families in Society: The Journal of Contemporary Human Services, 78*, 413–419.

Department of Defense. (2011, October 28). *Repeal of "Don't Ask, Don't Tell" (DADT): Quick Reference Guide*. Retrieved February 9, 2012, from http://www.defense.gov/home/features/2010/0610_dadt/Quick_Reference_Guide_Repeal_of_DADT_APPROVED.pdf

Department of Defense. (2013, September 9). *Military family support*. Retrieved September 25, 2013, from http://www.defense.gov/home/features/2012/0212_familysupport/

Ender, M. G., Rohall, D. E., Brennan, A. J., Matthews, M. D., & Smith, I. (2012). Civilian, ROTC, and military academy undergraduate attitudes towards homosexuals in the U.S. military: A research note. *Armed Forces & Society*. doi:10.1177/0095327X11410856

Gates, G. J. (2010, May). *Lesbian, gay, and bisexual men and women in the US military: Updated estimates*. Los Angeles, CA: The Williams Institute. Retrieved November 8, 2011, from http://williamsinstitute.law.ucla.edu/research/census-lgbt-demographics-studies/lesbian-gay-and-bisexual-men-and-women-in-the-us-military-updated-estimates-2/

Gates, G. J., & Ost, J. (2004). *The gay atlas*. Washington, DC: The Urban Institute.

Goldberg, A. E. (2007). (How) does it make a difference? Perspectives of adults with lesbian, gay, and bisexual parents. *American Journal of Orthopsychiatry, 77*, 550–562.

Goldberg, A. E. (2010). *Lesbian and gay parents and their children: Research on the family life cycle*. Washington, DC: APA Books.

Goldberg, A. E., & Kuvalanka, K. (2012). Marriage (In)equality: The perspectives of adolescents and emerging adults with lesbian, gay, and bisexual parents. *Journal of Marriage and Family, 74*, 34–52.

Goldberg, A. E., & Smith, J. Z. (2011). Stigma, social context, and mental health: Lesbian and gay couples across the transition to adoptive parenthood. *Journal of Counseling Psychology, 58*, 139–150.

Hatzenbuehler, M. L., Keyes, K. M., & Hasin, D. S. (2009). State-level policies and psychiatric morbidity in lesbian, gay, and bisexual populations. *American Journal of Public Health, 99*, 2275–2281.

Hatzenbuehler, M., McLaughlin, K. A., Keyes, K. M., & Hasin, D. S. (2010). The impact of institutional discrimination on psychiatric disorders in lesbian, gay, and bisexual populations: A prospective study. *American Journal of Public Health, 100*, 452–459.

Herek, G. M. (2009). Hate crimes and stigma-related experiences among sexual minority adults in the United States: Prevalence estimates from a national probability sample. *Journal of Interpersonal Violence*. doi:10.1177/0886260508316477

Knobloch, L. K., & Theiss, J. A. (2012). Experiences of U.S. military couples during the post-deployment transition: Applying the relational turbulence model. *Journal of Social and Personal Relationships*. doi:10.1177/0265407511431186

Lawrence et al. v. Texas. (2003). Retrieved September 11, 2005, from http://caselaw.lp.findlaw.com/scripts/getcase.pl?court=us&vol=000&invol=02-102

McCarroll, J. E., Ursano, R. J., Liu, X., Thayer, L. E., Newby, J. H., & Norwood, A. E. (2000). Deployment and the probability of spousal aggression by U.S. Army soldiers. *Military Medicine, 165*, 41–44.

Meyer, I. H. (2003). Prejudice, social stress, and mental health in lesbian, gay, and bisexual populations: Conceptual issues and research evidence. *Psychological Bulletin, 129*, 674–697.

National Gay and Lesbian Task Force. (2012, January 20). *State nondiscrimination laws in the U.S.* Retrieved February 19, 2012, from http://www.thetaskforce.org/downloads/reports/issue_maps/non_discrimination_1_12.pdf

Obama, B. (2010, April 15). *Presidential memorandum: Hospital visitation*. Retrieved February 19, 2012, from http://www.whitehouse.gov/the-press-office/presidential-memorandum-hospital-visitation

Obama, B. (2010, June 2). *Presidential memorandum: Extension of benefits to same-sex domestic partners of federal employees*. Retrieved January 30, 2012, from http://www.whitehouse.gov/the-press-office/presidential-memorandum-extension-benefits-same-sex-domestic-partners-federal-emplo

Office of the Attorney General. (2012, February 17). *Re: McLaughlin v. Panetta, No 11-11905 (D. Mass)*. Retrieved February 19, 2012, from http://talkingpointsmemo.com/documents/2012/02/letter-from-the-attorney-general-to-congress-on-litigation-involving-the-defense-of-marriage-act-1.php?page=1

Office of the Inspector General, U.S. Department of Defense. (2000). *Military environment with respect to the homosexual conduct policy* (Report No. D-2000-101). Washington, DC: Author.

Oswald, R., Cuthbertson, C., Lazarevic, V., & Goldberg, A. (2010). Measuring community climate. *Journal of GLBT Family Studies, 6*, 214–228.

Oswald, R. F., & Holman, E. G. (2013). Place matters: LGB families in community context. In A. E. Goldberg & K. A. Allen (Eds.), *LGBT-parent families: Possibilities for new research and implications for practice* (pp. 193–208). New York: Springer.

Park, N. (2011). Military children and families: Strengths and challenges during peace and war. *American Psychologist, 66*, 65–72.

Philpott, T. (2011, February 2). Gay numbers won't be tracked. *Today in the Military: Headlines*. Retrieved December 10, 2011, from http://www.military.com/features/0,15240,226620,00.html

Public Law No. 104-199. (1996). *Defense of Marriage Act*. Retrieved October 8, 2011, from http://thomas.loc.gov/cgi-bin/bdquery/z?d104:HR03396:#

RAND Corporation. (2010). *Sexual orientation and U.S. Military Personnel Policy: An update of RAND's 1993 study*. Arlington, VA: Author.

Riggle, E. D. B., Rostosky, S. S., & Horne, S. G. (2010). Psychological distress, well-being, and legal recognition in same-sex couple relationships. *Journal of Family Psychology*. doi:10.1037/a0017942

Ristock, J. (2002). *No more secrets: Violence in lesbian relationships*. New York: Routledge.

Rostosky, S. S., Riggle, E. D. B., Horne, S. G., & Miller, A. D. (2009). Marriage amendments and psychological distress in lesbian, gay, and bisexual adults. *Journal of Counseling Psychology, 56*, 56–66.

Servicemembers Legal Defense Network. (n.d. A). *About "Don't Ask, Don't Tell": History of the issue*. Retrieved February 9, 2012, from http://www.sldn.org/pages/history-of-the-issue

Servicemembers Legal Defense Network (n.d. B). *Family benefits*. Retrieved February 20, 2012, from http://www.sldn.org/pages/family-benefits

Shapiro, D. N., Peterson, C., & Stewart, A. J. (2009). Legal and social contexts and mental health among lesbian and heterosexual mothers. *Journal of Family Psychology, 23*, 255–262.

Shecter, E., Tracy, A. J., Page, K. V., & Luong, G. (2008). Shall we marry? Legal marriage as a commitment event in same-sex relationships. *Journal of Homosexuality, 54*, 400–422.

Stacey, J., & Biblarz, T. J. (2001). (How) Does sexual orientation of parents matter? *American Sociological Review, 65*, 159–183.

Terp, D. M. (2011). *When Joanie comes marchin' home: An exploratory study of community-based mental health services for lesbian military families*. Unpublished Master's Thesis. Smith College School of Social Work, Northampton, MA. Retrieved February 19, 2012, from http://dspace.nitle.org/bitstream/handle/10090/23010/TERP%20thesis%206-14-2011.pdf?sequence=1

The Brookings Institution. (2010, May 19). Panel Discussion: *Lessons learned from the service of gays and lesbians in allied militaries*. Washington, DC: Author. Retrieved July 17, 2012, from http://www.brookings.edu/~/media/events/2010/5/19%20military%20service/20100519_military_service.pdf

van Gelderen, L., Gartrell, N., Bos, H., & Hermanns, J. (2009). Stigmatization and resilience in adolescent children of lesbian mothers. *Journal of GLBT Family Studies, 5*, 268–279.

Part III
Single Service Members

Chapter 9
Pre-deployment Well-Being Among Single and Partnered National Guard Soldiers: The Role of Their Parents, Social Support, and Stressors

Melissa A. Polusny, Christopher R. Erbes, Emily Hagel Campbell, Hannah Fairman, Mark Kramer, and Alexandria K. Johnson

Abstract Families are a key source of support for National Guard Soldiers, yet little is known about the influence of parents on Soldiers' pre-deployment well-being. In this chapter, we examine the potential role family may play in the psychological well-being of National Guard Soldiers. We present initial findings from the Readiness and Resilience in National Guard Soldiers (RINGS-2) study—an ongoing, prospective investigation of 2,089 National Guard Soldiers and their families. Single versus partnered Soldiers were compared on measures of pre-deployment well-being (post-traumatic stress symptoms, depression symptoms, and alcohol misuse). Prior to deployment, partnered Soldiers had higher PTSD and depression symptoms than single Soldiers, while single Soldiers reported greater alcohol misuse than partnered Soldiers. Multiple linear regression analyses examined the role of family contextual factors in understanding Soldiers' pre-deployment well-being. Findings demonstrated the important role families can play in Soldiers' well-being prior to deployment, both as a source of support and strain.

Keywords National guard/reserve component • Psychological well-being • Adult child-parent relationships

The views expressed in this article are those of the authors and do not reflect the official policy or position of the Department of Veterans Affairs, Department of the Army, or Department of Defense.

M.A. Polusny, Ph.D., L.P. (✉) • C.R. Erbes, Ph.D.
Minneapolis VA Health Care System, One Veterans Drive, Minneapolis, MN 55417, USA

Center for Chronic Disease Outcomes Research, Minneapolis, MN, USA

University of Minnesota Medical School, Minneapolis, Minneapolis, MN, USA
e-mail: melissa.polusny@va.gov; Christopher.Erbes@va.gov

E.H. Campbell • H. Fairman • M. Kramer, Ph.D. • A.K. Johnson
Center for Chronic Disease Outcomes Research, Minneapolis, MN, USA

S. MacDermid Wadsworth and D.S. Riggs (eds.), *Military Deployment and its Consequences for Families*, Risk and Resilience in Military and Veteran Families, DOI 10.1007/978-1-4614-8712-8_9, © Springer Science+Business Media New York 2014

Introduction

Our nation's "citizen soldiers"—National Guard and Reserve component troops—have been deployed at unprecedented levels in support of Operation Enduring Freedom (OEF) in Afghanistan and Operations Iraqi Freedom (OIF) and New Dawn (OND) in Iraq. Most National Guard Soldiers and their families are remarkably resilient across the deployment cycle (Cozza, Chun, & Polo, 2005). Yet, studies indicate National Guard Soldiers are at greater risk for post-traumatic stress disorder (PTSD) and related mental health problems following combat deployment compared to active duty component troops (for review see Griffith, 2010). Some have speculated that the elevated rates of mental health problems observed in National Guard Soldiers may be due to the unique challenges and stressors faced by citizen Soldiers who are simultaneously faced with preparing for deployment to potentially dangerous and hostile environments and disruptions to civilian employment and extended separation from home and family (Griffith, 2010).

Social support has been shown to lessen the negative effects of stressors on individuals (Cohen & Wills, 1985). Families, particularly spouses or romantic partners, have been shown to be a key source of support for military personnel across the deployment cycle (Erbes, Meis, Polusny, & Compton, 2011; Wiens & Boss, 2006). Our experience with National Guard/Reserve component Soldiers suggests that extended family, especially parents, can serve as a major source of support not only for single Soldiers, but for those who are married or partnered as well. However, little attention has focused on understanding the influence of parents on Soldiers' psychological well-being.

This chapter begins by discussing the unique challenges and stressors National Guard Soldiers face when preparing for deployment. Next, we briefly summarize the theoretical and empirical literature guiding our study of the role of family in the well-being of National Guard Soldiers. We then present baseline, pre-deployment findings from the Readiness and Resilience in National Guard Soldiers (RINGS-2) study—an ongoing prospective study of a large cohort of National Guard Soldiers and their families. Key indicators of Soldiers' psychological well-being prior to deployment will be compared in married/partnered versus single Soldiers. The influence of family stressors, concerns, and social support, especially parental support, on Soldiers' pre-deployment psychological well-being will be examined.

United States National Guard and Reserve Component

The U.S. National Guard is a direct descendent of early colonial militias and remains a reserve component composed of state National Guard service members or "citizen Soldiers" who generally hold civilian jobs or attend school and serve part-time in the National Guard (Griffith, 2010). As a dual state-Federal force, each state National Guard may be called up for active duty by its respective state governor to assist in state emergencies such as natural disasters and civil disturbances. National Guard units may also be called up by Congress for active duty to supplement regular armed forces; however, this rarely occurred prior to the terrorist attacks of September 11, 2001. With ongoing conflicts in two combat theaters, the US military has relied on unprecedented deployments of National Guard/ Reserve Component troops to support these military operations. Since 2001, more than 630,000 National Guard/Reserve component service members (45 % of all OEF/OIF/OND veterans) deployed to Afghanistan or Iraq (VA Office of Public Health, 2011).

Mobilization and preparing for prolonged deployment to a hostile combat theater environment has been identified as one of the most stressful aspects of military life (Peebles-Kleiger & Kleiger, 1994). For National Guard Soldiers, such deployments violate commonly held expectations about the role of citizen Soldiers captured by the former recruiting slogan "one weekend a month, two weeks a year." For citizen Soldiers, preparing for deployment may be especially stressful because of the anticipated effects deployment may have on two important life domains: civilian employment and family. Unlike the active duty force, citizen Soldiers tend to rely primarily on civilian employment for their livelihood with military service supplementing their income (Griffith, 2010). When called up for active duty, deployment may cause financial hardship for some citizen Soldiers and their families if military income is less than the Soldier's civilian income. In a recent survey of 4,034 deployed National Guard Soldiers, Riviere, Kendall-Robbins, McGurk, Castro, and Hoge (2011) found that financial hardship and job loss were independently associated with poorer mental health even after controlling for level of combat exposure, gender, age, and rank.

Citizen soldiers are typically older than active duty Soldiers and are more likely to leave behind families when they deploy. Nearly half of enlisted Soldiers and two thirds of officers serving in the National Guard are married (Office of Army Demographics, 2010). In a retrospective, cross-sectional study of Veterans who had served in the first Gulf War (Vogt, Samper, King, King, & Martin, 2008) found that Veterans who had served in the National Guard/Reserve component were more likely to report family/relationship disruptions during the deployment than those who had served as active duty service members. Moreover, deployment may be especially stressful for citizen Soldiers and their families who may be less prepared for prolonged separations and may receive less support during deployments (Griffith, 2010).

Social Support and Soldier Well-Being

Hobfoll's Conservation of Resources theory offers a useful conceptual framework for understanding how families might contribute to Soldiers' resilience or psychological well-being across the deployment cycle. According to this theory, individuals are motivated to accumulate and conserve resources, while stressors have deleterious effects on psychological well-being to the extent that they threaten, decrease, or overwhelm existing physical, social, and psychological resources (Hobfoll, 1989, 2002). Guided by the Conservation of Resources framework, we conceptualize family support as a key social resource that can offset the stressors associated with mobilization and preparing for deployment. However, during the period prior to deployment, family members may face their own stressors as they prepare practically and emotionally for family separation and the anxiety of deployment (McCarroll, Hoffman, Grieger, & Holloway, 2005). Family members' responses to these stressors can be a source of additional strain and worry for the soldier (MacDermid, 2010). It is therefore possible that family can serve as an important social resource for deploying Soldiers, but also that families can serve as a source of stress or strain, particularly if the family is in a state of conflict or distress related to the anticipated deployment.

Our previous work has examined the impact of family support and Soldiers' concerns about their families on Soldiers' well-being before, during, and after deployment. In a longitudinal study of over 2,600 National Guard Soldiers assessed in-theater while deployed to Iraq and 1 year after returning home, we found family support during deployment was a significant protective factor for reduced risk of developing PTSD symptoms (Gewirtz, Polusny, DeGarmo, Khaylis, & Erbes, 2010). Using data from a separate prospective, longitudinal study of 522 National Guard Soldiers deployed to Iraq, we found Soldiers' perceptions of social support following deployment was a significant protective factor associated with lower risk of developing PTSD even after controlling for pre-deployment risk factors and combat exposure (Polusny et al., 2011). Soldiers' concerns about family, job and other life disruptions before and during deployment were also predictive of both PTSD and depression symptoms following deployment when controlling for other risk factors (Erbes, 2011).

Taken together, these findings suggest military families' responses to deployment-related stressors and challenges may be an important factor in Soldiers' psychological well-being across the deployment cycle. Previous studies also suggest lack of social support following deployment is an important resource loss that erodes Soldiers' resilience and increases vulnerability to PTSD. However, this resource loss hypothesis assumes social support was present prior to deployment and that the stresses and strains of deployment depleted this resource. Yet, studies examining the influence of family support on the well-being of National Guard Soldiers prior to deployment are lacking.

Relationship Status and Well-Being

The view that intimate partner relationships are a key source of social support that may buffer against stress associated with preparing for deployment is consistent with extensive family and sociological literatures documenting a wide range of psychological and health benefits associated with marriage. Studies have consistently found that being married is a protective factor associated with psychological well-being for most people (Gove, Hughes, & Style, 1983; Horwitz, White, & Howell-White, 1996; Kim & McKenry, 2002), and the social integration literature would suggest that some of the benefits of marriage extend to cohabitating and partnered individuals as well (Hughes & Gove, 1981; Kim & McKenry, 2002; Musick & Bumpass, 2011).

Within military populations, the few studies examining the influence of marital/intimate partner relationship status on Soldiers' psychological well-being have produced mixed results. While some studies have found higher rates of post-deployment mental health problems among married Soldiers (Lapierre, Schwegler, & LaBauve, 2007; Seal, Bertenthal, Miner, Sen, & Marmar, 2007), others have found single or unmarried Soldiers suffer greater mental health problems (Iversen et al., 2008). It is possible that the role of marriage as a protective factor for military personnel may vary across the deployment cycle. For example, being in a supportive intimate relationship may be associated with enhanced psychological well-being or greater mental treatment seeking following deployment. Consistent with this hypothesis, we found that National Guard Soldiers with the highest levels of PTSD following deployment were more likely to seek mental health care when they were in supportive intimate relationships (Meis, Barry, Erbes, Kehle, & Polusny, 2010). Yet, being married/partnered may also coincide with additional family stressors during mobilization that erode Soldiers' psychological well-being prior to deployment. Indeed, we have shown that Soldiers' worries and concerns about family well-being prior to and during deployment are predictive of Soldiers' mental health symptoms post-deployment (Erbes, 2011). Unfortunately, the majority of studies that have examined differences between single and married/partnered Soldiers have focused on service members' post-deployment mental health, and to our knowledge, the influence of relationship status on pre-deployment mental health has not been examined.

Soldiers and Their Parents

A growing body of literature has examined the impact of deployment on military families (MacDermid & Riggs, 2011). However, this research has primarily focused on the spouses and children of deployed service members, and studies examining the role of parents in the well-being of their deploying adult children are scant. Parent involvement in the lives of their adult children has increased over the past 30 years, with most parents and their adult children having frequent contact (Fingerman, Cheng, Tighe, Birditt, & Zarit, 2012). Given this frequent contact, it is not surprising that parents provide a critical source of emotional, financial, and practical support for their adult children (Fingerman et al., 2012), and increasingly this role of providing continued support is extending beyond the transition to young adulthood (Sage & Johnson, 2012). The literature on parent–adult child relationships shows that parental support is strongly associated with psychological well-being in adult children (Fingerman et al., 2012). Not only do parents continue to provide critical support to their adult children, but parents commonly continue to experience a wide variety of worries for their adult children including worries about their adult children's health, safety, relationships, and finances (Hay, Fingerman, & Lefkowitz, 2008). To our knowledge, few studies have examined the role of parents in the psychological well-being of service members.

Three studies have described the experiences and concerns of parents whose sons and daughters have been deployed. Orme and Kehoe (2011) reported findings from a qualitative study of 32 family members (n = 20 parents) of Australian Army Reservists. Family members were asked about their view of positive and negative effects of the deployment. Most (69 %) reported some positive views of the deployment, such as pride in their family member's service or maturation of the service member as a result of the deployment. Families also reported a number of challenges during the deployment, such as difficult or infrequent communication, feelings of loneliness while separated, and anxiety about uncertainty and lack of information.

As part of a larger study of the families of deployed Dutch military personnel, Andres and Moelker (2009) examined the experiences of 1,098 parents (55 % response rate) of Soldiers who had recently returned from either a peacekeeping mission to Bosnia-Herzegovina (19 %), combat deployment in Afghanistan (77 %), or other deployment (4 %). Regardless of whether the service member lived at home with parents or not, parents reported strong, cohesive, supportive relationships with their adult children. In addition, parents reported considerable worries about their deployed sons and daughters, with parents reporting significantly more worry when their adult child was deployed to a more hazardous mission area (e.g., Afghanistan).

Crow and Myers-Bowman (2011) conducted a qualitative, internet-based study of parents (n = 42) of US military service members (primarily active duty) deployed to OEF/OIF. Themes commonly reported by parents included strong reactions of fear, worry, and concern for their children's safety and well-being. Parents also described having mixed emotions about the deployment and a sense of pride in their child's military service. Finally, parents reported experiencing a number of challenges during the deployment including frustrations about communicating with their deployed children and difficulties with separation.

Recently, Worthen, Moos, and Ahern (2012) reported results of a qualitative study of 11 OEF/OIF Veterans living with their parents following separation from the military. In-depth interviews were conducted with Veterans about their experiences living with their parents. Themes commonly reported by recently returned OEF/OIF Veterans included both feeling appreciative of parents' instrumental and emotional support as well as experiencing conflicts with parents around readjusting to civilian life and redefining roles in the family.

Taken together, these studies suggest parents are an important source of support for their deployed sons and daughters, that parents feel pride for their children and see some benefit to deployment, but also that parents themselves may experience considerable distress and worry during their child's deployment. Additionally, these studies suggest conflicts may emerge in adult child–parent relationships as Veterans face the challenges of transitioning back to civilian life following deployment. Although an important first step in addressing the large gap in knowledge about parents of deployed service members, to the best of our knowledge, no published studies have examined the role of parents in predicting the psychological well-being of service members at any point during the deployment cycle.

In sum, theory and prior studies point to the importance of family in increasing available social resources for deploying National Guard Soldiers, and thus enhancing Soldiers' well-being before, during, and after deployments. Families may also be a potential source of stress and strain diminishing resources and potentially eroding Soldiers' resilience. Although married or partnered Soldiers may be particularly likely to benefit from family support, extended family, especially parents, may be an important resource for both single and partnered Soldiers. In this chapter, we will present initial findings from an ongoing longitudinal study of National Guard Soldiers and their families that address the following questions: (a) To what extent do the psychological benefits of marriage observed within the civilian literature extend to married/partnered National Guard Soldiers prior to deployment?, (b) To what extent does family context relate to the well-being of National Guard Soldiers prior to deployment?, and (c) To what extent do parents in particular play in the well-being of single compared to partnered Soldiers prior to deployment? We hypothesized that single National Guard Soldiers would show poorer well-being prior to deployment compared to partnered Soldiers. We hypothesized that Soldiers' pre-deployment family stressors and their concerns about the impact of deployment on their family would be predictive of Soldiers' pre-deployment well-being. Finally, we hypothesized parental support/frequency of communication with their adult children would be associated with greater Soldier well-being, especially among single Soldiers with parents experiencing more concerns and worries about their children.

The Readiness and Resilience in National Guard Soldiers Project

The Readiness and Resilience in National Guard Soldiers (RINGS) Project is an ongoing collaboration between the Minneapolis Veterans Affairs Health Care System, the University of Minnesota, and the Minnesota Army National Guard (MNARNG). With the support of the MNARNG, our research team has conducted a series of longitudinal studies assessing Soldiers and their family members before, during and after multiple deployments to OEF/OIF/OND (Erbes, 2011; Erbes et al., 2011; Gewirtz et al., 2010; Polusny et al., 2011). The overall goal of the RINGS research program is to generate information on individual differences (e.g., personality, history, and biological variables) and contextual-environmental factors (e.g., family functioning, occupational status) that promote resilience and recovery among National Guard service members following deployment. Information generated by the RINGS Project has been used to advance understanding of the needs and challenges of National Guard service members and to develop interventions that promote the well-being of service members and their families.

The RINGS-2 Study

One focus of the RINGS Project is the study of how contextual-family environment factors may influence resilience and recovery of National Guard service members. The RINGS-2 study is an ongoing prospective, longitudinal investigation of an entire National Guard Brigade Combat Team and their families that examines the impact of family well-being across the deployment cycle on Veterans' post-deployment mental health. The RINGS-2 study involves a cohort of 2,089 National Guard Soldiers who completed measures of baseline mental health functioning as well as individual/family risk and protective factors about 2–6 months prior to deployment to OEF or OND (Time 1). Spouses/partners of this cohort also completed a similar battery of baseline measures. Following this baseline assessment, Soldiers and spouses/partners were followed over a period of approximately 18 months. Spouses/partners were surveyed about 4 months (Time 2) and 9 months (Time 3) after Soldiers were deployed to OEF or OND. Coinciding with Time 3, in-theater data was collected from Soldiers deployed to OND using a secure website and online survey tool. Three months following Soldiers' return from deployment, both Soldiers and their spouses/partners will complete a final wave of data collection (Time 4). At Time 1, survey data was collected from the parents of a subset of deploying Soldiers. Parents were surveyed about their perceptions of support and communication with their deploying son or daughter as well as their expectations and concerns related to the upcoming deployment. This chapter will focus on findings from Soldiers' pre-deployment self-reports of mental health and family concerns as well as parents' self-reports.

Below, we present analyses and initial pre-deployment findings from the RINGS-2 study. We examine differences between single and partnered Soldiers on key indicators of psychological well-being prior to deployment. To elucidate factors influencing pre-deployment well-being for single versus partnered Soldiers, we examine the role of family as a source of potential support or strain. Additionally, our review of several lines of existing research suggests that parents may also play an important role in fostering the resilience of National Guard service members, especially among single Soldiers who are unable to reap the benefits of social support from a close intimate partner. We explore this hypothesis by examining whether parents' support and their worries/concerns are predictive of Soldiers' pre-deployment well-being.

Time 1 Data Collection

Details of the study procedures, sample, and measures collected at Time 1 are summarized here. The RINGS-2 study was approved by the Minneapolis VA Medical Center and University of Minnesota Institutional Review Boards as well as the relevant Army National Guard command. From January to August 2011, all National Guard Soldiers preparing to deploy to OEF or OND were invited to voluntarily participate in the study. Recruitment of participants took place during Family Preparation Academies, which are mandatory day-long pre-deployment training events held by the National Guard for service members and their families. The investigators provided a briefing to service members and their family members on the study, including a description of the purpose of the study, procedures, risks and benefits. Soldiers in a committed relationship were asked to nominate their spouse/partner to participate in the study, and all Soldiers were invited to nominate another family member (e.g., parent, step-parent) to complete a brief pre-deployment survey. Due to military regulations, Soldiers were not provided monetary compensation for their participation. However, all Soldiers were offered a small gift (padfolio and pen). Partners were compensated $20 for their participation at each wave of the larger study. Of the 2,688 Soldiers approached, 2,089 Soldiers completed a pre-deployment survey (78 % response rate). Of the 1,289 spouses or partners nominated by Soldiers, 1,067 partners completed a pre-deployment survey either in person at the Family Preparation Academy event or later by mail (83 % response rate). A total of 642 family members (527 of whom were parents) completed the brief pre-deployment survey at a Family Preparation Academy event.

Pre-deployment Soldier Cohort

The pre-deployment cohort of National Guard Soldiers (n = 2,089) was representative of the deploying Brigade Combat Team from which they were recruited. Given the high rate of soldier participation in the pre-deployment survey, it is not surprising that participants were quite similar in terms of demographics to the larger brigade. For example, 92 % of the pre-deployment participants vs. 94 % of the brigade were male; 89 % vs. 96 % were Caucasian, 90 % were enlisted (the same percentage of the brigade); 17 % vs. 12 % had a college degree or greater education; and 69 % vs. 60 % were deploying on their first deployment to OEF/OIF/OND.

The literature has suggested numerous definitions of the "single Soldier." In this chapter, we defined "single Soldiers" as never married, divorced or separated Soldiers not in an intimate partner relationship at Time 1. We defined "partnered Soldiers" as married, cohabitating, or engaged Soldiers as well as unmarried Soldiers in a committed intimate partner relationship at Time 1. Table 9.1 displays demographics characteristics of the pre-deployment cohort by relationship status (single versus partnered). Single Soldiers (21 %) were less likely than partnered Soldiers (36 %) to indicate they had been previously deployed to OEF/OIF/OND. However, among those who had previously deployed, there were no differences between single and partnered Soldiers in the mean level of prior combat exposure. A total of 265 (38 %) of single Soldiers and 262 (19 %) of partnered Soldiers had a parent complete the pre-deployment family survey, with the majority of parents (64 %) being mothers. The subsample of Soldiers with parents participating in the study differed from the larger pre-deployment Soldier cohort in several ways. Soldiers with a parent participating in the study were more likely than Soldiers without a participating parent to be younger, enlisted rank, female, and deploying

Table 9.1 Demographic characteristics of the pre-deployment soldier cohort by single versus partnered soldier relationship status

| | Soldier relationship status | | | | |
| | Single soldiers (N = 699) | | Partnered soldiers (N = 1,385) | | |
Characteristic	N	(%)	N	(%)	p
Age					<.0001
18–19	34	(4.99)	16	(1.18)	
20–24	344	(50.44)	381	(28.04)	
25–29	190	(27.86)	379	(27.89)	
30–39	86	(12.61)	359	(26.42)	
>40	28	(4.11)	224	(16.48)	
Gender					.0019
Female	73	(10.53)	91	(6.92)	
Male	620	(89.47)	1,283	(93.38)	
Rank					<.0001
Enlisted	656	(94.12)	1,205	(87.26)	
Officer/Warrant Officer	41	(5.88)	176	(12.74)	
Race					0.67
White	614	(88.60)	1,226	(89.23)	
Non-White	79	(11.40)	148	(10.77)	
Ethnicity					.64
Hispanic	24	(3.47)	55	(4.02)	
Non-Hispanic	658	(95.22)	1,299	(95.03)	
Education					<.0001
High school diploma	246	(35.50)	354	(25.73)	
Some college	379	(54.69)	730	(53.05)	
≥4 year college degree	67	(9.67)	292	(21.2)	
Prior OEF/OIF Deployment Status					<.0001
Yes	148	(21.17)	496	(35.81)	
No	551	(78.83)	889	(64.19)	

for the first time. While Soldiers with a participating parent perceived themselves to have greater social support than Soldiers without a parent participating in the study, there were no differences between groups in term of pre-deployment well-being on measures of depressive symptoms or alcohol misuse.

Measures

The pre-deployment soldier survey included a wide range of measures of potential risk and protective factors as well as measures of current well-being. Baseline mental health measures assessed symptoms of PTSD, depression, and alcohol misuse. PTSD was measured using the 17-item PTSD Checklist-Stressor Specific Version

(PCL-S; (Weathers, Litz, Herman, Huska, & Keane, 1993). Respondents were asked to rate the severity of each symptom during the past month on a Likert scale (1 = not at all to 5 = extremely, range = 17–85). The PCL-S has excellent test-retest reliability and high overall convergent validity (Blanchard, Jones-Alexander, Buckley & Forneris, 1996; Weathers et al., 1993). In the current sample, Cronbach's alpha was .96. Depression was measured using the 8-item depression scale from the Patient Health Questionnaire (PHQ-8) (Kroenke et al., 2009). Respondents were asked to rate the severity of each symptom occurring over the past 2 weeks on a four-point frequency scale (*Not at all, Several days, More than half the days, Nearly every day*). The PHQ-8 has demonstrated good psychometric properties (Kroenke et al., 2009; Kroenke, Spitzer, & Williams, 2001). In the current sample, Cronbach's alpha was .90. Alcohol misuse was assessed using the 10-item Alcohol Use Disorders Identification Test (AUDIT) developed by the World Health Organization (WHO) as a screening device for excessive drinking (Bush, Kivlahan, McDonell, Fihn, & Bradley, 1998). Respondents were asked to rate each item on a five-point scale (0 to 4), with most items scored in terms of frequency (i.e., *Never, Less than monthly, Monthly, Weekly, Daily or almost daily*). The AUDIT has demonstrated excellent reliability and sensitivities and specificities comparable to other self-report screening measures (Reinert & Allen, 2002). In the current sample, Cronbach's alpha was .85.

Soldiers' exposure to combat from previous deployments was assessed using the 15-item Combat Experiences scale from the Deployment Risk and Resilience Inventory (DRRI; King, King, & Vogt, 2003). The Combat Experiences scale was designed to assess objective events and circumstances with regard to stereotypical warzone experiences, such as firing upon enemies and witnessing casualties of war. Respondents were asked to indicate the frequency of occurrence (i.e., *Never, A few times over entire deployment, A few times each month, A few times each week, Daily or almost daily*) of each event during the most recent previous deployment. This scale has demonstrated good internal consistency (Vogt, Proctor, King, King, & Vasterling, 2008). In the current sample, Cronbach's alpha was .93. A modified version of the DRRI Concerns about Life and Family Disruptions scale assessed the extent to which Soldiers were worried or concerned about the impact of the pending deployment on their life and family. In the current sample, Cronbach's alpha was .90. A pre-deployment family stressors scale comprised of 15-items was used to identify whether respondents had experienced a range of stressful events (e.g., loved one passed away, financial problems, relationship infidelity) during the prior 3 months. Social support was assessed using the 19-item Medical Outcomes-Social Support Survey (MOS-SSS; Sherbourne & Stewart, 1991). Respondents were asked respondents to rate the frequency others were available to provide various components of functional support, including emotional, informational, tangible, affectionate, and positive social interaction. The MOS-SSS has demonstrated excellent psychometric properties (Sherbourne & Stewart, 1991). In the current sample, Chronbach's alpha was .98. A number of demographic variables were assessed including age, gender, race/ethnicity, and relationship status. Military demographics provided by Soldiers included current rank and prior deployment status.

As an extension of the larger RINGS-2 study, the pre-deployment family survey was designed to provide family members an opportunity to share their concerns related to their Soldier's upcoming deployment. As a proxy for the construct of parent support, frequency of communication in the parent–adult child relationship was assessed using a single item adapted from (Greenwell & Bengtson, 1997) that asked the parent to rate how frequently they typically communicated (i.e., in person, phone) with the Soldier prior to deployment. Parents' concerns about the Soldier were assessed using 9-items tapping a range of specific concerns (e.g., concerns about the Soldier's physical and emotional well-being, length of the deployment, and availability of supports for the Soldier) that parents may have related to their adult child's deployment. Parents were asked to rate each item on a 5-point Likert scale (1 = Not at all concerned to 5 = Very Concerned). In the current sample, Cronbach's alpha was .88.

Analyses and Results

Next, we summarize findings comparing single and partnered Soldiers on pre-deployment measures of psychological well-being, describe parents concerns about the deployment of their sons and daughters, and examine how parental support/frequency of communication and concerns may be associated with Soldiers' pre-deployment well-being. Overall, 6 % of the pre-deployment soldier cohort met criteria for probable PTSD, defined as a total PCL score of 50 or greater and endorsing DSM-IV diagnostic criteria by rating at least one intrusion symptom, three avoidance symptoms, and two hyperarousal symptoms at the moderate level (Arbisi et al., 2012; Hoge et al., 2004). Similarly, 6 % of Soldiers met criteria for probable depression, defined as a score of 10 or greater on the PHQ-8 (Kroenke et al., 2009). Nearly one quarter (23 %) of Soldiers met criteria for probable alcohol misuse, defined as a total AUDIT score of 8 or greater (Saunders, Aasland, Babor, de la Fuente, & Grant, 1993).

Single Versus Partnered Soldiers' Reports

We tested for unadjusted differences in baseline mental health (PTSD symptoms, depression symptoms, and alcohol misuse) as well as risk and protective factors by relationship status (single vs. partnered) using independent *t* tests. As shown in Table 9.2, partnered Soldiers had significantly higher PTSD and depression symptoms than single Soldiers. In contrast, single Soldiers reported significantly greater alcohol misuse than partnered Soldiers. Single Soldiers reported fewer pre-deployment family stressors and less concern about the impact of deployment on their life and family; however, single Soldiers also reported lower levels of perceived social support than partnered Soldiers.

Table 9.2 Soldier pre-deployment mental health concerns, social support, and family stressors by single versus partnered soldier relationship status

| | Soldier relationship status | | | | |
| | Single soldiers | | Partnered soldiers | | |
Mental health concerns	M	(SD)	M	(SD)	p
PTSD symptoms	24.68	(11.12)	26.24	(12.39)	.005
Depression symptoms	2.23	(3.73)	2.64	(3.92)	.03
Alcohol misuse	5.98	(4.99)	5.13	(4.40)	.0002
Social support	73.67	(17.54)	78.27	(15.57)	<.0001
Pre-deployment family stressors	1.12	(1.72)	1.27	(1.81)	.07
Pre-deployment life/family concerns	29.60	(12.14)	42.22	(12.61)	<.0001

Parental Support/Frequency of Communication and Concerns About Deployment

A subset of the Soldiers' parents completed a brief survey (n=527) prior to the deployment, with single (n=265) and partnered (n=262) Soldiers approximately equally represented. Most parents (63 %) reported at least daily or almost daily communication with their adult child, 22 % reported communicating a few times a week, and 11 % reported at least weekly communication. Parents of single Soldiers reported similar levels of communication with their adult child ($p=.47$) and similar levels of concerns about the deployment ($p=.09$) compared to parents of partnered Soldiers. In general, parents indicated being most concerned about their soldier's physical (i.e., being injured or killed) or emotional well-being, the length of their soldier's deployment (i.e., whether the deployment would be extended), and the availability of support (i.e., chaplains, mental health professionals) during and after deployment.

Predictors of Soldiers' Pre-deployment Mental Health

The prediction of pre-deployment mental health (PTSD symptoms, depression symptoms, and alcohol misuse) was assessed through a series of multiple linear regression analyses conducted separately for single Soldiers and partnered Soldiers. Variables were entered in four steps. In the first step, we entered Soldiers' demographic and military service characteristics (gender, age, military rank, and prior combat exposure). In the second step, we entered the MOS-Social Support total score, Pre-deployment Family Stressors total score, and the Concerns about Impact on Life/Family total score. In the third step, we entered parent reports of the extent of their communication with their soldier (Parent Support/Frequency of Communication) and the Parents Concerns about Deployment total score. To test for interaction between parent support and level of parent concern, we computed an interaction term that was entered in the final step. Following the recommendation of (Aiken & West, 1991), we centered the continuous Parents Concerns about

Deployment score, and used the centered score in computing the interaction term. Total scores on the PCL, PHQ-8, and AUDIT served as dependent variables. Table 9.3 displays the unstandardized and standardized regression coefficients (β) for each variable in the final model after entry of all variables.

For the prediction of pre-deployment PTSD symptom severity in single Soldiers, the final model yielded R = .48, F(10, 218) = 6.40, $p < .0001$). Significant independent predictors of pre-deployment PTSD symptoms in the final model included social support, pre-deployment family stressors, and the interaction between parent support/frequency of communication and parent concerns. After step 1, with all sociodemographic variables in the equation predicting PTSD symptoms for single Soldiers, $R^2 = 0.04$, F(4, 224) = 2.13, $p < .08$). After step 2, addition of social support, pre-deployment family stressors, and family concerns to the prediction of pre-deployment PTSD symptom severity resulted in a significant increase in R^2, $R^2 = 0.20$, F(3, 221) = 15.43, $p < .0001$ (R^2 change = 0.17). After step 3, parent support/ frequency of communication and parent concerns did not show significant main effects for pre-deployment PTSD severity, $R^2 = 0.21$, F(2, 219) = 1.11, $p < .33$). However, after step 4, results revealed a significant interaction between parent support/frequency of communication and parent concerns in the prediction of single Soldiers' pre-deployment PTSD severity, $R^2 = 0.23$, F(1, 218) = 4.38, $p < .04$ (R^2 change= 0.02). A significant interaction means that the effect of one variable (i.e., parent support) changes depending on the level of another variable (a moderator, i.e., level of parent concern). To further explore the interaction, we examined the association between parent support/frequency of communication and single Soldiers' PTSD severity separately for parents reporting high and low parent concern using a median split. Parent support/frequency of communication was associated with lower pre-deployment PTSD symptoms for parents high in parent concerns ($\beta = -.16$, $p = .08$); for those with low parent concerns, parent support/frequency of communication was not associated with single Soldiers' pre-deployment PTSD ($\beta = -.05$, $p = .60$).

For the prediction of pre-deployment PTSD symptom severity in partnered Soldiers, the final model yielded R = .49 ($R^2 = .24$), F(10, 213) = 6.68, $p < .0001$). The only significant independent predictors were social support, life/family concerns, and pre-deployment family stressors, accounting for 22.4 % of the variance in pre-deployment PTSD severity. After step 2, addition of social support, pre-deployment family stressors, and family concerns to the prediction of pre-deployment PTSD symptom severity resulted in a significant increase in R^2, R^2 change = 0.22, F(3, 216) = 21.14, $p < .0001$). In contrast to results for single Soldiers, greater family concerns was associated with pre-deployment PTSD symptoms for partnered parents. Additionally, the interaction between parent support/frequency of communication and parent concerns was associated with pre-deployment PTSD severity for single Soldiers but not partnered Soldiers. However, formal testing of the statistical significance of differences in the magnitude of effects across models predicting PTSD symptoms separately for single and partnered Soldiers revealed no differences in regression parameter estimates.

Table 9.3 Final Model: Multiple linear regression analyses predicting Soldiers' pre-deployment mental health in single versus partnered National Guard Soldiers

	PTSD						Depression						Alcohol misuse					
	Single soldiers			Partnered soldiers			Single soldiers			Partnered soldiers			Single soldiers			Partnered soldiers		
Predictor	B	SE	β	B	SE	β	B	SE	β	B	SE	β	B	SE	β	B	SE	β
Step 1																		
Gender	−2.68	2.00	−.08	1.14	2.04	.03	−.30	.73	−.03	.36	.70	.03	−1.76	.92	−.13†	−2.24	.79	−.18**
Age	.16	.18	.07	.11	.12	.06	.02	.07	.02	−.04	.04	−.06	−.10	.09	−.10	−.00	.05	−.01
Rank	−3.28	3.60	−.06	−.58	3.51	−.01	1.08	1.37	.05	−1.02	1.23	−.05	−1.30	1.73	−.05	−1.93	1.39	−.10
Prior combat exposure	.28	.15	.13†	.07	.10	.04	.01	.06	.02	−.01	.04	−.02	.13	.07	.14†	.05	.04	.07
Step 2																		
Social support	−.13	.04	−.19**	−.10	.05	−.12*	−.05	.02	−.19**	−.07	.02	−.22***	−.02	.02	−.08	−.03	.02	−.08
Pre-deployment life/family concerns	.08	.06	.08	.17	.06	.17**	−.02	.02	.05	.06	.02	.18**	−.01	.03	−.03	−.03	.02	−.08
Pre-deployment family stressors	2.36	.46	.32***	2.82	.49	.36***	.49	.17	.19**	.88	.17	.31***	.22	.21	.07	.40	.19	.13*
Step 3																		
Parent support	−1.33	.81	−.11	−.03	.87	−.00	−.26	.30	−.06	.04	.30	.01	.23	.38	.04	.25	.34	.05
Parent pre-deployment concerns	.31	.17	.22†	.06	.23	.03	.09	.06	.18	−.02	.08	−.04	.14	.08	.23†	.12	.09	.19
Step 4																		
Parent support × concerns interaction	−.21	.10	−.25*	.03	.14	.03	−.10	.04	−.32**	.05	.05	.13	−.07	.05	−.20	−.04	.05	−.12

†$p < .10$, *$p < 0.05$, **$p < 0.01$, ***$p < 0.001$

For the prediction of pre-deployment depression symptom severity in single Soldiers, the final model yielded R = .35 (R^2 = .12), F(10, 232) = 3.14, $p < .001$). Significant independent predictors of pre-deployment depression symptoms in the final model included social support, pre-deployment family stressors, and the interaction between parent support/frequency of communication and parent concerns. As with the prediction of PTSD for single Soldiers, none of the sociodemographic variables entered on step 1 were significantly associated with single Soldiers' pre-deployment depression, R^2 = 0.007, F(4, 238) = 0.41, $p < .80$). After step 2, addition of social support, pre-deployment family stressors, and family concerns to the prediction of pre-deployment depression symptom severity resulted in a significant increase in R^2, R^2 change = 0.08, F(3, 235) = 6.40, $p < .0001$. After controlling for these predictors, there were no main effects for parent support/frequency of communication or parent concerns on the prediction of pre-deployment depression symptom severity in single Soldiers, R^2 change = 0.01, F(2, 233) = 1.47, $p < .23$. However, there was a significant interaction between parent concerns and parent support/frequency of communication in the prediction of single Soldiers' depression symptoms, R^2 change = 0.03, F(1, 232) = 6.78, $p < .01$. Again, there was a trend toward greater parent support/frequency of communication being associated with lower pre-deployment depression symptoms for parents high in parent concerns ($\beta = -.11$, $p = .25$); parent support was not associated with single Soldiers' pre-deployment depression symptoms ($\beta = .01$, $p = .89$) among parents reporting low concerns.

For the prediction of pre-deployment depression in partnered Soldiers, the final model yielded R = .49 (R^2 = .24), F (10, 231) = 7.44, $p < .0001$). The only significant independent predictors of pre-deployment depression severity in partnered Soldiers were social support, pre-deployment family stressors, and family concerns, accounting for 23 % of the variance in pre-deployment depressive symptoms (R^2 change = 0.23, F(3, 234) = 23.34, $p < .0001$). Parent support/frequency of communication and parent concerns were not associated with pre-deployment depressive symptoms in partnered Soldiers, nor was the interaction between them. However, the regression coefficient for the interaction term was significantly greater ($p = .017$) in the single soldier model ($B = -.32$, $p < .01$) compared to the partnered soldier model ($B = .05$, ns).

For the prediction of pre-deployment alcohol misuse in single Soldiers, the final model yielded R = .26 (R^2 = .07), F(10, 233) = 1.65, $p < .10$). None of the variables entered in the final model were significant independent predictors; however, male gender, prior combat exposure, and parent's concerns approached significance. A different picture emerged for the partnered Soldiers. For the prediction of pre-deployment alcohol misuse in partnered Soldiers, the final model yielded R = .30 (R^2 = .09), F(10, 231) = 2.29, $p < .01$). Male gender and pre-deployment family stressors were significant independent predictors of partnered Soldiers' pre-deployment alcohol misuse. After accounting for sociodemographic variables, results showed that social support, pre-deployment family stressors, and family concerns accounted for an additional 3.0 % of the variance in pre-deployment alcohol misuse among partnered Soldiers. For step 2, R^2 change = 0.03, $F(3, 234) = 2.30$, $p < .08$). However, formal comparisons revealed that the effects of predictors across single and partnered soldier models were not statistically significant.

Discussion

Results from these initial analyses of pre-deployment data from the RINGS-2 study continue to highlight the important role that family, including parents, play in the psychological well-being of National Guard Soldiers. Compared to single Soldiers, partnered Soldiers reported significant greater pre-deployment PTSD and depression symptom severity. This may be due to the fact that partnered Soldiers also reported experiencing greater pre-deployment family stressors and worries about family disruptions during the mobilization and pre-deployment phase of the deployment. However, results of regression analyses showed that while pre-deployment family stressors played an important role in predicting PTSD and depression for both single and partnered Soldiers, Soldiers' concerns about the impact of deployment on life and family was associated with poorer pre-deployment psychological well-being for partnered Soldiers only. The finding that greater family concerns were uniquely associated with pre-deployment mental health for partnered Soldiers is consistent with findings from our previous work showing these family concerns continue to be predictive of Soldiers' post-deployment mental health (Erbes et al., 2011). It further highlights the possibility that family relationships can be both a source of support and strain in the context of a deployment.

Results also suggest that parental support may carry different implications for the well-being of single compared to partnered Soldiers. For single Soldiers, parental support/frequency of communication was associated with lower PTSD and depression symptoms, but only for those single Soldiers with parents who were high in concerns about the deployment. When parents were low in their concerns about the deployment, parental support/frequency of communication no longer had a protective effect on Soldiers' psychological well-being. It is possible that parents with greater concerns were more emotionally invested in their Soldier's well-being, more aware of how their Soldier was functioning, or more effective in offering support to their Solider. Further research is needed to examine the implications of this interaction. These results highlight the importance of parental support in the context of single Soldiers' well-being prior to deployment and are consistent with findings in the civilian literature showing parents continue to be an important source of social and emotional support for their adult children (Conger & Conger, 2002; Hay et al., 2008) especially when adult children are unmarried and not romantically involved with an intimate partner (Fingerman, Miller, Birditt, & Zarit, 2009). For partnered Soldiers, parental support/frequency of communication and parental concerns about the deployment were not associated with Soldiers' well-being and did not contribute to predicting PTSD or depression beyond the role of family and general social support.

In contrast to the greater risk for mental health symptoms among partnered compared to single Soldiers, the reverse was found for alcohol misuse. Results showed that single Soldiers reported significantly greater pre-deployment alcohol misuse compared to partnered Soldiers. This findings is consistent with an extensive literature showing greater alcohol misuse among single compared to partnered individuals (Leonard & Rothbard, 1999). In addition, we found that family contextual factors were differentially associated with alcohol misuse based on Soldiers' relationship status. Whereas pre-deployment family stressors were independently associated with alcohol misuse in partnered Soldiers, results revealed no significant independent predictors of alcohol misuse in single Soldiers. While family contextual factors may play an important role in single Soldiers' psychological well-being, families appear to have little association with single Soldiers' alcohol use.

While the RINGS-2 study represents an important advance in the study of Soldiers and their families across the deployment cycle, the findings reported here had several limitations. First, although we obtained pre-deployment Soldier data from nearly 80 % of the entire brigade, only a subset of Soldiers had parents who attended the Family Preparation Academies and were subsequently invited to participate in the study. Parents who attended these pre-deployment training events are likely more supportive and/or concerned than parents who did not attend these events. Additionally, participants in the sample were primarily Caucasian, and most Soldier-parent dyads consisted of sons and mothers. Thus, we are unable to examine race or gender differences in the role of parent support in Soldiers' pre-deployment well-being. Since the subsample of parents included in this study may be unique, findings on the role of parents on Soldiers' well-being should be considered preliminary and replication is needed. Second, our pre-deployment survey of parents was necessarily brief, and consequently our assessment of parental support/frequency of communication relied on a single item. Future studies should incorporate more comprehensive measures of the quality of parent–adult child relationships (Pitzer, Fingerman, & Lefkowitz, 2011). Because of the brevity of the survey, we were unable to assess a number of important factors, such as parent well-being, that may contribute to the impact of family context on soldier well-being. Third, the cross-sectional nature of these findings precludes making inferences regarding causality or the direction of the observed associations.

Despite these limitations, this study advances the literature on single and partnered Soldiers and their families. To our knowledge, this is the first study to examine the relationship between parental support/frequency of communication and Soldier well-being prior to deployment using both Soldier and parent reports. Overall, the current findings support the hypothesis that family can serve as both a source of support and strain for deploying Soldiers, depending on Soldiers' current relationship status. On the one hand, parents play an important role in supporting single Soldiers as they are mobilized and prepare for deployment. This seems to be especially the case when parents themselves have greater concerns about the deployment and the impact of the deployment on the Soldiers' well-being. On the other hand, families can be the source of stressors, worries and concerns, especially for married or partnered Soldiers, which may begin to erode Soldiers' well-being even prior to deployment.

These initial findings from the RINGS-2 study highlighting the importance of parents as part of the family context of Soldiers suggest that the Department of Defense, VA, military family organizations, and researchers should consider broadening their focus on military families to include the parents of Soldiers. Future research is needed to understand the needs and concerns of parents of deploying Soldiers and how parents may influence Soldiers' mental health and resilience across the deployment cycle. Consistent with the overall goals of the RINGS Project, we will continue to track Soldier and family well-being over time during and after the current deployment. Thus, we will be able to examine the implications of parental contact and support once Soldiers return from this deployment, and to further evaluate the influence of family well-being across the deployment cycle on Soldiers' resilience.

Acknowledgements This research was supported by a Service Directed Research (SDR) grant from the Department of Veterans Affairs Health Services Research & Development (SDR #398). This material is the result of work supported with resources and the use of facilities at the Minneapolis VA Health Care System, Minneapolis, MN. The authors would like to acknowledge Lieutenant Colonel Barbara O'Reilly, Major Aaron Krenz, and the Minnesota Army National Guard for their ongoing support of the Readiness and Resilience in National Guard Soldiers (RINGS) Project.

References

Aiken, L. S., & West, S. G. (1991). *Multiple regression: Testing and interpreting interactions.* Thousand Oaks, CA: Sage.

Andres, M. D., & Moelker, R. (2009). Parent's voice. The intergenerational relationship, worry, appraisal of the deployment, and support among parents of deployed personnel. In G. Caforio (Ed.), *Military sociology. Essays in honor of Charles C Moskos* (Vol. 2, pp. 119–145). Bingley: Emerald.

Arbisi, P., Kaler, M. E., Kehle, S., Erbes, C., Polusny, M. A., & Thuras, P. (2012). The predictive validity of the PTSD Checklist in a non-clinical sample of combat exposed National Guard troops. *Psychological Assessment, 24*(4), 1034–1040.

Blanchard, E. B., Jones-Alexander, J., Buckley, T. C., & Forneris, C. A. (1996). Psychometric properties of the PTSD Checklist (PCL). *Behaviour Research and Therapy, 34,* 669–673.

Bush, K., Kivlahan, D. R., McDonell, M. B., Fihn, S. D., & Bradley, K. A. (1998). The AUDIT alcohol consumption questions (AUDIT-C): An effective brief screening test for problem drinking. *Archives of Internal Medicine, 158,* 1789–1795.

Cohen, S., & Wills, T. A. (1985). Stress, social support, and the buffering hypothesis. *Psychological Bulletin, 98,* 310–357.

Conger, R. D., & Conger, K. J. (2002). Resilience in Midwestern families: Selected findings from the first decade of a prospective, longitudinal study. *Journal of Marriage and Family, 64,* 361–373.

Cozza, S. J., Chun, R. S., & Polo, J. A. (2005). Military families and children during Operation Iraqi Freedom. *Psychiatric Quarterly, 76,* 371–378.

Crow, J. R., & Myers-Bowman, K. S. (2011). "A fear like I've never felt": Experiences of parents whose adult children deployed to combat zones. *Marriage & Family Review, 47,* 164–195.

Erbes, C. R. (2011). Couple functioning and PTSD in returning OIF soldiers: Preliminary findings from the Readiness and Resilience in National Guard Soldiers project. In S. M. Wadsworth & D. Riggs (Eds.), *Risk and resilience in U.S. military families* (pp. 47–67). New York: Springer.

Erbes, C. R., Meis, L. A., Polusny, M. A., & Compton, J. S. (2011). Couple adjustment and post-traumatic stress disorder symptoms in National Guard veterans of the Iraq war. *Journal of Family Psychology, 25*, 479–487.

Fingerman, K. L., Cheng, Y., Tighe, L., Birditt, K. S., & Zarit, S. (2012). Relationships between young adults and their parents. In A. Booth, S. L. Brown, N. S. Landale, W. D. Manning, & S. M. McHale (Eds.), *Early adulthood in a family context* (pp. 59–85). New York: Springer.

Fingerman, K. L., Cheng, Y., Wesselmann, E. D., Zarit, S., Furstenberg, F., & Birditt, K. S. (2012). Helicopter parents and landing pad kids: Intense parental support of grown children. *Journal of Marriage and Family, 74*, 880–896.

Fingerman, K., Miller, L., Birditt, K., & Zarit, S. (2009). Giving to the good and the needy: Parental support of grown children. *Journal of Marriage and Family, 71*, 1220–1233.

Gewirtz, A. H., Polusny, M. A., DeGarmo, D. S., Khaylis, A., & Erbes, C. R. (2010). Posttraumatic stress symptoms among National Guard soldiers deployed to Iraq: Associations with parenting behaviors and couple adjustment. *Journal of Consulting and Clinical Psychology, 78*, 599–610.

Gove, W. R., Hughes, M., & Style, C. B. (1983). Does marriage have positive effects on the psychological well-being of the individual? *Journal of Health and Social Behavior, 24*, 122–131.

Greenwell, L., & Bengtson, V. L. (1997). Geographic distance and contact between middle-aged children and their parents: The effects of social class over 20 years. *Journal of Gerontology B: Psychological Sciences and Social Sciences, 52*, S13–S26.

Griffith, J. (2010). Citizens coping as soldiers: A review of deployment stress symptoms among reservists. *Military Psychology, 22*, 176–206.

Hay, E. L., Fingerman, K. L., & Lefkowitz, E. S. (2008). The worries adult children and their parents experience for one another. *The International Journal of Aging & Human Development, 67*, 101–127.

Hobfoll, S. E. (1989). Conservation of resources. A new attempt at conceptualizing stress. *American Psychologist, 44*, 513–524.

Hobfoll, S. E. (2002). Social and psychological resources and adaptation. *Review of General Psychology, 6*, 307–324.

Hoge, C. W., Castro, C. A., Messer, S. C., McGurk, D., Cotting, D. I., & Koffman, R. L. (2004). Combat duty in Iraq and Afghanistan, mental health problems, and barriers to care. *New England Journal of Medicine, 351*, 13–22.

Horwitz, A. V., White, H. R., & Howell-White, S. (1996). Becoming married and mental health: A longitudinal study of a cohort of young adults. *Journal of Marriage and Family, 58*, 895–907.

Hughes, M., & Gove, W. R. (1981). Living alone, social integration, and mental health. *American Journal of Sociology, 87*, 48–74.

Iversen, A. C., Fear, N. T., Ehlers, A., Hacker, H. J., Hull, L., Earnshaw, M., et al. (2008). Risk factors for post-traumatic stress disorder among UK Armed Forces personnel. *Psychological Medicine, 38*, 511–522.

Kim, H. K., & McKenry, P. C. (2002). The relationship between marriage and psychological well-being: A longitudinal analysis. *Journal of Family Issues, 23*, 885–911.

King, D. W., King, L. A., & Vogt, D. S. (2003). *Manual for the Deployment Risk and Resilience Inventory (DRRI): A collection of measures for studying deployment-related experiences of military veterans.* Boston, MA: National Center for Posttraumatic Stress Disorder.

Kroenke, K., Spitzer, R. L., & Williams, J. B. (2001). The PHQ-9: Validity of a brief depression severity measure. *Journal of General Internal Medicine, 16*, 606–613.

Kroenke, K., Strine, T. W., Spitzer, R. L., Williams, J. B., Berry, J. T., & Mokdad, A. H. (2009). The PHQ-8 as a measure of current depression in the general population. *Journal of Affective Disorders, 114*, 163–173.

Lapierre, C. B., Schwegler, A. F., & LaBauve, B. J. (2007). Posttraumatic stress and depression symptoms in soldiers returning from combat operations in Iraq and Afghanistan. *Journal of Traumatic Stress, 20*, 933–943.

Leonard, K. E., & Rothbard, J. C. (1999). Alcohol and the marriage effect. *Journal of Studies on Alcohol, 13*, 139–146.

MacDermid, S. M. (2010). Family risk and resilience in the context of war and terrorism. *Journal of Marriage and Family, 72*, 537–556.

MacDermid, S., & Riggs, D. S. (2011). *Risk and resilience in U.S. military families.* New York: Springer.

McCarroll, J. E., Hoffman, K. J., Grieger, T. A., & Holloway, H. C. (2005). Psychological aspects of deployment and reunion. In P. W. Kelley (Ed.), *Military preventive medicine: Mobilization and deployment* (pp. 1395–1424). Falls Church, VA: Surgeon General of the Army.

Meis, L. A., Barry, R. A., Erbes, C. R., Kehle, S. M., & Polusny, M. A. (2010). Relationship adjustment, PTSD symptoms, and treatment utilization among coupled National Guard solliders deployed to Iraq. *Journal of Family Psychology, 24*, 560–567.

Musick, K., & Bumpass, L. L. (2011). *Re-examining the case for marriage: Union formation and changes in well-being* (California Center for Population Research On-Line Working Paper Series, PWP-CCPR-2006-003). Los Angeles, CA: California Center for Population Research.

Office of Army Demographics. (2010). *FY10 Army profile.* Washington, DC: Department of the Army.

Orme, G. J., & Kehoe, E. J. (2011). Left behind but not left out? Perceptions of support for family members of deployed reservists. *Australian Defence Force Journal, 185*, 26–33.

Peebles-Kleiger, M. J., & Kleiger, J. H. (1994). Re-integration stress for Desert Storm families: Wartime deployments and family trauma. *Journal of Traumatic Stress, 7*, 173–194.

Pitzer, L., Fingerman, K. L., & Lefkowitz, E. S. (2011). Development of the parent adult relationship questionnaire (PARQ). *International Journal of Aging and Human Development, 72*, 111–135.

Polusny, M. A., Erbes, C. R., Murdoch, M., Arbisi, P. A., Thuras, P., & Rath, M. B. (2011). Prospective risk factors for new-onset post-traumatic stress disorder in National Guard soldiers deployed to Iraq. *Psychological Medicine, 41*, 687–698.

Reinert, D. F., & Allen, J. P. (2002). The Alcohol Use Disorders Identification Test (AUDIT): A review of recent research. *Alcoholism: Clinical and Experimental Research, 26*, 272–279.

Riviere, L. A., Kendall-Robbins, A., McGurk, D., Castro, C. A., & Hoge, C. W. (2011). Coming home may hurt: Risk factors for mental ill health in US reservists after deployment in Iraq. *British Journal of Psychiatry, 198*, 136–142.

Sage, R. A., & Johnson, M. K. (2012). Extending and expanding parenthood: Parental support to young children. *Sociology Compass, 6*, 256–270.

Saunders, J. B., Aasland, O. G., Babor, T. F., de la Fuente, J. R., & Grant, M. (1993). Development of the Alcohol Use Disorders Identification Test (AUDIT): WHO collaborative project on early detection of persons with harmful alcohol consumption–II. *Addiction, 88*, 791–804.

Seal, K. H., Bertenthal, D., Miner, C. R., Sen, S., & Marmar, C. (2007). Bringing the war back home: Mental health disorders among 103,788 US veterans returning from Iraq and Afghanistan seen at Department of Veterans Affairs facilities. *Archives of Internal Medicine, 167*, 476–482.

Sherbourne, C. D., & Stewart, A. L. (1991). The MOS social support survey. *Social Science and Medicine, 32*, 705–714.

VA Office of Public Health. (2011). *Analysis of VA health care utilization among Operation Enduring Freedom (OEF), Operation Iraqi Freedom (OIF), and Operation New Dawn (OND) Veterans.* Arlington, VA: Department of Veterans Affairs.

Vogt, D. S., Proctor, S. P., King, D. W., King, L. A., & Vasterling, J. J. (2008). Validation of scales from the deployment risk and resilience inventory in a sample of Operation Iraqi Freedom Veterans. *Assessment, 15*, 391–403.

Vogt, D. S., Samper, R. E., King, D. W., King, L. A., & Martin, J. A. (2008). Deployment stressors and posttraumatic stress symptomatology: Comparing active duty and National Guard/Reserve personnel from Gulf War I. *Journal of Traumatic Stress, 21*, 66–74.

Weathers, F. W., Litz, B. T., Herman, D. S., Huska, J. A., & Keane, T. M. (1993). The PTSD Checklist (PCL): Reliability, validity, and diagnostic utility. In F. W. Weathers, B. T. Litz, D. S. Herman, J. A. Huska, & T. M. Keane (Eds.), Paper presented at the Annual Meeting of the International Society for Traumatic Stress Studies. San Antonio, TX.

Wiens, T. W., & Boss, P. (2006). Maintaining family resiliency before, during, and after military separation. In C. A. Castro, A. B. Adler, & T. W. Britt (Eds.), *Military life: The psychology of serving in peace and combat* (pp. 13–38). Westport, CT: Praeger Security International.

Worthen, M., Moos, R., & Ahern, J. (2012). Iraq and Afghanistan veterans' experiences living with their parents after separation from the military. *Contemporary Family Therapy, 34,* 362–375.

Chapter 10
Towards a Better Understanding of Post-Deployment Reintegration

Donald R. McCreary, Jennifer M. Peach, Ann-Renée Blais, and Deniz Fikretoglu

Abstract Although researchers have examined the 6–12 month period after which service members return home from an overseas deployment, their studies often focus on members' mental and physical health (e.g., whether or not the member is displaying symptoms of post-traumatic stress disorder or a minor traumatic brain injury). In this chapter, we take a different approach to the post-deployment reintegration period, focusing instead on the positive and negative experiences and perceptions associated with three domains that returning service members have told us are important: reintegrating back into a garrison work environment, reintegrating back into one's family, and integrating the deployment experiences into one's personal identity. In addition, the chapter describes the development and validation of the Post-Deployment Reintegration Scale (PDRS), which we created to support our research, as well as the construction and use of norms for the PDRS. Finally, we

D.R. McCreary, Ph.D. (✉)
Psychology Group, Individual Behavior and Performance Section,
Defence Research and Development Canada – Toronto,
1133 Sheppard Avenue West, Toronto, ON, Canada M3C 2K9

Individual Behavior and Performance Section, Defence Research and Development
Canada – Toronto, 1133 Sheppard Avenue West, Toronto, ON, Canada, M3C 2K9
e-mail: Don.McCreary@drdc-rddc.gc.ca

J.M. Peach, Ph.D.
Director General Military Personnel Research & Analysis, Department of National Defence,
285 Coventry Road, Ottawa, ON, Canada K1K 3X6
e-mail: Jennifer.Peach@forces.gc.ca

A.-R. Blais, Ph.D. • D. Fikretoglu, Ph.D.
Psychology Group, Individual Behavior and Performance Section,
Defence Research and Development Canada – Toronto,
1133 Sheppard Avenue West, Toronto, ON, Canada M3C 2K9
e-mail: Ann-Renee.Blais@drdc-rddc.gc.ca; Deniz.Fikretoflu@drdc-rddc.gc.ca

S. MacDermid Wadsworth and D.S. Riggs (eds.), *Military Deployment and its Consequences for Families*, Risk and Resilience in Military and Veteran Families,
DOI 10.1007/978-1-4614-8712-8_10, © Springer Science+Business Media New York 2014

focus on single service members, looking at the degree to which marital status and whether or not someone has dependents influence the post-deployment reintegration experiences and perceptions captured by the PDRS.

Keywords Post-deployment reintegration • Family reintegration • Work reintegration • Personal reintegration • Single-service members

Background

The military deployment cycle is often thought of as a three-stage process. The initial part is the pre-deployment stage, where service members train for the upcoming mission. This training period can last upwards of 12 months and may often take members away from home for extended periods of time. The deployment stage covers the period during which members are in the theater of operations. Deployments tend to be 6–15 months long (depending on the mission, the country deploying the service members, and their role on those deployments). Finally, there is the post-deployment reintegration period, where returning military personnel re-establish themselves back into both their regular jobs and their prior social networks, as well as put their deployment experiences into perspective. The reintegration process starts as soon as service members arrive back home and may last several months (Thompson & Gignac, 2002).

The challenges faced by individuals during the post-deployment reintegration period can be persistent and stressful (e.g., Bartone, Adler, & Vaitkus, 1998; Orsillo, Roemer, Litz, Ehlich, & Friedman, 1998; Wilson & Krauss, 1985). Indeed, researchers have recently shown that individuals returning from a deployment are at increased risk for a wide range of mental health concerns, including PTSD (Basham, 2008; Ford et al., 2001; Hoge et al., 2004; Wain, Bradley, Nam, Waldrep, & Cozza, 2005), depression and anxiety (Adler, Bliese, McGurk, Hoge, & Castro, 2009; Morissette et al., 2011; Wright, Foran, Wood, Eckford, & McGurk, 2012), alcohol and drug use (Jacobson et al., 2008; Tucker, Sinclair, & Thomas, 2005), and both suicide and alcohol-related death (Hendin & Pollinger-Haas, 1991; Thoresen & Mehlum, 2004). Additional research suggests that returning service members are at greater risk for increased levels of aggression (McCarroll et al., 2000; Wright et al., 2012), reckless driving and danger seeking (Killgore et al., 2008), marital problems (Basham, 2008; Sayers, 2011), burnout (Harrington, Bean, Pintello, & Mathews, 2001; Hourani, Williams, & Kress, 2006; Tucker et al., 2005), difficulty finding meaning in life (Bowling & Sherman, 2008), and negative attitudes towards work (Yerkes & Holloway, 1996). Data also have shown that rates of mental health symptoms tend to increase throughout the post-deployment reintegration period (e.g., Bliese, Wright, Adler, Thomas, & Hoge, 2007; Milliken, Auchterlonie, & Hoge, 2007; Thomas et al., 2010).

The majority of the research studying the reintegration stage of the deployment cycle has typically focused on the links between stressors or trauma experienced during the members' deployment and post-deployment clinical issues or psychosocial problems. In comparison, studies focusing on the positive impacts of deployment on reintegration are less common. Still, researchers have found that deployment can have several benefits, including exposing members to new environments, heightening their world awareness, and developing new strengths and skills (Basham, 2008). Deployment also has been associated with a renewed sense of purpose and meaning *vis a vis* members' jobs and life in general (e.g., Litz, Orsillo, Friedman, Ehlich, & Batres, 1997; Maguen, Vogt, King, King, & Litz, 2006; Mehlum, 1995), happiness when reconnected with their families (Pincus, House, Christenson, & Adler, 2001), and strengthened relationships with others (Newby et al., 2005). Similarly, research on post-traumatic growth indicates that combat exposure can lead to both costs and growth (Aldwin, Levenson, & Spiro, 1994; Tedeschi & Calhoun, 1996), while Adler, Zamorski, and Britt (2011) suggest that, in addition to emotional, cognitive, and social benefits, reintegration can have both positive and negative outcomes in the physical domain. Positive physical outcomes can include enjoying the comforts of home again, relief from extreme temperatures, and the ability to prepare a meal, while negative outcomes can include hypervigilance to threat and difficulty sleeping.

In 2002, a group of researchers at Defence Research and Development Canada's Toronto laboratory (including the third and first authors of this chapter) began a more in-depth study of the post-deployment reintegration stage. At that time, there was a lot less research on post-deployment reintegration, and much of it was focused on studying the adverse clinical consequences of deployment (e.g., Orsillo et al., 1998). Over the next several years, we developed a general model outlining the prominent non-clinical aspects of post-deployment reintegration, a measurement tool to assess the model (Blais, Thompson, & McCreary, 2009), as well as norms for the measure (Fikretoglu & McCreary, 2010) so that users had an effective way to communicate information about the aspects of post-deployment reintegration the model and its measure assessed. The primary purpose of this chapter is to describe this program of research. Additionally, we will focus on single service members, with and without children, in order to better understand their experiences in the post-deployment reintegration period.

Developing a Model of PDR

When thinking about service members' post-deployment reintegration experiences, our original team (Blais, Thompson, Febbraro, Pickering, & McCreary, 2003) was guided by two overarching goals. First, we felt that our understanding of post-deployment reintegration and its effects on individual service members should not be focused solely on the negative, adverse, or clinical aspects of this period. That is, members' experiences can be both positive and negative. Focusing on only one of these two dimensions can seriously misrepresent both the content and process of the reintegration stage of the deployment cycle.

Our second goal was to highlight the fact that reintegration was not a unidimensional construct. In an initial study led by one of our original team members (Thompson & Gignac, 2002), focus groups were conducted with Canadian Forces

(CF) members returning from an overseas deployment. Findings suggested that there were four main themes associated with post-deployment reintegration: (1) reintegrating back into one's work environment; (2) reintegrating back into one's family; (3) reintegrating back into one's Western, privileged culture; and (4) dealing personally with one's deployment experiences.

Thus, in our model, service members' perceptions and experiences of their post-deployment reintegration period should be focused on both the positive and negative aspects of reintegrating in each of these domains. However, as we note in the next section, it was difficult to operationalize the cultural reintegration dimension. After several attempts to develop and validate items that addressed cultural reintegration, we decided to drop that domain from our model of post-deployment reintegration, leaving only the work, family, and personal domains (although some items were included in the two personal domain subscales that reflect the intersection between the personal and the cultural aspects of post-deployment reintegration; see Blais et al., 2009, for a more in-depth discussion of why these aspects of the model are salient).

Development and Validation of the Post-Deployment Reintegration Scale

To study post-deployment reintegration from the context of our model, we developed the Post-Deployment Reintegration Scale (PDRS). This was done using an iterative process, over a series of studies.[1] A brief overview of these studies and their findings are presented in this section. For more detailed information, see Blais et al. (2009).

Post-Deployment Reintegration Scale: Development

The initial version of the PDRS contained 64 positive and negative items in the four initial domains: Work, Family, Personal, and Cultural (Blais et al., 2003). However, an exploratory factor analysis (EFA) on the responses from 374 CF personnel who

---

[1] To get the large sample sizes of deployed CF members required to develop and validate the PDRS, we received permission to include the scale in the CF's post-deployment Human Dimensions of Operations (HDO) survey, a large, regularly given omnibus set of questionnaires designed to give CF commanders a broad overview of a wide range of potential post-deployment personnel issues (e.g., Brown, 2005a, 2005b, 2005c). Including the PDRS in the post-deployment HDO survey was desirable for two reasons. First, our team felt that individuals needed time to adjust; time to develop post-deployment reintegration-related experiences and perceptions. As we had little information about how that process worked, we felt that the timing provided by the HDO survey was an appropriate starting point. Second, the HDO survey also included other measures that we could use to assess the validity of the PDRS.

had returned from a deployment to Afghanistan 6 months earlier suggested that there was a fair degree of overlap between the personal and cultural dimensions of the PDRS. To address this issue, we worked with a subject matter expert (i.e., a senior Army officer with numerous overseas deployments) to refine several existing items and to add additional ones. The revised version of the PDRS had a total of 81 items and was administered to 474 CF service members who had also deployed to Afghanistan approximately 6 months earlier. The findings from an analysis with a subsample of that data revealed, again, that there were statistical problems with the cultural reintegration items. Thus, we decided to drop the cultural domain from our model, moving the items that best reflected the intersection between the personal and cultural domains into the personal reintegration domain. We then used a second subsample to test the remaining six-factor, three domain (positive and negative dimensions of work, family, and personal post-deployment reintegration) model. The EFA revealed the expected latent factor structure and Cronbach alpha estimates of internal consistency ranged between .78 and .91.

However, because multivariate statistics can sometimes be difficult to replicate, we felt it was important to be rigorous and repeat our EFA in an independent sample of 519 CF members who had deployed to Afghanistan. The sample was randomly split into two, and these two new EFAs both replicated the earlier one, showing that the six-factor, three domain model is best represented in the PDRS. In addition, those six scales showed appropriate levels of internal consistency, with Cronbach alphas ranging from .78 to .89.

Given these findings, we were confident that the item structure of the PDRS matched our post-deployment reintegration model. The final version of the PDRS (which we sometimes refer to as the Army PDRS, because it was developed and validated solely on Army personnel) can be found in Table 10.1. In that Table, the items are organized by their subscales, though the item numbers to their left reflect their actual position in the scale when it is presented to participants.

Post-Deployment Reintegration Scale: Validation

In addition to the construct validation offered by the exploratory factor analyses, Blais et al. (2009, Study 3) also reported findings from analyses that examined the correlations between the PDRS subscales and several personal and organizational variables (described below) which were logically expected to be related to the PDRS model. With regard to psychological well-being, findings showed that, as expected, higher scores on the negative work, family, and personal aspects of post-deployment reintegration were correlated with higher levels of self-reported symptoms of depression and post-traumatic stress disorder.

Service members who reported higher levels of overall deployment-related stress also reported higher levels of negative family and personal reintegration experiences and perceptions. The deployment-related stress measure used in the HDO survey at that time could also be broken down into five subscales: military career,

Table 10.1 Items and instructions for the post-deployment reintegration scale (Blais et al., 2009)

	Scale instructions: There are no right or wrong answers to the following questions. People may have differing views, and we are interested in what *your* experiences are. **Please indicate the extent to which each of the statements below is true for you since returning from [insert deployment name]:**
Item	**Work Positive**
1.	I am glad I went on the tour.
7.	I am applying job-related skills I learned during my deployment.
10.	I am better able to deal with stress.
20.	I feel I am a better soldier.
27.	I am proud of having served overseas.
34.	I have developed stronger friendships.
Item	**Work Negative**
5.	I find military bureaucracy more frustrating.
12.	I feel my current work duties are less meaningful.
17.	Day to Day work tasks seem tedious.
22.	Garrison life has been boring.
30.	I feel a lower sense of accomplishment at work.
32.	I have considered leaving the military.
Item	**Family Positive**
2.	I feel closer to my family.
8.	I have become more responsive to my family's needs.
13.	I have become more involved in my family relationships.
23.	I have realized how important my family is to me.
28.	I have a greater willingness to be with my family.
36.	I more fully appreciate the time I spend with my family.
Item	**Family Negative**
4.	There has been tension in my family relationships.
11.	I feel the tour has had a negative impact on my personal life.
15.	I feel my family has had difficulty understanding me.
18.	The tour has put a strain on my family life.
25.	Getting back "into sync" with family life has been hard.
31.	I feel my family resented my absence.
Item	**Personal Positive**
6.	I am more aware of problems in the world.
14.	I have a better understanding of other cultures.
19.	I have realized how well off we are in Canada.
24.	I have a greater appreciation of the value of life.
29.	I have a greater appreciation of the conveniences taken for granted in Canada.
33.	I more fully appreciate the rights and freedoms taken for granted in Canada.
Item	**Personal Negative**
3.	Putting the events of the tour behind me has been tough.
9.	I have had difficulty reconciling the devastation I saw overseas with life in Canada.
16.	I have been confused about my experiences during the tour.
21.	It has been hard to get used to being in Canada again.
26.	Being back in Canada has been a bit of a culture shock.
35.	Focusing on things other than the tour has been difficult.

work, family, combat, and external conditions. The findings showed that the negative PDRS scales tended to be correlated with most aspects of deployment stress and, as might be expected, were more strongly associated with deployment stress than the positive subscales from the PDRS.

The PDRS subscales also were correlated with several organizational measures, in logically predictable ways. For example, higher Work Positive scores on the PDRS were correlated with higher levels of positive job-related affect. Furthermore, this correlation was higher than those between the Family Positive scale and positive job-related affect, as well as between the Personal Positive scale and positive job-related affect. Similarly, higher scores on the negative PDRS subscales, especially the Work Negative PDRS scores, were correlated with higher levels of negative job-related affect. Work Negative PDRS scores also were correlated with an increased likelihood of wanting to leave the CF in the next year.

We have also explored the consistency of responses to the PDRS over time (McCreary, Blais, & Thompson, 2008). This is commonly done in the development of self-report questionnaires because many psychological constructs (e.g., personality traits) are expected to be stable over time. Our assumption for the PDRS was not one of stability, but rather one of change and adaptation. That is, we expected there to be statistically significant differences in PDRS scores over time, especially as service members started to feel more comfortable in their traditional environments, and re-established their relationships and routines. One hundred fourteen CF personnel returning from a deployment to Afghanistan completed the PDRS at approximately 5 months post-reintegration, and again approximately 6 months later. Paired sample t-tests showed no significant differences between the 5- and 11-month scores on any of the six PDRS subscales. Ongoing work is exploring why this might be the case. For example, it may be that some people's post-deployment reintegration experiences and perceptions improve over time, while others may get worse or stay the same. In a sample such as the one we described here, if there are different subsets of people experiencing these three reintegration processes, those positive and negative changes across groups may average out statistically to no change, effectively masking an important phenomenon. If these three groups exist, we hope to be able to identify them and study the reasons for the differences.

Post-Deployment Reintegration Scale: Updated Findings

The previous section of this chapter summarized our previously published findings from the initial development and validation of the PDRS (Blais et al., 2009). Since then, over 3,000 PDRS data points have been generated. Those additional cases have allowed us to develop a more detailed understanding of the PDRS. In this section we will be presenting three updated findings from our PDRS research that we think are highly pertinent: (1) differences in mean scores between the PDRS positive and negative subscales; (2) correlations among all six subscales; and (3) norms for the PDRS subscales.

As with the PDRS development, we relied on the CF post-deployment HDO survey to collect all of our follow-up data. A total of 3,006 CF personnel completed the survey between August 2004 and February 2007. All had returned from the NATO mission in Afghanistan approximately 6 months prior to the data collection (Fikretoglu & McCreary, 2010). The questionnaire package was administered in mass-testing sessions on military bases by a Personnel Selection Officer or was mailed to augmentees and individuals who transferred to new units. The sample was composed primarily of Regular Force members (93.3 %), who were male (88.6 %). Over half the sample was married (59.7 %) with children (52.8 %). See Table 10.2 for a more detailed description of the sample's demographic characteristics.[2]

The Relationships Among the Post-Deployment Reintegration Scale's Subscales

When we compared the means from the positive subscales to their corresponding negative subscales (i.e., Work Positive to Work Negative; Family Positive to Family Negative; Personal Positive to Personal Negative), it became clear that CF members were reporting more positive than negative post-deployment experiences in all three domains. As shown in Table 10.3, the effect size statistics for our t-tests demonstrated that the mean differences between the positive and negative subscales in all three analyses were all either large or very large (Hyde, 2005), with the differences in the Family and Personal domains being the largest.

Additionally, the positive and negative subscales tend to be orthogonal (Table 10.4). That is, returning service members are reporting both positive and negative post-deployment reintegration experiences and perceptions. Another way of saying this is that having a lot of positive post-deployment reintegration experiences and perceptions does not preclude the same people from also reporting a lot of negative post-deployment reintegration experiences and perceptions. However, the correlations also demonstrate that reintegration experiences of the same valence are correlated, suggesting there is a tendency for good and bad experiences to permeate across domains.

---

[2] Before beginning our data analyses, we screened the data for univariate normality, outliers, and assessed missing data (Kline, 2010). None of the PDRS scale items met Kline's criteria for excessive skewness or kurtosis. To check for outliers we standardized items and noted any with absolute values greater than 3.29. Responses to items 1, 9, 16, and 27 contained outliers. We used the Windsor technique (Kline, 2010) to trim values that had absolute z-score values greater than 3.29 back to the next highest score, eliminating all item-level outliers. In all, 330 of the 3,006 participants had missing data on some of the PDRS items. To minimize missing data, we computed the mean for each subscale if participants had completed at least half the items in the subscale. We next assessed each subscale for normality and used the Windsor technique to trim back scores on the Personal Negative subscale. Third, we excluded cases which had no score on at least one of the subscales, resulting in 2,974 valid cases for each sub-scale (i.e., 32 excluded cases).

Table 10.2 Demographic characteristics of the post-deployment reintegration scale norming sample (N = 2,974)

Variable	Category	N	%
Military Status	Regular Force	2,775	93.3
	Reserve Force	154	5.2
Military Rank	Junior Non-Commissioned Member	1,973	66.3
	Senior Non-Commissioned Officer	546	19.00
	Junior Officer	255	8.6
	Senior Officer	123	4.1
Augmentee Status	Augmentee	595	20.0
	Non-Augmentee	2,242	75.4
Total Tours	1	1,116	37.5
	2	697	23.4
	3	498	16.7
	4+	596	20.0
Age	17–21	63	2.1
	22–26	506	17.0
	27–31	463	15.6
	32–36	389	13.1
	37–41	336	11.3
	42–46	222	7.5
	47+	85	2.9
Education	Some High School	154	5.2
	High School	943	31.7
	Some University/College	548	18.4
	University/College Degree or above	425	14.3
Gender	Male	2,634	88.6
	Female	286	9.6
First Language	Anglophone	2,588	87.0
	Francophone	338	11.4
Marital Status	Single	1,151	38.7
	Married	1,774	59.7
Children	0	1,570	52.8
	1	486	16.3
	2	556	18.7
	3+	285	9.6

Note: Numbers and percentages are rounded. Variables for which the categories do not add up to 100 % have missing values, which have not been included in this table due to space limitations
Note: Junior Non-Commissioned Member includes the ranks of Private, Corporal and Master Corporal. Senior Non-Commissioned Officer includes Sergeant, Warrant Officer, Master Warrant Officer, and Chief Warrant Officer. Junior Officer includes Second Lieutenant, Lieutenant, and Captain. Senior Officer includes Major, Lieutenant-Colonel, Colonel, and General

Post-Deployment Reintegration Scale Norms

To assist in interpreting scores from the PDRS, we created norms for the Canadian Forces as a whole, as well as specific subgroups within the CF (Fikretoglu & McCreary, 2010). The CF norms are presented in Table 10.5. It is important to note

Table 10.3 Descriptive statistics for each post-deployment reintegration scale subscale and mean differences within each domain (N = 2,974)

PDRS	Mean	SD	Skewness	Kurtosis	t-Test between positive and negative scales within domains	Effect size (Cohen's d)
Work Negative	2.80	1.08	0.22	−0.87	$t(2973) = -28.88***$	−0.76
Work Positive	3.51	.76	−0.38	−0.22		
Family Negative	2.01	.94	0.93	0.19	$t(2973) = -46.24***$	−1.18
Family Positive	3.15	.99	−0.28	−0.62		
Personal Negative	1.83	.82	1.06	0.48	$t(2973) = -90.43***$	−1.80
Personal Positive	3.40	.92	−0.48	−0.26		

$***p < .001$

Note: Skewness values of less than three and kurtosis values of less than ten are not considered serious enough departures from univariate normality to warrant further attention (Kline, 2010). Effect sizes can be categorized into the following groups: close to zero (<0.10), small (0.11–0.35), moderate (0.36–0.65) large (0.65–1.00) or very large (> 1.00) (Hyde, 2005)

Table 10.4 Correlations among post-deployment reintegration scale subscales (N = 2,974)

	WN	WP	FN	FP	PN	PP
Work Negative (WN)	(.85)					
Work Positive (WP)	−.05	(.74)				
Family Negative (FN)	.47	−.09	(.88)			
Family Positive (FP)	−.01 (*ns*)	.42	.03 (*ns*)	(.89)		
Personal Negative (PN)	.49	.05	.67	.14	(.86)	
Personal Positive (PP)	.09	.55	.12	.56	.25	(.84)

Note: All correlations are significant at p < .01 unless indicated above. Numbers in parentheses are reliability coefficients for each scale

Table 10.5 Norms for the full CF sample

	Mean (SD)	95% CI	Much below average	Below average	Average	Above average	Much above average
WN	2.79 (1.08)	2.76–2.84	NA	1.00–1.70	1.71–3.87	3.88–4.95	4.96–5.00
WP	3.51 (.76)	3.48–3.53	1.23–1.98	1.99–2.74	2.75–4.27	4.28–5.00	NA
FN	2.01 (.94)	1.98–2.04	NA	1.00–1.06	1.07–2.95	2.96–3.89	3.90–4.83
FP	3.15 (.99)	3.11–3.18	1.00–1.16	1.17–2.15	2.16–4.14	4.15–5.00	NA
PN	1.83 (.82)	1.80–1.86	NA	NA	1.01–2.65	2.66–3.47	3.48–4.29
PP	3.40 (.92)	3.37–3.44	1.00–1.55	1.56–2.47	2.48–4.32	4.33–5.00	NA

Note: N = 2,974, *SD* Standard Deviation, *CI* Confidence Interval, *WN* Work Negative, *WP* Work Positive, *FN* Family Negative, *FP* Family Positive, *PN* Personal Negative, *PP* Personal Positive

that, unlike many clinical scales, the PDRS was neither designed nor validated to be used in a diagnostic manner. As such, these norms were developed to be used as comparison points for group-level means only. Thus, we recommend against comparing an individual's scores to the norms as a way of determining whether that individual is reintegrating at, above, or below average. Instead, the PDRS could be used alongside other information, such as interviews, focus groups, and other surveys, to determine whether a group (such as individuals from a particular tour) is experiencing more or fewer reintegration difficulties than experienced by previous tours (Fikretoglu & McCreary, 2010).

Post-Deployment Reintegration in CF Single Service Members

Military members, as a group, embody a wide variety of intersecting demographic characteristics. They vary, for example, as a function of their age, gender, racial or ethnic background, and education level. One demographic group that military researchers seldom focus on is the single service member. That is, while it is true that many researchers commonly ask research participants about their marital status, it is rare that researchers focus on the unique aspects of single service members themselves. This is surprising since their numbers are not trivial. For example, in our large PDRS norms sample, single service members represent 39 % of respondents. What little there is known about single service members shows that they are more likely to engage in a wider array of unhealthy behaviors, including excessive alcohol use and smoking (Bray, Spira, & Lane, 2011; Jones & Fear, 2011).

When people do mention the concept of single service members, the assumption tends to be that they are all young, single, never-married, and without children. But not all single service members fall into this category. Some single service members have children, while others do not. Those with children may be single parents, or they may share custody. Furthermore, some single service members may also be responsible for taking care of their aging parents. An additional issue is that single service members with dependents (be they children or aging parents) may be older, and consequently possess more life experience, than members without dependents. Thus, it is evident that there are many different types of single service member (in the same way that there is heterogeneity among married service members), and that their post-deployment reintegration experiences and perceptions may be different depending on both the member's marital status and family responsibilities.

Typical studies, including our own, rarely ask about the more complex living arrangements that all service members may face, such as shared child custody and time spent looking after aging or ill parents. However, in our large sample of CF members, we do know that 22 % were single and that 74 % of single service members did not have a dependent (which was the terminology used in the survey demographics section). Single members without dependents had a median age between 27 and 31 years, while those with dependents had a median age between 32 and 36 years. In contrast, among married service members (including common-law), only 30 % had no dependents. Those without dependents were, on average, between 27 and 31 year of age; those with dependents were, on average, between 32 and 36 years old.

With this notion of the diversity of single service members in mind, we approached our large CF dataset with the following empirical question: do single

Table 10.6 Comparing mean scores on four PDRS subscales based on relationship and family status

	WN		WP		FN		FP	
	M	SD	M	SD	M	SD	M	SD
Single								
No dependents (N = 983)	2.96	1.08	3.58	.75	1.85	.86	2.80	1.01
Dependents (N = 150)	2.77	1.13	3.44	.81	2.37	1.11	3.21	1.00
Married								
No dependents (N = 584)	2.83	1.05	3.57	.74	1.98	.91	3.20	.90
Dependents (N = 1,175)	2.63	1.05	3.44	.76	2.11	.97	3.41	.90

Note: Data from the Positive Personal and Negative Personal subscales are not included here since none of the regressions were statistically significant; *WN* Work Negative, *WP* Work Positive, *FN* Family Negative, *FP* Family Positive. Values for the Personal Negative and Personal Positive scales are not shown because there were no statistically significant effects for this dimension

service members (with and without dependents) differ from similar married service members on their PDRS scores? To this end, we examined the role of marital status (single vs. married), the presence of dependents (none vs. one or more), and the interaction between to two, using multiple regression.

We conducted six hierarchical multiple regression analyses, one for each PDRS subscale score. In those analyses, the PDRS subscale scores were the dependent variables. We entered the independent variables in two steps. In Step 1, we entered age (centered at its grand mean) as a covariate because both single and married service members without dependents appeared to be younger than service members with dependents, as well as two dummy-coded variables representing marital status (1 = married, 0 = single) and dependents (1 = yes, 0 = no). In Step 2, we added the interaction between marital status and dependents to the Step 1 model. In line with Aiken and West (1991), and because we did not have strong theoretical expectations of interactions, we followed a step-down procedure: In the presence of a non-significant interaction, we interpreted the results associated with the Step 1 model only. Means and standard deviations are shown in Table 10.6. The results of the regression analyses are shown in Table 10.7.

While we will not focus extensively on the results associated with respondents' age, it is important to note that we did find significant main effects for Age at Step 1 in five of the six analyses. That is, after controlling for both Marital Status and the presence or absence of Dependents, older individuals reported lower levels of both positive and negative post-deployment reintegration perceptions and experiences in all PDRS domains except the Personal Positive. The magnitude of the association between Age and PDRS scores, as measured by Beta coefficients, ranged from $-.07$ to $-.23$. The strongest associations were with the Work Negative (Beta = $-.23$) and Work Positive (Beta = $-.12$) subscales.

Together, the main effects of Age, Marital Status, and Dependents accounted for about 6 % of the variance in Work Negative scores, $F(3, 2036) = 43.36$, $MSE = 1.13$, $p < .001$. However, neither Marital Status nor Dependents were significant predictors of negative work reintegration. The main effects of Age, Marital Status, and

Table 10.7 Summary of hierarchical regression analyses predicting PDRS scores

	PDRS score							
	WN		WP		FN		FP	
Predictor	ΔR²	B(SE)	ΔR²	B(SE)	ΔR²	B(SE)	ΔR²	B(SE)
Step 1	.060*		.022*		.022*		.086*	
Age		0.16 (0.02)*		−0.06 (0.01)*		−0.06 (0.02)*		−0.04 (0.02)*
Marital status (MS)		−0.01 (0.06)		0.04 (0.04)		0.06 (0.05)		0.44 (0.05)*
Dependents (D)		−0.08 (0.06)		−0.10 (0.04)*		0.26 (0.05)*		0.27 (0.05)*
Step 2	.000		.000		.008*		.001	
Age		−0.16 (0.02)*		−0.06 (0.01)*		−0.07 (0.02)*		−0.04 (0.02)*
Marital status (MS)		0.02 (0.07)		0.04 (0.05)		0.18 (0.06)*		0.48 (0.06)*
Dependents (D)		−0.02 (0.11)		−0.13 (0.08)		0.62 (0.10)*		0.40 (0.10)*
MS × D		−0.09 (0.13)		0.04 (0.09)		−0.47 (0.11)*		−0.17 (0.12)
Total R²	.060*		.022*		.030*		.089*	

*p < .05

Note: *WN* Work Negative, *WP* Work Positive, *FN* Family Negative, *FP* Family Positive. Except for Age, none of the predictors were significantly associated with the Personal Negative and Positive scores, so we did not include these results in the table

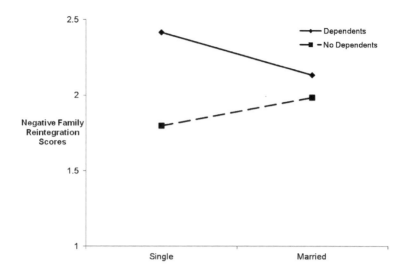

Fig. 10.1 Interaction between marital status and dependents when predicting family negative scores from the post-deployment reintegration scale

Dependents together explained about 2 % of the variance in Work Positive scores, $F(3, 2036) = 15.27$, $MSE = 0.57$, $p < .001$. Having dependents was associated with significantly lower Work Positive scores, $B = -0.10$, $SE = 0.04$, $\beta = -.07$, $t(2036) = -2.43$, $p = .02$, 95 % CI [−.18, −.02].

Jointly, the main effects of Age, Marital Status, and Dependents accounted for about 0.5 % of the variance in Personal Negative scores, $F(3, 2036) = 3.19$, $MSE = 0.66$, $p = .02$. However, neither Marital Status nor Dependents were significant predictors of negative personal reintegration. The main effects of Age, Marital Status, and Dependents together explained about 0.2 % of the variance in positive personal reintegration, $F(3, 2036) = 1.37$, $MSE = 0.83$, $p = .25$. None of the predictors had a significant predictive association with scores on the Personal Positive scale.

The interaction between Marital Status and Dependents was a significant predictor of negative family reintegration, $B = -0.47$, $SE = 0.11$, $t(2035) = -4.12$, $p < .001$, 95 % CI [−.69, −.25]. At Step 2, the model accounted for about 3 % of the variance in Family Negative scores, up from about 2 % at Step 1, $F(4, 2035) = 15.94$, $MSE = 0.87$, $p < .001$, $F(3, 2036) = 15.48$, $MSE = 0.88$, $p < .001$, and $\Delta F(1, 2035) = 16.95$, $p < .001$. An investigation of the simple slopes revealed that, for married participants, whether or not they had dependents did not have a significant effect on their negative family scores, $B = 0.15$, $SE = 0.06$, $t(2035) = 2.56$, $p = .06$. However, for single participants, having dependents resulted in significantly higher scores on the Family Negative scale than not having dependents, $B = 0.61$, $SE = 0.10$, $t(2035) = 6.18$, $p = .004$. Figure 10.1 displays the interaction.

The main effects of Age, Marital Status, and Dependents together explained about 9 % of the variance in Family Positive, $F(3, 2036) = 63.80$, $MSE = 0.89$,

$p < .001$. Having dependents or being married was associated with significantly higher Family Positive scores, respectively, $B = 0.27$, $SE = 0.05$, $\beta = .14$, $t(2036) = 5.25$, $p < .001$, 95 % CI [.17, .37] and $B = 0.44$, $SE = 0.05$, $\beta = .22$, $t(2036) = 8.62$, $p < .001$, 95 % CI [.34, .54].

These findings suggest that being a single service member or having dependents rarely influences post-deployment reintegration-related experiences and perceptions. The one area, however, where these two demographic variables seemed to be associated with poorer reintegration was in the family domain. Being married or having dependents had significant main effects on the positive family scores, each uniquely predicting higher levels of Family Positive scores on the PDRS. For the Family Negative scores, marital status and having dependents interacted, such that, for married individuals, whether or not they had dependents did not have a significant impact on their scores, whereas, for single individuals, having dependents translated into significantly higher scores than not having dependents. This suggests there may be stressors associated with being single with dependents that increase the risk for having difficulty adjusting in the family domain (e.g., Drummet, Coleman, & Cable, 2003). However, given that the overall effect sizes were relatively low and the sample size large, there is the possibility that these effects are methodological artifacts.

Summary

Our aim with this chapter has been to convey the importance of post-deployment reintegration by noting that very little research has focused on the stressors and non-clinical strains of the post-deployment period itself. To address this research gap, we developed a model that focused on people's positive and negative experiences and perceptions in three general areas where the post-deployment reintegration process is most salient: at work, within the family, and within one's personal and world views. Next we developed a way to effectively measure the positive and negative aspects of the work, family, and personal aspects of post-deployment reintegration. Finally, we focused on: (1) new developments with our post-deployment reintegration measure (e.g., the relationships between scales and developing norms so that users would have a way of effectively interpreting findings from it); and (2) describing the ways in which single service members (with and without dependents) differed from married service members (also with and without dependents) on the PDRS.

Research on post-deployment reintegration has important implications for both service members and the clinicians or practitioners who work with them through difficult times. Important for both of these groups is our focus on the positive, as well as the negative, aspects of post-deployment reintegration. As psychological researchers, we often focus on the negative aspects of people's lives, in order to identify ways in which to improve people's quality of life. But as the positive psychology movement has shown, we have done this to the detriment of identifying people's strengths and the ways in which they often thrive in difficult situations (Seligman &

Csikszentmihalyi, 2000). An overly negative focus in military psychology research may lead service members to over-estimate their likelihood of developing psychological disorders such as post-traumatic stress disorder or depression. It may also lead them to focus solely on the negative, as opposed to the positive, aspects associated with post-deployment reintegration. It also ignores the clinical wisdom that we can use or build upon people's existing strengths to address their weaknesses. For example, if someone is doing well in the family domain, but is struggling in the work domain, it might be beneficial for the practitioner to get them to think about how their interpersonal strengths that served them well in the family domain can be applied in the work domain. Thus, including both positive and negative aspects of reintegration in our model reminds both service members and clinicians of the importance of balancing the negative with the positive.

Another implication for practitioners is that, while there are general trends in post-deployment reintegration, there also are subgroup differences. Our examination of the role that marital status and having dependents have on post-deployment reintegration shows that, overall, single and married service members tend to be very similar on their self-reported PDRS experiences and perceptions. However, whereas the process was similar for married service members with or without dependents, single service members with dependents reported more Family Negative experiences than their counterparts without dependents (even after controlling for age). As such, it is important to note that single parent families may be an at-risk group within military settings. Whether the seemingly higher levels of negative family reintegration experiences and perceptions for this group are due to pre-existing vulnerability factors (single parents may be less educated and may come from disadvantaged SES backgrounds; Ambert, 2006), the added stressors of single parenthood, a confound related to the high statistical power in our sample, or some combination of all three, is one important target for future research, as findings would help to address questions around both the nature and the timing of interventions to support these individuals.

While we have learned a lot, there is still so much more that needs to be understood about the post-deployment reintegration period. One of the main issues, in our minds anyway, has to do with the process itself. More specifically, we are cognizant of the fact that our research typically captured people at approximately the 6 month point of the post-deployment reintegration stage. Part of the reason for this is that we used the CF Human Dimensions of Operations survey as a vehicle for getting the large sample sizes we needed for development and validation purposes. A second reason for wanting this timeframe was that previous work by Thompson and Gignac (2002) suggested that it may take people 4 or more months to fully adapt to being home again. However, we are aware that people may respond differently at different time points in the reintegration process. For example, Adler, Britt, Castro, McGurk, and Bliese (2011) noted that anger and alienation were the key themes that emerged from their interviews with U.S. service members who had been home from deployment for only a week. Similarly, one of our smaller studies reassessed a small group of people again at approximately 11 months post-deployment, where we noted that there were really no apparent differences in PDRS scores from Time 1 to Time 2.

Thus, in conclusion, the following question needs to be asked: what factors influence the post-deployment reintegration process? Based on the findings we presented here, as well as in Blais et al. (2009), it would appear that combat-related stressors are not strongly associated with PDRS scores. However, post-traumatic stress disorder symptoms are more highly correlated with PDRS scores, so perhaps traumatic experiences on deployment are indirectly related with some aspects of the post-deployment reintegration experience. But what about the various social contexts in which returning service members find themselves (e.g., Reservists who return to a civilian job)? How do these influence the post-deployment reintegration process? What roles do factors such as peer support, leadership, and work-life balance (just to name a few) play in enhancing or detracting from the reintegration experience? How do other individual differences influence this process (e.g., men vs. women, enlisted vs. officer)? Do these factors influence the different reintegration domains equally or do some influence some domains more than others? All of these questions, and more, will provide service members and health care practitioners a better understanding of the complex nature of the post-deployment reintegration period.

Acknowledgements The authors wish to thank Dr. Megan Thompson, who is a co-creator of the Post-Deployment Reintegration Scale. We also thank Dr. Angela Febbraro and Dr. Donna Pickering for their assistance in the initial stage of the scale's development, Major Gary Ivey for his help with the data used in this chapter, as well as the many members of the Canadian Forces (especially those in the Personnel Selection Branch) who helped and encouraged us in this endeavor.

References

Adler, A. B., Bliese, P. B., McGurk, D., Hoge, C. W., & Castro, C. A. (2009). Battlemind debriefing and battlemind training as early interventions with soldiers returning from Iraq: Randomization by platoon. *Journal of Consulting and Clinical Psychology, 77*, 928–940.

Adler, A. B., Britt, T. W., Castro, C. A., McGurk, D., & Bliese, P. D. (2011). Effect of transition home from combat on risk-taking and health-related behaviors. *Journal of Traumatic Stress, 24*, 381–389.

Adler, A. B., Zamorski, M., & Britt, T. W. (2011). The psychology of transition: Adapting to home after deployment. In A. B. Adler, P. B. Bliese, & C. A. Castro (Eds.), *Deployment psychology: Evidence-based strategies to promote mental health in the military* (pp. 153–174). Washington, DC: American Psychological Association.

Aiken, L. S., & West, S. G. (1991). *Multiple regression: Testing and interpreting interactions.* Newbury Park, CA: Sage.

Aldwin, C. M., Levenson, M. R., & Spiro, A., III. (1994). Vulnerability and resilience to combat exposure: Can stress have lifelong effects? *Psychology and Aging, 9*, 34–44.

Ambert, A.-M. (2006). *One parent families: Characteristics, causes, consequences, and issues.* Ottawa, ON: The Vanier Institute.

Bartone, P. T., Adler, A. B., & Vaitkus, M. A. (1998). Dimensions of psychological stress in peacekeeping operations. *Military Medicine, 163*, 587–593.

Basham, K. (2008). Homecoming as safe haven or the new front: Attachment and detachment in military couples. *Clinical Social Work Journal, 36*, 83–96.

Blais, A. R., Thompson, M. M., Febbraro, A., Pickering, D., & McCreary, D. R. (2003). *The development of a multidimensional measure of post-deployment reintegration: Initial psychometric analyses & descriptive results* (Technical Report TR 2003–142). Toronto, ON: Defence Research and Development Canada.

Blais, A.-R., Thompson, M. M., & McCreary, D. (2009). The development and validation of the Army post-deployment reintegration scale. *Military Psychology, 21*, 365–386.

Bliese, P. D., Wright, K. M., Adler, A. B., Thomas, J. L., & Hoge, C. W. (2007). Timing of post-combat mental health assessments. *Psychological Services, 4*, 141–148.

Bowling, U. B., & Sherman, M. D. (2008). Welcoming them home: Supporting service members and their families in navigating the tasks of reintegration. *Professional Psychology: Research and Practice, 39*, 451–458.

Bray, R. M., Spira, J. L., & Lane, M. E. (2011). The single service member: Substance use, stress, and mental health issues. In S. MacDermid Wadsworth & D. Riggs (Eds.), *Risk and resilience in U.S. military families* (pp. 325–342). New York, NY: Springer Science + Business Media.

Brown, K. J. (2005a, February). *Human dimensions of operations survey: Norm development 2004* (Sponsor Research Report 2005–02). Ottawa, ON: Director Human Resources Research and Evaluation. National Defence Headquarters.

Brown, K. J. (2005b). *Human dimensions of operations survey: Revision and two year validation* (Technical Note 2004–10). Ottawa, ON: Director Human Resources Research and Evaluation, National Defence Headquarters.

Brown, K. J. (2005c). *Human dimensions of operations survey: The way forward* (Sponsor Research Report 2005–08). Ottawa, ON: Director Human Resources Research and Evaluation, National Defence Headquarters.

Drummet, A. R., Coleman, M., & Cable, S. (2003). Military families under stress: Implications for family life education. *Family Relations, 52*, 279–287.

Fikretoglu, D., & McCreary, D. R. (2010). *Development of norms for the post-deployment reintegration scale* (Technical Report, 2010–168). Ontario, ON: Defence Research and Development Canada Toronto.

Ford, J. D., Campbell, K. A., Storzbach, D., Binder, L. M., Anger, W. K., & Rohlman, D. S. (2001). Posttraumatic stress symptomatology is associated with unexplained illness attributed to Persian Gulf War military service. *Psychosomatic Medicine, 63*, 842–849.

Harrington, D., Bean, N., Pintello, D., & Mathews, D. (2001). Job satisfaction and burnout: Predictors of intentions to leave a job in a military setting. *Administration in Social Work, 25*, 1–16.

Hendin, H., & Pollinger-Haas, A. (1991). Suicide and guilt as manifestations of PTSD in Vietnam combat veterans. *American Journal of Psychiatry, 148*, 586–591.

Hoge, C. W., Castro, C. A., Messer, S. C., McGurk, D., Cotting, D. I., & Koffman, R. L. (2004). Combat duty in Iraq and Afghanistan, mental health problems, and barriers to care. *The New England Journal of Medicine, 351*, 13–22.

Hourani, L. L., Williams, T. V., & Kress, A. M. (2006). Stress, mental health, and job performance among active duty military personnel: Findings from the 2002 Department of Defense health-related behaviors survey. *Military Medicine, 171*, 849–856.

Hyde, J. S. (2005). The gender similarities hypothesis. *American Psychologist, 60*, 581–592.

Jacobson, I. G., Ryan, M. A. K., Hooper, T. I., Smith, T. C., Amoroso, P. J., Boyko, E. J., et al. (2008). Alcohol use and alcohol-related problems before and after military combat deployment. *The Journal of the American Medical Association, 300*, 663–675.

Jones, E., & Fear, N. T. (2011). Alcohol use and misuse within the military: A review. *International Review of Psychiatry, 23*, 166–172.

Killgore, W. D. S., Cotting, D. I., Thomas, J. L., Cox, A. L., McGurk, D., Vo, A. H., et al. (2008). Post-combat invincibility: Violent combat experiences are associated with increased risk-taking propensity following deployment. *Journal of Psychiatric Research, 42*, 1112–1121.

Kline, R. B. (2010). *Principles and practice of structural equation modeling* (3rd ed.). New York: Guilford.

Litz, B. T., Orsillo, S. M., Friedman, M., Ehlich, P., & Batres, A. (1997). Post-traumatic stress disorder associated with peacekeeping duty in Somalia. *American Journal of Psychiatry, 154*, 178–184.

Maguen, S., Vogt, D., King, L. A., King, D. W., & Litz, B. T. (2006). Posttraumatic growth among Gulf War I veterans: The predictive role of deployment-related experiences and background characteristics. *Journal of Loss and Trauma, 11*, 373–388.

McCarroll, J. E., Ursano, R. J., Liu, X., Thayer, L. E., Newby, J. H., Norwood, A. E., et al. (2000). Deployment and the probability of spousal aggression by U.S. Army soldiers. *Military Medicine, 165*, 41–44.

McCreary, D. R., Blais, A.-R., & Thompson, M. M. (2008, August). *A longitudinal investigation of post-deployment reintegration in Canadian soldiers.* Presented at the annual meeting of the American Psychological Association, Boston, MA, USA.

Mehlum, L. (1995). Positive and negative consequences of serving in a UN peacekeeping mission: A follow-up study. *Internal Review of Armed Forces Medical Services, 68*, 289–295.

Milliken, C. S., Auchterlonie, J. L., & Hoge, C. W. (2007). Longitudinal assessment of mental health problems among active and reserve component soldiers returning from the Iraq war. *Journal of the American Medical Association, 298*, 2141–2148.

Morissette, S. B., Woodward, M., Kimbrel, N. A., Meyer, E. C., Kruse, M. I., Dolan, S., et al. (2011). Deployment-related TBI, persistent postconcussive symptoms, PTSD, and depression in OEF/OIF veterans. *Rehabilitation Psychology, 56*, 340–350.

Newby, J. H., McCarroll, J. E., Ursano, R. J., Fan, Z., Shigemura, J., & Tucker-Harris, Y. (2005). Positive and negative consequences of a military deployment. *Military Medicine, 170*, 815–819.

Orsillo, S. M., Roemer, L., Litz, B. T., Ehlich, P., & Friedman, M. J. (1998). Psychiatric symptomatology associated with contemporary peacekeeping: An examination of post-mission functioning among peacekeepers in Somalia. *Journal of Traumatic Stress, 11*, 611–625.

Pincus, S. H., House, R., Christenson, J., & Adler, L. E. (2001). The emotional cycle of deployment: A military family perspective. *Journal of the Army Medical Department, Apr–Jun*, 15–23.

Sayers, S. L. (2011). Family reintegration difficulties and couples therapy for military veterans and their spouses. *Cognitive and Behavioral Practice, 18*, 108–119.

Seligman, M. E. P., & Csikszentmihalyi, M. (2000). Positive psychology: An introduction. *American Psychologist, 55*, 5–14.

Tedeschi, R. G., & Calhoun, L. G. (1996). The posttraumatic growth inventory: Measuring the positive legacy of trauma. *Journal of Traumatic Stress, 9*, 455–471.

Thomas, J. L., Wilk, J. E., Riviere, L. A., McGurk, D., Castro, C. A., & Hoge, C. W. (2010). Prevalence of mental health problems and functional impairment among active component and National Guard soldiers 3 and 12 months following combat in Iraq. *Archives of General Psychiatry, 67*, 614–623.

Thompson, M. M., & Gignac, M. A. M. (2002). The experience of Canadian Forces augmentees. In A. V. P. Essens, E. Tanercan, & D. Winslow (Eds.), *The human in command: Peace support operations* (pp. 235–263). Amsterdam: Mets & Schilt/KMA.

Thoresen, S., & Mehlum, L. (2004). Risk factors for fatal accidents and suicides in peacekeepers: Is there an overlap? *Military Medicine, 169*, 988–993.

Tucker, J. S., Sinclair, R. R., & Thomas, J. L. (2005). The multilevel effects of occupational stressors on soldiers' well-being, organizational attachment, and readiness. *Journal of Occupational Health Psychology, 10*, 276–299.

Wain, H., Bradley, J., Nam, T., Waldrep, D., & Cozza, S. (2005). Psychiatric interventions with returning soldiers at Walter Reed. *Psychiatric Quarterly, 76*, 315–360.

Wilson, J. P., & Krauss, G. E. (1985). Predicting post-traumatic stress disorder among Vietnam veterans. In W. E. Kelly (Ed.), *Post-traumatic stress disorder and the war veteran patient* (pp. 102–147). New York: Brunner/Mazel.

Wright, K. M., Foran, H. M., Wood, M. D., Eckford, R. D., & McGurk, D. (2012). Alcohol problems, aggression, and other externalizing behaviors after return from deployment: Understanding the role of combat exposure, internalizing symptoms, and social environment. *Journal of Clinical Psychology, 68*, 782–800.

Yerkes, S. A., & Holloway, H. C. (1996). War and homecomings: The stressors of war and of returning from war. In R. J. Ursano & A. E. Norwood (Eds.), *Emotional aftermath of the Gulf War* (pp. 25–42). Washington, DC: American Psychiatric Press.

Chapter 11
Young Veterans and the Transition to Civilian Employment: Does Marital Status Matter?

Meredith Kleykamp and Sidra Montgomery

Abstract The sequencing and timing of employment, education, and family formation differs between veterans and nonveterans due to the overlapping nature of military service with other commitments such as higher education and civilian labor force participation. Labor market opportunities and outcomes for these young veterans are an important step in their transition to adulthood, likely influencing and being influenced by, in particular, family decisions, such as marriage and becoming a parent. Using nationally representative data, we examine how veteran and marital status influence labor force participation, employment, earnings, and college enrollment. In summary, veterans appear to do worse than their peers in terms of labor force participation and employment. The veteran "penalty" in labor force participation is only significant for married veterans, compared against married nonveterans. All veterans, single, married, divorced or separated, male or female appear to have lower odds of employment than civilians. Accounting for compositional differences only increases this gap. Among those who do find paid work, male veterans appear to out earn their civilian peers.

Keywords Veterans • Military • Employment • College • Labor force • Earnings

M. Kleykamp, Ph.D. (✉) • S. Montgomery
Department of Sociology, University of Maryland, 2112 Art-Sociology Bldg.,
College Park, MD 20742, USA
e-mail: kleykamp@umd.edu; sidra26@umd.edu

S. MacDermid Wadsworth and D.S. Riggs (eds.), *Military Deployment and its Consequences for Families*, Risk and Resilience in Military and Veteran Families,
DOI 10.1007/978-1-4614-8712-8_11, © Springer Science+Business Media New York 2014

Introduction

The Military and the Transition to Adulthood

The transition to adulthood for young adults is marked by several significant events including finishing school, gaining full-time employment, financial independence, marriage, and becoming a parent (Furstenburg, 2010). Following the completion of high school three main pathways emerge for young adults including higher education, the civilian labor market, and the military. Military service often coincides with critical windows during the life course when young adults are making important decisions about marriage, education, and work (Teachman & Tedrow, 2007). The military is an institution that plays an important role in the transition to adulthood for young adults who volunteer to serve, and transitioning *out* of the military is an important, often overlooked aspect of that process. Today, young service members who transition out of the post-9/11 military are becoming young veterans in a civilian economy still recovering from a recession. The sequencing and timing of employment, education, and family formation differs between veterans and nonveterans due to the overlapping nature of military service with other commitments such as higher education and civilian labor force participation (Teachman & Tedrow, 2007). Labor market opportunities and outcomes for these young veterans are an important step in their transition to adulthood, likely influencing and being influenced by, in particular, family decisions, such as marriage and becoming a parent.

How are young veterans doing in the transition to the civilian labor market in comparison to their civilian peers? In the sections that follow, we briefly review research on the employment, earnings, and college enrollment outcomes for veterans of the all-volunteer force and research on the importance of marital status as a moderating influence on the transition to the labor market. We analyze nationally representative data from 2005–2010 to understand how young veterans differ from their non-serving peers in these key labor market domains. We maintain a sharp focus on variation in these outcomes along both gender and marital status divisions, given differences in the opportunity structure for maintaining a military career and family for women, and because of the importance of family formation as a part of the transition to adulthood.

Post-Service Outcomes for Veterans in the All-Volunteer Force (AVF)

Scholars have theorized that differences in labor market outcomes between veterans and nonveterans originate from the selectivity of military service members (and thus veterans) and/or human capital changes induced by service. Sorting out the relative influence of selection from the changes related to service is an ongoing challenge in research on military veterans. In this paper, we are not able to tackle the question of selection but rather, we present differences between veterans and nonveterans as the data reveal and discuss the implications of such differences for future research. We discuss likely selection mechanisms and their anticipated influence on our findings throughout.

Employment

Although popular reporting has documented high unemployment rates among young OEF/OIF veterans, nearly 12 % of whom are unemployed, there are few detailed analyses investigating why (Bureau of Labor Statistics, 2012). High unemployment among recent veterans stands in stark contrast to the experiences of earlier cohorts who experienced an employment advantage over nonveterans. Veterans in the 1980s were more likely to be employed than their nonveteran counterparts, perhaps as a result of hiring preferences for veterans in the public sector (Angrist, 1998). A recent study of differentials between veterans and nonveterans is the only comprehensive study of hiring and employment for post-9/11 veterans (Bureau of Labor Statistics, 2012). However, using an audit method, Kleykamp (2009, 2010) sent fictitious resumes matched on certain characteristics in response to job advertisements in two major metropolitan areas to examine if hiring preferences (measured by callbacks for an interview) differed by veteran status. Veterans whose military work experience was highly transferable to the civilian labor market were preferred over comparable nonveterans, regardless of gender and race, while veterans with non-transferable work experience, such as those in heavily combat-oriented jobs, were treated less favorably by employers. These findings suggest a possible connection between combat experience, military occupational specialty, and veterans' unemployment.

Earnings

The majority of research on veterans labor market outcomes focus on post-service earnings. This focus, without an attendant examination of employment, misses an important dimension (gaining paid work) that stratifies veterans and their civilian peers. It is not inconceivable to observe both high veteran unemployment and high veteran earnings if finding gainful employment is a primary hurdle for veterans. In an environment like this, those veterans who do find work may be highly selective, and thus expected to out-earn their civilian peers. Overall, previous research has found significant differences between veterans' and nonveterans' earnings based on race/ethnicity, gender, and socioeconomic status (Cooney, Segal, Segal, & Falk, 2003; Phillips, Andrisani, Daymont, & Gilroy, 1992; Teachman & Call, 1996; Teachman & Tedrow, 2007; Xie, 1992). Military service appears to be beneficial for the earnings and income of nonwhite veterans yet detrimental for white veterans in comparison to their peers (Angrist, 1998; Phillips et al., 1992; Teachman & Tedrow, 2007). Although most military service members earn more than comparable civilian peers during military service (when accounting for cash and in kind payments), only nonwhite veterans show long-run increases in earnings in the civilian labor market. White veterans, however, experience an earnings deficit in comparison to nonveterans in the transition years immediately following military service (although the gap appears to close several years after military service) (Angrist, 1998). Our analyses focus on a relatively young cohort of veterans and as such, veteran–nonveteran differences we identify may reflect the transitory effect of transitioning from military to civilian life, rather than a more permanent difference from non-serving peers. Although differences, good or bad, may be temporary, they are nevertheless experienced as real during that transition, and are seen as real by politicians, advocates, and the public.

The earnings premium for nonwhite veterans has been suggested as evidence in support of the military as a bridging environment for racial minorities, especially considering that nonwhite service members are more highly concentrated in support and administrative occupational roles (Kleykamp, 2009; Xie, 1992). However, racial differences in the veteran premium may stem from several selective processes. Some have suggested racial differences in selectivity into military service, with the military "creaming" the more advantaged African Americans, and "dredging" the less advantaged whites (Mare and Winship, 1984). If black veterans are more advantaged relative to their non-veteran black peers, and white veterans are disadvantaged relative to their white non-serving peers before service, it may appear that military service benefits blacks but not whites. African Americans are also less likely to serve in combat occupations in the military and are more likely to work in jobs with greater civilian transferability, which may partly account for the greater returns to their military experience if combat occupational experience is not transferrable to the civilian labor market.

There are gender differences in the earnings gap among veterans and between veterans and nonveterans. Some recent research suggests that while male veterans have higher median earnings than nonveterans, after controlling for demographic characteristics and work status factors, male veterans appear to earn less than their nonveteran peers (Holder, 2007). The same study found that female veterans have higher earnings than their nonveteran counterparts, attributing this difference to female veterans' greater likelihood of working full-time and year-round than female nonveterans. In contrast, Cooney et al. (2003) found that women veterans suffered deficits in their earnings and family income in comparison to their nonveteran peers, and only black women veterans were able to close the earnings gap.

A more recent study, with careful controls for selection, found that those in the military out-earn their peers while in service, and these gains continue into the future, with no significant gender differences in that pattern. As long as 15 years after enlisting (many years after most who serve leave the military), Army enlistees had roughly 11 % higher earnings than their peers (Loughran, Martorell, Miller, & Klerman, 2011). The same study found the highest returns to military service among those from the lower end of the AFQT (Armed Forces Qualification Test) distribution, and that the gains in earnings were not likely to come as a result of later investments in higher education. Similarly, Teachman and Tedrow (2007) found that less educated veterans have higher earnings than comparable nonveterans but the delayed entry into the civilian labor market for more educated male veterans likely leads to the deficit in their earnings compared with peers (Teachman & Tedrow, 2007). In short, the evidence on military service and earnings is mixed, and highly contingent on study populations, methods, and models.

College Enrollment

Employment and earnings are central indicators of labor market success, but we also conceive of college enrollment as an important labor market outcome. A college education influences labor force outcomes; the college-educated have better job opportunities and higher pay than their non-graduate peers. One of the benefits available to young service members is the GI Bill, which provides financial resources for veterans (with an honorable discharge) to pursue higher education as well as other vocational training for up to 10 years after separation from the military. Despite the availability of the GI Bill, veterans lag behind their peers in education upon separation and the gap continues to grow over time (Cohen, Warner, & Segal, 1995; Teachman, 2007). The years that most young adults pursue higher education coincide with the prime years for military service, thus forcing individuals who join the military to attain higher education at later ages (Loughran et al., 2011). This makes it more difficult for young veterans to 'catch up' to their nonveteran peers. Teachman (2007) found that only veterans with higher Armed Forces Qualification Test (AFQT) successfully closed the educational gap, all others lagged behind their nonveteran peers. The Post-9/11 GI Bill, passed in 2009, may make it easier for young veterans to access higher education through the addition of benefits such as increased funding for tuition and books, and a monthly housing allowance. It will be several years before research will be able to assess whether and how these changes to the GI Bill have an impact on the educational profiles of young veterans. Although many enlist in the military for educational benefits, it may be difficult to utilize these benefits if young adults have established families and households during their time in the military.

Why Marital Status?

Marriage is part of the transition to adulthood for many young people, and it is often linked with other markers of the transition such as financial independence, full-time employment, and parenthood (Aronson, 2008). Given that the timing of military service coincides with important years in the transition to adulthood, it is not surprising that the military institution has some association with marriage for service members. After age 22, the majority of new enlistees are married, and enlistees are roughly twice as likely to be married as civilians of the same age (Department of Defense, 2010). Many who enter single marry within the course of their service, leading to higher rates of marriage and childbearing among military members than their civilian same-age peers (Department of Defense, 2010). The plurality (48 %) of the young post-9/11 veterans in our analyses are single and never married (versus 69 % of the non-veterans who are never married), implying that more than half of the young veterans we analyze are or were married, and that they are 30 % *less* likely to be single and never married than their civilian peers.

Hogan and Seifert (2010) report that among young adults (ages 23–25) the odds of being married were three times greater for those with military service in comparison to those who have never served. Marriage rates in the military for young adults are consistently higher than their civilian peers, for both men and women (Hogan & Seifert, 2010; Lundquist & Smith, 2005). In parallel to the high marital rates seen in the military institution, there are also higher rates of divorce. Women in the military have a significantly higher chance of divorce than both men in the military and women in the civilian world, while men in the military are less likely than their civilian counterparts to be divorced (Karney & Crown, 2007; Kelty, Kleykamp, & Segal, 2010). After leaving the military, divorce rates for veterans are higher in comparison to their nonveteran peers (Karney & Crown, 2007). While the focus of this section is on single soldiers and veterans, in our analysis, the experience of single veterans must be understood in comparison with the experiences of their current or formerly married counterparts.

Marital Status and Labor Market Outcomes

Marital status is associated with labor market outcomes, such as labor force participation, earnings, and educational attainment. These associations stem from the bi-directional influences of labor market participation on marriage, and marriage on labor market outcomes. Labor market characteristics affect an individual's position in the marriage market (i.e. their "marriageability") and influence an individual's ability to form and maintain a marital relationship. But, marital status also influences individuals' labor force participation, earnings, and educational attainment. In both of these relationships, there are important differences between men and women. The following sections provide an overview of current research on marriage and family status and their relationship to selected labor market outcomes.

Labor Force Participation

Women's labor force participation has substantially increased over the past century, but women's labor force participation rates began to level off in the 1990s (Goldin, 2006; Waldman, 1983). The majority of women, regardless of their marital status, are likely to be in the labor force in some capacity. Marriage brings more financial stability, contributing to married women's employment and earnings often being valued as "secondary" within the household, and often leading to lower labor force participation among married women (Cohen & Bianchi, 1999; Goldin, 2006; Waite, 1995; Pettit & Hook, 2005). Gender-based segregation of women and men into gender-stereotyped jobs persists in the labor market, with consequences for work quality and earnings (Cotter, Hermsen, & Vanneman, 2004).

Previous research has also shown that married men work more and achieve more in the labor force (Nock, 1998; Waite, 1995). Historically, men have been the sole financial provider in marriage. With more women entering the work place, Oppenheimer (1988) argues that the economic determinants of marriage are changing. The importance of women's potential in the labor market for marriage formation has increased, while the expectations for men's labor market status have remained much the same (Oppenheimer, 1988; Sweeney, 2002). A man's financial security, labor force position, and earnings potential are positively associated with his likelihood of marriage and entry into marriage as opposed to cohabitation (Kalmijn & Luijkx, 2005; Xie, Raymo, Goyette, & Thornton, 2003). Kalmijn and Luijkx (2005) also found that marriage serves as a protective factor for men's employment, speculating that the pressures of the breadwinning role in marriage work to keep men employed.

Earnings

Although women's participation in the labor force has been increasing over the past century, women still earn less, and continue to have lower wages for performing the same jobs as their male counterparts (Blau & Kahn, 2007; Cotter et al., 2004). Chandler, Kamo, and Werbel (1994) found that women's marital status matters less than the timing of marriage; delaying marriage significantly increases women's wages by providing an extended period of career formation free of spousal and family demands. Women with children experience a 7 % wage penalty for motherhood in the labor force, with penalties being even higher for married mothers than for unmarried mothers (Budig & England, 2001; Budig & Hodges, 2010). Married men, however, are consistently shown to earn a "marriage premium" in the labor market because they earn more than other men (Nock, 1998; Waite, 1995). Similar to labor force participation, men with financially stability and economic potential for their earnings are more likely to make a marital commitment in the first place (Xie et al., 2003). Marital and family status is negatively associated with the earnings of women, but it is positively associated with the earnings of men.

School Enrollment

College enrollment may be the one area where women outperform men. The gender gap in educational achievement leveled out around 1982, and women now outperform men in high school graduation rates, entry into college, and completion of a college degree. Women are more likely to enroll in college, older women are more likely to return to college, and there are more women than men in every age range attending college. Regardless of marital status, women who complete some form of higher education will likely have better employment opportunities, earnings, and will be able to achieve a higher standard of living (Buchmann, 2009; Buchmann & DiPrete, 2006). The same social processes facilitating women's entry into the labor market in large numbers also influence trends in delaying marriage and childbearing and pursuing higher education during the young adult years (Buchmann, 2009; Goldin, 2006).

Marriage and family status have been shown to have mixed effects on education. Teachman and Polonko (1988) found that marriage has a negative effect on women's educational attainment, while for men parenthood has more of a negative effect than marriage. Taniguchi and Kaufman (2005) examined nontraditional students (24 and above), and found that married students do not differ from the never-married students in their degree completion rate. Married students are more likely to complete their college degree than divorced students. The presence of young children is negatively correlated with degree completion for both men and women. While there are mixed results about the effect of marriage on educational outcomes for men and women, it is clear that women represent an increasing majority in higher education.

Marital Status and Veterans' Transitions Out of the Military

The important life course transition out of the military and into the civilian labor market may be influenced by young veterans' marital status. Marriage could provide young veterans with greater financial resources and social support, enabling the veteran to seek a wider variety of post-service opportunities, especially if the veteran's spouse is working and contributing to the household economy. For women veterans, marital status may be strongly connected to the reasons for separation from the military, due to desires to start or continue to raise a family. Single veterans may have less social support and fewer resources to smooth over periods of transitional instability, such as looking for work or deciding what to pursue. But, being single may allow for more flexibility and less constraint in choosing from opportunities that are available. If the patterns identified in previous research on civilians— that marriage increases labor force attachment among men—hold, then male married veterans may have more constraints in the transition out of the military. Single veterans (especially those without children) may be better able to take advantage of the educational benefits that are provided by the military to go back to school and earn an advanced degree, if they do not have other expectations about supporting a family and household. Through the following analyses we seek to better understand whether marriage enables or constrains the post-service options for young veterans.

Data and Methods

The Current Population Survey (CPS) is a monthly survey of approximately 60,000 households, and is the primary source of national labor force statistics in the U.S. Our empirical investigation relies on two distinct series of the CPS from 2005 to 2010. We model four key labor market outcomes for post-9/11 veterans by gender: labor force participation, employment, earnings, and college enrollment. We use the merged outgoing rotation group (MORG) series of the CPS, which affords us a larger sample than any single monthly series, to measure labor force participation, employment status, and earnings. We use the October series of the CPS to measure college enrollment. The CPS uses a complex design wherein it surveys individuals for 4 sequential months, rotating them out of the observation sample for 8 months, and then surveys them again for 4 sequential months. Individuals surveyed in month 4 and month 8 of the period in which they are observed are in the outgoing rotation groups, and are asked additional labor force questions. Although all basic monthly CPS surveys collect information on college enrollment, the question is asked only of those aged 18–24. We use the October supplement because it asks more detailed questions about college enrollment of the full adult sample. Because veterans are likely to enroll in college at older ages, relying on data from those under 24 would fail to capture many veterans pursuing college degrees as "non-traditional" students.

All CPS respondents are asked about their veteran status and the last period in which they served. Because we do not have detailed service dates, we define a cohort of recent veterans as those who served at some point after September 11, 2001 (the most recent category of service recorded in the data). Because we are interested in the transition to adulthood, we limit our sample to those young adults age 18–30. We pool the 2005–2010 survey data to ensure a large sample of these young recent veterans for our analyses, which necessarily limits our ability to analyze trends within this period of time.

Outcome Measures

Individuals in the labor force include those employed, or unemployed but looking for work, while those not in the labor force are not actively seeking work. Employed persons are those who did any work for pay in the reference week of the survey and those who have a job but were temporarily absent from it in the reference week. We analyze employment or unemployment among those in the labor force. We measure earnings as hourly (or hourly-equivalent) wages or salary (in 2010 dollars) following the dominant practice in labor economics research (Lemieux, 2006). Because earnings show a non-normal, right-skewed distribution, we model the natural log of hourly earnings in regression analyses. In addition to the age limitations, we limit our samples to workers who have non-zero wage information. All samples used for our analyses exclude imputed earners. We also exclude high and low outliers from our samples: following Lemieux (2006), we drop those who report hourly earnings below $1/hour or above $100/hour in 1979 dollars. Topcodes change across the CPS years and we again follow Lemieux (2006), and multiply the weekly wages of those with topcoded earnings by 1.4. Without adjustments for topcoding, wages among the highest earners are underestimated. Finally, we measure college enrollment as those individuals currently enrolled in a 2- or 4-year college degree program. We limit our analyses of enrollment to individuals with at least a high school or equivalent degree, but who have not yet attained a Bachelor's or higher degree. While some may pursue a second degree, these are likely to be unusual cases, and sample size limitations prohibit their inclusion in the multivariate analysis of enrollment.

Table 11.1 presents key descriptive statistics on the analytic sample for each of our four main outcomes of interest. We present descriptive statistics on control variables for each of the four analytic samples in Table 11.4 of the Appendix. These unadjusted figures provide initial clues into the challenges facing young veterans' transition into the civilian labor market. Overall, never- and formerly-married veterans appear to have greater attachment to the labor force, whereas married veterans have lower labor force participation rates. Approximately 45 % of married female veterans are out of the labor force compared with 33.9 % of married, non-veteran women. Among those in the labor force, veterans show higher unemployment rates than nonveterans across all groups, with the greatest veteran/nonveteran disparity occurring among married men. Unemployment among married non-veteran men stood at 5.7 % compared against 13.9 % unemployment among married male veterans.

However, once employed, veterans appear to out earn their nonveteran counterparts, especially among married men. Married male veterans earn an average of nearly $1.50 more per hour than their peers (roughly a 10 % earnings premium among married male veterans). Veterans are also more likely to be enrolled in college than their non-serving peers, with the exception of single men and women. While the GI Bill likely facilitates college enrollment for veterans, it appears single veterans may not be taking full advantage of that opportunity to exceed enrollment rates of their peers.

As noted earlier, these average differences do not account for the compositional differences between veterans and nonveterans, in particular differences in average age, education, ethno-racial identification, region of residence, or the presence of children, nor do they account for occupation or industry of employment all of which have been shown to influence labor market outcomes, and which likely vary by gender, veteran status and marital status. We briefly describe our analytical approach before presenting results from the models of the four outcomes of interest.

Analytical Strategy

Our analysis consists of multivariate regression models of the four outcomes of interest. For labor force participation, employment (among those in the labor force)

Table 11.1 Descriptive statistics for labor force participation, employment, earnings and college enrollment by gender, veteran status, and marital status

	Male						Female					
	Nonveteran			Veteran			Nonveteran			Veteran		
	Single	Married	Other	Single	Married	Other	Single	Married	Other	Single	Married	Other
Labor Force Status (%)[a]												
Employed	66.1	88.9	77.9	69.6	84.0	75.5	64.0	62.3	66.7	68.0	46.8	70.0
Unemployed	9.1	4.9	9.7	11.2	7.0	14.1	6.7	3.8	7.5	11.3	7.6	10.4
NILF	24.8	6.1	12.4	19.3	9.0	10.4	29.3	33.9	25.8	20.7	45.6	19.6
N	141,350	40,797	5,239	1,957	1,486	377	128,523	60,572	10,499	381	450	156
Unemployment (among LF) (%)[a]												
Unemployed	9.5	5.7	10.1	14.2	13.9	13.0	12.1	5.2	11.1	13.7	7.7	15.8
Employed	89.3	94.9	89.4	88.8	94.3	86.6	91.7	94.6	90.3	88.0	88.8	93.6
N	105,739	38,389	4,593	1,536	1,327	327	91,379	40,637	7,880	293	256	120
Earnings (hourly in 2010 $s)[a]	12.1	15.3	13.4	13.8	16.8	14.7	11.4	13.9	11.6	12.1	13.4	14.3
N	55,782	22,939	2,405	874	845	179	52,602	25,849	4,528	162	154	83
College Enrollment (%)[b]												
Enrolled	38.7	11.0	15.7	29.8	22.3	20.4	49.0	16.4	20.6	37.3	29.2	50.7
Not Enrolled	61.3	89.0	84.3	70.2	77.7	79.6	51.0	83.6	79.4	62.7	70.8	49.3
N	32,102	7,816	1,252	616	460	130	28,524	11,611	2,421	126	128	49

Source: [a]Current Population Survey, MORG Series (2005–2010)
Source: [b]Current Population Survey, October Series (2005–2010)
Note: NILF refers to those Not in the Labor Force

and college enrollment, we separately estimate logistic regression models of the probability of experiencing those outcomes. We also model the natural log of hourly earnings with a standard OLS regression model. Our models statistically evaluate differences in these four outcomes by veteran status and marital status, and by the interaction of veteran and marital status. Models include several variables expected to influence those outcomes in addition to our key correlates of interest. Table 11.4 of the Appendix details these additional variables. We run our regression analyses separately for men and women, as labor force dynamics differ between men and women, and utilize sample weights in both the descriptive and multivariate analyses.

We interpret these models as offering preliminary evidence for veteran/nonveteran differences net of controls for other compositional differences which might be driving observed differences. To simplify the interpretation of our regression models, we use our model results to generate predicted mean differences between veterans and their civilian peers adjusted for compositional differences. All categorical variables are dummy-coded, with the reference categories noted at the bottom of Table 11.2. Because many reports in national summary publications (e.g. Bureau of Labor Statistics, 2012) typically present only basic, unadjusted comparisons, these compositionally-adjusted differences provide more compelling evidence about the extent of veteran/nonveteran differences in key labor market outcomes that likely relate to the military experience itself. But, because we cannot adjust for the self- and institutional-selection of individuals into and out of military service, we cannot make any strong claims about the extent to which veteran/nonveteran differences are really the results of the military experience, and not the selective forces that influence entering or leaving the military or the occupational or other experiences during service.

Results

Table 11.2 presents the results of the four regression models. These models are not nested, but rather four separate models, with slightly different analytical samples that use a (mostly) common set of covariates. Estimates for the labor force, employment and enrollment outcomes are reported as odds ratios, while the estimates for earnings reflect unstandardized coefficients in the log dollars scale. In the sections that follow, we discuss each model's results separately, and present additional information to aid in the interpretation of the model results. The key covariates of interest, veteran status, marital status, and the interaction of the two are the primary focus of the analysis but we attend to important estimates on some controls.

Across all models, the main effects of veteran status and marital status provide information about the average difference in outcomes between the reference group and the focal group, at the reference level of the other variable, net of the effect of the additional variables in the model. For example, the estimate associated with

Table 11.2 Estimates from regression models of labor force participation, employment, earnings, and college enrollment, by gender (standard errors in parenthesis, 95 % confidence intervals in brackets)

	Labor force participation		Employment		Earnings		College enrollment	
	Odds ratio		Odds ratio		ln($)		Odds ratio	
	Male	Female	Male	Female	Male	Female	Male	Female
Veteran: Served since 9/11/01	0.9	1.22	0.83+	0.63*	0.05**	0.05	1.54	1.48
	(0.06)	(0.19)	(0.08)	(0.14)	(0.02)	(0.03)	(0.41)	(0.99)
	[0.78,1.03]	[0.91,1.64]	[0.68,1.00]	[0.41,0.97]	[0.01,0.08]	[−0.01,0.11]	[0.92,2.58]	[0.40,5.49]
Married	1.93***	0.63***	1.98***	1.43***	0.08***	0.05***	0.73*	0.60***
	(0.06)	(0.01)	(0.08)	(0.05)	(0.01)	(0.00)	(0.11)	(0.06)
	[1.82,2.05]	[0.61,0.65]	[1.84,2.14]	[1.34,1.54]	[0.07,0.08]	[0.04,0.06]	[0.55,0.97]	[0.49,0.74]
Other	1.29***	1.01	0.99	0.91+	0.02**	−0.02**	0.65+	0.77
	(0.07)	(0.03)	(0.06)	(0.05)	(0.01)	(0.01)	(0.16)	(0.14)
	[1.17,1.43]	[0.96,1.07]	[0.88,1.11]	[0.83,1.00]	[0.01,0.04]	[−0.03,−0.01]	[0.39,1.06]	[0.54,1.08]
Veteran* Married	0.72*	0.49***	0.99	0.72	0.03	−0.08	1.67	1.44
	(0.09)	(0.09)	(0.17)	(0.24)	(0.02)	(0.05)	(0.77)	(1.31)
	[0.55,0.92]	[0.34,0.71]	[0.70,1.40]	[0.37,1.38]	[−0.02,0.07]	[−0.18,0.02]	[0.68,4.10]	[0.24,8.55]
Veteran* Other	1.28	0.97	0.8	2.24+	0.00	0.09	1.6	4.3
	(0.28)	(0.27)	(0.18)	(1.09)	(0.04)	(0.06)	(1.33)	(4.07)
	[0.84,1.95]	[0.56,1.68]	[0.52,1.25]	[0.86,5.80]	[−0.07,0.08]	[−0.03,0.21]	[0.31,8.20]	[0.67,27.47]
Age	2.63***	2.01***	1.11*	0.98	0.10***	0.07***	0.19***	0.21***
	(0.07)	(0.05)	(0.05)	(0.05)	(0.01)	(0.01)	(0.03)	(0.03)
	[2.49,2.78]	[1.92,2.10]	[1.02,1.21]	[0.90,1.08]	[0.09,0.11]	[0.06,0.08]	[0.14,0.25]	[0.16,0.28]
Age^2	0.98***	0.99***	1	1	0.00***	0.00***	1.03***	1.03***
	0.00	0.00	0.00	0.00	0.00	0.00	0.00	0.00
	[0.98,0.98]	[0.99,0.99]	[0.99,1.00]	[0.99,1.00]	[−0.00,0.00]	[−0.00,0.00]	[1.02,1.04]	[1.02,1.03]
High School/GED	1.73***	1.90***	1.24***	1.52***	0.13***	0.12***		
	(0.04)	(0.03)	(0.04)	(0.05)	(0.01)	(0.01)		
	[1.66,1.80]	[1.84,1.97]	[1.17,1.31]	[1.42,1.63]	[0.12,0.14]	[0.117,0.13]		

(continued)

Table 11.2 (continued)

	Labor force participation Odds ratio		Employment Odds ratio		Earnings ln($)		College enrollment Odds ratio	
	Male	Female	Male	Female	Male	Female	Male	Female
Some College	1.15***	2.16***	1.81***	2.36***	0.18***	0.20***	10.98***	9.08***
	(0.02)	(0.04)	(0.06)	(0.09)	(0.01)	(0.01)	(1.00)	(0.79)
	[1.10,1.20]	[2.09,2.24]	[1.70,1.93]	[2.19,2.53]	[0.17,0.19]	[0.19,0.21]	[9.19,13.13]	[7.65,10.78]
BA or higher	1.91***	3.74***	2.44***	2.85***	0.39***	0.42***		
	(0.06)	(0.09)	(0.13)	(0.15)	(0.01)	(0.01)		
	[1.80,2.02]	[3.57,3.91]	[2.21,2.70]	[2.57,3.16]	[0.38,0.40]	[0.41,0.44]		
Black	0.58***	0.80***	0.47***	0.50***	−0.11***	−0.06***	1.21	1.03
	(0.01)	(0.02)	(0.02)	(0.02)	(0.01)	(0.01)	(0.14)	(0.11)
	[0.56,0.61]	[0.77,0.83]	[0.44,0.50]	[0.47,0.53]	[−0.12,−0.10]	[−0.07,−0.05]	[0.96,1.52]	[0.84,1.26]
Hispanic	1.24***	0.75***	1.15***	0.87***	−0.12***	−0.04***	0.88	1
	(0.03)	(0.01)	(0.03)	(0.03)	(0.00)	(0.00)	(0.09)	(0.09)
	[1.20,1.29]	[0.73,0.78]	[1.09,1.22]	[0.82,0.93]	[−0.12,−0.11]	[−0.05,−0.04]	[0.72,1.08]	[0.83,1.20]
Other	0.53***	0.50***	0.89*	0.82***	−0.01	0.01	1.51**	1.34*
	(0.01)	(0.01)	(0.040)	(0.041)	(0.01)	(0.01)	(0.210)	(0.170)
	[0.50,0.55]	[0.48,0.53]	[0.82,0.96]	[0.74,0.91]	[−0.02,0.00]	[−0.00,0.02]	[1.15,1.98]	[1.04,1.73]
Urban residence	0.96+	0.96*	1.12***	1.05	0.11***	0.14***	1.44***	1.40***
	(0.02)	(0.02)	(0.03)	(0.03)	(0.00)	(0.00)	(0.15)	(0.13)
	[0.93,1.00]	[0.92,0.98]	[1.06,1.18]	[0.99,1.12]	[0.10,0.12]	[0.13,0.15]	[1.18,1.77]	[1.16,1.69]
Any children <6 at home?	1.82***	0.603***	0.88**	0.66***	0.03***	−0.02***	0.56***	0.54***
	(0.07)	(0.01)	(0.04)	(0.02)	(0.01)	(0.00)	(0.09)	(0.05)
	[1.69,1.96]	[0.59,0.62]	[0.82,0.96]	[0.62,0.70]	[0.02,0.04]	[−0.03,−0.01]	[0.41,0.78]	[0.46,0.65]
Mining			1.07	20.42***	0.24***	0.16***		
			(0.13)	(15.02)	(0.02)	(0.04)		
			[0.83,1.37]	[4.83,86.37]	[0.20,0.28]	[0.08,0.23]		

Construction	0.74***	0.78*	0.04***	0.04**
	(0.03)	(0.08)	(0.01)	(0.01)
	[0.68,0.80]	[0.63,0.95]	[0.03,0.05]	[0.01,0.06]
TCU	1.19**	1.11	0.04***	0.03**
	(0.07)	(0.09)	(0.01)	(0.01)
	[1.072,1.326]	[0.94,1.31]	[0.03,0.06]	[0.01,0.06]
Trade	1.12**	0.94	−0.17***	−0.19***
	(0.05)	(0.06)	(0.01)	(0.01)
	[1.03,1.21]	[0.83,1.05]	[−0.18,−0.16]	[−0.21,−0.18]
Services/FIRE	0.88***	1.1	−0.10***	−0.09***
	(0.04)	(0.06)	(0.01)	(0.01)
	[0.81,0.95]	[0.98,1.23]	[−0.11,−0.09]	[−0.11,−0.08]
Government	1.80***	1.64***	0.19***	0.10***
	(0.18)	(0.18)	(0.01)	(0.01)
	[1.48,2.18]	[1.33,2.04]	[0.16,0.21]	[0.08,0.13]
Agriculture, forest, fisheries	0.56***	1.15	−0.13***	−0.12***
	(0.04)	(0.15)	(0.01)	(0.02)
	[0.49,0.64]	[0.89,1.48]	[−0.15,−0.10]	[−0.15,−0.09]
Unclassified	0.75*	0.60**	−0.18***	−0.22***
	(0.11)	(0.11)	(0.03)	(0.05)
	[0.56,0.99]	[0.42,0.86]	[−0.25,−0.11]	[−0.31,−0.13]
Manual	0.54***	0.49***	−0.15***	−0.23***
	(0.03)	(0.03)	(0.01)	(0.01)
	[0.50,0.59]	[0.44,0.55]	[−0.16,−0.14]	[−0.24,−0.21]

(continued)

Table 11.2 (continued)

	Labor force participation Odds ratio		Employment Odds ratio		Earnings ln($)		College enrollment Odds ratio	
	Male	Female	Male	Female	Male	Female	Male	Female
Service			0.60***	0.69***	−0.19***	−0.17***		
			(0.03)	(0.03)	(0.01)	(0.00)		
			[0.55,0.66]	[0.64,0.75]	[−0.20,−0.18]	[−0.18,−0.16]		
Farm, forest, fish			1.14	0.51***	−0.24***	−0.26***		
			(0.11)	(0.07)	(0.02)	(0.02)		
			[0.94,1.38]	[0.40,0.67]	[−0.27,−0.21]	[−0.30,−0.23]		
Private Sector					0.10***	0.08***		
					(0.01)	(0.01)		
					[0.09,0.12]	[0.07,0.09]		
Constant					0.71***	0.98***		
					(0.07)	(0.07)		
					[0.56,0.85]	[0.83,1.12]		
N	191,206	200,581	151,911	140,565	83,024	83,378	42,376	42,859
Pseudo R²/R² (earnings)	0.13	0.08	0.06	0.06	0.36	0.37	0.32	0.30
BIC	4.13E+08	5.31E+08	2.15E+08	1.63E+08	76,891.05	76,491.57	1.57E+11	1.62E+11

Source: Current Population Survey, MORG Series, 2005–2010 and Current Population Survey, October Series, 2005–2010 (for enrollment model)

Legend: +p<0.10, *p<.05; **p<.01; ***p<.001

Note: Reference is: Non-veteran, never married, less than HS (high school graduate for enrollment model), white, rural, no children <6, manufacturing industry, managerial occupation veteran status tells us about the average difference between veterans and non-veterans, among the never married. The interaction effects tell us whether there are dissimilar effects of veteran status across marital status categories. Estimates reflect the additional difference between veteran and nonveterans among the married, or among the other category, relative to the never married. The interpretation of interaction effects can be challenging, especially when using non-linear models like logistic regression. To ease interpretation, we also provide a table of the predicted outcomes implied by the model results for each of the four outcomes. These predicted outcomes can be interpreted as the average outcome for the described groups, adjusted for the compositional differences across the groups. That is, if veterans are older on average than nonveterans, the predicted outcomes are computed holding age across the groups at the overall mean of the sample. While the regression model results provide a compact means of evaluating statistically significant differences across groups, the predicted outcome values inform us about the magnitude, or practical significance of observed differences.

Labor Force Participation

The first model in Table 11.2 presents estimates of a logistic regression model of the probability of being in the labor force, displayed in odds ratio form. Consistent with the findings of previous research, marriage is associated with higher labor force participation for men and lower participation for women. Divorced and separated men are also more likely to be in the labor force than their single peers. There are no statistically significant differences between veteran and nonveteran single men or women. Marriage appears to be associated with reduced labor force participation for both male and female veterans. Married veterans show about 30 % lower odds and married women veterans approximately half the odds of being in the labor force compared against nonveterans. The control variables are associated with labor force participation in expected ways. Notably, the presence of a young child is associated with reduced labor force participation for women, while correlating with higher participation among men.

We used the regression estimates to generate predicted probabilities of being in the labor force for six groups, separately by gender: single, married, and other veterans, and single, married, and other nonveterans. Table 11.3 presents these predicted outcome values, paralleling the presentation of the unadjusted means in Table 11.1. The most striking difference in labor force participation is between veteran and nonveteran married women. While 63.1 % of married nonveterans were in the labor force, only 51.8 % of married veteran women were. While women had overall lower labor force participation than their male peers, married veteran women had the lowest overall labor force participation of all groups. We speculate that the very low attachment to the labor force among married women veterans may stem from their leaving military service in order to pursue family formation. The military and family have been described as "greedy institutions", especially for women who serve and wish to raise children (Segal, 1986). Further research is needed to reveal whether our speculated mechanism is supported by empirical evidence, as our data are not sufficient for testing this hypothesis.

Married male veterans are also less likely than their peers to be in the labor force. The arguments about work–family role conflict about women's "opting out" of the labor force may be less likely to hold for male veterans, given prior research on gender, family, and labor force participation.

Employment

Popular media, veterans' advocates and lawmakers have highlighted high unemployment among young veterans as an important social problem. Our analyses provide initial information about whether high veteran unemployment rates stem from compositional differences between veterans and their peers. The second set of model results presented in Table 11.2 suggests this is not the case. Veterans do appear to have significantly lower rates of employment than similar nonveterans. In fact, controlling for compositional differences reveals slightly greater veteran/nonveteran disparities than observed from the unadjusted means. The interaction between marital status and veteran status was not statistically significant suggesting married and unmarried veterans are similarly disadvantaged in terms of unemployment. Male veterans had about 17 % lower odds of being employed, and female veterans had approximately 37 % lower odds of being employed relative to nonveterans.

Marriage is associated with higher odds of employment, with married men showing nearly twice the odds of being employed and women showing nearly 50 % higher odds of employment over their never married peers. Models of employment include broad industry and occupation categories, with manufacturing and management as the reference categories respectively. Some industries offer greater opportunity for employment, with transportation, communication and utilities and government having higher odds, and construction and unclassified industries showing lower odds of employment relative to the beleaguered manufacturing industry. Both the manual labor and service occupations are associated with lower odds of employment compared with managerial and professional occupations.

An examination of the predicted employment rates (Table 11.3), net of the influence of demographic, industry, and occupation controls reveals important gender patterns. Veterans appear to have lower employment rates across all marital status categories, but the veteran/nonveteran disparities are greater among women. Among men, single veterans show approximately a 2 percentage point disadvantage in employment rates, while among women this disparity rises to approximately 8 percentage points. Although the dominant story about high veteran unemployment

Table 11.3 Predicted outcome values by gender, veteran status and marital status (95 % confidence intervals in brackets)

	Nonveteran			Veteran		
	Single	Married	Other	Single	Married	Other
Male						
In Labor	78.6	86.9	82.2	76.9	81.6	84.0
Force (%)	[78.4, 78.8]	[86.3, 87.5]	[80.9,83.5]	[74.8, 79.1]	[78.7, 84.5]	[79.3, 88.7]
Employed (%)	89.6	94.4	89.5	87.8	93.3	85.2
	[89.4, 89.8]	[94.1, 95.7]	[88.5, 90.5]	[85.8, 89.8]	[91.5, 95.0]	[80.6, 89.8]
Earnings	11.5	12.4	11.8	12.0	13.3	12.4
(hourly, in 2010 $s)	[11.4, 11.5]	[12.3, 12.4]	[11.6 12.0]	[11.7, 12.4]	[12.9, 13.8]	[11.6, 13.2]
Enrolled in	33.3	28.94	27.3	39.6	42.5	40.0
College (%)	[32.2, 34.4]	[25.3, 32.6]	[20.8, 33.7]	[32.0, 47.2]	[31.8, 53.2]	[17.9, 62.1]
Female						
In Labor	72.1	63.1	72.4	75.6	51.8	75.4
Force (%)	[71.8, 72.4]	[62.6, 63.6]	[71.4, 73.3]	[70.6, 80.6]	[46.9, 56.7]	[67.7, 83.1]
Employed (%)	91.9	94.9	91.2	87.9	88.2	93.5
	[91.7, 92.1]	[93.8, 94.4]	[90.5, 91.9]	[83.5, 92.2]	[83.3, 93.0]	[85.5, 98.5]
Earnings	10.7	11.3	10.5	11.3	11.9	12.1
(hourly, in 2010 $s)	[10.7, 10.8]	[11.2, 11.4]	[10.4, 10.7]	[10.6, 12.0]	[10.1, 11.9]	[11.0, 13.4]
Enrolled in	40.7	32.8	36.5	47.1	44.8	65.9
College (%)	[39.5, 42.0]	[30.2, 35.5]	[31.4, 41.7]	[25.9, 68.3]	[25.3, 64.3]	[47.2, 84.6]

Source: Current Population Survey, MORG Series, 2005–2010 and Current Population Survey, October Series, 2005–2010 (for enrollment model)

features male veterans, the problem of unemployment may be most pronounced among female veterans.

Earnings

The third set of model results (Table 11.2) provides coefficient estimates of the natural log of hourly earnings among those with valid earnings. A rule of thumb for interpretation of estimates on a logged dependent variable is to interpret them as percent differences. For example, among men, veterans appear to have 5 % higher earnings than nonveterans. That point estimate is similar for women, but not statistically significant at conventional levels. None of the veteran marital status interactions were statistically significant either, indicating the veterans' earnings premium among men holds across all marital status categories. Coefficient estimates on the control variables operate in expected ways. Married men and women have higher earnings than the never married. Men with young children at home out earn their peers without young children, while women with young children have lower earnings than other women. Consistent with results from other models in this analyses and prior research, parenting appears to benefit men, while disadvantaging women in the labor force. How do these estimates translate to real dollars? Single male veterans earn roughly $0.55 per hour more than nonveterans.

College Enrollment

Nearly all veterans serving after 9/11 have access to generous educational benefits through the GI Bill. We expect that veterans would have higher enrollment rates than their nonveteran peers. The final set of models in Table 11.2 reveals no statistically significant differences between veteran and nonveterans in college enrollment. The October CPS data contain only one-fourth the number of observations than the MORG data used for the previous three models. Married men and women are less likely to be enrolled in college. It also appears that education begets more education, with those who have some college being more likely to be currently enrolled than counterparts with only a high school education. This may reflect students currently in a degree program, who would have some college, unless in their first semester in school. Also consistent with the "model minority" literature, respondents of the "other" race or ethnicity, most of who are of Asian origin, are more likely to be enrolled in college than their white peers. As seen in other models, women with young children at home are less likely to be in college, but so are men with young children at home.

In summary, veterans appear to do worse than their peers in terms of labor force participation and employment. The veteran "penalty" in labor force participation is only significant for married veterans, compared against married nonveterans. All veterans, male or female appear to have lower odds of employment than civilians. Accounting for compositional differences only increases this gap. In other words, the basic group differences often reported in the media understate the effect of military service on employment, since veterans have other characteristics that are associated with *higher* employment rates. Among those who do find paid work, male veterans appear to out earn their peers. We interpret this result cautiously. Given the veteran disadvantage in hiring, it seems plausible that those veterans who do find work may be especially skilled or desirable and they command a wage premium, or they may work in better-compensated segments of the economy not captured by our rough industry and occupation categories.

Military service, college enrollment, marriage, and attachment to the labor force are all indicators of the transition to adulthood. Single men and women (regardless of veteran status) are more likely to be enrolled in college. Married men especially are more likely to be attached to the labor force than their single peers. Viewed through the lens of a "normative" life course, this makes sense, as young people are expected to attend college, establish a career, and get married. Military service doesn't fit neatly into a normative patterning of these key life transitions, but neither does it totally dismantle them. Rather it appears to push this somewhat normative or expected patterning of events into older ages. Although the veteran by marital status interactions were not statistically significant, the direction and magnitude suggest that married veterans may be re-ordering this conventional path, putting service and marriage before college and work.

Implications

Implications for Future Research

Our data analyses are coarse, and mostly descriptive, but they raise important avenues for future research. Below we delineate several of the many directions for future research. Longitudinal data are required to document and trace the sequencing of these key life course transitions. Marriage appears to be associated with lower attachment to the labor force among married male veterans than married male nonveterans. If we characterize the transition to adulthood as culminating with a civilian career, it appears that military service may draw out that process, leaving veterans disadvantaged relative to their nonveteran single peers, who may already have completed college and found work. Others though have characterized military service as one of several paths in the transition to adulthood, because it allows the mostly noncollege population an opportunity to pursue a relatively well-paid career with regular opportunities for promotion, extensive benefits and a generous pension (Kelty et al., 2013). Seen in this light, military service is not disadvantageous, but rather leaving the military is. Second, future research should investigate veteran unemployment and the mechanisms behind veterans' employment problems (see Kleykamp (2012) for a more extended discussion on the topic). Previous work has examined discrimination in hiring, but future work might also examine how differing military occupational experiences improve or degrade employment chances. In particular, future research should attend to the distinction between military roles that have civilian equivalence, such as medical, clerical, and other administrative roles versus the combat occupations such as infantry, armor, and others with little to no civilian equal, and how those groups fare in finding civilian work. Differences by characteristics like rank, branch of service, or combat exposure likely play important roles in the civilian employment outcomes of veterans. Those who retire from the military after a 20-year career may be less attached to the labor force because of the steady, albeit reduced, income provided by their retirement pension. Those in our analysis are too young to have served long enough to retire, but differences between officers and enlisted veterans, or Army versus Air Force may play a role in influencing veterans' labor force outcomes. Combat-exposed veterans may suffer physical or mental scars that impede their successful transition to civilian work, but little secondary data collects such detailed information on the military experiences of veterans. The CPS data used for this analysis does not contain these measures.

Future research should also better understand how veterans search for work, and what kinds of work they are expecting to find. We suspect there may be some mismatch between the expectations veterans have for the kinds of jobs they will get, and those employers are willing to offer them. Because recent veterans can voluntarily "quit" their military employment and receive unemployment compensation (covered by their former employer, the Department of Defense), they may use unemployment compensation as a buffer to search for ideal employment, and not have to settle for less-than-desired work.

Finally, while we examine how marriage or single status correlates with labor market outcomes, it is also the case that civilian labor market outcomes may influence marriageability among veterans. If single veterans find it difficult to find good civilian jobs, their lack of employment may hinder their prospects in another market—the marriage market. We think such issues would be fertile territory for future research.

Implications for Practitioners and Service Providers

Our analyses provide little guidance about the reasons why or the mechanisms generating several differences between veterans and nonveterans. For that reason, we are cautious in recommending any particular actions or policies on the basis of these particular findings. Employment is the most clear problematic labor market outcome for veterans. Young veterans are experiencing higher rates of unemployment than their peers, when demographically they appear to have characteristics that should advantage them in finding work. We acknowledge that young veterans may be experiencing high rates of unemployment due to the transition between military and civilian work, and that these employment problems may be transitory. Veterans may be using unemployment benefits to engage in extended job searches, seeking ideal employment, or moving in search of work or other activities that act to pause their employment outcomes not preclude them. With time, they may settle down, find work, and reach parity with their peers. However, for now, for whatever reason, they are less likely to be employed than their peers. We have no information or data to evaluate how unemployed veterans view their unemployment. Because unemployment is defined and measured as those who are without a job but actively seeking work, we assume the status is not one that is desired.

Practitioners and service providers should be made aware of this primary challenge for veterans and should consider how employment challenges intersect with their particular mission. For example, health care providers, particularly mental health care providers, should consider the relationships between conditions like anxiety, depression and PTSD and the search for good civilian employment. Just as these health conditions may influence veterans' search for work, an unsuccessful job search may exacerbate, or contribute to mental health problems. Those working in the physical health professions too should be attentive to the implications of physical injury or disability on employment, and connect injured veterans with services available to them for vocational training and rehabilitation.

More, and perhaps different, employment services need to be provided to soldiers *before* they transition out of the military services. Given the high unemployment rates observed among veterans, the current suite of employment transition service would appear to be less effective than intended. Such programs are not likely to be effective if designed as "one size fits all" training or briefings. Individualized career counseling, resume preparation, and job search strategies are needed. A junior enlisted infantryman has very different employment transition needs than does a medical doctor, and services need to be tailored to each.

Transition counseling should also include information about the GI Bill and college choice options. Although our data cannot reject the possibility that veterans and nonveterans are enrolled in college at the same rates, veterans do have privileged access to college benefits that may provide a long-run advantage in employment and earnings if used to attain a college degree. Recent evidence suggests many veterans are using GI Bill benefits at for-profit colleges (United States Senate, 2010). The long-term value of these degree programs is unclear and there is reason to be concerned that the long-run benefits to the GI Bill may not be realized, if veterans use these college benefits for degree programs that offer little payoff, or if they do not matriculate. Other research suggests veterans may be more likely to attain an Associate's degree, but less likely to attain the more valuable Bachelor's degree (Loughran et al., 2011). We encourage the development of stronger programs for helping soon-to-separate soldiers and recent veterans to make smart choices about college and the use of their GI Bill benefits.

Appendix

Table 11.4 Descriptive statistics for control variables (all numbers in percent unless noted)

Variable	Labor force participation		Employment		Earnings		College enrollment	
	Male	Female	Male	Female	Male	Female	Male	Female
Veteran: Served since 9/11/01	1.9	0.5	2.0	0.5	2.1	0.4	3.0	0.8
Single	74.8	64.7	70.4	65.6	69.4	65.2	78.5	68.3
Married	22.2	29.9	26.4	28.6	27.5	29.2	18.0	25.7
Other	2.9	5.4	3.3	5.8	3.1	5.7	3.5	6.0
Age (in years)	24.0	24.0	24.6	24.4	24.6	24.5	23.6	23.5
<High School	17.8	13.8	15.5	9.1	14.3	8.0		
High School/GED	32.4	27.1	33.6	25.9	32.6	24.8	48.0	40.0
Some College	32.8	37.1	31.6	38.2	32.1	38.4	52.0	60.0
BA or higher	17.0	22.0	19.4	26.9	21.0	28.8		
White	60.1	60.6	61.3	64.4	61.7	65.2	61.3	59.2
Black	12.5	14.2	10.9	13.7	10.1	12.9	13.1	16.1
Hispanic	20.3	17.8	21.5	15.4	21.7	15.3	18.6	18.0
Other	7.1	7.4	6.4	6.5	6.5	6.6	7.0	6.7
Urban residence	86.2	86.1	86.2	86.3	86.8	86.7	85.1	84.8
Any children <6 at home?	14.0	28.4	16.7	25.1	17.0	24.1	14.3	30.8
Manufacturing			10.9	5.0	11.8	5.1		
Mining			0.7	0.1	0.7	0.1		
Construction			14.3	1.2	12.7	1.1		
Trans., Comm., Util.			7.0	3.3	7.3	3.4		
Trade			28.9	30.9	29.5	29.8		
Services/FIRE			30.8	55.4	31.2	56.3		
Government			2.9	2.7	3.3	3.0		
Agriculture, forest, fisheries			4.0	1.1	3.1	1.0		
Unclassified			0.5	0.2	0.5	0.2		
Managerial			20.1	27.1	21.3	28.9		
Manual			37.3	5.6	36.4	5.3		
Service			40.6	66.5	40.9	65.2		
Farm, forest, fish			1.9	0.8	1.5	0.6		
Private Sector			91.7	87.9	91.2	87.2		
N	191,206	200,581	151,911	140,565	83,024	83,378	42,376	42,859

Source: Current Population Survey, MORG Series, 2005–2010 and Current Population Survey, October Series, 2005–2010 (for enrollment model)

References

Angrist, J. (1998). Estimating the labor market impact of voluntary military service using social security data on military applicants. *Econometrica, 66*, 249–288.

Aronson, P. (2008). The markers and meanings of growing up. *Gender & Society, 22*, 56–82.

Blau, F. D., & Kahn, L. M. (2007). The gender pay gap: Have women gone as far as they can? *Academy of Management Perspectives, 21*(1), 7–23.

Buchmann, C. (2009). Gender inequalities in the transition to college. *Teachers College Record, 111*(10), 2320–2346.

Buchmann, C., & DiPrete, T. (2006). The growing female advantage in college completion: The role of family background and academic achievement. *American Sociological Review, 71*(4), 515–541.

Budig, M., & England, P. (2001). The wage penalty for motherhood. *American Sociological Review, 66*, 204–225.

Budig, M., & Hodges, M. (2010). Differences in disadvantage: Variation in the motherhood penalty across White women's earnings distribution. *American Sociological Review, 75*(5), 705–728.

Bureau of Labor Statistics. (2012). *Employment situation of veterans—2011*. Washington, DC: U.S. Department of Labor. Retrieved June 24, 2012, from http://www.bls.gov/news.release/vet.nr0.htm

Chandler, T., Kamo, Y., & Werbel, J. (1994). Do delays in marriage and childbirth affect earnings? *Social Science Quarterly, 75*(4), 838–853.

Cohen, P. N., & Bianchi, S. M. (1999). Marriage, children, and women's employment: What do we know? *Monthly Labor Review, 122*(12), 22–31.

Cohen, J., Warner, R. L., & Segal, D. R. (1995). Military service and educational attainment in the all-volunteer force. *Social Science Quarterly, 76*, 88–104.

Cooney, R. T., Segal, M. W., Segal, D. R., & Falk, W. W. (2003). Racial differences in the impact of military service on the socioeconomic status of women veterans. *Armed Forces & Society, 30*, 53–85.

Cotter, D., Hermsen, J., & Vanneman, R. (2004). *Gender inequality at work. The American people: Census 2000*. New York, NY: Russell Sage.

Department of Defense. (2010). *Population representation in the military services*. Retrieved November 7, 2011, from http://prhome.defense.gov/MPP/ACCESSION%20POLICY/PopRep2010/faq/faq.html

Furstenburg, F. F. (2010). On a new schedule: Transitions to adulthood and family change. *The Future of Children, 20*, 67–87.

Goldin, C. (2006). The quiet revolution that transformed women's employment, education, and family. *The American Economic Review, 96*(2), 1–21.

Hogan, P. F., & Seifert, R. F. (2010). Marriage and the military: Evidence that those who serve marry earlier and divorce earlier. *Armed Forces & Society, 36*, 420–438.

Holder, K. (2007). *Exploring the veteran-nonveteran earnings differential in the 2005 American Community Survey*. In Conference Paper, American Sociological Association Annual Meeting.

Kalmijn, M., & Luijkx, M. (2005). Has the reciprocal relationship between employment and marriage changed for men? An analysis of the life histories of men born in the Netherlands between 1930 and 1970. *Population Studies, 59*(2), 211–231.

Karney, B. R., & Crown, J. S. (2007). *Families under stress: An assessment of data, theory, and research on marriage and divorce in the military* (MG-599-OSD, 2007). Santa Monica, CA: RAND Corporation. Retrieved October 5, 2011, from http://www.rand.org/pubs/monographs/MG599

Kelty, R., Kleykamp, M., & Segal, D. R. (2010). The military and the transition to adulthood. *The Future of Children, 20*, 181–207.

Kleykamp, M. (2009). A great place to start? *Armed Forces & Society, 35*, 266–285.

Kleykamp, M. A. (2010). *Women's work after war* (Upjohn Institute Working Paper No. 10-169). Kalamazoo, MI: W.E. Upjohn Institute for Employment Research.

Kleykamp, M. (2012). Labor market outcomes among veterans and military spouses. In J. M. Wilmoth & A. London (Eds.), *Life course perspectives on military service*. London: Routledge.

Lemieux, T. (2006). Increasing residual wage inequality: Composition effects, noisy data, or rising demand for skill? *American Economic Review, 96*, 461–498.

Loughran, D. S., Martorell, P., Miller, T., & Klerman, J. A. (2011). *The effect of military enlistment on earnings and education* (TR-995-A, 2011). Santa Monica, CA: RAND Corporation. Retrieved October 2, 2011, from http://www.rand.org/pubs/technical_reports/TR995

Lundquist, J. H., & Smith, H. L. (2005). Family formation among women in the U.S. military: Evidence from the NLSY. *Journal of Marriage and Family, 67*, 1–13.

Mare, R. D., & Winship, C. (1984). The paradox of lessening racial inequality and joblessness among black youth: Enrollment, enlistment, and employment, 1964–1981. *American Sociological Review, 49*, 39–55.

Nock, S. L. (1998). *Marriage in men's lives*. New York: Oxford University Press.

Oppenheimer, V. K. (1988). A theory of marriage timing. *American Journal of Sociology, 94*(3), 563–591.

Pettit, B., & Hook, J. (2005). The structure of women's employment in comparative perspective. *Social Forces, 84*, 779–801.

Phillips, R. L., Andrisani, P. J., Daymont, T. N., & Gilroy, C. L. (1992). The economic returns to military service: Race-ethnic differences. *Social Science Quarterly, 73*, 340–359.

Segal, M. (1986). The military and the family as greedy institutions. *Armed Forces & Society, 13*(1), 1–38.

Sweeney, M. M. (2002). Two decades of family change: The shifting economic foundations of marriage. *American Sociological Review, 67*(1), 132–147.

Taniguchi, H., & Kaufman, G. (2005). Degree completion among nontraditional college students. *Social Science Quarterly, 86*(4), 912–927.

Teachman, J. (2007). Military service and educational attainment in the all-volunteer era. *Sociology of Education, 80*, 359–374.

Teachman, J. D., & Call, V. R. A. (1996). The effect of military service on educational, occupational, and income attainment. *Social Science Research, 25*, 1–31.

Teachman, J. D., & Polonko, K. A. (1988). Marriage, parenthood, and the college enrollment of men and women. *Social Forces, 67*(2), 512–523.

Teachman, J., & Tedrow, L. (2007). Joining up: Did military service in the early all volunteer era affect subsequent civilian income? *Social Science Research, 36*, 1447–1474.

United States Senate Health, Education, Labor and Pensions Committee. (2010). *Benefitting whom? For-profit education companies and the growth of military educational benefits*. Retrieved November 7, 2011, from http://harkin.senate.gov/documents/pdf/4d0bbba63cba1.pdf

Waite, L. J. (1995). Does marriage matter? *Demography, 32*(4), 483–508.

Waldman, E. (1983). Labor force statistics from a family perspective. *Monthly Labor Review, 106*(12), 16–20.

Xie, Y. (1992). The socioeconomic status of young male veterans, 1964–1984. *Social Science Quarterly, 73*, 379–396.

Xie, Y., Raymo, J. M., Goyette, K., & Thornton, A. (2003). Economic potential and entry into marriage and cohabitation. *Demography, 40*(2), 351–367.

Chapter 12
Recent Developments in the Uneasy Tension Between Family and Career: Competency-Related Perceptions of Women and Mothers

Jenny M. Hoobler

Abstract In this chapter I summarize my own research, other current research, and theory, as well as provide anecdotal evidence from the popular press regarding career-related perceptions of women and mothers at work. Women are often categorized as less career-dedicated and career-competent because of real or perceived caregiving roles, which tend to be devalued even in contemporary work environments. I conclude with the significance of this phenomenon for career-active female spouses of military personnel and women seeking leadership positions in the military, as well as ideas for future research and implications for practitioners.

Keywords Women • Mothers • Career • Stereotypes • Caregiving • Military

As recent evidence from the business world and academic literature suggest, others' perceptions may be critical to especially women's career progress. Social identity categorization processes form the basis of these career-related perceptions. In this chapter I present recent research findings from the management, psychology, and military psychology literatures, and anecdotal examples from government and business leaders to illustrate that, especially for mothers and women—even single women—supervisors' and other superiors' perceptions matter career-wise. And these perceptions contribute to an uneasy tension between family and career.

An example comes from the gaffe made by former Governor of Pennsylvania, Ed Rendell, regarding the career potential of now Secretary of Homeland Security, Janet Napolitano. At a December 2008 news conference in Philadelphia, Rendell, then the National Governors' Association chairman, did not realize he was standing next to a live microphone. He had this to say about Napolitano, President Obama's

J.M. Hoobler, Ph.D. (✉)
Department of Managerial Studies, College of Business Administration, University of Illinois at Chicago, 601 S. Morgan Street, 2212 University Hall, MC 243, Chicago, IL 60607, USA
e-mail: jhoobler@uic.edu

S. MacDermid Wadsworth and D.S. Riggs (eds.), *Military Deployment and its Consequences for Families*, Risk and Resilience in Military and Veteran Families, DOI 10.1007/978-1-4614-8712-8_12, © Springer Science+Business Media New York 2014

choice for Secretary of Homeland Security: "Janet's perfect for that job. Because for that job, you have to have no life. Janet has no family. Perfect. She can devote, literally, 19–20 hours a day to it" (Tapper & Jaffe, 2008). Unpacking Rendell's perceptions of Secretary Napolitano involves examining how people's social identity categories, identities such as being a single person, a woman, and someone with or without caregiving responsibilities, color perceptions of a person's suitability for a top job, and, in general, perceptions of their career competency and dedication.

The Power of Others' Perceptions

The perceptions of those who have power and control decisions, whether that person is the governor of Pennsylvania or simply your own direct supervisor, are important, whether they are accurate or not. This is because they often bring with them privileges, opportunities, social validation, and a host of other resources for the person who is the target of those perceptions. This idea is not new to the management literature. Extensive work has been done on both (1) people's reliance on social identity categories (e.g., their race, gender, age) to judge others in the workplace, and (2) the intentional manipulation of others' perceptions in the workplace, that is, impression management (e.g., "those behaviors individuals employ to protect their self-images, influence the way they are perceived by significant others, or both," Wayne & Liden, 1995, p. 232), and ingratiation ("a set of interpersonal influence tactics that function to enhance one's interpersonal attractiveness and ultimately 'gain favor' with another individual," Westphal & Stern, 2007, p. 270). For the purposes of this article I focus on the first body of knowledge—the reliance on social identity categories to judge others—and provide illustrative examples of this research below.

   In interviewing and other workplace situations, people tend to judge others not just by their experience, the quality of their ideas and how well they convey them, and how they conduct themselves interpersonally, but by social identity categories—often surface-level demographic factors. The research on the psychology of job interviewing, for example, is in part based on the ideas behind social identity theory—that individuals categorize themselves and others using social categories (like race, gender, and age) and attach values to these identities (Gaertner & Dovidio, 2000; Tajfel, 1982). By evaluating those who have similar identities to one's self more positively than dissimilar others, this allows the maintenance of positive self-identities (Steele, 1988). In support of this, field studies have demonstrated that when the interviewer and the applicant are of the same race, this leads to both more positive overall assessments of the job candidate, and increases the likelihood of a job offer (e.g., Goldberg, 2005). Also underscoring the weight of racial perceptions in the job search process is Bertrand and Mullainathan's (2004) field experiment to determine whether employers discriminate against African-American applicants. Responding to job ads in major Chicago and Boston newspapers, they submitted multiple résumés from phantom job seekers and randomly assigned first names on the résumés, choosing from one set of names that is particularly common among blacks and from another set common among whites. Apart from their names, the phantom applicants had the same experience, education, and skills, so employers had no reason to distinguish between them. Yet applicants with typically white-sounding names were 50 % more likely to be called for interviews than were those with black-sounding names.

Another example of the power of social categorization in the workplace illustrates the particular importance of *supervisors*' perceptions. Powell's (2004) study explored why there are so few black and other ethnic minority managers in local governments in the United Kingdom. Powell examined the results of 360-degree feedback evaluations in local government jobs. 360-degree feedback is where performance evaluations of one employee are solicited from many parties, for example, the employee's supervisor, colleagues, and customers, in the effort to obtain a more comprehensive view of the employee's performance, i.e., the full "360-degree" picture. The intention is to avoid the effects of interpersonal biases inherent to receiving feedback in the traditional manner, from one person, typically the employee's direct supervisor. Powell (2004) found that black managers were consistently rated lower than white managers by their supervisors, but rated higher than white managers by their colleagues. This contradicts existing research findings that extol the virtues of 360-degree evaluation processes by arguing that supervisors' perceptions correlate with peer perceptions. But perhaps more importantly, it sheds light on the hazards of relying on supervisors' perceptions alone. If employees are awarded raises, given promotions, assigned to plum projects or prime working hours based on these evaluations, supervisors' perceptions likely translate into not only psychological, but also career and financial consequences for the employees they supervise.

While business practitioners, as in the supervisors example above, often use surface-level social identifiers (Harrison, Price, & Bell, 1998) such as those that are visible in momentary observations of others like race, sex, and age, to make judgments about others, *researchers* fall prey to this in some fashion as well. The design of research studies often includes shallow ways of measuring substantive differences between people. For example, the practice of grouping study respondents into nominal categories to explore theoretical differences between groups is rather standard practice. Checking a box to self-report respondents' race (as in "are you black, white, Hispanic, …?") is often used as a proxy for deep-level diversity, that is, differences among individuals in terms of non-immediately recognizable characteristics including personalities, values, attitudes, and culture (Harrison et al., 1998; Jackson, May, & Whitney, 1995). Hence, surface-level demographic factors are assumed to reflect deeper, meaningful differences between people and predict their behavior and attitudes. An example might be a researcher who finds in her dataset that respondents who were over age 50 tended to report lower intentions to leave their organization, and then concludes from this that Baby Boomers have a stronger work ethic than do younger workers, allowing age to approximate work values when work values were in fact not measured. Some scholars (e.g., Cox & Nkomo, 1990) have for many years cautioned against these types of research designs that make a large leap between theory and operationalization of study variables, yet these types of studies continue to be published.

Social Identity Categorization and Career Outcomes

According to Feldman's (1981, 1986) work on social categorization, supervisors make assumptions about employees based on external, surface-level cues which then influence the information that is salient, attended to, and recalled in relation to that employee (Shore, Barksdale, & Shore, 1995). Moreover, supervisors then make resource allocations according to these categorizations, including bestowing constructive feedback, allowing participation in decision-making, and assigning challenging projects to their employees (Liden, Wayne, & Stillwell, 1993). These allocations can have implications for career progress. For example, the decision to develop an employee, that is, provide that employee with organizational experiences that expand his or her skills and experience, is often an interpersonal one: Direct supervisors can serve as gate-keepers to whether employees are given the chance to e.g., attend training classes, or serve on committees that will expand their knowledge and give them "face time" with important persons internal and external to their organization. Van Velsor and Hughes (1990) and Lyness and Thompson (1997, 2000) have shown that development of this type is important to career success: Both male and female senior managers felt that organizational development experiences, such as being placed in roles and tasks that are challenging and unique, had a significant impact on their career achievements such as the degree to which they were satisfied with their careers and the hierarchical levels they attained.

Supervisors tend to allocate career-related resources such as organizational development opportunities in less than optimal ways. Humans are cognitive misers, and akin to the social identity categorization processes described above, supervisors tend to use "short-cuts" in the cognitive process of deciding which employees are worthy of the time, dollars, and energy required for organizational development. My own research has demonstrated that women, as opposed to men, tend to not fit with the view of the ideal worker as one who is unencumbered by caregiving responsibilities and therefore free to work as many hours as the job dictates (Acker, 2006; Lewis, 1997). As a result, women tend to receive fewer organizational development opportunities (Hoobler, Lemmon, & Wayne, In Press; King et al., In Press). I turn now to expand on the social categorization of women as caregivers, and the impact this has on their careers.

Gender and Career Perceptions

Gender Social Role Theory

Gender social role theories (Eagly, 1987; Eagly & Karau, 2002) hold that men and women are perceived as having disparate natural tendencies. The gender-typical roles (e.g., breadwinner versus homemaker) credited to men and women shape expectations about what is appropriate behavior for each. Research over many years and across various academic disciplines consistently finds that men are generally perceived as more active, risk-taking, and competent, whereas women are seen as more expressive, communal, nurturing, and supportive (c.f., Diekman & Eagly, 2000). In the business world, this theoretical reasoning forms the basis of what has been called the "think leader, think male" paradigm (Schein, 1973, 1975)—the persistent view held by both men and women that the prototype of a successful leader is more likely to involve a man and masculine behaviors including risk-taking, aggressiveness, and decisiveness (Heilman, 2001) than typical female conceptualizations.

Not only are men and women perceived as having different characteristics, but the characteristics of men have also traditionally held more value in the workplace. The caregiving traits women are perceived as having ("nurturing, supportive") are central to roles that are often unpaid and/or hidden in the private sphere of the home. As well, evidence shows that women are in fact the ones to perform the lion's share of parenting and caring for the elderly or sick (Navaie-Waliser, Spriggs, & Feldman, 2002), which reinforces the stereotype that this is what women do and what they seem to be good at. So, in value and in practice, caregiving roles create a double-bind for women, career-wise. Not only are traditionally feminine characteristics associated with caregiving prowess perceived to be incongruent with leadership roles, these caregiving roles are both under- or not rewarded in the external labor market (Lewis, 2001; Liff & Ward, 2001; Littleton, 1997).

So evidence exists that people are less likely to associate women with leadership abilities than men, but also that women's caregiving roles mean women are less focused and less competent in their careers. For example, Mattis (2002) presents this stereotype used in "myth-busting" training in the Bank of Montreal's Advancement of Women Initiative: "Because of child-rearing responsibilities, women are less committed to their careers" (p. 321). Research evidence supports that being a woman is associated with perceptions of decreased managerial ability (Powell, Butterfield, & Parent, 2002), less effective leadership (Eagly, Johannesen-Schmidt, & Van Engen, 2003), and fewer attributions for organizational successes (Heilman & Haynes, 2005). This evidence continues to proliferate 40 years after Schein coined the term "think leader, think male" (Schein, 1973, 1975).

Single Women

Because stereotypes of women as less suited for career and leadership roles seem to be at least in part rooted in women's association with caregiving roles (Hoobler, Wayne, & Lemmon, 2009), the question becomes, if a woman is not a mother, does not care for elderly or sick family members or friends, and is not married or part-nered, do these perceptions of caregiving roles apply, and do they still serve to devalue her status in the workplace? The anecdotal answer to this question seems to be "yes," according to a recent quote from the CEO of Glencore, the world's largest diversified commodities trading company and employer of 52,000 people.

"Women are quite as intelligent as men, [but]…they have a tendency not to be so involved quite often and they're not so ambitious in business as men because they've better things to do. Quite often they like bringing up their children and all sorts of other things… Pregnant ladies have nine months off. Do you think that means that when I rush out, what I'm absolutely desperate to have is young women who are about to get married in my company, and that I really need them on board because I know they're going to get pregnant and they're going to go off for nine months?"
    - Simon Murray, Chairman, Glencore, quoted in *The Sunday Telegraph*, 4/24/11 (Cave, 2011)

Mr. Murray's interviewer summarized that Mr. Murray has "lively opinions" (Cave, 2011) on, among other things, women. His perceptions seem to be at the same time echoed in the Rendell comments regarding Secretary Napolitano above. Yet Murray's comments depart from Rendell's comments in important ways as well. Commonalities these perceptions share include the idea that judging women's suitability for leadership roles is tightly linked to their caregiver identities. Napolitano was seen as suitable for her role as Secretary of Homeland Security because she had "no family," (a common misconception of single workers; Casper, Weltman & Kwesiga, 2007) yet judging her work competence was nevertheless tied to family considerations—a link not usually considered in judging male job applicants. The Murray quote goes further to suggest that women who do not occupy caregiving roles (not married/partnered, with no children) will inevitably do so, and this will disrupt their career commitment. This has been termed the "ticking womb" fallacy—that all women are on the cusp of leaving their career to pursue family roles, when in reality, many will not. While women as compared to men, do have more career interruptions and lower labor force participation, married and unmarried women without children actually more closely mirror men (as compared to women without children) in both labor force participation and career earnings (Bertrand, Golden, & Katz, 2010). So, while the presence of children does have an impact on women's time away from work and their earnings, not every career woman has children. In fact, women in leadership roles are less likely than their male counterparts to be a parent (Galinksy et al., 2003)—a point I will revisit in discussing women's leadership in the military below.

I return now to the question of career perceptions of single women. Initial research suggests that single women face perceptions that they are less career competent and dedicated, despite not having children nor a spouse/partner. Research my colleagues and I (Hoobler et al., 2009) did at a U.S. Fortune 100 transportation firm suggests that, even when female employees did not have children, did not have elder-care responsibilities, and were not married or partnered, their supervisors (both men and women) still felt these women experienced family-to-work conflict (negative spillover from family responsibilities onto work roles). So, perhaps the "ticking womb" idea does persist. Just being female was associated with supervisors' perceptions of family-to-work conflict. Interestingly, we found that it was actually the male employees, as opposed to the female employees, who reported that their family life spilled over to affect work to a higher degree. Further, from our research it was not just women of child-bearing age who were perceived by their

supervisors to have higher family-to-work conflict, but rather age had no bearing ⌣⌣
these perceptions of women.

However, the research does strike a note of positivity for a different test case group: single women at the upper echelons of organizations. Single women in high-status positions are perceived as career competent because they fit the modern mold of the professional woman (Fiske, Cuddy, Glick, & Xu, 2002)—low in warmth but high in competence. The "think leader, think male" paradigm explains these findings. Women who have made it in the leadership realm should either possess or are attributed with non-traditional gender social roles, those more commonly ascribed to men, e.g., low warmth. So for women who have already "made it," stereotypes about caregiving roles do not seem to apply nor do they seem to negatively skew others' perceptions of them. But this presents a catch-22: These women were able to ascend to the top jobs, when, at the same time, caregiving roles would have seemed to have played a role in judging their competency "on the way up." Perhaps there is something inherently different about the women who make it as top leaders, for instance, in personality or behavioral styles. Or there may be something different about the workplaces and/or industries in which these women are able to succeed. I address these ideas in the "how career women can 'win'" section below.

Parental and Marital Status

In this section, I discuss career-related perceptions of both mothers and fathers. As for mothers, as I conveyed above, via the "ticking womb" metaphor, some harbor the assumption that all women are, or are about to be, mothers. By extension, the belief is that women will at some point eschew their career for caregiving roles. Moreover, this stereotype does not extend to just women with young children, or women of childbearing age, but rather all women (Hoobler et al., 2009). So the question becomes whether or not, when women in fact do become mothers, there is an additional negative impact on others' career-related perceptions of them. From my own research I have found that indeed working mothers are seen as having more family-to-work conflict than working women who are child-free (supplemental analyses from Hoobler et al., 2009). And there is a good deal of research that supports, in real dollars, a "child penalty" for mothers, that is, that women with children tend to earn lower wages than women without children (e.g., Budig & England, 2001; and see Economic Disparities section below). But perhaps the good news is that our research has found that single mothers do not experience a "double penalty" (i.e., for being both a woman and a mother) as far as others' perceptions of their career competence.

But, marriage does seem to be career-limiting from a perceptual standpoint—for both men and women. Again from our research in a Fortune 100 transportation firm, both men and women who were married or partnered were assumed by their supervisors to have greater family-to-work conflict than those employees who were not married, which was a surprising finding for my colleagues and me. We assumed that married employees would be seen as more stable, more reliable, and more financially tied to the organization and therefore less likely to quit. We do not know if supervisors held these perceptions (i.e., stability and reliability) regarding married employees. But what we do know is that married workers were seen as more likely to let their family responsibilities collide with work roles. This contradicts the popular idea that there is a marriage premium for men (Heilman & Okimoto, 2008), based on the stability and reliability ideas advanced above.

As far as the presence of children, there are interesting differences in comparing the career-related perceptions of mothers to career-related perceptions of fathers. Both mothers and fathers are perceived as less committed to their jobs than are nonparents (Fuegen, Biernat, Haines, & Deaux, 2004). And both mothers and fathers are perceived as less interested in achievement than workers who are not parents (Heilman & Okimoto, 2008). However, only mothers are seen as less competent, compared to workers who are not parents (Heilman & Okimoto, 2008). So, in sum, it seems that all parents face perceptions that they have less time and energy to devote to work roles, yet only for women is the presence of children associated with perceptions that she can perform job tasks less effectively than nonparent peers. In fact, mothers who violate gender roles by being employed full-time are perceived as both less nurturing (less competent in their caregiving role than fathers, e.g., Bridges & Etaugh, 1995) plus perceived as less professionally competent than full-time employed fathers (Etaugh & Folger, 1998).

Do Perceptions Relate to Economic Disparities?

Many studies have documented the persistence of a gender pay gap, whereby women are paid from 9 to 18 cents to the dollar (depending on how experience, education, and other human capital factors are taken into consideration) less than men are paid in the United States (Blau & Kahn, 2007). While some of this disparity can be explained by the different occupational choices that men and women make, and the divergent salaries that accompany these choices, evidence of gender discrimination as an explanation for the remaining gender pay gap exists (Goldin & Rouse, 2000).

Bertrand et al. (2010) released a longitudinal study of the interplay between gender, family demographics, and career and salary achievement of highly-educated workers in the U.S. corporate and financial sectors. They found that the gender pay gap between MBA (Masters of Business Administration) students directly following graduation is less than 12 %, meaning women earn about 12 % less than their male counterparts. However, 15 years out, this gap widens substantially to 38 %. As far as explanations for these gaps, they find no main effects of marriage/partnership and they conclude that the gender wage gap is almost entirely due to the presence of children. First, women with children average an 8-month labor force deficit (meaning time away from paid labor—which has a compounded effect on lifetime earnings) due to career interruptions, while women with no children have just a 1.5-month deficit. These career interruptions include time away from work upon birth of a child or, less often, upon adoption of a child. Bertrand and scholars also found that MBA women's earnings dropped by, on average about $45,000 two years following the birth of a first child, which had a close to $80,000 impact on earnings per year in subsequent years. They found that women with no children outearned mothers to the extent that their wages were more similar to men's than they were to mothers'. Perhaps surprisingly, there was no additional impact of a second birth on earnings, possibly signifying that career allowances for children (e.g., part-time work, finding a more family-friendly position, leaving the workforce) tend to be made at the time or shortly after the first child comes along.

I present these results from the Bertrand and colleagues (2010) study in an effort to explore whether there is a financial impact of the career-related perceptual differences of men and women (akin to discrimination) that I have presented above. While tying these findings together may be a crude exercise, I do feel a few ideas may be hypothesized. First, remember that both married/partnered men and women were perceived to let their family roles spill over to work roles to a greater extent than non-married/-partnered employees. From Bertrand and colleagues' (2010) study this perception does not seem to result in a significant monetary impact on career success. So, perhaps bosses think that married people are less successful at focusing specifically on career roles, but this does not seem to impact the degree to which they may be given higher paying jobs and granted promotions and raises. Second, remember that both mothers and fathers tend to be viewed as less committed to careers. Bertrand and colleagues' (2010) findings suggest that mothers as opposed to fathers, in even this highly career-focused sample of MBAs, do tend to act in ways that put family ahead of career. In their study, nine years past graduation, females were about 12 % less likely than their male peers to be working outside the home, and had spent on average half a year more outside of the workforce. A woman with at least one child was about 20 % less likely to work in a given year than the average man, over the 16 years of the study. In contrast, a woman without children was only 3 % less likely to be employed as compared to the average man in the study.

There are many ways to interpret the overlay of these findings onto career-related perceptions of mothers and fathers. The most obvious interpretation would be that supervisors and others in the workplace are legitimate in their perceptions that mothers are less committed and interested in achievement (salary being one measure of objective achievement) than nonparents. This could be a conclusion drawn from the fact that even highly-educated career women are more likely than their male counterparts to pursue what have been called "mommy track[1]" types of jobs (part-time work, etc.) or exit the labor force altogether. A word of caution against generalizing this interpretation: Not all mothers pursue these alternative ways of

---

[1] As Hill, Martinson, Ferris, and Baker (2004) point out, fewer women appear to be on what has been termed the "mommy track," as it is often not feasible for economic reasons. And, as an anonymous reviewer suggested, perhaps it is time to let go of the term "mommy track" because it may serve to increase negative stereotypes about working mothers.

working nor do they all exit the workforce upon birth or adoption of a child, even for a temporary period of time. A second possible interpretation of these findings would be that supervisors' perceptions of mothers become self-fulfilling prophecy. That is, because supervisors hold the expectation that mothers will take a career off-ramp upon having children, they treat them in ways that make their exodus easier. This treatment could include lower expectations, less challenging projects, and low-profile work. Because mothers may feel their career is "not going anywhere" anyway (Beiner, 2007), they may choose to leave their organizations.

Military Implications

Military Spouses

Others' career-related perceptions of women and mothers are relevant to military families and military careers in two main ways. First, there has recently been an upsurge of interest in supporting the careers of military spouses. These spouses are likely to be female, given that members of the military are still overwhelmingly male (Febbraro & Gill, 2010) and that same-sex spouses are still the minority of military families. Assumptions about female spouses as caregivers are likely even more exaggerated in a military context for at least three reasons. First, the threat of turnover of military spouse career women in the organizations in which they work is likely very high. While women in general are seen by employers as a high "flight risk" due to the possibility of leaving to pursue caregiving roles (Lyness & Judiesch, 2001), military spouses are likely to be seen as an even greater flight risk due to the mobile, transitive lifestyle of their spouses' military postings. Second, the caregiving roles of female military spouses are highly salient to others due to the likelihood of single parenting during times of husbands' deployment. Third, perceptions of military spouses' careers being "secondary careers," that is, subordinate to their husbands' careers, may be commonplace in that others may assume the spouses' careers are not essential for benefits and compensation—the assumption being that the military is the primary provider for the family. Moreover, under the terms of some Status of Forces Agreements (SOFAs; agreements that establish the rights and privileges of foreign personnel and their dependents while present in a host country), military spouses are forbidden from off-base employment altogether (Cohen, 2011). So, for these reasons, the effects I have detailed above of women being associated with caregiving roles and this serving to derail perceptions of women as competent and committed to their careers, should be magnified for military spouses. As such these women may face an even steeper climb to obtain desired career resources such as organizational development opportunities and to achieve desired career outcomes such as positive performance evaluations, promotions, and raises.

Women's Leadership in the Military

The second way in which these career-related perceptions of women and mothers are relevant to military careers and military families is in considering women's leadership within the military hierarchy. Many studies of women in the military are underpinned by the theme of career and family being uneasy bedfellows. Theorists have argued that the military is a "total institution," whereby its views and demands supplant any competing family or personal commitments (Febbraro & Gill, 2010, p. 686). Indeed, family is the main reason women decide to leave military careers (Febbraro & Gill, 2010; Harris, 2009). Eighty percent of women who plan to leave the Army, inclusive of those who have recently experienced promotions, leave due to family issues (Harris, Steinberg, & Scarville, 1994). About a quarter of married active duty women are married to active duty military men (Office of the Deputy Under Secretary of Defense & Military Community and Family Policy, 2012). Thus, the issue of maintaining relationships given geographical separation and the challenges of raising children during deployment are likely to contribute to women's decisions to leave the Services. As Ganderton (2002) explains, military culture places a high value on "face time"–which work and family scholars suggest is directly oppositional to what children need when growing up, which is time with their parents (Smith, 2001). To get family time, individuals are frequently dependent on the willingness of their superiors to grant access to the still-lacking family friendly policies that do exist (Holden & Tanner, 2001), which suggests that the power of the direct superior is important in the attempt to balance family and career.

As far as attitudes toward women's leadership in the military, while representation of women in leadership positions has improved to a certain extent, traditional stereotypes persist. Matthews, Ender, Laurence, and Rohall (2009) found that 29.6 % of ROTC (Reserve Officers' Training Corps), 38.1 % of West Point first-year cadets, and 35.3 % of civilians surveyed either answered "should not" or "don't know" to the question of whether women should serve as military commanders. Returning to the traditional stereotype of women as caregivers, Febbraro and Gill's (2010) research shows that caregiver stereotypes extend to women's occupational segregation within military jobs. As evidence, they point to women in the Israeli Defense Forces being most often "posted to clerical, support, or 'caretaking' roles" such as teaching or social welfare, which are "consistent with traditional gender-role expectations, stereotypes, and norms" (p. 673). Moreover, these are positions unlikely to be imbued with power and high rank. And, as of the writing of this chapter, women in the U.S. and U.K. are still not officially[2] allowed to serve in combat roles. This exclusion has been argued to negatively impact women's career advancement (DeCew, 1995). Febbraro and Gill (2010) argue this occupational segregation is rooted in assumptions and stereotypes about women's lack of emotional

---

[2] As an exception to this, and as the documentary film *Lioness* (Room 11 Productions) illustrates, the U.S. policy banning women from serving in direct ground combat has been, in practice, violated during the Iraq War.

toughness and the belief that mixed-gender units will undermine the "male bonding" central to the cohesion required of combat units (Febbraro & McCann, 2003).

Women in the military often occupy lower level officer positions and can feel isolated in their workgroups. In 2004, women comprised 15 % of both the U.S. enlisted and officer force, yet U.S. military women are disproportionately represented in the lower enlisted and lower officer levels in all four branches of the Service (Moskos, 2007). Stoever, Schmaling, Gutierrez, Fonseca, and Blume (2007) found that, in their study of officers, being a woman was a negative predictor of pay grade, even after controlling for education and years of service. Rosabeth Moss Kanter's theory of tokenism (1977) in the workplace holds that when a demographic group (here, women) equals less than fifteen percent of a work group, as they do in many work groups within the military, they will be viewed predominantly as a member of that distinctive demographic group, and there will be pressure for them to occupy limited or stereotypically gender appropriate roles. As well, they likely face increased scrutiny of their labors and work product, and report isolation and polarization from the rest of the workgroup. This theory explains a number of findings regarding negative outcomes for women leaders in the military. For example, female officers are more likely to be underevaluated on performance reviews by male superiors when units are not gender balanced (Pazy & Oron, 2001). Kanter's theory would predict that only when the number of women in military workgroups exceeds 15 % can women's status be uplifted from tokenism to individual achievement, and gender power differentials begin to be remedied.

How Can Career Women "Win?"/Implications for Practitioners

The foregoing chapter has documented in detail the somewhat dismal plight of women in business and military careers. These circumstances notwithstanding, how can women "win," that is, how can they be successful in careers where they are likely to be viewed stereotypically? In this section I offer two suggestions. First, many women have reframed their definitions of career success. Instead of objective indicators of career success such as hierarchical position in organizations (e.g., division commander, vice-president, or CEO) or top salaries or pay grades, they will pursue other, perhaps more subjective career goals. In this vein, Mainiero and Sullivan (2005) write, rather than opting-out of paid work altogether or pursuing linear, hierarchical views of career progress, many women tend to pursue what these scholars call "kaleidoscope careers." They find that "many women [have] examined the opportunities, roadblocks, and possibilities, then forged their own approach to a career without regard for traditional career models and standard measures of achievement" (p. 108). These women tend to look at their needs and desires and adjust their career strivings to best fit their circumstances at the time—circumstances like spouses' geographical moves, the need to reduce stress or pursue achievement or education milestones, the desire for a challenge, or the need for flexibility or security. Finding careers that allow for these factors, reevaluating individual needs periodically over the life course, and making changes to satisfy emergent needs is what the kaleidoscope career is all about. However, let me be clear. Nothing in this discussion is intended to signal that women and mothers are not or should not be interested in more objective indicators of career success. While the popular press may make sensational claims that women are not interested in the top jobs and the large salaries that accompany them (Hoobler et al., In Press; Mainiero & Sullivan, 2005), the research evidence paints a different picture. In fact, Eagly, Karau, Miner, and Johnson (1994) found that while men had a slightly higher overall motivation to manage (that is, the motivation to perform typical role requirements related to being a manager in a business organization), women actually scored higher than men on certain managerial tasks (e.g., the desire to be a figurehead, the desire to perform certain administrative tasks). And a report of what women in upper echelons in companies want finds that a full 55 % say their goal is to be CEO (Catalyst, 2003). So, while many women find that spinning the kaleidoscope to make personal and family desires drop into place along with career strivings, a good many women are defining career success in ways that would have traditionally been seen as consistent with masculine values: advancement in hierarchies and attaining ever-increasing salaries. The important message is that a one-size-fits-all career is not the best for everyone nor the best at all times across the life course. Mainiero and Sullivan (2005) offer detailed suggestions for how organizations may remake themselves to aid in the creation of kaleidoscope careers.

Second, women should find companies with organizational cultures that fit their individual career goals. For mothers, it may be crucial to find an employer that values their many social identities, and where participating in caregiving roles is not something that will detract from perceptions of competency and dedication (Hoobler, 2007). But also for single women, "family-friendly" organizations that value work-life balance and have human resource policies in place that demonstrate organizational commitment to multiple employee social identities is still recommended. These are likely to be organizations where more women are employed (hence avoiding the tokenism effects detailed above). Moreover, the research has demonstrated that family-friendly cultures make for better workplaces for *all* employees—including nonparents, men, and fathers.

Catalyst (Galinksy et al. 2003), a leading non-profit research organization, suggests that organizations should engage in the following initiatives to ensure the development of the next generation of leaders—both men and women: systematic career development and management for both genders; an inclusive work environment that values diversity, provides equal opportunities, and guards against discrimination; and attention to work-life needs, including addressing the existence of cultural values and expectations of very long work hours, providing role models that support involvement in activities outside of work, and rethinking existing career paths. Inherent to these recommendations is that the organization must play a role in creating workplaces that are gender equitable. While interpersonal processes (e.g., supervisors' perceptions) are important to women's career advancement, the organization has responsibility for this as well.

The good news is that many women do make it work—balancing both perceptions of themselves and outside commitments with satisfying career progress. Ezzedeen and Ritchey (2009) found that through a complex mix of value systems, personal and professional social support, and life-course strategies akin to the kaleidoscope career idea, executive women were able to advance their careers and at the same time maintain balance and satisfaction. They end their manuscript with a suggestion that "women must embrace certain beliefs about their life roles and revisit what society considers appropriate. Women can reasonably expect to live with some disapproval when they bend social norms; however, …[women] also indicated that times were changing and gender roles were in flux" (p. 405). So, this chapter does draw a picture of the challenges women and mothers face in the workplace, but with an eye toward perceptions and stereotypes improving in upcoming decades and for successive generations.

Future Research

I conclude with the following suggestions for future research related to workplace perceptions of women and mothers. First, we must understand why social role theory-based stereotypes endure. Virginia Schein's research illustrating "think leader, think male" is now, as mentioned, nearly 40 years old. Why do these perceptions allying males with leadership prowess persist? Boyce and Herd (2003) asked the tough question of whether there is legitimacy in "think leader, think male in the military." That is, they ask whether the U.S military's success in "achieving national and international military objectives throughout America's history" (p. 376) is in part attributed to its masculine culture and requisite masculine leadership. They conclude that especially in these turbulent, dynamic times of global terrorism, the unprecedented need for smaller, more flexible special operations forces (Burns, 2002) that are trained in a wide variety of skills including humanitarian, peace-keeping, and other unconventional efforts, requires a new kind of leadership. This leadership may take the form of a more flexible leadership style (Thompson, 2000) that may be more charismatic and higher in consensus building, with overtones of a more traditionally feminine leadership approach. So, in the contemporary military climate, perhaps there is space to clear out old archetypes of leadership effectiveness. There would be great value in testing the effectiveness of and best contexts for new, alternative leadership styles.

The second research recommendation is to more fully document the choices that women are making in regard to family life due to career considerations. The extant research has shown that career-focused women tend to put off having children until later in life and are less likely than their male counterparts to have children at all (Galinksy et al. 2003; Lundberg & Pollak, 2007). Military women are more likely than military men to have never married: Of battalion commanders, only 20.3 % of women had children as compared to 98 % of men (Harris, 2009). Furthermore, as an anonymous reviewer suggested, research is needed to test whether, as this reviewer suspects, female officers may plan their fertility around their military careers (e.g., delaying having children or timing births around tours and deployments). Indeed research should uncover the family choices women make, including the extremes of not marrying and opting to forego motherhood, based in part on job schedules but also on women's concern for others' perceptions of their career competency. These choices seem to signal a social problem and the need for cultural transformation of masculine-typed work organizations.

Third, the research on career-related perceptions of single workers who are child-free is sparse and can be hard to compare study-to-study. I feel more research attention is due this work subgroup. For example, future research could explore whether being single does enhance perceptions of career competency and commitment, perhaps depending on the industry in which singles are employed. It is easy to imagine that in industries where long, billable hours are required, for example, in advertising and the legal profession, or in military deployments, this could be the case. Family responsibilities can be perceived by others as a source of stability, encumbrance, or somewhere in between the two, and these views may depend on the perceiver, the job, and the post.

The final research idea comes from the dismantling of the "Don't Ask, Don't Tell" policy in the U.S. Military. Research could explore how non-traditional family structures including same-sex partnerships affect others' perceptions of responsibility for caregiving, and, by extension, career competency and dedication. One research question could be: Do same-sex partner mothers find that both parents are saddled with others' perceptions of decreased competency?

Conclusion

In business and military organizations, there exists an uneasy tension between family and career. This is in part rooted in women and mothers' assumed caregiving roles being incompatible with perceptions of what it takes to be successful in and dedicated to modern-day organizations. Until such stereotypes are eliminated, solutions lie in women finding organizations that fit with current career and personal life goals, and reevaluating these as needs and desires change.

References

Acker, J. (2006). Inequality regimes: Gender, class, and race in organizations. *Gender & Society, 20*(4), 441–464.
Beiner, T. M. (2007). Not all lawyers are equal: Difficulties that plague women and women of color. *Syracuse Law Review, 58*, 317–331.
Bertrand, M., Golden, C., & Katz, L. F. (2010). Dynamics of the gender gap for young professionals in the financial and corporate sectors. *American Economic Journal: Applied Economics, 2*(3), 228–255.

Bertrand, M., & Mullainathan, S. (2004). Are Emily and Greg more employable than Lakisha and Jamal? A field experiment on labor market discrimination. *American Economic Review, 94*(4), 991–1013.

Blau, F. D., & Kahn, L. M. (2007). The gender pay gap. *The Economists' Voice, 4*(4), 1–6.

Boyce, L. A., & Herd, A. M. (2003). The relationship between gender role stereotypes and requisite military leadership characteristics. *Sex Roles, 49*(7–8), 365–378.

Bridges, J. S., & Etaugh, C. (1995). College students' perceptions of mothers: Effects of maternal employment-childrearing pattern and motive for employment. *Sex Roles, 32*(11–12), 735–751.

Budig, M. J., & England, P. (2001). The wage penalty for motherhood. *American Sociological Review, 66*(2), 204–225.

Burns, R. (2002, November 13). Special operations role grows. *The Fayetteville Observer*, p. 11A.

Casper, W. J., Weltman, D., & Kwesiga, E. (2007). Beyond family-friendly: The construct and measurement of singles-friendly work cultures. *Journal of Vocational Behavior, 70*(3), 478–501.

Catalyst. (2003). *Women in US corporate leadership: 2003*. Retrieved October 20, 2011, from http://www.catalystwomen.org

Cave, A. (2011, April 24). *Glencore's Simon Murray: England today looks economically absolutely shambolic*. The Telegraph. Retrieved October 20, 2011, from http://www.telegraph.co.uk/finance/financetopics/profiles/8469647/Glencores-Simon-Murray-England-today-looks-economically-absolutely-shambolic.html

Cohen, C. F. (2011). *Maintaining career continuity as a military spouse*. National Military Spouse Network. Retrieved August 13, 2012, from http://www.nationalmilitaryspousenetwork.org/

Cox, T., & Nkomo, S. M. (1990). Invisible men and women: A status report on race as a variable in organization behavior research. *Journal of Organizational Behavior, 11*(6), 419–432.

DeCew, W. J. (1995). The combat exclusion and the role of women in the Military. *Hypatia, 10*(1), 56–73.

Diekman, A. B., & Eagly, A. H. (2000). Stereotypes as dynamic constructs: Women and men of the past, present, and future. *Personality and Social Psychology Bulletin, 26*(10), 1171–1188.

Eagly, A. H. (1987). *Sex differences in social behavior: A social role interpretation*. Hillsdale, NJ: Erlbaum.

Eagly, A. H., Johannesen-Schmidt, M. C., & Van Engen, M. L. (2003). Transformational, transactional, and laissez-faire leadership styles: A meta-analysis comparing men and women. *Psychological Bulletin, 129*(4), 569–591.

Eagly, A. H., & Karau, S. J. (2002). Role congruity theory of prejudice toward female leaders. *Psychological Review, 109*(3), 573–598.

Eagly, A. H., Karau, S. J., Miner, J. B., & Johnson, B. T. (1994). Gender and motivation to manage in hierarchic organizations: A meta-analysis. *Leadership Quarterly, 5*(2), 135–159.

Etaugh, C., & Folger, D. (1998). Perceptions of parents whose work and parenting behaviors deviate from role expectations. *Sex Roles, 39*(3–4), 215–223.

Ezzedeen, S. R., & Ritchey, K. G. (2009). Career advancement and family balance strategies of executive women. *Gender in Management: An International Journal, 24*(6), 388–411.

Febbraro, A. R., & Gill, R. M. (2010). Gender and military psychology. In J. C. Chrisler & D. R. McCreary (Eds.), *Handbook of gender research in psychology* (pp. 671–696). New York: Springer.

Febbraro, A. R., & McCann, C. (2003, May). *Demystifying the "feminine mythtique": Or, women and combat can mix. Gazette on the Net*. Pentagon, VA: On-line Publication of the U.S. Marine Corps.

Feldman, J. M. (1981). Beyond attribution theory: Cognitive processes in performance appraisal. *Journal of Applied Psychology, 66*(2), 127–148.

Feldman, J. M. (1986). A note on the statistical correction of halo error. *Journal of Applied Psychology, 71*(1), 173–176.

Fiske, S. T., Cuddy, A. J. C., Glick, P., & Xu, J. (2002). A model of (often mixed) stereotype content: Competence and warmth respectively follow from perceived status and competition. *Journal of Personality and Social Psychology, 82*(6), 878–902.

Fuegen, K., Biernat, M., Haines, E. L., & Deaux, K. (2004). Parents in the workplace: How gender and parental status influence judgments of job-related competence. *Journal of Social Issues, 60*(4), 737–754.

Gaertner, S. L., & Dovidio, J. F. (2000). *Reducing intergroup bias: The common ingroup identity model*. Philadelphia, PA: Psychology Press.

Galinksy, E., Salmond, K., Bond, J. T., Brumit Kropf, M., Moore, M., & Harrington, B. (2003). *Leaders in a global economy: A study of executive women and men*. New York: Families and Work Institute, Catalyst, and the Center for Work & Family.

Ganderton, S. L. (2002). *Work-life balance: Implementing flexible initiatives to improve retention and complete integration of women in the Canadian Forces*. Toronto, ON: Canadian Forces College.

Goldberg, C. B. (2005). Relational demography and similarity-attraction in interview assessments and subsequent offer decisions. *Group & Organization Management, 30*(6), 597–624.

Goldin, C., & Rouse, C. (2000). Orchestrating impartiality: The impact of "blind" auditions on female musicians. *American Economic Review, 90*(4), 715–741.

Harris, G. L. A. (2009). Women, the military, and academe: Navigating the family track in an up or out system. *Administration & Society, 41*(4), 391–422.

Harris, B. C., Steinberg, A. G., & Scarville, J. (1994). Why promotable female officers leave the army. *Minerva's Quarterly Report on Women in the Military, 12*, 1–23.

Harrison, D. A., Price, K. H., & Bell, M. P. (1998). Beyond relational demography: Time and the effects of surface- and deep-level diversity on work group cohesion. *Academy of Management Journal, 41*(1), 96–107.

Heilman, M. E. (2001). Description and prescription: How gender stereotypes prevent women's ascent up the organizational ladder. *Journal of Social Issues, 57*(4), 657–674.

Heilman, M. E., & Haynes, M. C. (2005). No credit where credit is due: Attributional rationalization of women's success in male–female teams. *Journal of Applied Psychology, 90*(5), 905–916.

Heilman, M. E., & Okimoto, T. G. (2008). Motherhood: A potential source of bias in employment decisions. *Journal of Applied Psychology, 93*(1), 189–198.

Hill, E. J., Martinson, V. K., Ferris, M. Z., & Baker, R. (2004). Beyond the mommy track: The influence of new-concept part-time work for professional women on work and family. *Journal of Family and Economic Issues, 25*(1), 121–136.

Holden, N. J., & Tanner, L. M. (2001). *An examination of current gender integration policies in TTCP countries* (Director Strategic Human Resource Coordination Personnel Operational Research Team & Director Military Gender Integration and Employment Equity; ORD Report R2001/01). Ottawa, ON: Department of National Defense.

Hoobler, J. M. (2007). On-site or out-of-sight? Family-friendly childcare provisions and the status of working mothers. *Journal of Management Inquiry, 16*(4), 372–380.

Hoobler, J. M., Lemmon, G., & Wayne, S. J. (In Press). Women's managerial aspirations from a human capital perspective. *Journal of Management*.

Hoobler, J. M., Wayne, S. J., & Lemmon, G. (2009). Bosses' perceptions of family-work conflict and women's promotability: Glass ceiling effects. *Academy of Management Journal, 52*(5), 939–957.

Jackson, S. E., May, K. E., & Whitney, K. (1995). Understanding the dynamics of diversity in decision-making teams. In R. A. Guzzo & E. Salas (Eds.), *Team decision-making effectiveness in organizations* (pp. 204–261). San Francisco, CA: Jossey-Bass.

Kanter, R. M. (1977). *Men and women of the corporation*. New York, NY: Basic Books.

King, E. B., Botsford, W., Hebl, M.R., Kazama, S., Dawson, J. F., & Perkins, A. (2012). Benevolent sexism at work: Gender differences in the distribution of challenging developmental experiences. *Journal of Management, 38*(6),1835–1866.

Lewis, S. (1997). "Family friendly" employment policies: A route to changing organizational culture or playing about at the margins? *Gender, Work, & Organization, 4*(1), 13–23.

Lewis, S. (2001). Restructuring workplace cultures: The ultimate work-family challenge? *Women in Management Review, 16*(1), 21–29.

Liden, R. C., Wayne, S. J., & Stillwell, D. (1993). A longitudinal study on the early development of leader-member exchanges. *Journal of Applied Psychology, 78*(4), 662–674.

Liff, S., & Ward, K. (2001). Distorted views through the glass ceiling: The construction of women's understandings of promotion and senior management positions. *Gender, Work and Organization, 8*(1), 19–36.

Littleton, C. A. (1997). Reconstructing sexual equality. In D. T. Meyers (Ed.), *Feminist social thought: A reader* (pp. 715–734). New York, NY: Routledge.

Lundberg, S., & Pollak, R. A. (2007). The American family and family economics. *Journal of Economic Perspectives, 21*, 3–26.

Lyness, K. S., & Judiesch, M. K. (2001). Are female managers quitters? The relationships of gender, promotions, and family leaves of absence to voluntary turnover. *Journal of Applied Psychology, 86*(6), 1167–1178.

Lyness, K. S., & Thompson, D. E. (1997). Above the glass ceiling? A comparison of matched samples of female and male executives. *Journal of Applied Psychology, 82*(3), 359–375.

Lyness, K. S., & Thompson, D. E. (2000). Climbing the corporate ladder: Do female and male executives follow the same route? *Journal of Applied Psychology, 85*(1), 86–101.

Mainiero, L. A., & Sullivan, S. E. (2005). Kaleidoscope careers: An alternate explanation for the "opt-out" revolution. *Academy of Management Executive, 19*(1), 106–123.

Matthews, M. D., Ender, M. G., Laurence, J. H., & Rohall, D. E. (2009). Role of group affiliation and gender on attitudes toward women in the military. *Military Psychology, 21*, 241–251.

Mattis, M. C. (2002). Best practices for retaining and advancing women professionals and managers. In R. J. Burke & D. L. Nelson (Eds.), *Advancing women's careers: Research and practice* (pp. 309–332). Malden, MA: Blackwell Publishers.

Moskos, C. (2007). Diversity in the armed forces of the United States. In J. Soeters & J. van der Meulen (Eds.), *Cultural diversity in the armed forces: An international comparison* (pp. 15–30). New York, NY: Routledge.

Navaie-Waliser, M., Spriggs, A., & Feldman, P. H. (2002). Informal caregiving: Differential experiences by gender. *Medical Care, 40*(12), 1249–1259.

Office of the Deputy Under Secretary of Defense, Military Community and Family Policy. (2012). *2011 Demographics profile of the U.S. Military*. Caliber, an ICF Consulting Company. Retrieved January 30, 2013, from http://www.militaryonesource.mil/12038/Project%20 Documents/MilitaryHOMEFRONT/Reports/2011_Demographics_Report.pdf

Pazy, A., & Oron, I. (2001). Sex proportion and performance evaluation among high ranking military officers. *Journal of Organizational Behavior, 22*(6), 689–702.

Powell, S. (2004). Interview with Beverly Alimo-Metcalfe. *Journal of Health Organization and Management, 18*(6), 393–398.

Powell, G. N., Butterfield, D. A., & Parent, J. D. (2002). Gender and managerial stereotypes: Have the times changed? *Journal of Management, 28*(2), 177–193.

Schein, V. A. (1973). The relationship between sex role stereotypes and requisite management characteristics. *Journal of Applied Psychology, 57*(2), 95–100.

Schein, V. A. (1975). The relationship between sex role stereotypes and requisite management characteristics among female managers. *Journal of Applied Psychology, 60*(3), 340–344.

Shore, L. M., Barksdale, K., & Shore, T. H. (1995). Managerial perceptions of employee commitment to the organization. *Academy of Management Journal, 38*(6), 1593–1615.

Smith, H. (2001). *Juggling work and family*. PBS

Steele, C. M. (1988). The psychology of self-affirmation: Sustaining the integrity of the self. *Advances in Experimental Social Psychology, 21*, 261–302.

Stoever, C. J., Schmaling, K. B., Gutierrez, C. A., Fonseca, C., & Blume, A. W. (2007). Predicting pay grade in the U.S. military by gender and ethnic minority status. *Journal of Applied Social Psychology, 37*(8), 1667–1680.

Tajfel, H. (1982). *Social identity and intergroup relations*. Cambridge: Cambridge University Press.

Tapper, J., & Jaffe, M. (2008, December 3). *Napolitano perfect for homeland security because she has 'no life'*. Rendell. ABCNews. Retrieved October 20, 2011, from http://abcnews.go.com/blogs/politics/2008/12/rendell-napolit/

Thompson, M. D. (2000). Gender, leadership orientation, and effectiveness: Testing the theoretical models of Bowman and Deal and Quinn. *Sex Roles, 42*(11–12), 969–992.

Van Velsor, E., & Hughes, M. W. (1990). *Gender differences in the development of managers: How women managers learn from experience*. Greensboro, NC: Center for Creative Leadership.

Wayne, S. J., & Liden, R. C. (1995). Effects of impression management on performance ratings: A longitudinal study. *Academy of Management Journal, 38*(1), 232–260.

Westphal, J. D., & Stern, I. (2007). Flattery will get you everywhere (especially if you are a male Caucasian): How ingratiation, boardroom behavior, and demographic minority status affect additional board appointments at U.S. companies. *Academy of Management Journal, 50*(2), 267–288.

Part IV
Family Sequelae of Wounds and Injuries

Chapter 13
The Effects of Wounds of War on Family Functioning in a National Guard Sample: An Exploratory Study

Lisa Gorman, Adrian Blow, Michelle Kees, Marcia Valenstein, Chris Jarman, and Jim Spira

Abstract When a service member is injured in the line of duty, whether the injury is physical, psychological, or a combination, family members and relationships are impacted. This chapter looks at the etiology of self-reported deployment injury among a sample of National Guard service members who deployed to Iraq and Afghanistan between 2006 and 2009. This study explores how physical injuries relates to family functioning and mental health outcomes in the early post deployment phase of reintegration. In particular, we were interested in service members' and spouses' reports of relationship adjustment and parenting stress, and how

L. Gorman, Ph.D. (✉)
Michigan Public Health Institute, Okemos, MI, USA
e-mail: lgorman@mphi.org

A. Blow, Ph.D. • C. Jarman
Department of Human Development and Family Studies, Michigan State University,
East Lansing, MI, USA
e-mail: blowa@msu.edu; Jarmanch@msu.edu

M. Kees, Ph.D.
Department of Child and Adolescent Psychiatry, University of Michigan,
Ann Arbor, MI, USA
e-mail: mkees@med.umich.edu

M. Valenstein, M.D.
Department of Veterans Affairs Health Services Research and Development,
University of Michigan, Ann Arbor, MI, USA

Department of Psychiatry, University of Michigan, Ann Arbor, MI, USA
e-mail: marciav@med.umich.edu

J. Spira, Ph.D.
Pacific Islands Division, US Department of Veterans Affairs, Honolulu, HI, USA

National Center for PTSD, Honolulu, HI, USA

VA Healthcare, Honolulu, HI, USA
e-mail: James.Spira@va.gov

S. MacDermid Wadsworth and D.S. Riggs (eds.), *Military Deployment and its*
Consequences for Families, Risk and Resilience in Military and Veteran Families,
DOI 10.1007/978-1-4614-8712-8_13, © Springer Science+Business Media New York 2014

families with a self-reported injury fared in comparison to families without an injury. Preliminary findings with this sample suggest that a deployment injury may have more of an effect on the service members' mental health and parenting stress than on their spouse or significant other at this early readjustment period.

Keywords National Guard • Injury • Family functioning

Understanding Resilience in Wounded Warriors

When a service member is injured in the line of duty, whether the injury is physical, psychological, or a combination, family members and relationships are impacted. While there is a growing body of literature on the effects of service member deployment to war and their related psychological concerns on family functioning (Erbes, Meis, Polusny, Compton, & MacDermid Wadsworth, 2012; Gewirtz, Polusny, DeGarmo, Khaylis, & Erbes, 2010; Gorman, Blow, Ames, & Reed, 2011), little is known about the effects of physical wounds on family functioning. In her comprehensive review of the literature on families in the times of the most recent wars, MacDermid Wadsworth concludes that there are many gaps when it comes to our understanding of family adaptation to physical wounds acquired in war (MacDermid Wadsworth, 2010). She makes the compelling argument an injury to a service member leads to many changes for families that can include a change in family roles and structures as well as the overall family emotional climate. The current exploratory study aimed to identify the impact of a physical injury acquired during deployment on family functioning using two measures (relationship adjustment and parental stress), while also examining psychological symptoms (PTSD, depression, and alcohol use) of the service members and their spouses. A deployment injury was hypothesized to predict lower general family functioning and greater level of psychological distress in both service members and their spouses.

Background

Physical Injury

The injuries sustained by service members during combat can potentially affect all members of the family system. The injuries may have either a physical or psychological etiology or a combination of the two, with varying levels of disability in each category. One method of injury surveillance for Iraq and Afghanistan are the medical evacuation records. Between March 2003 and August 2010, the number of non-hostile injuries (n = 10,383) was greater than the number of evacuees wounded in action (n = 8,954) (Fischer, 2010). Often non-combat related injuries are fractures, inflammation/pain, and dislocation, and causes are sports/physical training, fall/jumps, and motor vehicle-related incidents (Hauret, Taylor, Clemmons, Block, &

Jones, 2010). Amputations represented 1,621 of the evacuees during the same time period (Fischer, 2010). There are no studies we could find that describe the impact of either combat or non-combat related injury on military family functioning.

Psychological Effect of Injury

In contrast to the number of studies looking at injury and family functioning outcomes, there is a good deal of evidence to suggest that injury places service members at risk for psychological difficulties. Grieger and colleagues (2006) examined the rates and predictors of PTSD and depression among injured service members during and following hospitalization. Physical severity at 1 month was associated with both depression and PTSD at 7 months (Grieger et al., 2006). Compared to their peers who were in the same combat situations but were not injured, the prevalence of PTSD in the injured group was significantly higher (Koren, Norman, Cohen, Berman, & Klein, 2005).

Physical injuries that are readily apparent may make it easier for family members to adapt to the inevitable changes surrounding such injuries. Invisible wounds such as TBI or PTSD present military families with different struggles. Service members with these types of injuries often face an array of difficulties including impaired decision making, irritability, memory loss, sleep problems, dizziness, intrusive traumatic memories, reduced processing speed, headaches, tinnitus, and other cognitive deficits (Kelly, Amerson, & Barth, 2012; MacGregor, Dougherty, Tang, & Galarneau, 2012). The psychological injuries are those that cannot readily be identified by non-professionals and have no apparent physical impairments. Often assessed through standardized measures, the service members report the level of psychological symptoms they are experiencing and the interference of these symptoms on daily living. Traumatic brain injury (TBI), the signature service member wound of this era, is the loss of brain function due to an open or closed wound to the head and subsequent biochemical events in the brain (Weinstein, Salazzar, & Jones, 1995). While TBI has a physical component, mild TBI has a strong association with PTSD and physical health problems (Hoge et al., 2008) among returning Veterans. Thus, family difficulties may be compounded by the ways in which such invisible physical injuries affect relationships.

The presence of both physical and psychological injuries is another salient challenge facing thousands of wounded veterans and their families. The asymmetric nature of war currently waged by enemy combatants (e.g., improvised explosive devices, explosively formed penetrators, etc.) coupled with US forces' improved body armor, field trauma care, and evacuation methods have resulted in higher survival rates among US forces; yet these advances have also increased the incidence of long and arduous recoveries from blast injuries. Frequently, survival after such trauma entails physical, neurological, and psychological recuperation that may then interact to exacerbate the underlying injury or prolong treatment. The compounded effects of multiple traumas likely present service members and their families with particularly difficult challenges (Kelly et al., 2012).

Family Adaptation to Injury

Relatively little is known about how military spouses and significant others cope with and adapt to life after the return of a recently wounded service member. Because the severity of impairment varies across injured veterans, the range of responses will likely vary considerably. Similarly, almost nothing is known about the factors that predispose families of wounded service members to increased risk and stress, or about families who may possess or enact certain protective factors. Factors such as parental stress during long deployments as well as dyadic stress before, during, and after deployment are obvious areas of interest when investigating risk factors for impaired family functioning in the face of injuries. But it is also essential to investigate the potentially powerful protective factors some families are able to muster.

In this chapter, we focus on physical wounds as the independent variable and we explore how these physical injuries relate to family and mental health outcomes in the early post deployment phase of reintegration. We are not necessarily excluding the possibility that both physical and psychological injury may coexist. In previous studies including our own, it is evident that psychological difficulties affect families. For example, studies show that depression is a strong predictor of poor family outcomes for both service members and spouses, (Blow et al., 2013), that PTSD affects dyadic adjustment (Allen, Rhoades, Stanley, & Markman, 2010; Meis, Barry, Kehle, Erbes, & Polusny, 2010; Riggs, Byrne, Weathers, & Litz, 1998), and in particular the PTSD cluster of dysphoria (feelings of isolation, loss of interest in activities, irritability, and sleep disturbance) has a negative effect on dyadic functioning (Erbes et al., 2012). PTSD also affects parenting; Gewirtz et al. (2010) found that PTSD affects parenting and that those with higher PTSD symptoms experience more parenting challenges. In spite of the growing body of literature related to the effects of psychological symptoms in combat veterans on family well-being, there is a dearth of studies focused on the impact of physical wounds on family functioning.

Cozza and colleagues have observed child distress in clinical treatment facilities of the moderate and severely injured service members, but far less is known about the family outcomes of those service members who were injured and have now returned to community life. In military treatment facilities, families with distress prior to the injury were at risk for higher levels of child distress and poorer family functioning following a deployment injury (Cozza et al., 2010). Cozza et al. (2010) found that family disruption (changes in living arrangements, schedules, and parenting time) was a greater prediction of child distresses than injury severity. Further, families who had a high level of deployment stress prior to the injury were more likely to have the spouse report high levels of child distress following the injury (Cozza et al., 2010). Even though Cozza and colleagues looked at disruption to child/family schedules, parental discipline, and impact on time spent with children, the study could have been benefited by measuring both parents' perception of parenting stress.

Systems Framework

The systems framework (Broderick & Smith, 1979) is the theoretical guide for our study question and hypotheses. To understand the complexity of a deployment injury on the individual, the couple relationship, and the parent–child dyad, it is necessary to take into account the interconnectedness of members of the family as well as multiple levels of influence. This perspective shows how the family system is a unit of inter-related personalities within a network of systems that can support, interfere with, or damage the family (Loukas, Twitchell, & Piejak, 1998). Strong, mutually supportive linkages between microsystems are needed for optimal nego-tiation of challenging circumstances, a concept beneficial in guiding research with this population. From a systemic perspective, family processes can reduce the stress of a deployment related injury.

Research Question and Hypotheses

This exploratory study is the first to our knowledge to examine the relationship between the physical wounds of war and family functioning in a sample of National Guard service members who had recently returned from OIF/OEF deployment. We set out to answer/the following question:

What are the effects of combat injury on family functioning? We operationalized combat injury as a physical wound (self-report of a physical injury) and tested the following hypotheses:

H1: Physical injury in a service member will lead to higher levels of family distress for both the service member and his/her spouse.

H2: Physical injury in a service member will lead to higher levels of psychological distress for both the service member and his/her spouse.

Methods

Participants and Procedure

Participants were recruited from National Guard members and their spouses/signifi-cant others attending yellow ribbon reintegration events between October 2006 and September 2009. The 2-day reintegration programs took place approximately 45–90 days following the service member's return home from a 12 month deployment in either Operation Iraqi Freedom (OIF) or Operation Enduring Freedom (OEF). The study was announced to potential participants during a large meeting during the rein-tegration weekend and volunteer participants filled out the anonymous/confidential survey which took approximately 30–40 minutes to complete. The study was approved by the Institutional Review Boards at Michigan State University and the University of Michigan.

The participants completing surveys collected between October 2007 and August 2008 received a $10 gift card incentive for participation. There were 327 service members (40 % response rate) and 217 spouses and significant others (36 % response rate) in the first sample of data collected. The study participants who completed a survey in 2009 were paid a higher incentive of $25 with an overall response rate of 72 %. The 2009 sample had 579 service members and 321 spouses/significant others completing the survey. The two samples were combined for the analyses of this study for a total of 906 National Guard members and 538 spouses/significant others (N = 1,444) who were surveyed between 2007 and 2009. While the state where data was collected made every effort to have no more than one year deployment for three years of dwell time at home, it is possible that some participants could have volunteered and completed a survey for two separate deployments.

Because this study was interested in family outcomes, only those service members who had a spouse or significant other completing a survey were included in the subsample for this study; 525 linked couples in committed relationships and 364 linked couples were parents. Table 13.1 summarizes the demographic characteristics. The data set contains the following Military Occupational Specialties: infantry, cavalry, transportation, service personnel, medical support, military police, and security forces with the largest representation from infantry/cavalry. The service member sample was largely male while the spouse sample was overwhelmingly female. Caucasians made up 83 % of the sample with participation of African Americans (7 %), Hispanics (3.5 %), Native Americans (1.5 %), Asian Americans (2 %), and Multi-ethnic (1 %). In comparison to National Guard demographics (DOD, 2006) at the national level our sample includes more males (89 % versus 83 % nationally), more married (55.5 % versus 51 % nationally), and more with children (60 % versus 43 % nationally).

Measures

Relationship adjustment and parental stress were the outcome variables related to family functioning. We were also interested in PTSD, depression and alcohol use. Self-report of injury was the independent variable used in analysis.

PTSD Symptoms

PTSD for the service member was measured by the Posttraumatic Stress Disorder Checklist-Military Version (PCL-M) (Weathers, Litz, Herman, Huska, & Keane, 1993) a 17 item self-report measure of DSM-IV symptoms of PTSD. The total PCL Cronbach's alpha for this study was 0.94 for service members. Using the

Table 13.1 Service member and spouse demographic variable for data collected in 2007–2008; 2009 and combined for injury analysis

Characteristic	Service member			Spouse		
	2007–2008 (n = 200)	2009 (n = 325)	Combined (n=525)	2007–2008 (n = 200)	2009 (n = 325)	Combined (n = 525)
Age						
18–21, n (%)	0 (0)	42 (13.0)	42 (8.0)	7 (3.5)	70 (21.5)	77 (14.7)
22–30, n (%)	50 (25.0)	130 (40.5)	180 (34.5)	59 (29.5)	112 (35.0)	171 (32.7)
31–40, n (%)	68 (34.0)	89 (28.0)	157 (30.1)	73 (36.5)	94 (29.0)	167 (31.9)
41–50, n (%)	68 (34.0)	52 (16.0)	120 (23.0)	47 (23.5)	39 (12.0)	86 (16.4)
51 and over, n (%)	14 (7.0)	9 (2.5)	23 (4.4)	14 (7.0)	8 (2.5)	22 (4.2)
Gender						
Female, n (%)	5 (2.5)	13 (4.0)	18 (3.5)	192 (97.5)	310 (95.5)	502 (96.1)
Male, n (%)	190 (97.5)	312 (96.0)	502 (96.5)	5 (2.5)	15 (4.5)	20 (3.8)
Ethnicity						
African American, n (%)	22 (11.0)	13 (4.5)	35 (7.2)	17 (8.5)	13 (4.5)	30 (6.3)
Caucasian, n (%)	158 (80.0)	249 (87.0)	407 (83.9)	165 (83.5)	234 (84.0)	399 (83.3)
Hispanic, n (%)	3 (1.5)	12 (4.0)	15 (3.1)	3 (1.5)	16 (6.0)	19 (4.0)
Native American, n (%)	5 (2.5)	4 (1.5)	9 (1.8)	2 (1.0)	5 (1.5)	7 (1.5)
Asian American, n (%)	4 (2.0)	3 (1.0)	7 (1.4)	4 (2.0)	5 (1.5)	9 (1.9)
Multi-Ethnic, n (%)	3 (1.5)	3 (1.0)	6 (1.2)	3 (1.5)	2 (.5)	5 (1.0)
Other, n (%)	3 (1.5)	3 (1.0)	6 (1.2)	4 (2.0)	6 (2.0)	10 (2.0)
Education						
≤High School Diploma, n (%)	33 (16.5)	106 (33.5)	139 (26.9)	40 (20)	63 (20)	103 (20.2)
≤Associates Degree, n (%)	113 (56.5)	160 (50.5)	273 (52.8)	79 (49.0)	188 (61.0)	287 (56.4)
Bachelor's degree, n (%)	41 (20.5)	40 (12.5)	81 (15.7)	47 (24.0)	46 (15.0)	93 (18.3)
≥Graduate degree, n (%)	13 (6.5)	11 (3.5)	24 (4.6)	14 (7.0)	13 (4.0)	27 (5.3)
Military Rank						
Enlisted, n (%)	161 (80.5)	275 (91.5)	436 (85.5)	N/A	N/A	N/A
Officer (w/WO), n (%)	39 (19.5)	27 (8.5)	66 (12.9)	N/A	N/A	NA

Missing data—Percentages are calculated based on number of responses for each variable. Not all participants responded to all questions

reference point of 30 days, respondents were asked to answer each item related to their most distressing military event using a 5-point Likert type. Spouses did not complete the PCL in wave one, but did complete the 17-item PCL-C (Weathers et al., 1993) in wave 2.

Depressive Symptoms

Depression was measured using the Beck Depression Inventory Second Edition BDI-II (Beck, Steer, & Brown, 1996) for the first wave and the Patient Health Questionnaire PHQ-9 (Kroenke, Spitzer, & Williams, 2001) for the second wave of data collection. The BDI-II is a 21 item self-report inventory that is effective in discriminating among individuals with various levels of depression ranging from minimal to severe. The measure had a high internal consistency with a Cronbach's alpha of 0.91. Similar to other studies (Bryant et al., 2008; Segal et al., 2006), we used a total score of 14 or greater on the BDI-II as meeting the criteria for likely depression. The PHQ-9 is a self-report instrument that assesses 9 DSM-IV symptoms of depression over a 2 week period, with total scores ranging from 0 to 27 (Kroenke et al., 2001). Cut off scores of 10 or higher indicate depressive symptoms. The PHQ-9 has acceptable reliability with a Cronbach's alpha of 0.84 for this study. In order to standardize analyses for depression in the current study, we created a single standardized variable for depression across the entire sample by standardizing the BDI within sample one and standardizing the PHQ-9 within sample two.

Hazardous Alcohol Use

Alcohol use was assessed with the Alcohol Use Disorders Identification Test (AUDIT; Saunders, Aasland, Babor, de la Fuente, & Grant, 1993). This 10 item instrument is scored on a 5-point Likert scale, with total scores ranging between 0 and 40. An AUDIT score of 8 or higher indicates alcohol misuse. The instrument has good internal consistency, with a Cronbach's alpha of .80.

Physical Injury

Physical injury was self-reported by the service member. Participants responded to a series of questions about their most recent deployment as well as a series of questions about a previous deployment experience. If the service member responded yes to "Were you wounded or injured?" during the most recent deployment or during a previous deployment they were classified as having a deployment related injury.

Relationship Distress

Relationship distress was measured with the Revised Dyadic Adjustment Scale (Busby, Christensen, Crane, & Larson, 1995). The RDAS is a 14 item Likert-type scale and has multiple response choices. The total RDAS Cronbach's alpha for this study was 0.88 for both service members and spouses. A criterion cutoff score to distinguish between distressed and non-distressed couples was established for the RDAS, with a score of 47 and below representing distressed, and a score of 48 and above representing non-distressed couples (Crane, Middleton, & Bean, 2000).

Parenting Stress

Parental stress was measured using the Parental Stress Scale (Berry & Jones, 1995). The measure contains 18 Likert items with lower total scores reflecting less stress associated with parenting. The test-retest reliability for the scale is r =.81 and the internal consistency is α = .83.

Combat Exposure

Combat exposure was assessed on the service members' most recent deployment experience and a previous deployment experience for those service members with multiple deployments utilizing the four remaining variables of the combat exposure assessment. Combat exposure for the study analysis was computed based on four standardized items. We computed recent deployment exposure and previous deployment exposure utilizing the maximum of these two understanding that for some service members' a previous deployment experience may have been more traumatic or vice versa. The correlation between maximum exposure and the injury variable was .257, p < .05.

Analysis

Multilevel modeling (MLM) was used to test whether deployment injury predicted lower family functioning or higher levels of psychological distress for service members and their spouses. This data analytic approach allows for non-independence between service members' and their spouses' scores, and (unlike mixed-model ANOVA) it does not exclude cases in which one partner has missing data. Since MLM uses all available data in its estimates, missing data were not imputed. The MIXED procedure with SPSS software was used in the analysis. The estimation method was restricted maximum likelihood. In these analyses we tested whether there were mean differences as a function of injury status, role (i.e., service member versus spouse), and the interaction between injury status and role. The means, standard deviations, and F-tests are reported in the findings.

Results

For this study, 513 service members (M = 49.52, SD = 9.59) and 512 spouses (M = 49.29, SD = 9.85) completed the Revised Dyadic Adjustment Scale (RDAS). Of the participants completing the RDAS, 41 % (n=211) of service members and 38 % (n = 193) of spouses reported clinically distressed relationships. Of the paired couples, 363 service members (M = 36.40, SD = 9.42) and 360 spouses (M = 35.80,

SD = 9.90) completed the Parental Stress Scale (PSS). This demonstrated that participants were experiencing parenting stress; 46 % of service member (n = 165) who were parents (n = 363) and 43 % of spouses (n = 154) who were parents (n = 360) met the cutoff criteria for parental stress.

For this study, paired-sample t tests were conducted to compare the means of service members' and spouses' scores on family functioning variables. There was not a significant difference in the report of dyadic adjustment $t(503) = .752$, ns or parental stress $t(342) = .805$, ns. Our preliminary analysis suggests that service members and their spouses were similar in the report of dyadic adjustment and parental stress. Scores on family function variables were highly correlated.

A primary aim of the study was to understand how an injury affects family functioning. For this sample, 499 service members responded to the question, "Were you wounded or injured in your most recent deployment?" Eleven percent (n = 55) reported that they had been wounded or injured. Service members were also asked if they had been wounded or injured in a previous deployment with 305 respondents and 220 non respondents. We attribute the missing data to the frequency of service members who were on their first deployment (n = 278). A total of 38 service members reported that they had been injured in a previous deployment. When an additional variable was created to combine these two questions, there were 74 reports of being wounded or injured in any deployment.

Because we were interested in the looking at psychological symptoms as an outcome variable, we also did some frequency analysis of psychological injuries in the entire sample. We found that service members in the sample were experiencing symptoms to meet the cutoff criteria for depression (21 %; n = 109), PTSD (13 %; n=63), and hazardous alcohol use (27 %; n = 140). Spouses were also experiencing symptoms consistent with depression (21 %; n = 110), PTSD (13 %; n=62), and hazardous alcohol use (11 %; n = 57). We created a dichotomous variable for psychological injury if the individual met the strict screening criteria for one or more behavioral health issues. Service members (43 %; n = 218) and spouses (33 %; n = 159) indicated clinical ranges of psychological functioning 45–90 days post-deployment.

Testing the Effects of Injury on Service Members' and Spouses' Outcomes

Multilevel modeling was used to test whether deployment injury predicted lower family functioning or higher levels of psychological distress for service members and their spouses. This data analytic approach allows for non-independence between service members' and their spouses' scores, and (unlike mixed-model ANOVA) it does not exclude cases in which one partner has missing data. In these analyses we tested whether there were mean differences as a function of injury status, role (i.e., service member versus spouse), and the interaction between injury status and role. The means, standard deviations, and F-tests are reported in Table 13.2.

Table 13.2 Results from a multilevel model to test effects of deployment injury on service members' and spouses' report of relationship adjustment, parental stress, and psychological functioning (alcohol use, depression, and PTSD)

	No injury		Deployment injury						
	Service member	Spouse	Service member	Spouse		Injury main effect	Role main effect	Interaction
Dyadic Adjustment								
M	49.97	49.41	48.17	48.54	F	1.31	0.02	0.80
(SD)	(9.26)	(9.61)	(11.00)	(10.75)	(df)	(471)	(471)	(471)
Parental Stress								
M	35.87	35.91	39.61	35.72	F	3.09	4.87*	5.14*
(SD)	(9.02)	(9.70)	(10.19)	(11.10)	(df)	(354)	(347)	(347)
Alcohol Use								
M	5.52	3.42	7.03	3.17	F	1.47	60.46**	5.40*
(SD)	(5.59)	(3.81)	(7.28)	(4.53)	(df)	(478)	(476)	(476)
Depression (BDI)								
M	7.65	9.01	14.22	8.74	F	5.70*	4.21*	11.59**
(SD)	(6.79)	(8.93)	(8.86)	(8.02)	(df)	(194)	(193)	(193)
Depression (PHQ)								
M	5.49	5.62	7.96	7.52	F	12.76**	0.09	0.28
(SD)	(5.25)	(4.63)	(5.74)	(5.97)	(df)	(298)	(298)	(298)
Zdepression								
M	−0.11	−0.02	0.49	0.19	F	18.18**	1.91	5.77*
(SD)	(0.95)	(0.98)	(1.11)	(1.10)	(df)	(495)	(493)	(493)
PTSD (Sample 1)								
M	29.71	–	46.00	–	F	36.82**	–	–
(SD)	(11.65)	–	(19.24)	–	(df)	(192)	–	–
PTSD (Sample 2)								
M	28.58	27.71	38.40	31.60	F	18.24**	6.60*	3.97*
(SD)	(13.22)	(12.54)	(14.97)	(16.67)	(df)	(279)	(278)	(278)

Couple adjustment as measured by the RDAS (Busby et al., 1995) was the first family functioning variable examined in the study of 525 paired couples. As can be seen in Table 13.2, there were no significant differences for service members or spouses in dyadic adjustment as a function of injury. The MLM analysis was repeated controlling for combat exposure with no change in outcome of dyadic adjustment for injury main effect, role (service member verses spouse), or an interaction between injury and role.

Parental stress was the second family functioning variable of interest. The analysis examining parental stress was restricted to families with children, and included a total of 364 paired couples. The role main effect suggests that parental stress was higher for service members (M = 36.40, SD = 9.42) than for spouses (M = 35.80, SD = 9.90). However, this effect was qualified by a significant interaction with injury status such that there was no role difference in parental stress for couples in the no injury group, F(1,284) = .01, p = .94, but there was a significant role difference for deployment injury couples, F(1,51) = 4.68, p = .035. As shown in the table, service members who reported a deployment injury had significantly higher parental stress than their spouses. The MLM analysis of parental stress was repeated controlling for the service members' combat exposure. There were no statistically significant changes in our findings.

Alcohol use also showed a significant role main effect such that on average service members reported higher levels of hazardous alcohol use (M = 5.78, SD = 5.87), than their spouses (M = 3.50, SD = 4.06). In addition, the interaction between injury status and role was statistically significant. Examination of the means suggests that injury status did not affect spouses' alcohol use, $F(1,489) = .25$, p = .62) but it did affect service members' hazardous alcohol use, $F(1, 492) = 4.08$, p = .04. Injured service members reported higher alcohol use than non-injured service members.

As we noted earlier, as can be seen in Table 13.2, three variables were used to test the effects of deployment injury on depression: The BDI scores for sample 1, the PHQ scores for sample 2, and the z score for the BDI and PHQ of the full data set. In all three analyses there was a significant main effect for injury. The injury main effect suggests that depressive symptoms were higher for individuals within a family where the service member reported a deployment related injury (BDI M = 11.48, SD = 8.82; PHQ M = 7.74, SD = 5.83) than for individuals in families where there was no deployment injury reported (BDI M = 8.33, SD = 7.94; PHQ M = 5.56, SD = 4.94). The role main effect in sample 1 suggests that the overall depression scores was higher for spouses (M = 8.91, SD = 8.76) than for service members (M = 8.52, SD = 7.41). This effect was qualified by a significant interaction with injury status such that there was not a statistically significant role difference in BDI scores for couples in the no injury group, $F(1,168) = 3.60$, p = .06, but there was a significant role difference for deployment injury couples, $F(1,26) = 5.73$, p = .024. As shown in the table, service members in sample 1 who reported a deployment injury had significantly higher depression scores than their spouses. When we controlled for combat exposure the main effect of injury dropped to $F(1,194) = 3.73$, p = .055, while the main effects for role and interaction remained statistically significant.

However, for sample 2, examination of the means suggests that injury status affected both the spouses', $F(1, 294) = 5.93$, p = .015) and the service members depression scores, $F(1,297) = 8.48$, p = .004. As seen in the table, the spouses in the non-injured couples had higher levels of depression than the service members. However, within the couples where a service member had reported a deployment injury, the reverse was true; the service members had higher depression scores than the spouses.

The PCL-M was completed by all service members in the study to assess their level of PTSD symptoms, and in the second sample, spouses also received the PCL-C to assess PTSD symptoms. Overall, there was a significant injury effect on PTSD for service members $F(1,478) = 51.33$, p = .000. Service members who reported a deployment injury had higher levels of PTSD (M = 41.25, SD = 16.98) than non-injured service members (M = 29.02, SD = 12.61). In sample 1, univariate analyses showed a significant main effect for injury on PTSD symptoms for the service members. In addition to the significant main effect for injury, in sample 2 there were also main effects for role. However, this effect was qualified by a significant interaction with injury status such that there was no role difference in PTSD for couples in the no injury group, $F(1,326) = 1.56$, $p = .213$, but there was a significant role difference for deployment injury couples $F(1,18) = 6.26$, $p = .022$. As can be seen in the table, if there is no injury the PTSD is low for both service member and the spouse. When there is a deployment injury, PTSD is significantly higher for the service member than the spouse.

Discussion

Findings from this study give us insight into the early reintegration processes for service members who have sustained an injury, in particular, the processes that influence how they relate to their intimate partners and children. An earlier study by our research team (Blow et al., 2013) reported that psychological injuries such as depression have a strong negative effect on both service members and spouses dyadic adjustment post deployment. In the present study, we were interested in understanding how self-reported physical injuries were related to the psychological injuries and family functioning variables. Our findings suggest that physical injuries only had an effect on the psychological adjustment of service members but not spouses at this early readjustment period. This included service members drinking more than their spouses, being more depressed, and having higher levels of PTSD. In addition, service members who experienced a physical injury were more depressed and had more symptoms of PTSD than service members who did not report an injury. When it came to family, a physical injury had no effect on dyadic adjustment; however it did have an effect for service members in terms of parenting stress. Specifically, service members who reported a deployment injury had significantly higher parental stress than their spouses.

These findings suggest that service members are struggling with all of the normal losses and transitions related to adjusting to life after a physical injury, and mental health factors are exacerbated in this process. Spouses on the other hand appear to be relatively unaffected at the 45–90 day post deployment event. This is perhaps because of their compassion for their partner's condition and understanding related to the source of the concern and that the service member has not been home long enough for compassion fatigue to set in. This supposition for compassion and understanding related to the source of concern is based on similar findings of Renshaw et al. (2011) who showed that there is an attribution process related to how spouses interpret mental health symptoms post deployment; they are more understanding if symptoms are attributed to a war injury.

The cross-sectional nature of this study limits our ability to make causal inferences or predict the long-term adjustment of either psychological health or family outcomes for either service members or the spouses and significant others. The existing bodies of literature suggest that there is some burden associated with caring for veterans with PTSD (Calhoun, Beckham, & Bosworth, 2002). In addition to caregiver burden, Calhoun and associates found spouses of veterans with PTSD had poorer psychological adjustment than did spouses of veterans with PTSD. The spouse who experiences exhaustion and burnout in caring for or wanting to help a distressed partner who has undergone a traumatic even may experience secondary traumatic stress (Dirkzwager, Bramsen, Ader, & van der Ploeg, 2005; Figley, 1998). It is simply too early in the reintegration process for our study sample to know whether spouses will remain unaffected by the service member injury over the life-course. We speculate that difficulties in parenting for service members may be related to life changes as a result of the injury leading to changes in parenting activities.

An obvious limitation of the study was the inability to look at the interface of self-reported injury, family outcomes, and traumatic brain injury (TBI), the signature wound of conflicts in Iraq and Afghanistan. The study team collected TBI self-report data in the 2009 subsample with preliminary analysis showing 3 % of the service members in the subsample met the criteria for likely TBI. Because the sample size was not large enough to ensure adequate power for TBI analyses it was not included in our findings. Future studies should look at the effects of TBI on family outcomes within this population.

Another limitation was that a physical injury was assessed by the service members self-report of being injured or not, but we do not know the extent of these injuries. We do not know if injury was classified as non-combat related or if the participant is a Purple Heart recipient. We do not know if the injury required evacuation or the extent that the service member completed the mission for which they trained. We do not know whether the recovery took place on the forward operating base, at a military treatment facility that required the family to relocate, or if the recovery is ongoing. We also do not know whether the injury resulted in disability compensation or if the injury will delay the service member's ability to return to civilian employment. Finally, we do not know the amount of time that has passed since the injury. Despite the limitation of the study, it identifies some obvious gaps in the literature and the need to better understand the implication of service related injuries on psychological and family outcomes.

Implications

Based on background literature and clinical experiences, we would anticipate that the young amputee seeing his unit buddies for the first time since the improvised explosive device caused him to lose consciousness would be in a very different place at the reintegration event 45–90 day post deployment than his fifty year old counterpart who was evacuated for stress injuries. We would also anticipate that these two service members would vary in present and future familial processes related to their reintegration and long term adjustment. Even though the study is limited in that it contains a spectrum of deployment related injuries without specification, it begins to raise question and shed light onto the need to understand not only those with severe combat related injuries but also other types of deployment related injuries.

On both ends of the spectrum, both the service member and their family/support systems will have to make sense of their experiences and grapple with how the deployment injury will or will not define their subsequent life experiences. The military and civilian supports should be sensitive to ecological factors that influence both psychological and family outcomes of the injured service members. The prevention and intervention strategies should build on positive coping strategies and familial processes that promote individual and family resilience.

Findings from this study suggest that injured service members may need individually oriented interventions as they adjust to life after deployment including interventions for depression, PTSD, and alcohol misuse. In addition, they may need both individual and family based interventions related to parenting and establishing a new parental role post deployment injury. Programs to support wounded warriors and their families often focus on the severely injured service members. However, as Cozza et al. (2010) suggests, identification and intervention with families of combat injured families experiencing distress and disruption is needed regardless of injury severity.

References

Allen, E. S., Rhoades, G. K., Stanley, S. M., & Markman, H. J. (2010). Hitting home: Relationships between recent deployment, posttraumatic stress symptoms, and marital functioning for army couples. *Journal of Family Psychology, 24*(3), 280–288.

Bay, E., Blow, A. J., & Xie, Y. (2012). Interpersonal relatedness and psychological functioning following traumatic brain injury (TBI): Implications for marital and family therapists. *Journal of Marital and Family Therapy, 38*, 556–567.

Bay, E., Hagerty, B., Williams, R. A., & Kirsch, N. (2005). Chronic stress, salivary cortisol response, interpersonal relatedness, and depression among community-dwelling survivors of traumatic brain injury. *Journal of Neuroscience Nursing, 36*(6), 55–65.

Bay, E., Hagerty, B. M., Williams, R. A., Kirsch, N., & Gillespie, B. (2002). Chronic stress, sense of belonging, and depression among survivors of traumatic brain injury. *Journal of Nursing Scholarship, 34*(3), 221–226.

Beck, A., Steer, R., & Brown, G. (1996). *Beck depression inventory* (2nd ed.). San Antonio, TX: Psychological Corporation.

Berry, J. O., & Jones, W. H. (1995). The parental stress scale: Initial psychometric evidence. *Journal of Social and Personal Relationships, 12*(3), 463–472.

Blow, A., Gorman, L., Ganoczy, D., Kees, M., Kashy, D., Valenstein, M., et al. (2013). Hazardous drinking and family function in National Guard veterans and spouses postdeployment. *Journal of Family Psychology, 27*(2), 303–313. doi:10.1037/a0031881.

Broderick, C., & Smith, J. (1979). The general systems approach to the family. In W. Burr, R. Hill, F. I. Nye, & I. Reiss (Eds.), *Contemporary theories about the family* (Vol. 2, pp. 112–129). New York: Free Press.

Bryant, R., Mastrodomenico, J., Felmingham, K., Hopwood, S., Kenny, L., Kandris, E., et al. (2008). Treatment of acute stress disorder. *Archives of General Psychiatry, 65*(6), 659–667.

Busby, D. M., Christensen, C., Crane, D. R., & Larson, J. H. (1995). A revision of the Dyadic Adjustment Scale for use with distressed and nondistressed couples: Construct hierarchy and multidimensional scales. *Journal of Marital and Family Therapy, 21*, 289–308.

Calhoun, P. S., Beckham, J. D., & Bosworth, H. B. (2002). Caregiver burden and psychological distress in partners of veterans with chronic posttraumatic stress disorder. *Journal of Traumatic Stress, 15*, 205–212.

Cozza, S. J., Guimond, J. M., McKibben, J. B. A., Chun, R. S., Arata-Maiers, T. L., Schneider, B., et al. (2010). Combat-injured service members and their families: The relationship of child distress and spouse–perceived family distress and disruption. *Journal of Traumatic Stress, 23*, 112–115.

Crane, D., Middleton, K., & Bean, R. (2000). Establishing criterion scores for the Kansas marital satisfaction scale and the revised dyadic adjustment scale. *The American Journal of Family Therapy, 28*, 53–60.

Dirkzwager, A. J. E., Bramsen, I., Ader, H., & van der Ploeg, H. M. (2005). Secondary traumatization in partners and parents of Dutch peacekeeping soldiers. *Journal of Family Psychology, 19*, 217–226.

Erbes, C., Meis, L., Polusny, M., Compton, J., & MacDermid Wadsworth, S. (2012). An examination of PTSD symptoms and relationship functioning in U.S. soldiers of the Iraq war over time. *Journal of Traumatic Stress, 25*, 187–190.

Figley, C. R. (1998). *Burnout in families: The systemic costs of caring*. New York: CRC.

Fischer, H. (2010) *U.S. military casualty statistics: Operation New Daw, Operation Iraqi Freedom, and Operation Enduring Freedom* (Congressional Research Service for Congress: CRS 7-5700). Retrieved October 28, 2012, from http://www.fas.org/sgp/crs/natsec/RS22452.pdf

Gewirtz, A., Polusny, M., DeGarmo, D., Khaylis, A., & Erbes, C. (2010). Posttraumatic stress symptoms among National Guard soldiers deployed to Iraq: Associations with parenting behaviors and couple adjustment. *Journal of Consulting and Clinical Psychology, 78*(5), 599–610. doi:10.1037/a0020571.

Gorman, L., Blow, A. J., Ames, B., & Reed, P. (2011). National Guard families after combat: Mental health, use of mental health services, and perceived treatment barriers. *Psychiatric Services, 62*(1), 28–34.

Gorman, L., Blow, A. J., Kashy, D. A., Fitzgerald, H. E., Ames, B., Spira, J., et al. (Under Review). Psychological symptoms and functioning of National Guard couples following combat zone deployment. *Journal of Marriage and Family*.

Grieger, T. A., Cozza, S. J., Ursano, R. J., Hoge, C., Martinez, P. E., Engel, C. C., et al. (2006). Posttraumatic stress disorder and depression in battle-injured soldiers. *American Journal of Psychiatry, 163*, 1777–1783.

Hauret, K. G., Taylor, B. J., Clemmons, N. S., Block, S. R., & Jones, B. H. (2010). Frequency and causes of nonbattle injuries air evacuated from Operations Iraqi Freedom and Enduring Freedom U.S. Army, 2001-2006. *American Journal of Preventative Medicine, 38*, S94–S107.

Hoge, C. W., McGurk, D., Thomas, J., Cox, A., Engel, C., & Castro, C. (2008). Mild traumatic brain injury in US soldiers returning from Iraq. *The New England Journal of Medicine, 358*(5), 453–463.

Koren, D., Norman, D., Cohen, A., Berman, J., & Klein, E. M. (2005). Increased PTSD risk with combat-related injury: A match comparison study of injured and uninjured soldiers experiencing the same combat events. *The American Journal of Psychiatry, 162*, 276–278.

Kroenke, K., Spitzer, R. L., & Williams, J. B. (2001). The PHQ-9: Validity of a brief depression severity measure. *Journal of General Internal Medicine, 16*(9), 606–613. doi:jgi01114 [pii].

Loukas, A., Twitchell, G. R., & Piejak, L. A. (1998). The family as a unit of interacting personalities. In L. L'Abate (Ed.), *Handbook of family psychopathology*. New York: Guilford.

MacDermid Wadsworth, S. M. (2010). Family risk and resilience in the context of war and terrorism. *Journal of Marriage and Family, 72*, 537–556.

Meis, L. A., Barry, R. A., Kehle, S. M., Erbes, C. R., & Polusny, M. A. (2010). Relationship adjustment, PTSD symptoms, and treatment utilization among coupled national guard soldiers deployed to Iraq. *Journal of Family Psychology, 24*(5), 560–567. doi:10.1037/a0020925.

Renshaw, K. D., Allen, E. S., Rhoades, G. K., Blais, R. K., Markman, H. J., & Stanley, S. M. (2011). Distress in spouses of service members with symptoms of combat-related PTSD: Secondary traumatic stress or general psychological distress? *Journal of Family Psychology, 25*(4), 461–469.

Riggs, D. S., Byrne, C. A., Weathers, F. W., & Litz, B. T. (1998). The quality of the intimate relationships of male Vietnam veterans: Problems associated with posttraumatic stress disorder. *Journal of Traumatic Stress, 11*(1), 87–101.

Saunders, J., Aasland, O., Babor, T., de la Fuente, J., & Grant, M. (1993). Development of the Alcohol Use Disorders Identification Test (AUDIT): WHO Collaborative Project on early detection of persons with harmful alcohol consumption - II. *Addiction, 88*, 791–804.

Schwab, K. A., Ivins, B., Cramer, G., Johnson, W., Sluss-Tiller, M., Kiley, K., et al. (2007). Screening for traumatic brain injury in troops returning from deployment in Afghanistan and Iraq: Initial investigation of the usefulness of a short screening tool for traumatic brain injury. *Journal of Head Trauma Rehabilitation, 22*, 377–389.

Segal, Z., Kennedy, S., Gemar, M., Hood, K., Pedersen, R., & Buis, T. (2006). Cognitive reactivity to sad mood provocation and the prediction of depressive relapse. *Archives of General Psychiatry, 63*, 749–755.

Tanielian, T., & Jaycox, L. H. (2008). *Invisible wounds of war: Psychological and cognitive injuries, their consequences, and services to assist recovery*. Santa Monica, CA: Rand Monographs.

Weathers, F. W., Litz, B. T., Herman, J. A., Huska, J. A., & Keane, T. M. (1993). *The PTSD Checklist (PCL): Reliability, validity and diagnostic utility*. Paper presented at the 9th Annual Conference of the ISTSS, San Antonio, TX.

Chapter 14
Resources and Coping Strategies Among Caregivers of Operation Iraqi Freedom (OIF) and Operation Enduring Freedom (OEF) Veterans with Polytrauma and Traumatic Brain Injury

Joan M. Griffin, Greta Friedemann-Sánchez, Kathleen F. Carlson, Agnes C. Jensen, Amy Gravely, Brent C. Taylor, Sean M. Phelan, Kathryn Wilder-Schaaf, Sherry Dyche Ceperich, and Courtney Harold Van Houtven

Abstract Family caregivers with adequate resources manage stress from caregiving more effectively, minimizing their risk for poor health. What resources caregivers have and how they use them may vary, however, by care recipients' level of functional dependence and relationship to the caregiver. Using a cross-sectional mailed survey, we assessed the coping behaviors and social, family, financial, and internal resources used by caregivers of US veterans who sustained war-related polytrauma and traumatic brain injuries. We compared the resources of those caring for veterans needing high and moderate levels of care and parent and spousal caregivers.

J.M. Griffin, Ph.D. (✉)
Department of Veterans Affairs, Minneapolis Health Care System, Center for Chronic Disease Outcomes Research, One Veterans Drive, Minneapolis, MN 55417, USA

Department of Medicine, University of Minnesota Medical School, Minneapolis, MN, USA
e-mail: joan.griffin2@va.gov

G. Friedemann-Sánchez, Ph.D.
Humphrey School of Public Affairs, University of Minnesota, 301 19th Ave. S, Minneapolis, MN 55455, USA
e-mail: frie0013@umn.edu

K.F. Carlson, Ph.D.
Department of Veterans Affairs, Portland Center for the Study of Chronic, Comorbid Mental and Physical Disorders, Portland Veterans Affairs Medical Center, Portland, OR, USA

Department of Public Health and Preventive Medicine, Oregon Health and Science University, 3710 SW US Veterans Road, Portland, OR 97239, USA
e-mail: Kathleen.carlson@va.gov

A.C. Jensen, B.S. • A. Gravely, M.A.
Department of Veterans Affairs, Minneapolis Health Care System,
Center for Chronic Disease Outcomes Research, One Veterans Drive,
Minneapolis, MN 55417, USA
e-mail: agnes.jensen2@va.gov; amy.gravely@va.gov

S. MacDermid Wadsworth and D.S. Riggs (eds.), *Military Deployment and its Consequences for Families*, Risk and Resilience in Military and Veteran Families, DOI 10.1007/978-1-4614-8712-8_14, © Springer Science+Business Media New York 2014

Spouses had fewer social and family resources and less self-esteem than parents. Parents had higher incomes, but less access to health insurance than spouses. Those caring for veterans with high needs compared to moderate needs were lonelier, but otherwise, resources did not differ. Caregivers, especially spouses, lacked many resources that could help them manage stress from caregiving.

Keywords Family • Caregiver • Veterans • Polytrauma • Traumatic brain injury • Strain • Resources • Social support • Parents • Spouse

Research on caregiving consistently shows that, although there are positive aspects of providing care to someone (Cohen, Colantonio, & Vernich, 2002), caregivers face physical, emotional, cognitive, financial and social challenges from caregiving (Baronet, 1999; Degeneffe, 2001; Raina et al., 2004; Schulz & Martire, 2004). These challenges can exceed caregivers' ability to manage the required demands, which in turn may affect their ability to self-care or provide appropriate support for

B.C. Taylor, Ph.D.
Department of Veterans Affairs, Minneapolis Health Care System,
Center for Chronic Disease Outcomes Research, One Veterans Drive,
Minneapolis, MN 55417, USA

Department of Medicine, University of Minnesota Medical School, Minneapolis, MN, USA

Division of Epidemiology and Community Health, University of Minnesota School
of Public Health, Minneapolis, MN 55417, USA
e-mail: brent.taylor2@va.gov

S.M. Phelan, Ph.D., M.P.H.
Division of Health Care Policy and Research, 200 First St. SW, Rochester, MN 55905, USA
e-mail: phelan.sean@mayo.edu

K. Wilder-Schaaf, Ph.D.
Department of Veterans Affairs, Hunter Holmes McGuire Veterans Affairs Medical Center,
1201 Broad Rock Blvd, Richmond, VA, USA

Department of Physical Medicine & Rehabilitation, Neuropsychology & Rehabilitation
Psychology Service, Virginia Commonwealth University, Richmond, VA 23235, USA
e-mail: Kathryn.WilderSchaaf@va.gov

S.D. Ceperich, Ph.D.
Hunter Holmes McGuire Veterans Affairs Medical Center, Richmond, VA, USA

Department of Psychology, Virginia Commonwealth University School of Medicine,
1201 Broad Rock Blvd, Richmond, VA 23249, USA
e-mail: sherry.ceperich@va.gov

C.H. Van Houtven, Ph.D.
Center for Health Services Research in Primary Care, Durham VA Medical Center,
Durham, NC, USA

Division of General Internal Medicine, Department of Medicine, Duke University
Medical Center, Duke University, 508 Fulton St, Durham, NC 27705, USA
e-mail: Courtney.Vanhoutven@duke.edu

care recipients. Although the stressors that a caregiver faces may differ depending on a care recipient's condition and severity, caregivers often rely on internal and external resources to help them cope and buffer the negative effects of stress (Killeen, 1990; Lazarus & Folkman, 1984). Resources can include anything from material and emotional assets to helpful or harmful coping behaviors. Examples of adaptive resources include adequate income, family members who are reliable and can provide emotional and practical support, and the confidence that they can provide high quality care. Maladaptive resources are harmful behaviors or avoidance of one's personal commitments and responsibilities that are used to cope with caregiving challenges and difficult situations.

Caregivers with adequate and beneficial resources have been shown to manage stress more effectively and minimize their risk for poor health outcomes (Acton & Kang, 2001; Sorensen, Pinquart, & Duberstein, 2002; Van Houtven et al., 2013). Those with inadequate resources or maladaptive coping strategies, however, are less able to buffer the impact of caregiving challenges (Abe, Kashiwagi, & Tsuneto, 2003; Folkman, 1997; Gottlieb & Wolfe, 2002). For example, caregivers who use excessive alcohol consumption to cope with the strain of caregiving may put themselves or their care recipient at risk for poor health or injury (Bristowe & Collins, 1988; Homer & Gilleard, 1990). In order to promote psychological resiliency and reduce health risks, clinicians, social workers, policy makers, and researchers often look to develop or enhance beneficial resources or intervene to reduce risk from potentially harmful coping behaviors. Assessing the availability of emotional, social, financial and material resources and understanding the variation within a population of caregivers are important steps in identifying how best to intervene and provide caregiving support.

In this paper, we present data on the resources relied upon by one group of caregivers, those providing care to Operation Iraqi Freedom (OIF) and Operation Enduring Freedom (OEF) service members and veterans with traumatic brain injuries (TBI)/polytrauma (defined as a traumatic brain injury and at least one other injury to one or more body systems). Our previous work shows that within the military and veteran population who has sustained TBI and polytrauma injuries, there is great variation in the severity of injuries and types of ongoing neurobehavioral symptoms (Sayer et al., 2009). Likewise, there is variation in their need for long-term and ongoing care and assistance, but of those that need care, more parents than spouses take on the responsibilities of providing that care (Griffin et al., 2012). Given that parent and spouse caregivers of this population are relatively young and will likely need to draw on their resources for years to come, it is critical to assess variation in available resources across caregiver characteristics in order to determine the segments of the population in greatest need of support. Our analysis is exploratory in nature; however, based on evidence in the general caregiving literature, we hypothesize that resources will vary by severity of the care recipients' injuries and their level of need, and the relationship between the care recipient and the caregiver (Bernard & Guarnaccia, 2003; Blacher, 2001; Eakes, 1995; Li, Seltzer, & Greenberg, 1997). On one hand, military and veteran benefits (e.g., health insurance and survivor benefits) are structured to support spouses, not parents, but on the other, based on a life course perspective (Elder, Kirkpatrick Johnson, & Crosnoe,

2003) which assumes that the sum of social and historical experiences and personal development influences behavior, parents may have developed more external (i.e., social support, caregiving assistance, assets) and internal resources (i.e., self-efficacy, self-esteem, healthy behaviors) over time from which they draw.

Method

In 2005, the US Department of Veterans Affairs (VA) designated four inpatient Polytrauma Rehabilitation Centers (PRCs), one in each of the following cities: Minneapolis, Minnesota; Tampa, Florida; Palo Alto, California; and Richmond, Virginia. Skilled in providing care for the complex and unique rehabilitation needs of those moderately and severely injured in OEF/OIF, treatment teams at these centers demonstrate expertise in comprehensive interdisciplinary rehabilitation for polytrauma/TBI. Many US service members with polytraumatic injuries/TBI first receive acute care at military hospitals overseas or stateside, and then are transferred to a PRC for inpatient rehabilitation (Friedemann, Sayer, & Pickett, 2008; Sigford, 2008). Those receiving inpatient care at a PRC present with an average of five injuries, including penetrating and non-penetrating head injuries, and six physical or cognitive impairments. They are admitted at different levels of consciousness, and with recent amputations, multiple fractures, burns, visual and hearing loss, pain, and post-traumatic stress disorder, among other consequences from their trauma (Friedemann-Sanchez, Sayer, & Pickett, 2008; Sayer et al., 2008). Eighty-eight percent have some cognitive impairment (Sayer et al., 2008).

Our investigation on caregiver resources is based on data from the Family and Caregiver Experiences Study (FACES), a cross-sectional study that characterized the caregiving experiences of those providing care to the service members and veterans (whom we refer to as care recipients heretofore) treated and discharged from a PRC. Mailed surveys were used to quantitatively describe who cares for care recipients with polytrauma/TBI, what caregiving tasks caregivers perform, and the resources they have and use.

Participants

From administrative and hospital discharge data we identified care recipients who: (1) served in the military during OEF/OIF; (2) had polytraumatic injuries, including a TBI; (3) received care from one of the four PRCs and were discharged between September, 2001 and February, 2009 to either an institution or a community setting; (4) had been discharged from a PRC for at least 3 months; and, (5) were still alive at the time the study was fielded.

Figure 14.1 presents a flow chart outlining participant response. We attempted to mail surveys to the next-of-kin for all 1,045 eligible care recipients. We were not able to reach 20 % (n = 209) either by mail or telephone. Of the 80 % of

Participant response flow chart

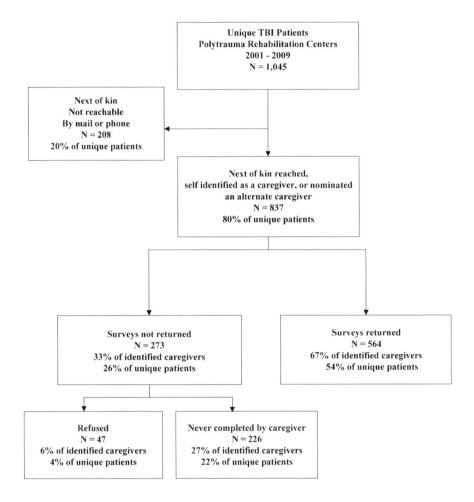

Fig. 14.1 Participant response flow chart

next-of-kin we did contact, 18 nominated an alternate person who they believed was the primary caregiver to receive the survey. A total of 564 surveys were completed and returned, which represents 53.9 % of the 1,045 next-of-kin originally identified, and 67 % (n = 564) of the 837 caregivers verified by phone or survey as the primary caregiver. Of those whom we identified as caregivers, only 47 refused participation (6 %). For the purposes of this study on resources, we included only those who reported that they were the parent or spouse of the care recipient. Those with any other relationship to the care recipient (i.e. sibling or grandparent) were excluded (n = 36).

No data on demographic characteristics were available for non-responding caregivers but information on their care recipients was available through VA administrative data. In order to assess potential response bias, we compared the age, gender, race and marital status of the care recipients of the 481 non-respondents to the 564 respondents and found no significant differences in care recipient characteristics. Similarly, we found no significant differences by the geographic location of injury (e.g., Iraq/Afghanistan versus the United States) or mechanism of injury (e.g., bullet/blast, motor vehicle crash, or fall). However, we did find that caregivers of those care recipients with lower functional status (as measured by FIM® rating, described below) at admission and discharge from the PRC were more likely to respond than caregivers of those with higher functional status.

Procedure

Care recipient demographics were collected using administrative and PRC discharge data, as were functional status measures. Injury details, including geographic location and mechanism of injury, were supplemented using administrative data.

Caregiver resources were collected from a mailed questionnaire that included questions about both the care recipient and caregiver. The survey was conducted over 6 months in late 2009, using Dillman's Tailored Design Method (Dillman, 2007). An introductory letter explaining the purpose of the study was mailed 5 days before the survey packet was sent. The initial survey packet included a cover letter, the questionnaire, and a postage-paid return envelope. Also included were instructions on how to nominate someone else in case the identified next-of-kin thought that another person more aptly fit the definition of primary caregiver. A $20 cash incentive was included in the initial survey packet. Potential participants were given the option to refuse participation by a toll-free telephone call or mail. Study staff telephoned participants 15 days after the initial mailing to verify delivery, whether the next-of-kin was, in fact, the caregiver and to answer questions about the questionnaire or study. A second mailing (with no incentive) was sent using an overnight delivery service to those who did not return the questionnaire within 21 days of the initial mailing. Study staff attempted a final telephone call with non-responding next-of-kin 15 days after the second survey mailing. If a next-of-kin nominated someone else as the current primary caregiver, that nominee then received an initial mailing and equivalent follow up. Study protocols were reviewed and approved by the Institutional Review Boards at all four PRC sites.

Measures

Demographics

In the questionnaire, caregivers were asked to report on their demographics using standard single-item questions about age, race, ethnicity, marital and employment status, number of years of schooling, annual income and their relationship to the care recipient. Caregivers were also asked to self-report their health status, using options from excellent to poor.

Care Recipient Characteristics

Caregivers were asked to report details on their care recipient's injuries, including the amount of time the care recipient spent in coma after the injury. In order to assess ongoing care needs of the care recipient, caregivers were asked whether the care recipient required help or support with activities of daily living (ADLs) or instrumental activities of daily living (IADLs). Using common assessments of ADLs and IADLs (Katz, Ford, Moskowitz, Jackson, & Jaffe, 1963; Lawton & Brody, 1969), caregivers reported what tasks they personally performed, help others provided (either from paid care attendants or unpaid family members and friends), or if no help was needed for specific tasks. Care recipients who needed help with any ADL were categorized as "high intensity" and those needing help with IADLs but not ADLs were categorized as needing "moderate intensity" help. For the analysis presented herein, we do not include the caregivers who reported that the care recipient did not need help with either ADLs or IADLs, since they were least likely to be actively providing day-to-day care that included caregiving-related demands that taxed or exceeded their resources. Our sample, therefore, is limited to the 369 parent and spouse caregivers who provide high and moderate intensity help. In order to assess other responsibilities that may affect the availability or access to resources, caregivers were also asked if in addition to caregiving, they worked for pay or were the care recipient's legal guardian.

Care recipients' functional independence was assessed at both admission to and discharge from the PRC using the FIM® rating (previously referred to as Functional Independence Measure). The FIM® rating is an 18-item functional assessment tool commonly used in rehabilitation populations. Ratings range from one, indicating the patient requires total assistance or "performs less than 25 % of the task," to seven, indicating that the patient is completely independent. Therefore, a rating from one to six indicates that the care recipient requires some assistance, supervision or support. Total ratings range from 18 to 126 and lower ratings indicate greater need of supervision or support.

Caregiver Resources

Caregivers were asked a series of questions to assess resources. Caregiver resources were categorized into social resources (e.g., social support, social isolation, availability of help, sources of assistance with care), family resources (e.g., family functioning), financial resources (e.g., household income, access to health insurance), internal resources (e.g., self-efficacy, self-esteem) and coping behaviors.

A modified version of the ENRICHD social support instrument (ESSI), a validated measure of social support was used to assess the emotional, instrumental, informational, and appraisal attributes associated with social support (Vaglio et al., 2004). The scale had excellent internal reliability ($\alpha = 0.91$) in our sample. Given the social isolation that often accompanies caregiving, we also assessed loneliness using three items from the UCLA Loneliness scale (Russell, 1996). This scale also had excellent internal reliability within our sample ($\alpha = 0.89$). Availability of help with caregiving was assessed by asking, "If or when you need help (from friends, family, etc) how much would you get?" with answers ranging from a great deal to no help. Caregivers were also asked who provides assistance to the care recipient. Answers included the primary caregiver only; caregiver and paid care providers; caregiver and unpaid family members or friends; caregiver and others (e.g., advocacy groups, veteran or military organizations); or caregiver and two or more of the aforementioned sources.

For family resources, caregivers were asked to complete the general functioning scale in the McMaster Family Assessment Device (FAD) (Epstein, Baldwin, & Bishop, 1983). This instrument is a commonly used assessment of a family's overall ability to cooperate with each other. It, too, had excellent internal reliability in our sample ($\alpha = 0.92$).

We assessed monetary resources (i.e. annual household income, including money from jobs and net income from business or a farm, and pensions, dividends, interest, Social Security and disability payments) and access to health insurance. Health insurance is a resource that enables caregivers to access health care services when needed and, in turn, may reduce the risk of caregivers forfeiting their own health for the sake of their care recipient.

Self-efficacy and self-esteem were measured to assess internal resources that caregivers may draw on to buffer stressors. Self-efficacy was measured using two items: "How confident are you that you can take care of your care recipient's physical needs" and "How confident are you that you can take care of your care recipient's emotional needs." Response options ranged from not at all confident to extremely confident. Self-esteem was measured using Rosenberg's self-esteem scale (Rosenberg, 1965), a validated, widely-used scale of self-esteem with excellent internal reliability in our sample ($\alpha = 0.90$).

Coping behaviors were measured in two ways. First, caregivers were asked how often, when under stress, they did any of the following things: eat, exercise, watch television, read, take medication to calm oneself, or talk to a counselor or therapist. Answers ranged from never to often, and were then recoded into often/sometimes and never/rarely. Second, they were asked a separate set of questions from the Behavioral Risk Factor Surveillance System (CDC) (2008), related to their drinking and smoking behavior.

Analysis Strategy

Simple summary statistics and tests of association were used to describe differences by relationship to care recipient and intensity of care recipient needs. First, we compared demographics and caregiver self-reported health status by these variables.

Second, we used indicators of the care recipient's injury severity (i.e., loss of consciousness and FIM® ratings) and indicators of the caregivers' ongoing responsibilities (i.e., hours spent caregiving and legal guardianship) and compared them by relationship and intensity of care recipient's current care needs. Third, we examined caregiver resources for all caregivers and then compared each set of resources by relationship and intensity of care recipient's current care needs. Finally, in order to determine if other variables explained the bivariate association between parents and spouses and care needs, we tested in a series of multiple linear regression models, the relationship between resources and two main predictors, relationship and care recipient needs. Indicators of each type of resources were chosen based on the bivariate analysis. Household income and education were included as covariates because of their strength of association with each resource. We first fit each model with the two main predictors and then fit each model with education and household income. Finally, we added whether the care recipient and caregiver lived together and whether the caregiver was the care recipient's legal guardian, two additional variables that may influence the availability of caregiver resources.

Results

In our sample, 60.2 % of caregivers were parents and 39.8 % were spouses. Nearly 32 % of caregivers reported that the injured care recipient had high intensity needs and 68 % had moderate intensity needs. Differences in demographics by relationship to the care recipient and the care recipient's intensity of need are reported in Table 14.1. As expected, parents were older than spouses, however, parents were relatively young (mean age, 55 years). Our sample included almost 20 % male caregivers. Most were fathers (31 % of all parents), rather than husbands (3 % of all spouses). More spouses (77.6 %) than parents (64.8 %) attended or graduated from college. Parents and spouses did not differ by race, ethnicity, or self-reported health. Of the parents, 64.4 % (n=143) were married and 30.6 % (n=68) were either divorced or separated (data not shown). The only significant demographic difference by intensity of need was that those caring for care recipients with moderate intensity needs were significantly more likely to be working for pay than those caring for care recipients with high intensity needs.

Data presented in Table 14.2 show the care recipient's injury characteristics by both the caregiver's relationship to the care recipient and the intensity of care recipient needs and includes corresponding p-values associated with overall differences across categories. Of the parents, over 51 % were caring for a care recipient who was in coma for more than a week after sustaining injuries, compared to 31 % of spouses. FIM® rating at both admission and discharge from the PRC were significantly lower (lower functional ability) for care recipients cared for by parents than for spouses. Likewise, significantly more parents than spouses had been named legal guardian for the injured care recipient. Over 43 % of spouses, however, reported currently spending 40 or more hours a week providing care to the injured care recipient, and for parents, 28 % reported working an equivalent number of hours.

Table 14.1 Bivariate differences in demographics and health status by relationship and intensity of care recipient's need

Variable	Relationship to care recipient			Level of care recipient care needs		
	Parent 60.2 % (n = 222)	Spouse 39.8 % (n = 147)	p-value	High need 31.7 % (n = 117)	Moderate need 68.3 % (n = 252)	p-value
Age			<0.001			<0.001
Under age 30	0	37.2 % (55)		14.5 % (17)	15.1 % (38)	
Age 30–44	5.9 % (13)	44.2 % (65)		23.9 % (28)	19.8 % (50)	
Age 45–59	66.7 % (148)	16.3 % (24)		47.0 % (55)	46.4 % (117)	
Age 60 or above	22.1 % (49)	0		10.3 % (12)	14.7 % (37)	
Missing	5.4 % (12)	2.0 % (3)		4.3 % (5)	4.0 % (10)	
Gender			<.001			0.56
Male	30.6 % (68)	3.4 % (5)		17.9 % (21)	20.6 % (52)	
Female	67.6 % (150)	95.9 % (141)		80.3 % (94)	78.2 % (197)	
Missing	1.8 % (4)	0.7 % (1)		1.7 % (2)	1.2 % (3)	
Race			0.87			0.35
White	73.0 % (162)	74.1 % (109)		68.4 % (80)	75.8 % (191)	
African American	10.4 % (23)	8.2 % (12)		12.8 % (15)	7.9 % (20)	
More than 1 race	3.2 % (7)	4.8 % (7)		2.6 % (3)	4.4 % (11)	
Other	5.0 % (11)	5.4 % (8)		6.0 % (7)	4.8 % (12)	
Unknown	8.6 % (19)	7.5 % (11)		10.3 % (12)	7.1 % (18)	
Ethnicity—Latino/ Hispanic	11.3 % (25)	8.8 % (13)	0.36	14.5 % (17)	8.3 % (21)	0.06
Highest year of education			0.04			0.08
≤ High school graduate	32.9 % (73)	21.1 % (31)		28.2 % (33)	28.2 % (71)	
Some college or trade school	40.5 % (90)	49.7 % (73)		51.3 % (60)	40.9 % (103)	
≥ Bachelors Degree	24.3 % (54)	27.9 % (41)		18.8 % (22)	29.0 % (73)	
Missing	2.3 % (5)	1.4 % (2)		1.7 % (2)	2.0 % (5)	
Self-reported health			0.86			0.24
Excellent	12.6 % (28)	12.9 % (19)		9.4 % (11)	14.3 % (36)	
Very good	23.9 % (53)	23.8 % (35)		22.2 % (26)	24.6 % (62)	
Good	34.7 % (77)	40.1 % (59)		35.0 % (41)	37.7 % (95)	
Fair	21.2 % (47)	17.7 % (26)		23.9 % (28)	17.9 % (45)	
Poor	5.4 % (12)	4.8 % (7)		7.7 % (9)	4.0 % (10)	
Missing	2.3 % (5)	0.7 % (1)		1.7 % (2)	1.6 % (4)	

Note: High needs include care recipients who need assistance with ADLs or ADLs and IADLs. Moderate needs include care recipients who need assistance with only IADLS, not ADLs

Table 14.2 Bivariate differences in care recipient's injury characteristics and caregivers responsibilities by relationship and intensity of care recipient's need

Variable	Relationship to care recipient			Level of care recipient care needs		
	Parent 60.2 % (n=222)	Spouse 39.8 % (n=147)	p-value	Parent 60.2 % (n=222)	Spouse 39.8 % (n=147)	p-value
Care recipient injury characteristics						
Length of coma/ loss of consciousness[a]			<.001			0.07
None	5.9 % (13)	10.9 % (16)		6.0 % (7)	8.7 % (22)	
30 min or less	9.0 % (20)	22.4 % (33)		15.4 % (18)	13.9 % (35)	
More than 30 min, but less than 1 week	18.5 % (41)	18.4 % (27)		14.5 % (17)	20.2 % (51)	
1 week or more	51.4 % (114)	30.6 % (45)		51.3 % (60)	39.3 % (99)	
Caregiver did not know coma status	12.6 % (28)	16.3 % (24)		8.5 % (10)	16.7 % (42)	
Caregiver did not respond to question	2.7 % (6)	1.4 % (2)		4.3 % (5)	1.2 % (3)	
Admission FIM® rating median (range)[b]						
Cognitive	18 (5–35)	27 (5–35)	<.001	17 (5–35)	25 (5–35)	<.001
Motor	53 (13–91)	76.5 (13–91)	<.001	34 (13–91)	70.5 (13–91)	<.001
Total	72 (18–126)	102 (18–126)	<.001	51 (18–126)	93 (18–126)	<.001
Discharge FIM® rating median (range)[b]						
Cognitive	30 (5–35)	32 (5–35)	<.001	27 (5–35)	31 (5–35)	<.001
Motor	85 (13–91)	90 (13–91)	<.001	76 (13–91)	89 (13–91)	<.001
Total	115 (18–126)	119 (18–126)	<.001	102 (18–126)	118 (18–126)	<.001
Caregiving responsibilities						
Hours per week spent providing care			<.001			<.001
Less than 5 h	39.6 % (88)	14.3 % (21)		8.6 % (10)	39.3 % (99)	
5–19 h	15.8 % (35)	17.0 % (25)		8.6 % (10)	19.8 % (50)	
20–39 h	7.7 % (17)	18.4 % (27)		12.0 % (14)	11.9 % (30)	
40–79 h	6.8 % (15)	13.6 % (20)		16.2 % (19)	6.4 % (16)	
80 h or more	21.6 % (48)	29.9 % (44)		49.6 % (58)	13.5 % (34)	
Did not quantify hours	8.6 % (19)	6.8 % (10)		5.1 % (6)	9.1 % (23)	
Caregiver is named care recipient's legal guardian	28.4 % (63)	9.5 % (14)	<.001	31.6 % (37)	15.9 % (40)	<.001

Note. High needs include care recipients who need assistance with ADLs or ADLs and IADLs. Moderate needs include care recipients who need assistance with only IADLS, not ADLs
[a]Caregiver proxy report
[b]The total FIM® rating is the sum of cognitive and motor ratings. The range for total FIM® rating is 18–126, for cognitive is 5–35, and for motor is 13–91

Table 14.3 Bivariate differences in caregiver's resources by relationship and intensity of care recipient's need

	Relationship to care recipient			Level of care recipient care needs		
	Parent 60.2 % (n = 222)	Spouse 39.8 % (n = 147)	p-value	Parent 60.2 % (n = 222)	Spouse 39.8 % (n = 147)	p-value
Social resources						
Availability of help from friends, family, etc[a]			<0.001			0.36
A great deal/some help	71.6 % (159)	51.7 % (76)		61.5 % (72)	64.7 % (163)	
A little help	13.1 % (29)	34.0 % (50)		23.1 % (27)	20.6 % (52)	
No help	10.8 % (24)	14.3 % (21)		12.8 % (15)	11.9 % (30)	
Missing	4.5 % (10)	0		2.6 % (3)	2.8 % (7)	
Who provides assistance to care recipient						
Primary caregiver only	41.4 % (92)	54.4 % (80)	0.01	31.6 % (37)	53.6 % (135)	<0.01
Caregiver and paid providers	21.2 % (47)	34.7 % (51)	<0.01	38.5 % (45)	21.0 % (53)	<0.01
Caregiver and unpaid family members/friends	23.9 % (53)	5.4 % (8)	<.001	14.5 % (17)	17.5 % (44)	0.48
Caregiver and others (e.g., advocacy groups, Veteran organizations)	3.6 % (8)	1.4 % (2)	0.19	5.1 % (6)	1.6 % (4)	0.05
Caregiver and <u>two</u> or more other sources	9.9 % (22)	4.1 % (6)	0.04	10.3 % (12)	6.3 % (16)	0.19
Social Support (range = 7–35, mean, sd)[b]	25.6 (7.4)	22.8 (6.6)	<.001	23.7 (7.2)	24.8 (7.2)	0.16
Loneliness (range = 3–15, mean, sd)[c]	6.3 (3.4)	8.6 (3.2)	<.001	7.9 (3.3)	7.0 (3.6)	0.02
Family resources						
Family functioning (range = 1–4, mean, sd)[c]	1.7 (0.6)	2.0 (0.6)	<.001	1.8 (0.6)	1.9 (0.6)	0.48
Financial resources						
Caregiver's household annual income			<0.01			0.29

(continued)

Table 14.3 (continued)

	Relationship to care recipient			Level of care recipient care needs		
	Parent 60.2 % (n=222)	Spouse 39.8 % (n=147)	p-value	Parent 60.2 % (n=222)	Spouse 39.8 % (n=147)	p-value
≤$30,000	23.9 % (53)	15.6 % (23)		21.4 % (25)	20.2 % (51)	
$30,001 to $50,000	18.9 % (42)	34.7 % (51)		31.6 % (37)	22.2 % (56)	
$50,001 to $80,000	25.2 % (56)	29.9 % (44)		23.1 % (27)	29.0 % (73)	
≥$80,000	17.1 % (38)	12.2 % (18)		14.5 % (17)	15.5 % (39)	
Missing	14.9 % (33)	7.5 % (11)		9.4 % (11)	13.1 % (33)	
Caregiver is currently working	45.5 % (101)	43.5 % (64)	0.47	29.9 % (35)	51.6 % (130)	<.001
Caregiver has health insurance	69.4 % (154)	87.1 % (128)	0.01	76.1 % (89)	76.6 % (193)	0.16
Internal resources						
Self-efficacy (range=1–5, mean, sd)[b]	3.6 (1.0)	3.5 (1.0)	0.17	3.7 (1.0)	3.5 (0.9)	0.14
Self-esteem (range=13–40, mean, sd)[b]	33.7 (4.8)	31.1 (6.2)	<.001	32.3 (5.9)	32.8 (5.4)	0.50
Coping strategies						
Eating[d]	66.2 % (147)	83.7 % (123)	<.001	69.2 % (81)	75.0 % (189)	0.75
Watching TV[d]	79.3 % (176)	77.6 % (114)	0.58	70.1 % (82)	82.5 % (208)	0.02
Reading, %[d]	71.2 % (158)	57.8 % (85)	.01	63.2 % (74)	67.1 % (169)	0.06
Taking medication to calm yourself[d]	19.4 % (43)	29.3 % (43)	0.06	27.4 % (32)	21.4 % (54)	0.35
Exercising[d]	57.7 % (128)	50.3 % (74)	0.29	47.0 % (55)	58.3 % (147)	0.10
Talking to a counselor or therapist[d]	12.6 % (28)	18.4 % (27)	0.11	12.8 % (15)	15.9 % (40)	0.86
Drinking behavior						
Binge drinker	17.6 % (39)	21.1 % (31)	0.79	12.0 % (14)	22.2 % (56)	0.08
Heavy drinker	5.9 % (13)	6.1 % (9)	0.83	6.0 % (7)	6.0 % (15)	0.62
Smoking behavior						
Current smoker	23.9 % (53)	23.8 % (35)	0.84	28.2 % (33)	21.8 % (55)	0.15

Note. High needs include care recipients who need assistance with ADLs or ADLs and IADLs. Moderate needs include care recipients who need assistance with only IADLS, not ADLs
[a]Caregivers provided responses to the question, "If or when you need help (from friends, family, etc.), how much would you get?"
[b]Higher score indicates better functioning
[c]Lower score indicates better outcome
[d]Caregivers who responded "sometimes or always"

For those caring for care recipients with high intensity needs, over 51 % reported the care recipient was in coma for more than 1 week after sustaining injuries, compared to 39 % of those caring for care recipients with moderate intensity needs who reported the care recipient was in coma for 1 week or more post-injury. As expected, median FIM® rating at admission and discharge was lower for those with high intensity needs than for those with moderate intensity needs. Significantly more caregivers of care recipients with high intensity needs (31.6 %) were named legal guardian, compared to those caring for care recipients with moderate needs (15.9 %).

In Table 14.3, we report the overall availability of resources, such as social or family resources, and then compare different resources by relationship to care recipient and care recipient's intensity of need. We found that nearly 50 % of caregivers provide care to the care recipient without regular assistance from others. Another 27 % provide care alongside paid care providers, and 17 % receive regular help from another unpaid family member or friend. Caregivers were also asked, during times that they need additional help if they receive it from family and friends, and the majority report they can count on a great deal or some help, however, over 12 % report they receive no help at all. Despite the fact nearly half of all caregivers report working for pay, 46 % have household incomes less than $50,000 a year. At least two-thirds of caregivers report eating, reading and watching television as ways they cope with stress, and 23 % say they take medication to calm themselves. Over half say they get some exercise, but less than 15 % see a therapist or counselor. Six percent report they drink heavily and nearly 20 % report binge drinking. Nearly 24 % are current smokers.

Spouses reported significantly less social support and report more loneliness than parents. More spouses reported being the only one providing care (54.4 %) compared to parents (41.4 %). When asked how much help with caregiving responsibilities they would get if needed, over 71 % of parents, but only 52 % of spouses reported that they would receive a great deal or some help. Spouses also reported significantly lower family functioning than parents. Over half of spouses report having household incomes of less than $50,000 a year, but they were significantly more likely to have health insurance coverage (87.1 %) than parents (69.4 %). Parents also had low household incomes, with nearly 43 % having annual incomes of less than $50,000. Although spouses and parents did not differ in their reports of self-efficacy, spouses reported significantly lower self-esteem. Spouses reported coping with stress by eating more often than parents, and parents reported reading to alleviate stress more often than spouses, but otherwise there were no significant differences in coping behaviors, including drinking and smoking behaviors.

Differences in resources by intensity of need were not as consistent as findings by relationship. Availability of social support and help when needed did not significantly differ between those caring for care recipients with high needs and moderate needs. More moderate intensity caregivers (53.6 %) than high intensity caregivers (31.6 %) reported being the only caregiver. However, high intensity caregivers were more socially isolated. Caregivers of care recipients with moderate and high intensity needs did not differ significantly by family functioning, access to health

Table 14.4 Summary of standardized linear regression coefficients for variables predicting social resources

Dependent variable	Independent variables	B (SE)	β
Caregiver Social Support			
Step 1:	Relationship to care recipient (ref: parent)	−2.77 (0.76)	−0.19***
	Intensity of need (ref: high needs)	0.99 (0.81)	0.07
Step 2:	Relationship to care recipient (ref: parent)	−2.72 (0.79)	−0.19***
	Intensity of need (ref: high needs)	0.81 (.83)	0.05
	Education	−0.92 (0.57)	−0.09
	Houschold income	1.63 (0.41)	0.23***
Step 3:	Relationship to care recipient (ref: parent)	−2.46 (0.94)	−0.17**
	Intensity of need (ref: high needs)	0.78 (0.85)	0.05
	Education	−0.99 (0.58)	−0.10
	Household income	1.58 (0.42)	0.23***
	Lives with veteran	−0.30 (1.01)	−0.02
	Legal guardian of veteran	0.44 (1.05)	0.02
Caregiver Loneliness			
Step 1:	Relationship to care recipient (ref: parent)	2.28 (0.36)	0.32***
	Intensity of need (ref: high needs)	−0.79 (0.38)	−0.11*
Step 2:	Relationship to care recipient (ref: parent)	2.29 (0.38)	0.32***
	Intensity of need (ref: high needs)	−0.77 (0.40)	−0.10*
	Education	0.41 (0.27)	0.09
	Household income	−0.68 (0.20)	−0.19**
Step 3:	Relationship to care recipient (ref: parent)	2.27 (0.46)	0.31***
	Intensity of need (ref: high needs)	−0.82 (0.41)	−0.11*
	Education	0.35 (0.28)	0.07
	Household income	−0.72 (0.20)	−0.21***
	Lives with veteran	−0.29 (0.49)	−0.04
	Legal guardian of veteran	−0.51 (0.50)	−0.06

Note. High needs include care recipients who need assistance with ADLs or ADLs and IADLs. Moderate needs include care recipients who need assistance with only IADLS, not ADLs
Statistical significance of t-test: * p<.05, ** p<.01, *** p<.001

insurance, self-efficacy, or self-esteem. Nor did they differ by most coping strategies, including talking to a counselor or therapist or alcohol and smoking behaviors. The only exception was for caregivers of those with moderate intensity needs, who reported watching more television to cope with stress (82.5 % vs. 70.1 %).

The standardized regression coefficients for indicators of social resources (i.e., social support and loneliness); family resources (i.e., family functioning); financial resources (i.e., health insurance coverage); and internal resources (i.e., caregiver self-esteem) are presented in Tables 14.4, 14.5, 14.6 and 14.7, respectively. The multivariate models mirror the bivariate findings shown in Table 14.3. Being a spouse was significantly associated with fewer social, family and internal resources,

Table 14.5 Summary of standardized linear regression coefficients for variables predicting family resources

Family functioning	Independent variables	B (SE)	β
Step 1:	Relationship to care recipient (ref: parent)	0.29 (0.07)	0.23***
	Intensity of need (ref: high needs)	0.07 (0.07)	0.05
Step 2:	Relationship to care recipient (ref: parent)	0.29 (0.07)	0.23***
	Intensity of need (ref: high needs)	0.07 (0.08)	0.05
	Education	0.07 (0.05)	0.08
	Household income	−0.06 (0.04)	−0.10
Step 3:	Relationship to care recipient (ref: parent)	0.38 (0.08)	0.30***
	Intensity of need (ref: high needs)	0.04 (0.08)	0.03
	Education	0.05 (0.05)	0.06
	Household income	−0.07 (0.04)	−0.11
	Lives with veteran	−0.26 (0.09)	−0.18***
	Legal guardian of veteran	−0.06 (0.09)	−0.04

Note. High needs include care recipients who need assistance with ADLs or ADLs and IADLs. Moderate needs include care recipients who need assistance with only IADLS, not ADLs
Statistical significance of t-test: *** p < .001

Table 14.6 Summary of standardized linear regression coefficients for variables predicting financial resources

Caregiver health insurance coverage	Independent variables	B (SE)	β
Step 1:	Relationship to care recipient (ref: parent)	0.09 (0.04)	0.15**
	Intensity of need (ref: high needs)	0.06 (0.04)	0.09
Step 2:	Relationship to care recipient (ref: parent)	0.11 (0.04)	0.17**
	Intensity of need (ref: high needs)	0.05 (0.04)	0.07
	Education	0.04 (0.03)	0.09
	Household income	0.08 (0.02)	0.26**
Step 3:	Relationship to care recipient (ref: parent)	0.12 (0.04)	0.19**
	Intensity of need (ref: high needs)	0.06 (0.04)	0.09
	Education	0.05 (0.03)	0.11
	Household income	0.09 (0.02)	0.28**
	Lives with veteran	0.004 (0.05)	0.005
	Legal guardian of veteran	0.07 (0.05)	0.09

Note. High needs include care recipients who need assistance with ADLs or ADLs and IADLs. Moderate needs include care recipients who need assistance with only IADLS, not ADLs
Statistical significance of t-test: ** p < .01

but spouses were significantly more likely to have health care insurance than parents. Intensity of care recipient need was significantly associated with caregiver loneliness, but not with other resources. After adjusting for education and household income in Step 2, and co-habitation and legal guardianship status in Step 3, there was little to no change in the associations between relationship to care recipient, intensity of care recipient needs and each resource.

Table 14.7 Summary of standardized linear regression coefficients for variables predicting internal resources

Caregiver self-esteem	Independent variables	B (SE)	β
Step 1:	Relationship to care recipient (ref: parent)	−2.62 (0.59)	−0.23***
	Intensity of need (ref: high needs)	0.25 (0.62)	0.02
Step 2:	Relationship to care recipient (ref: parent)	−2.73 (0.63)	−0.24***
	Intensity of need (ref: high needs)	0.11 (0.66)	0.01
	Education	0.68 (0.45)	0.09
	Household income	0.74 (0.32)	0.13*
Step 3:	Relationship to care recipient (ref: parent)	−2.57 (0.75)	−0.23***
	Intensity of need (ref: high needs)	0.34 (0.67)	0.03
	Education	0.64 (0.45)	0.08
	Household income	0.82 (0.32)	0.15*
	Lives with veteran	0.60 (0.80)	0.05
	Legal guardian of veteran	1.79 (0.83)	0.13*

Note. High needs include care recipients who need assistance with ADLs or ADLs and IADLs. Moderate needs include care recipients who need assistance with only IADLS, not ADLs
Statistical significance of t-test: * $p < .05$, *** $p < .001$

Discussion

This study provides novel and important information on informal caregiving provided to care recipients with TBI/polytrauma and points to a need for interventions that are tailored according to the caregiver's relationship with the care recipient. Our data show that parents provide care for more severely injured care recipients than spouses, but that they also have more social resources, greater family functioning, self-esteem, and, except for health insurance coverage, financial resources. Consistent with the life course perspective, these results likely reflect their past experiences and knowledge of how to gather, retain and use resources, as well as having already reached their peak earning years. The results also likely reflect the differences in the emotional relationship that distinguishes spouses from parents and children. Understanding the complexities of this relationship likely extends beyond the availability of resources we measured in our study; however, our data do suggest some possible explanations. With a traumatic injury, both parents and spouses take on a sudden new role as caregiver. However, with an adult child, parents revert back to a distant but familiar role of caring for their child. Although 30 % of the caregiving parents in our study were divorced, significantly more reported they had a great deal of help and that family and friends provided additional help and support than spousal caregivers, which for many families includes the other parent and/or stepparent of the care recipient or the care recipient's adult siblings. Spouses, however, are faced with taking on a new role and have to adjust their life as a spouse to include being a caregiver to their partner, and in that role, they may not have the same extensive network of functional family systems as parents. They also may experience the loss of their marital role, as they knew it prior to injury.

The financial value associated with caregiving has been documented (Arno, Levine, & Memmott, 1999), but far fewer studies have directly explored the role that having or not having economic resources has on caregiver or care recipient health (Friedemann-Sánchez & Griffin, 2011; Van Houtven et al., 2013). We found in our study that 21 % of caregivers had annual household incomes less than $30,000 a year and another 25 % had incomes between $30,000 and $50,000 a year. Although we cannot determine if income is low because of caregiving (e.g. due to quitting work to provide care) or whether it was low prior to the injury, having few financial resources likely limits how much additional help with care or respite from providing care can be purchased, and creates a vulnerability to any additional financial stress. Our results also show that parents are less likely to have health insurance. With rates of employment not significantly different between spouses and parents, the difference in health insurance coverage may be a reflection of spouses having access to insurance through the military. Therefore, particular attention to parents' own health needs and remedies for accessing care may be important to consider.

Recent legislation (Public Law 111-163, the Caregivers and Veterans Omnibus Health Services Act of 2010), signed into law in May, 2010, is aimed at improving resources for families of care recipients injured in the line of duty during Operation Iraqi Freedom (OIF) and Operation Enduring Freedom (OEF). Although the legislation authorizes resources to be developed for all caregivers, it also mandates a special set of unprecedented benefits and resources specifically for qualified caregivers of injured OEF/OIF veterans who need assistance with activities of daily living (ADLs) or supervision or protection because of the residual effects of their illnesses and injuries. These targeted benefits include financial stipends paid directly to the primary caregiver, social support and counseling services, caregiver-related training, and health insurance coverage. Based on our findings, we expect these stipends will likely benefit those who provide support to care recipients needing assistance with ADLs, supervision, or protection as a result of their injuries. Parent caregivers, in particular, may benefit from the availability of health insurance coverage.

Lessons from caregiving interventions for chronic conditions suggest that providing resources, such as targeted education, social support for caregivers, and training to improve mastery and self-efficacy can improve caregiver health. Additionally, some interventions, such as psychotherapy and training for caregivers can significantly improve care recipients' scores for various health outcome scales (Sorensen et al., 2002). A number of systematic reviews, however, shows that these positive effects are small and not long-lasting (Goy, Kansagara, & Freeman, 2010; Martire, Lustig, Schulz, Miller, & Helgeson, 2004). Interventions that have specifically targeted families of patients with TBI and polytrauma are far fewer than for other conditions, like dementia. Similar to the general caregiving literature, however, most show small effects and focus on resources, such as improving education or support (Boschen, Gargaro, Gan, Gerber, & Brandys, 2007). These conclusions have led some to suggest that multiple component interventions that include skills, training, and social support may be the best approach for improving outcomes (Lovasik, Kerr, & Alexander, 2001). With the passage of Public Law 111-163, the Veterans Health Administration (VHA) is developing and implementing multiple resources specifically for caregivers. Our study examined existing resources for caregivers <u>prior</u> to the implementation of this legislation for caregivers of OEF/OIF veterans with polytrauma/TBI. We found that although most caregivers had some degree of support or assistance providing care, mostly from family and friends, and engaged in wide varieties of coping behaviors, most had very limited income and were socially isolated. We also found that spouses and parents who provide care to injured care recipients had significantly different resources. With significant differences across groups, it is possible that different approaches for programs or services may be necessary to support caregivers based on their relationship to the care recipient. New interventions to develop and enhance resources may need to address these differences in order to have the intended and expected magnitude of effect.

Despite the many strengths of our study, such as its strong design that included all those in the target population, our relatively large sample size, low refusal rate, and the numerous resources on which caregivers reported, our study did have a number of limitations. First, our data were cross-sectional, and therefore, we are not able to determine if the availability and use of resources prior to the care recipient's injury has remained constant since the injury or if the differences between spouses and parents were present prior to the injury. In addition, the PRCs added staff, such as psychologists and educators over time as the TBI/polytrauma patient population grew, but because of the cross sectional nature of the data, we are not able to identify if caregivers of service members injured later had more resources available to them during rehabilitation or whether they utilized more resources after discharge than caregivers of service members injured earlier in the wars. Because of the timing of our survey, however, our data do provide a snapshot of what resources were and how they varied across groups prior to the passage of Public Law 111-163, creating an opportunity for future study to test the impact of new resources available post-legislation. Second, the resources we identified, although theoretically inclusive, may have been a limited set of resources caregivers use and rely on. For example, we did not inquire about information seeking or access to appropriate information, although both have been shown to have a protective effect on caregivers of dementia patients. Likewise, we did not examine whether caregivers had been able to or did seek support services, including adult day care or home health aides at the time of the survey, nor did we examine whether specific resources for issues related to intimacy or relationship functioning, were available. Third, it is possible that caregivers over- or under-reported their resources or the amount of care the care recipient needed. However, because our survey was implemented before the legislation that became Public Law 111-163 was introduced by Congress, it is unlikely that any reporting bias was due to anticipation about benefits.

Our research identifies a number of gaps in resources that health care providers could help to address. Acute rehabilitation providers, for example, are in a unique position to provide guidance to caregivers early on about ways to cope, especially during transitions from acute rehabilitation or hospitalization to home. Although there were no significant differences by relationship to care recipient or intensity of need, few spouses and parents reported seeking counseling or therapy (15 %) as a means of coping with stress. Increasing counseling or therapy services for all family members may improve overall family functioning and may help to encourage healthy coping behaviors. Offering counseling or therapy in a variety in settings (such as in-home, over the telephone or internet) and at times that accommodate caregivers who are sole care providers may be crucial to increasing use of these services. Our findings suggest that spouses providing care to care recipients may especially benefit from counseling or other interventions addressing problems with self-esteem, social support, and family functioning.

Providing enhanced support or resources for care recipients' caregivers may improve caregiver health as well as the health and safety of care recipients. Our prior research has suggested that care recipients with polytrauma/TBI whose care-givers reported worse physical and mental health had increased odds of incurring new injuries than those whose caregivers were in better health (Carlson et al., 2012). Prior caregiving studies of elders have also found that caregiver substance use is strongly associated with care recipient safety (Bristowe & Collins, 1988; Homer & Gilleard, 1990). Compared with the general U.S. adult population, there was a high proportion of binge drinking in our caregiver population (19 % compared to 15 %; 2010 BRFSS). The prevalence of heavy drinking and smoking was also elevated in this caregiving population. Overall enhanced support or, more specifically, educa-tional efforts and counseling focused on teaching positive coping strategies for care-givers may reduce harmful behaviors and ultimately improve both caregiver and care recipient outcomes.

Finally, additional research is needed to evaluate the impact of caregiver benefits from Public Law 111-163. We have hypothesized elsewhere that caregiving can have a cyclical and recursive pattern, so that caregivers with inadequate resources are less likely to manage stress and more likely to develop poor health (Friedemann-Sánchez & Griffin, 2011). Poor health, in turn, can then cause even greater stress, taxing individual resources further. Testing how targeted benefits to improve resources can affect caregiver and care recipient health could be used to improve and expand VA programs, but could also be used as a model on how best to support caregivers of non-veteran care recipients.

Conclusions

Caregivers of OEF/OIF care recipients with polytrauma/TBI have significant gaps in the resources that could help them buffer stress from caregiving. New programs being developed by the VA to support caregivers may help to fill these gaps. Spousal caregivers report fewer social, family, and internal resources than parents and parents have less access to health insurance than spouses. Both groups of caregivers, there-fore, may benefit from these new benefits and services. Health care providers can also provide early guidance to caregivers about resources, including available sup-port services and advice on self-care, which may help caregivers cope with stress related to caregiving.

Funding Support and Acknowledgements This research was supported by the Department of Veterans Affairs, Veterans Health Administration, Office of Research and Development and a grant from the Health Services Research and Development service (SDR-07-044). The findings and conclusions presented in this manuscript are those of the authors and do not necessarily represent the views of the Department of Veterans Affairs or HSR&D. The sponsor was not involved in any aspect of the study's design and conduct; data collection, management, analysis, or interpretation of data; or in the preparation, review or approval of the manuscript.

References

Abe, K., Kashiwagi, T., & Tsuneto, S. (2003). Coping strategies and its effects on depression among caregivers of impaired elders in Japan. *Aging and Mental Health, 7,* 207–211.

Acton, G. J., & Kang, J. (2001). Interventions to reduce the burden of caregiving for an adult with dementia: A meta-analysis. *Research in Nursing and Health, 24,* 349–360.

Arno, P. S., Levine, C., & Memmott, M. M. (1999). The economic value of informal caregiving. *Health Affairs (Millwood), 18,* 182–188.

Baronet, A. M. (1999). Factors associated with caregiver burden in mental illness: A critical review of the research literature. *Clinical Psychology Review, 19,* 819–841.

Bernard, L. L., & Guarnaccia, C. A. (2003). Two models of caregiver strain and bereavement adjustment: A comparison of husband and daughter caregivers of breast cancer hospice patients. *Gerontologist, 43,* 808–816.

Blacher, J. (2001). Transition to adulthood: Mental retardation, families, and culture. *American Journal on Mental Retardation, 106,* 173–188.

Boschen, K., Gargaro, J., Gan, C., Gerber, G., & Brandys, C. (2007). Family interventions after acquired brain injury and other chronic conditions: A critical appraisal of the quality of the evidence. *Neurorehabilitation, 22,* 19–41.

Bristowe, E., & Collins, J. B. (1988). Family mediated abuse of noninstitutionalized frail elderly men and women living in British Columbia. *Journal of Elder Abuse & Neglect, 1,* 45–64.

Carlson K. F., Meis, L. A., Jensen, A. C., Simon, A. B., Gravely, A. A., Taylor, B. C., Bangerter, A. K., Schaaf, K. W., & Griffin, J. M. (2012). Caregiver reports of subsequent Iinjuries among veterans with traumatic braint injury after discharge from inpatient polytrauma rehabilitation programs. *Journal of Head Trauma Rehabilitation, 27*(1),14–25.

Centers for Disease Control and Prevention (CDC). (2008). *Behavioral risk factor surveillance system survey questionnaire*. Atlanta, Georgia: U.S. Department of Health and Human Services, Centers for Disease Control and Prevention.

Cohen, C. A., Colantonio, A., & Vernich, L. (2002). Positive aspects of caregiving: Rounding out the caregiver experience. *International Journal of Geriatric Psychiatry, 17,* 184–188.

Degeneffe, C. E. (2001). Family caregiving and traumatic brain injury. *Health and Social Work, 26,* 257–268.

Dillman, D. A. (2007). *Mail and internet surveys*. Hoboken, NJ: The Tailored Method Design Wiley Press.

Eakes, G. G. (1995). Chronic sorrow: The lived experience of parents of chronically mentally ill individuals. *Archives of Psychiatry Nursing, 9,* 77–84.

Elder, G. H., Kirkpatrick Johnson, M., & Crosnoe, R. (2003). *The emergence and development of life course theory*. New York: Springer.

Epstein, N. B., Baldwin, L. M., & Bishop, D. S. (1983). The McMaster family assessment device. *Journal of Marital and Family Therapy, 9,* 171–180.

Folkman, S. (1997). Positive psychological states and coping with severe stress. *Social Science & Medicine, 45,* 1207–1221.

Friedemann, S., Sayer, N. A., & Pickett, T. (2008). Provider perspectives on rehabilitation of patients with polytrauma. *Archives of Physical Medicine & Rehabilitation, 89*(1), 171–178.

Friedemann-Sánchez, G., & Griffin, J. M. (2011). Defining the boundaries between unpaid labor and unpaid caregiving: Review of the social and health sciences literature. *Journal of Human Development and Capabilities, 12,* 511–534.

Friedemann-Sanchez, G., Sayer, N. A., & Pickett, T. (2008). Provider perspectives on the rehabilitation of patients with polytrauma. *Archives of Physical Medicine & Rehabilitation, 89,* 171–178.

Gottlieb, B. H., & Wolfe, J. (2002). Coping with family caregiving to persons with dementia: A critical review. *Aging and Mental Health, 6,* 325–342.

Goy, E., Kansagara, D., & Freeman, M. (2010). *A systematic evidence review of interventions for non-professional caregivers of individuals with dementia.* Portland, OR: Evidence-Based Synthesis Program (ESP) Center.

Griffin, J. M., Friedemann-Sanchez, G., Jensen, A. C., Taylor, B. C., Gravely, A., Clothier, B., et al. (2012). The invisible side of war: Families caring for US service members with traumatic brain injuries and polytrauma. *Journal of Head Trauma Rehabilitation, 27,* 3–13.

Homer, A. C., & Gilleard, C. (1990). Abuse of elderly people by their carers. *British Medical Journal, 301,* 1359–1362.

Katz, S., Ford, A., Moskowitz, R., Jackson, B., & Jaffe, M. (1963). Studies of illness in the aged. The index of ADL: A standardized measure of biological and psychosocial function. *JAMA: Journal of the American Medical Association, 185,* 914–919.

Killeen, M. (1990). The influence of stress and coping on family caregivers' perceptions of health. *International Journal of Aging and Human Development, 30,* 197–211.

Lawton, M. P., & Brody, E. M. (1969). Assessment of older people: Self-maintaining and instrumental activities of daily living. *Gerontologist, 9,* 179–186.

Lazarus, R. S., & Folkman, S. (1984). *Stress, appraisal, and coping.* New York: Springer.

Li, L. W., Seltzer, M. M., & Greenberg, J. S. (1997). Social support and depressive symptoms: Differential patterns in wife and daughter caregivers. *Journals of Gerontology B: Psychological Sciences and Social Sciences, 52,* S200–S211.

Lovasik, D., Kerr, M. E., & Alexander, S. (2001). Traumatic brain injury research: A review of clinical studies. *Critical Care Nursing Quarterly, 23,* 24–41.

Martire, L. M., Lustig, A. P., Schulz, R., Miller, G. E., & Helgeson, V. S. (2004). Is it beneficial to involve a family member? A meta-analysis of psychosocial interventions for chronic illness. *Health Psychology, 23,* 599–611.

Raina, P., O'Donnell, M., Schwellnus, H., Rosenbaum, P., King, G., Brehaut, J., et al. (2004). Caregiving process and caregiver burden: Conceptual models to guide research and practice. *BMC Pediatrics, 4,* 1.

Rosenberg, M. (1965). *Society and the adolescent self-image.* Princeton, NJ: Princeton, University Press.

Russell, D. W. (1996). UCLA loneliness scale. *Journal of Personality Assessment, 66,* 20–40.

Sayer, N. A., Chiros, C. E., Sigford, B., Scott, S., Clothier, B., Pickett, T., et al. (2008). Characteristics and rehabilitation outcomes among patients with blast and other injuries sustained during the Global War on Terror. *Archives of Physical Medicine & Rehabilitation, 89*(1), 163–170.

Sayer, N. A., Cifu, D. X., McNamee, S., Chiros, C. E., Sigford, B. J., Scott, S., et al. (2009). Rehabilitation needs of combat-injured service members admitted to the VA polytrauma rehabilitation centers: The role of PM&R in the care of wounded warriors. *Physical Medicine and Rehabilitation, 1*(1), 23–28.

Schulz, R., & Martire, L. M. (2004). Family caregiving of persons with dementia: Prevalence, health effects, and support strategies. *American Journal of Geriatric Psychiatry, 12,* 240–249.

Sigford, B. J. (2008). To care for him who shall have borne the battle and for his widow and his orphan (Abraham Lincoln): The Department of Veterans Affairs polytrauma system of care. *Archives of Physical Medicine and Rehabilitation, 89,* 160–162.

Sorensen, S., Pinquart, M., & Duberstein, P. (2002). How effective are interventions with caregivers? An updated meta-analysis. *Gerontologist, 42,* 356–372.

Vaglio, J., Jr., Conard, M., Poston, W. S., O'Keefe, J., Haddock, C. K., House, J., et al. (2004). Testing the performance of the ENRICHD Social Support Instrument in cardiac patients. *Health and Quality of Life Outcomes, 2,* 24–29.

Van Houtven, C. H., Friedemann-Sánchez, G., Clothier, B., Levison, D., Taylor, B. C., Jensen, A. C., et al. (2013). Is policy well-targeted to remedy financial strain among caregivers of severely injured U.S. Service Members? *Inquiry, 49*(4), 339–351.

Chapter 15
Combat-Related Posttraumatic Stress Disorder and Families

Tanja Frančišković, Aleksandra Stevanović, and Miro Klarić

Abstract A series of studies have demonstrated that post-traumatic stress disorder in war veterans may cause serious problems in husband–wife relationships. These problems reduce the relationship satisfaction in both partners and may cause redistribution of family roles. The increased burden placed on the wives may lead to burnout, transmission of post-traumatic symptoms and development of other mental disorders. In addition, PTSD symptoms have an immediate effect on the veterans' ability to fulfill their parental roles, which certainly affects the children's development. The 1991–1995 war in Croatia had many consequences on the war veterans, their families and civilians. For nearly two decades, the Regional Psychotrauma Center, in Rijeka, Croatia has been providing psychological help to war victims, majority of which are war veterans. Our clinical experiences, as well as the results of our studies, indicate that treatment of the traumatized veterans needs to include the wives. A systemic approach in treating the traumatized persons can improve individual functioning and couple functioning. Furthermore, it can minimize potential psychological effects on the children.

Keywords Combat PTSD • Family • War veterans

T. Frančišković (✉) • A. Stevanović
Department of Psychiatry and Psychological Medicine, School of Medicine,
University of Rijeka, Cambierieva 15, 51000 Rijeka, Croatia
e-mail: tanja.franciskovic@medri.uniri.hr; aleksandras@medri.uniri.hr

M. Klarić
Department of Psychiatry, University Hospital Mostar, K.M. Viševića Humskog 39, 88000
Mostar, Bosnia and Herzegovina
e-mail: klaricmiro@gmail.com

S. MacDermid Wadsworth and D.S. Riggs (eds.), *Military Deployment and its*
Consequences for Families, Risk and Resilience in Military and Veteran Families,
DOI 10.1007/978-1-4614-8712-8_15, © Springer Science+Business Media New York 2014

War affects not only war veterans, but also their families and the wider community (Mileti, Drabek, & Haas, 1975). Social support is one of the most helpful resources when facing trauma and plays an important role in the process of recovery (Bisson et al., 2007; Lincoln, Chatters, & Taylor, 2005; Neria, Nandi, & Galea, 2008). Families, as the most powerful social unit, can provide many forms of support to traumatized persons. In fact, family relationships can be an "antidote" to stress disorders (Figley, 1989). Posttraumatic stress disorder (PTSD) is one of the psychological disturbances that frequently affect war veterans. With its specific symptoms, PTSD exerts a profound effect on the veterans' social functioning, which can be best observed in family interactions. Family members, who should be the ones who provide emotional support, are hurt most deeply by the veterans' mental difficulties (Fullerton & Ursano, 1997; Koić, Frančišković, Mužinić-Masle, Đorđević, & Vondraček, 2002; Solomon, Waysman, Levy, et al., 1992).

The war that affected former Yugoslavia ended in the country's breaking up into a range of new states. The 4-year war left many victims, a great number of refugees and a ruined infrastructure. Tens of thousands of persons in Croatia and in Bosnia and Herzegovina joined the military forces or were mobilized for the war. Upon returning from the battlefront, many of them experienced various mental effects of psychological trauma and up to 26 % developed some symptoms of PTSD (Komar & Vukušić, 1999). We suggest that the situation was aggravated by the difficult social circumstances of living in a country in transition.

When one of the partners has health problems, the other partner is expected to give support. However, it is quite stressful and devastating to have a partner suffering from PTSD. Constantly providing support, but not receiving any at the same time can make a person feel helpless (Nelson Goff & Smith, 2005). Some common behavioral patterns of the wives of war veterans with PTSD have been identified through clinical work and scientific research by several authors. These women often take on the commitment of protecting their husbands against external factors that may irritate them. At the same time, they often protect their children from their husbands' "bad periods." Through excessive care for the traumatized, very often the entire family's life is subordinated to the veteran's needs; for instance, there is no loud music in the house, no visits from friends, etc. (Mason, 1990; Nelson Goff et al., 2006).

One of the common behavior patterns is also the excessive responsibility and too many duties taken by the wife of the war veteran. Many authors have described the "co-dependent" behavior of the Vietnam wives. These women took over the responsibility of resolving their husband's problems (Mason, 1990; Scaturo & Hardoby, 1988). Guilt, low self-esteem and fear are strong motives for assuming the role of the "responsible one" (Coughlan & Parkin, 1987; Verbosky & Ryan, 1988) or the "caregiver" in the family (Solomon, 1998). Since wives are mostly considered the "home keepers" (and very often see themselves that way too), they are inclined to assume most of (or all) responsibilities in the home in order to preserve the emotional climate in the family (Coughlan & Parkin, 1987; Mason, 1990; Verbosky & Ryan, 1988). Solomon (1998) described this as the "redistribution of roles and redivision of labor". Rabin & Nardi (1991) say that the wife's over-functioning is a way for her to avoid conflict by making fewer demands on the ill husband. This type of behavior may end up in a vicious circle: the over-functioning of the wife leads to under-functioning of the husband, who, in turn, increases his demands on the wife. Solomon (1998) describes the inclination of wife to feel responsible for his mental health even though she does not have much control over the husband's PTSD as a "compassion trap." Many wives give in to the AlAnon "Three C" concept—they believe they *cause* the husband's problems, they can *control* them and they can *cure* them (Harkness & Zador, 2004).

Wives of war veterans with PTSD tend to overprotect their traumatized partners from the trauma. Traumatic experience is not something that is easy to talk about. Veterans suffering from PTSD may isolate themselves from other people, even from their spouses, because it is too painful to talk about traumatic events. On the other hand, their wives may feel exhausted from hearing about traumatic events or they may feel uncomfortable seeing their partners in a situation that makes them vulnerable. In such instances, the wives often encourage their partners to "leave that behind" and go on with their lives (Gilbert, 1998). The avoidance of interaction can make both partners feel isolated and unsupported. Sometimes this isolation of the wife is done intentionally and sometimes it is the consequence of PTSD of the veteran, especially his avoidance symptoms. In addition, these couples often lack external support. A PTSD-affected spouse may stop the other partner from seeing other people, even members of the extended family. The couple may feel that others cannot understand what they are going through, while persons in their environment may not want to hear about their problems (Glassman, Magulac, & Darko, 1987; Maloney, 1988).

The Regional Psychotrauma Center in Rijeka, Croatia, has been providing help to war victims, most of whom are war veterans. From the beginning of the war in 1991, but also for years after, the Center was overwhelmed with war veterans seeking psychological help for their posttraumatic stress reactions. It took us several years to realize that success in treating PTSD-affected war veterans depended on the psychological state of their wives. Before we started working with wives, we had not fully understood the amount of pressure they had to live with. These women had not sought any help for years. They had even hesitated in responding to our invitations at first. We therefore decided to create psychotherapy programs that included war veterans' wives.

In this paper the psychological consequences of living with war veterans with PTSD will be discussed through our own clinical and scientific contributions, supported with the most relevant scientific and clinical insights in the field. The paper is divided into three major sections. In the first section the focus is on the effects of PTSD on war veterans' families through emotional burnout, caregiver burden and marital adjustment of veterans' wives. In the second section psychological consequences of living with combat PTSD with the emphasis on secondary traumatic stress are discussed. The third section focuses on the effect of combat PTSD on the children's psychosocial development.

The Effect of PTSD on War Veterans' Families

Emotional Burn-out, Caregiver Burden, and Marital Adjustment

Providing support to a family member diagnosed with PTSD can be quite difficult and stressful. This is especially difficult for wives, who are most often the main providers of support (Fullerton & Ursano, 1997; Kessler & McLeod, 1985). Most studies dealing with combat-related PTSD in war veterans and their families focus on the effects of PTSD on marital and cohabiting relationships. Posttraumatic Stress Disorder poses a risk of developing serious problems between partners. These problems reduce relationship satisfaction and affect the distribution of family roles. The increased burden placed on wives who are expected to provide constant support to their husbands may lead to burnout, transmission of post-traumatic symptoms and development of other mental disorders (Frančišković et al., 2007; Klarić, Frančišković, Pernar, et al., 2010).

In order to investigate the influence of combat PTSD on other family members we have conducted several studies.

In data collected during 2007, we investigated the influence of combat PTSD on veteran's partners through caregiver burden, emotional burnout (Klarić, Frančišković, Pernar, et al., 2010) and marital quality and relationship satisfaction (Klarić et al. 2011). The research was conducted with a sample from Mostar region, Bosnia and Herzegovina, where many war veterans' partners were themselves exposed to civilian war trauma. The sample comprised male veterans who had experienced war trauma. All veterans who were diagnosed with PTSD in Mostar Clinical Hospital and came for a doctor's appointment were asked to participate in the study, with a final sample of 154 couples entering the study. To form a control group, initial contact with veterans who did not suffer from PTSD was made through veterans' associations, and further recruitment was conducted using the snowballing method, with a final of 77 couples entering the study (Klarić, Frančiškovič, Pernar, et al., 2010; Klarić et al. 2011). Women whose husbands had PTSD reported significantly higher levels of somatic disturbances and PTSD symptoms, compared with wives of veterans without PTSD. The study also demonstrated that women with PTSD-diagnosed husbands had significantly higher scores in the Caregiver Burden Questionnaire and the Burnout Inventory. Subjective stress, subjective demand burden, and emotional burnout in relationships were even more obvious in couples in which both of the partners suffered from PTSD (Klarić, Frančišković, Pernar, et al., 2010). Also, veterans' PTSD was related to lower levels of marital adjustment of their wives, with the lowest adjustment found in couples where both partners had PTSD (Klarić et al., 2011).

Results supported the theoretical and scientific evidence found in the literature. Emotional burnout is a process associated with chronic accumulation of stressors which destroy a person's high ideals, motivation and dedication to life's goals. It is a condition of physical, emotional and mental exhaustion caused by long-term engagement in emotionally demanding situations (Figley, 1995, 1998). Such situations are quite frequent in couples in which one of the partners suffers from PTSD. Figley (1999) says that burnout occurs as a result of empathic engagement in providing help, but also as a result of an inability to find relief and rest through an interruption in the emotional engagement. Further on, an extensive exposure to stress, according to Figley, leads to "compassion fatigue," the extreme form of burnout. Compassion fatigue is an important concept in recognizing and understanding the effects of working or living with a traumatized person (Figley, 1999).

Low marital satisfaction found in our study among families of war veterans with PTSD also was not surprising. For instance, divorce rates in families of Vietnam War veterans are twice that in other families; family violence and communication and sexual problems are more frequent and problem-focused coping skills are poorer (Riggs, Byrne, Weathers, & Litz, 1998). More than 70 % of war veterans suffering from PTSD report a clinically significant level of stress in their relationships. Furthermore, there is a significant correlation between the level of relationship stress and the intensity of PTSD symptoms in war veterans, especially symptoms of avoidance and emotional numbness (Chrysos, Taft, King, & King, 2005; Dekel & Solomon, 2006; Jordan et al., 1992; Nelson Goff, Crow, Reisbig, & Hamilton, 2007; Riggs et al., 1998). Symptoms of re-experiencing traumatic events often affect the veteran's ability to be "present." Later, symptoms of avoidance and emotional numbness may interfere with his ability to identify, modulate and express emotions, which is a prerequisite of a healthy emotional relationship. Symptoms of arousal reduce veterans' feelings of security and reduce trust in other people. All this reduces the ability to connect with other people (Galovski & Lyons, 2004; Matsakis, 1998). Several other features of PTSD, such as unpredictable reactions and frequent aggressive outbursts, make relationship problems even more difficult. Later, the traumatized may find it hard to tolerate the feelings of vulnerability that develop in interpersonal relations (Harkness & Zador, 2004).

Many authors report that emotional emptiness resulting from veterans' self-absorption, isolation and irritability is one of the most serious effects of PTSD on family life (Lyons, 2001; Rosenheck & Thomson, 1986). The lack of emotional responsiveness and withdrawal from the family's emotional life can manifest in many forms. For instance, a PTSD-affected person may not pay any attention to family members, may spend hours in front of the television or not come home for days. As a result, such a person is absent from the children's development and from family routines (Rosenheck & Thomson, 1986) that are essential in creating feelings of identity and belonging. Also, veterans' withdrawal can make other family members feel guilty and responsible (Harkness & Zador, 2004; Lyons, 2001).

Impulsive outbursts of anger and violent and destructive behavior, which are frequently followed by periods of withdrawal and relative tranquility, can create additional problems. In some cases, veterans even become physically violent (Klarić, Frančišković, & Salčin Satriano, 2010). The unpredictable nature of fits of rage hurts the family atmosphere and causes tension, anxiety and hyper vigilance. It creates the feeling that one has to "walk on eggs" and bottle up emotions. It often happens that the veteran with PTSD and his family live separate lives, which leads to development of different sets of values (Harkness & Zador, 2004; Nelson Goff & Smith, 2005).

The Effect of War Veterans' PTSD on Marital Partners

Secondary Traumatic Stress

Studies show that persons in close contact with a traumatized person can also develop painful and severe symptoms of trauma (Figley, 1995, 1997; McCann & Pearlman, 1990; Pearlman & MacIan, 1995). The process is called secondary or vicarious traumatization. Secondary traumatization has been explored among emergency room workers (Andersen, Christensen, & Peterson, 1991; Marmar et al., 1999), therapists and healthcare professionals working with traumatized people (McCann & Pearlman, 1990; Pearlman & MacIan 1995) and partners and other family members of war veterans (Rosenheck & Nathan, 1985; Solomon, Waysman, Belkin, et al., 1992).

Recent studies increasingly focus on secondary traumatic stress. STS occurs as a result of being emotionally connected and providing care to someone with PTSD symptoms. It may develop as a result of knowing or hearing about traumatic events experienced by a significant other (Figley, 1995, 1998). Secondary traumatization involves the transmission of nightmares, intrusive thoughts, flashbacks and other symptoms typically experienced by individuals directly exposed to trauma. In a broader sense, secondary traumatization refers to any transmission of distress from someone who experienced trauma onto persons in close contact with the traumatized person. It includes a wide specter of manifestations (Dekel & Solomon, 2006; Galovski & Lyons, 2004) which develop as the result of a direct or an indirect exposure to primary traumatization of the spouse (Figley, 1989).

Our pilot study in 2002 focused on secondary traumatic stress, depression, anxiety and chronic pain in a sample of 80 women married to war veterans of the 1991–1995 war in Croatia, 40 of whom were being treated for PTSD (Koić et al., 2002). The results indicated that 30 % of the wives fulfilled criteria for secondary stress disorder. The results also showed that wives of the PTSD-diagnosed veterans had significantly more often reported chronic pain, mostly back pain and headaches, compared with wives of veterans without PTSD. In a similar study conducted in 2006, 32 of 56 women (57.1 %) whose husbands were treated with PTSD reported six or more symptoms of secondary traumatic stress, while only 3 women (5.3 %) did not report any symptoms. Twenty-two women (39.3 %) met criteria for secondary traumatic stress disorder according to the DSM-IV classification (Frančišković et al., 2007).

To gain more in-depth knowledge of the transmission of PTSD symptoms to wives of Croatian war veterans, we conducted a larger study that examined the level of secondary traumatic stress symptoms, current psychological symptoms and perception of quality of life in women whose husbands suffered from PTSD (N=50) (Stevanović, 2012). The research compared this group of women with women whose husbands did not have PTSD (N=50) and women whose husbands did not fight in the war (N=50). The research was carried out at the Center for Psychotrauma Rijeka. Thirty-six percent of the wives of PTSD-affected veterans met criteria for secondary traumatic stress disorder compared with only 8 % of wives of war veterans without PTSD. Wives of war veterans with PTSD reported higher levels of somatization, obsessive-compulsive symptoms, greater sensitivity in interpersonal relationships, as well as greater levels of depression, anxiety, hostility, phobias, paranoid ideations and psychoticism relative to the other two groups. Perceived quality of life for these women was significantly poorer as compared to the women whose husbands did not suffer from PTSD and women whose husbands did not take part in the war. The results also showed that the women with larger numbers of secondary traumatic stress symptoms also reported larger numbers of psychological symptoms and lower quality of life. Knowledge about the husband's traumatic experiences was the most important predictor of STS, while PTSD in war veterans had the strongest effect on wives' psychological symptoms. The study results suggested that a lack of knowledge about trauma protected the family members from developing STS symptoms. However, our clinical experience with wives of the Croatian war veterans indicates that the wall of silence erected by their husbands exhausts them and makes them feel helpless in their struggle to help their husbands.

Interestingly, women married to PTSD-affected veterans were statistically less satisfied with the quality of family relationships than the other two groups of women, but they still reported loving their husbands and not being able to imagine their lives without them. Similar to their veteran husbands, they described family as the most important thing in their lives.

Our results are in line with a series of studies that reveal that wives of PTSD-affected war veterans experience substantial emotional difficulties (Ben Arzi, Solomon, & Dekel, 2000; Dirkzwager, Bramsen, Adèr, & van der Ploeg, 2005). Higher frequency of STS symptoms has also been found in samples of Vietnam veterans' wives (Galovski & Lyons, 2004; Lyons, 2001), Israeli war veterans' wives (Ben Arzi, Solomon, & Dekel, 2000; Dekel, Solomon, & Bleich, 2005), wives of Dutch peace keepers (Dirkzwager et al., 2005) and among wives of U.S. war veterans from Iraq and Afanistan (Nelson Goff, Crow, Reisbig, & Hamilton, 2009). A study that explored the influence of combat-related PTSD on wives of Vietnam War veterans revealed that the women often felt "on the verge of breakdown." They reported significantly lower levels of happiness and life satisfaction and higher levels of demoralization, as compared to the wives of the War veterans without PTSD (Kulka et al., 1990). The veteran wives and members of their families often experienced emotional numbness, depression, anger and felt isolated and abandoned (Matsakis, 1998). Vietnam veteran wives reported an increased level of general psychopathology as compared to wives of the veterans without PTSD. Furthermore, these wives also reported higher levels of depression and anxiety, more problems with concentration, emotional exhaustion, headaches and sleeping problems and they were more likely to develop somatization disorders (Alessi, Ray, Ray, & Stewart, 2001; Ben Arzi, Solomon, & Dekel, 2000). Psychological profiles of war veteran wives reveal poorer social adjustment, greater interpersonal sensitivity, greater anxiety and higher levels of social introversion (Alessi et al., 2001; Beckham, Lytel, & Feldman, 1996; Calhoun, Beckham, & Bosworth, 2002; Dekel & Solomon, 2006; Galovski & Lyons, 2004; Solomon, Waysman, Levy, et al., 1992).

Effects of Combat Related PTSD on Parental Roles and Psychosocial Development of Children

Because of the emotional difficulties and specific patterns of behavior it can cause, persons suffering from PTSD can develop significant problems in parent–child relationships. Even though war veterans with PTSD often say that their children are their *raison d'etre*, they may lack sufficient patience or will to be a competent parent. It may be hard for a veteran to recognize that children's aggression could be age-appropriate or to tolerate such a behavior. This may lead veterans to avoid interactions with their children, or it could cause excessive reactions (Haley, 1984). Children of war veterans diagnosed with PTSD often describe their families as dysfunctional. PTSD symptoms directly affect the veterans' ability to fulfill their parental roles, which influences the children's development (Davidson & Mellor, 2001; Ruscio, Weathers, King, & King, 2002). In fact, parenthood in war veterans is often characterized by control, overprotection and excessive demands in relationships with the children. Such complicated relationships of war veterans and their children have been described in many studies (Dekel & Goldblatt, 2008; Harkness, 1991; Harkness & Zador, 2004; Jurich, 1983).

Klarić et al. (2008) examined the influence of fathers' PTSD on children. The sample of 154 war veterans suffering from combat-related PTSD and 77 war veterans who did not have PTSD reported the extent of their children's developmental, emotional and behavioral problems. The veterans with PTSD believed that their children had more problems compared to the children of the veterans without PTSD (Klarić et al. 2008). Results of a similar study of Vietnam war veterans revealed the same tendencies (Caselli & Motta, 1995).

In 2010 we conducted a pilot study aimed at assessing the relationship between fathers' chronic combat-related PTSD 15 years after the war, mothers' symptoms of secondary traumatization, and emotional and behavioral symptoms in their offspring. Seventy war veterans who were being treated for PTSD at the Center for psychotrauma Rijeka, their spouses, and their school-aged children were included. Emotional and behavioral symptoms in offspring were indirectly assessed by the mothers using the Child Behavior Check List (CBCL). The results did not show significant relationships between fathers' combat-related PTSD symptoms and children's emotional and behavior symptoms. However, symptoms of secondary traumatization in mothers were correlated with the presence of symptoms in offspring, suggesting a mediating role of mother's secondary traumatization between a veteran's war trauma and the psychological health of school-age offspring (Kaštelan, Frančišković, Stevanović, & Petrić, 2012). The pilot study was enlarged and the children of war veterans treated for PTSD were compared with a matching sample of children of war veterans without PTSD. It is important to mention that the two groups of children differed significantly only on subscales for withdrawn, anxious/depressed behavior, and the overall internalizing scale (Kaštelan, 2012).

Our results are partially consistent with previous studies. In 1985, Rosenheck and Nathan conducted a study comparing children of Vietnam War veterans and children of Holocaust survivors, discovering significant similarities. The children of

PTSD-diagnosed war veterans experienced behavioral difficulties, but specific problems had not been detected (Kulka et al., 1988). These children more often had authority problems, more frequently experienced depression, anger, hyperactivity and emotional pain and more frequently had problems in personal relationships. Furthermore, these children were more violent, had more behavioral disturbances, more often used drugs (Beckham, Feldman, Kirby, Hertzberg, & Moore, 1997) and more often sought psychiatric help (Davidson, Smith, & Kudler, 1989). They often manifested difficulties in academic careers, dyadic relationships and regulation of emotions, but it is hard to say whether these difficulties were consequences of the father's PTSD or the result of family violence (Harkness, 1991). In our research, however, we failed to find a significant relationship between fathers' PTSD symptoms and instead found a possible mediating role of mother's psychological well-being on emotional and behavioral problems in their children. Our results are most similar to those found in a Kuwait sample of children of prisoners of war. Children whose fathers had PTSD had significantly higher levels of depressive symptoms, but the symptoms were best predicted by mothers' level of PTSD, depression and anxiety symptoms (Al-Turkait & Ohaeri, 2008).

Conclusion

The results of our studies validate our experiences of working with wives of veterans suffering from PTSD, and showed that the veterans' war trauma and PTSD exerted a profound impact on their wives. Psychological work with both of the partners focusing on primary and secondary posttraumatic reactions should reduce and potentially prevent psychological problems in children who live with a dysfunctional father and an overburdened mother.

Clinicians working with traumatized war veterans and especially veterans who develop PTSD should bear in mind that living with a traumatized person can cause stress reactions in their partners. The treatment of traumatized veterans should certainly include wives, not only because wives provide needed support, but also to prevent the development of secondary symptoms among wives. A systemic approach in treating traumatized persons can improve individual functioning of both partners and reduce potential psychological consequences among their children.

References

Alessi, M. W., Ray, J. W., Ray, G. E., & Stewart, S. J. (2001). Personality and psychopathology profiles of veterans' wives: Measuring distress using the MMPI-2. *Journal of Clinical Psychology, 57*(12), 1535–1542.

Al-Turkait, F. A., & Ohaeri, J. U. (2008). Psychopathology status, behavior problems and family adjustment of Kuwaiti children whose fathers were involved in the first Gulf war. *Child and Adolescent psychiatry and Mental Health, 2*(1), 12. http://www.capmh.com/content/2/1/12.

Andersen, H. S., Christensen, A. K., & Peterson, G. O. (1991). Posttraumatic stress reactions amongst rescue workers after a major rail accident. *Anxiety Research, 4*, 245–251.

Beckham, J. C., Feldman, M. E., Kirby, A. C., Hertzberg, M. A., & Moore, S. D. (1997). Interpersonal violence and its correlates in Vietnam veterans with chronic posttraumatic stress disorder. *Journal of Clinical Psychology, 53*, 859–869.

Beckham, J. C., Lytel, B. L., & Feldman, M. E. (1996). Caregiver burden in partners of Vietnam veterans with posttraumatic stress disorder. *Journal of Consulting and Clinical Psychology, 64*, 1068–1071.

Ben Arzi, N., Solomon, Z., & Dekel, R. (2000). Secondary traumatization among wives of PTSD and post-concussion casualties: Distress, caregiver burden and psychological separation. *Brain Injury, 14*(8), 725–736.

Bisson, J. I., Ehlers, A., Matthews, R., Pilling, S., Richards, D., & Turner, S. (2007). Psychological treatments for chronic post-traumatic stress disorder: Systematic review and meta-analysis. *British Journal of Psychiatry, 190*, 97–104.

Calhoun, P. S., Beckham, J. C., & Bosworth, H. B. (2002). Caregiver burden and psychological distress in partners of veterans with chronic posttraumatic stress disorder. *Journal of Traumatic Stress, 15*, 205–212.

Caselli, L. T., & Motta, R. W. (1995). The effect of PTSD and combat level on Vietnam veterans' perceptions of child behavior and marital adjustment. *Journal of Clinical Psychology, 51*, 4–12.

Chrysos, E. S., Taft, C. T., King, L. A., & King, D. W. (2005). Gender, partner violence, and perceived family functioning among a sample of Vietnam veterans. *Violence and Victims, 20*, 549–559.

Coughlan, K., & Parkin, C. (1987). Women partners of Vietnam vets. *Journal of Psychosocial Nursing & Mental Health Services, 25*, 25–27.

Davidson, A. C., & Mellor, D. J. (2001). The adjustment of children of Australian Vietnam veterans: Is there evidence for the transgenerational transmission of war-related trauma? *Australian and New Zealand Journal of Psychiatry, 35*, 345–351.

Davidson, J., Smith, R., & Kudler, H. (1989). Familial psychiatric illness in chronic posttraumatic stress disorder. *Comprehensive Psychiatry, 30*, 339–345.

Dekel, R., & Goldblatt, H. (2008). Is there intergenerational transmission of trauma? The case of combat veterans' children. *American Journal of Orthopsychiatry, 78*, 281–289.

Dekel, R., & Solomon, Z. (2006). Marital relations among former prisoners of war: Contribution of posttraumatic stress disorder, aggression, and sexual satisfaction. *Journal of Family Psychology, 20*, 709–712.

Dekel, R., Solomon, Z., & Bleich, A. (2005). Emotional distress and marital adjustment of caregivers: Contribution of level of impairment and appraised burden. *Anxiety, Stress, & Coping, 18*, 71–82.

Dirkzwager, A. J., Bramsen, I., Adèr, H., & van der Ploeg, H. M. (2005). Secondary traumatization in partners and parents of Dutch peacekeeping soldiers. *Journal of Family Psychology, 19*(2), 217–226.

Figley, C. R. (1989). *Treating stress in families*. New York: Brunner/Mazel.

Figley, C. R. (1995). *Compassion fatigue: Coping with secondary traumatic stress disorder in those who treat the traumatized*. New York: Brunner/Mazel.

Figley, C. R. (1997). *Burnout in families: The systemic costs of caring*. Boca Raton, FL: CRC Press.

Figley, C. R. (1998). Burnout as systemic traumatic stress: A model for helping traumatized family members. In C. R. Figley (Ed.), *Burnout in families: The systematic costs of caring* (pp. 15–28). New York: CRC Press.

Figley, C. R. (1999). Compassion fatigue: Toward a new understanding of the cost of caring. In B. H. Stamm (Ed.), *Secondary traumatic stress: Self-care issues for clinicians, researchers, and educators*. Lutherville, MD: Sidran Press.

Frančišković, T., Stevanović, A., Jelušić, I., Roganović, B., Klarić, M., & Grković, J. (2007). Secondary traumatization of wives of war veterans with posttraumatic stress disorder. *Croatian Medical Journal, 48*(2), 177–184.

Fullerton, C. S., & Ursano, R. J. (1997). *Posttraumatic stress disorder: Acute and long term responses to trauma and disaster*. Washington, DC: American Psychiatric Press.

Galovski, T., & Lyons, J. (2004). Psychological sequelae of combat violence: A review of the impact of PTSD on the veteran's family and possible interventions. *Aggression and Violent Behavior, 9*, 477–501.

Gilbert, K. (1998). Understanding the secondary traumatic stress of spouses. In C. R. Figley (Ed.), *Burnout in families: The systematic costs of caring* (pp. 47–75). New York: CRC Press.

Glassman, J. N. S., Magulac, M., & Darko, D. F. (1987). Folie a familie: Shared paranoid disorder in a Vietnam veteran and his family. *American Journal of Psychiatry, 144*, 658–660.

Haley, S. (1984). The Vietnam veteran and his pre-school child: Child rearing as a delayed stress in combat veterans. *Journal of Contemporary Psychotherapy, 14*, 114–121.

Harkness, L. L. (1991). The effect of combat-related PTSD on children. National Center for PTSD. *Clinical Newsletter, 2*, 12–13.

Harkness, L., & Zador, N. (2004). Treatment of PTSD in families and couples. In J. P. Wilson, M. J. Friedman, & J. D. Lindy (Eds.), *Treating psychological trauma and PTSD* (pp. 335–353). New York: Guilford Press.

Jordan, B. K., Marmar, C. R., Fairbank, J. A., Schlenger, W. E., Kulka, R. A., Hough, R. L., et al. (1992). Problems in families of male Vietnam veterans with post-traumatic stress disorder. *Journal of Consulting and Clinical Psychology, 60*, 916–926.

Jurich, A. P. (1983). The Saigon of the family's mind: Family therapy with families of Vietnam veterans. *Journal of Marital and Family Therapy, 9*, 355–363.

Kaštelan A. (2012). *Psihičke smetnje djece iz obitelji veterana oboljelih od posttraumatskog stresnog poremećaja* (Unpublished doctoral dissertation). University of Rijeka, School of Medicine, Rijeka.

Kaštelan, A., Frančišković, T., Stevanović, A., & Petrić, D. (2012). *The relationship between father's combat-related Posttraumatic Stress Disorder, mother's secondary traumatization, and emotional and behavioural symptoms in their offspring; Pilot study*. Collegium antropologicum. (Accepted for publishing).

Kessler, R. C., & McLeod, J. D. (1985). Social support and mental health in community samples. In S. Cohen & S. L. Syme (Eds.), *Social support and health*. New York: Academic.

Klarić, M., Frančišković, T., Klarić, B., Kvesić, A., Kaštelan, A., Graovac, M., et al. (2008). Psychological problems in children of war veterans with posttraumatic stress disorder in Bosnia and Herzegovina: Cross-sectional study. *Croatian Medical Journal, 49*(4), 491–498.

Klarić, M., Frančišković, T., Pernar, M., Nemčić Moro, I., Miličević, R., Černi Obrdalj, E., et al. (2010). Caregiver burden and burnout in partners of war veterans with posttraumatic stress disorder. *Collegium Antropologicum, 34*(Suppl 1), 15–21.

Klarić, M., Frančišković, T., & Salčin Satriano, A. (2010). Family and psychotrauma. *Medicina Fluminensis, 46*(3), 309–317.

Klarić, M., Frančišković, T., Stevanović, A., Petrov, B., Jonovska, S., & Nemčić Moro, I. (2011). Marital quality and relationship satisfaction in war veterans and their wives in Bosnia and Herzegovina. *European Journal of Psychotraumatology, 2*, 8077. doi:10.3402/ejpt.v2i0.8077.

Koić, E., Frančisković, T., Mužinić-Masle, L., Đorđević, V., & Vondraček, S. (2002, April). *Chronic pain and secondary traumatization in the wives of the Croatian veterans treated for posttraumatic stress disorder*. Paper presented at 3rd World Congress in neurological rehabilitation, Venice, Italy.

Komar, Z., & Vukušić, H. (1999). Post-traumatic stress disorder in Croatian war veterans: prevalence and psychosocial characteristics. In D. Dekaris & A. Sabioncello (Eds.), *New insight in post-traumatic stress disorder (PTSD)* (Proceedings, pp. 42–44). Zagreb: Croatian Academy of Science and Arts.

Kulka, R. A., Schlenger, W. E., Fairbank, J. A., Hough, R. L., Jordan, K., Marmar, C., et al. (1990). *Trauma and the Vietnam War generation*. New York: Brunner/Mazel.

Kulka, R. A., Schlenger, W. E., Fairbank, J. A., Hough, R. L., Jordan, B. K., Marmar, C. R., et al. (1988). *Contracted reports of findings from the National Vietnam veterans readjustment study*. Research Triangle Park, NC: Research Triangle Institute.

Lincoln, K. D., Chatters, L. M., & Taylor, R. J. (2005). Social support, traumatic events, and depressive symptoms among African Americans. *Journal of Marriage and Family, 67*, 754–766.

Lyons, M. A. (2001). Living with post-traumatic stress disorder: the wives'/female partners/perspective. *Issues and Innovations in Nursing Practice, 34*, 69–77.

Maloney, L. J. (1988). Post traumatic stresses of women partners of Vietnam veterans. *Smith College Studies in Social Work, 58*, 122–143.

Marmar, C. R., Weiss, D. S., Metzler, T. J., Delucchi, K. L., Best, S. R., & Wentworth, K. A. (1999). Longitudinal course and predictors of continuing distress following critical incident exposure in emergency services personnel. *The Journal of Nervous and Mental Disease, 187*(1), 15–22.

Mason, P. H. C. (1990). *Recovering from the war: A woman's guide to helping your Vietnam veteran, your family, and yourself.* New York: Viking Penguin.

Matsakis, A. (1998). *Vietnam wives.* Washington, DC: Woodbine House.

McCann, I. L., & Pearlman, L. A. (1990). Vicarious traumatization: A framework for understanding the psychological effects of working with victims. *Journal of Traumatic Stress, 13*, 584–585.

Mileti, D., Drabek, T. E., & Haas, J. E. (1975). *Human systems in extreme environments.* Boulder, CO: University of Colorado, Institute of Behavioral Science.

Nelson Goff, B. S., Crow, J. R., Reisbig, A. M., & Hamilton, S. (2007). The impact of individual trauma symptoms of deployed soldiers on relationship satisfaction. *Journal of Family Psychology, 21*, 344–353.

Nelson Goff, B. S., Crow, J. R., Reisbig, A. M. J., & Hamilton, S. (2009). The impact of soldiers' deployments to Iraq and Afghanistan: Secondary traumatic stress in female partners. *Journal of Couple and Relationship Therapy, 8*, 291–305.

Nelson Goff, B. S., Reisbig, A. M., Bole, A., Scheer, T., Hayes, E., Archuleta, K. L., et al. (2006). The effects of trauma on intimate relationships: A qualitative study with clinical couples. *American Journal of Orthopsychiatry, 76*, 451–460.

Nelson Goff, B. S., & Smith, D. (2005). Systematic traumatic stress: The couple adaptation to traumatic stress model. *Journal of Marital and Family Therapy, 31*, 145–157.

Neria, Y., Nandi, A., & Galea, S. (2008). Post-traumatic stress disorder following disasters: A systematic review. *Psychological Medicine, 38*, 467–480.

Pearlman, L. A., & MacIan, P. S. (1995). Vicarious traumatization: An empirical study of the effects of trauma work on trauma therapists. *Professional Psychology, 26*, 558–565.

Rabin, C., & Nardi, C. (1991). Treating post-traumatic stress disorder couples: A psychoeducational program. *Community Mental Health Journal, 27*(3), 209–223.

Riggs, D. S., Byrne, C. A., Weathers, F. W., & Litz, B. T. (1998). The quality of the intimate relationships of male Vietnam veterans: Problems associated with posttraumatic stress disorder. *Journal of Traumatic Stress, 11*(1), 87–101.

Rosenheck, R., & Nathan, P. (1985). Secondary traumatization of children of Vietnam Veterans. *Hospital and Community Psychiatry, 36*(5), 538–539.

Rosenheck, R., & Thomson, J. (1986). "Detoxification" of Vietnam War trauma: A combined family-individual approach. *Family Process, 25*, 559–570.

Ruscio, A. M., Weathers, F. W., King, L. A., & King, D. W. (2002). Male warzone veterans' perceived relationships with their children: The importance of emotional numbing. *Journal of Traumatic Stress, 15*, 351–357.

Scaturo, D. J., & Hardoby, W. J. (1988). Psychotherapy with traumatized Vietnam combatants: An overview of individual, group, and family treatment modalities. *Military Medicine, 153*, 262–269.

Solomon, Z. (1998). The effect of combat-related post-traumatic stress disorder on the family. *Psychiatry, 51*, 323–329.

Solomon, Z., Waysman, M., Belkin, R., Levy, G., Mikulincer, M., & Enoch, D. (1992). Marital relations and combat stress reaction: The wives' perspective. *Journal of Marriage and Family, 54*, 316–326.

Solomon, Z., Waysman, M., Levy, G., Fried, B., Mikulincer, M., Benbenishty, R., et al. (1992). From front line to home front: A study of secondary traumatization. *Family Process, 31*, 289–302.

Stevanović, A. (2012). *Sekundarna traumatizacija supruga veterana oboljelih od posttraumatskog stresnog poremećaja* (Unpublished professional dissertation). University of Zagreb, Faculty of Philosophy, Zagreb.

Verbosky, S. J., & Ryan, D. A. (1988). Female partners of Vietnam veterans: Stress by proximity. *Issues in Mental Health and Nursing, 9*, 95–104.

Chapter 16
Community-Based Support and Unmet Needs Among Families of Persons with Brain Injuries: A Mixed Methods Study with the Brain Injury Association of America State Affiliates

Charles Edmund Degeneffe and Mark Tucker

Abstract This study examined service gaps and post-injury needs for families of persons with brain injuries as perceived by leadership of 28 Brain Injury Association of America state affiliates. Participants report that BIAA affiliates assist families with a variety of information, service referral, and emotional support services. Participants stressed that, while many community-based programs and professionals are available, they do not adequately meet family caregiver needs. Similarly, participant responses to a modified version of the Family Needs Questionnaire indicate that families have a great need for post-injury rehabilitation supports but that these needs are seldom fully met. Finally, participants emphasized a need for enhanced training and knowledge regarding brain injury. Clinical service and research implications are discussed for the general public and for the families of veterans.

Traumatic brain injury (TBI) is often referred to as the "silent epidemic" because, despite its high incidence, it receives less public attention than other, less common disabilities and illnesses (Degeneffe et al., 2008). Faul, Xu, Wald, and Coronado (2010) estimated that 1.7 million TBIs occur in the United States each year, most of which are concussions and other forms of mild TBI (Centers for Disease Control and Prevention [CDC], 2003). Of those injured, approximately 70,000–90,000 will experience functional impairment requiring long-term care and support (National Institutes of Health [NIH], 1999). TBI costs the United States approximately $60 billion per year in lost wages and medical care costs (Brain Injury Association of America [BIAA], 2011b). Further, the Faul et al. (2010) reports that approximately 795,000 persons experience non-traumatic forms of brain injuries because of strokes

C.E. Degeneffe, Ph.D., C.R.C., A.C.S.W. (✉) • M. Tucker, Ph.D., C.R.C.
Department of Administration, Rehabilitation and Postsecondary Education, Interwork Institute, San Diego State University, San Diego, CA, USA
e-mail: cdegenef@mail.sdsu.edu; mtucker@interwork.sdsu.edu

S. MacDermid Wadsworth and D.S. Riggs (eds.), *Military Deployment and its Consequences for Families*, Risk and Resilience in Military and Veteran Families, DOI 10.1007/978-1-4614-8712-8_16, © Springer Science+Business Media New York 2014

each year resulting in approximately $73.7 billion in health care, medication and lost productivity.

Brain injury is a disability that may result in a broad array of cognitive, physical, and emotional dysfunction (Degeneffe, 2001). Injured persons can experience great distress in coming to terms with the new realities of their post-injury lives which may lead to significant complications including abuse of drugs and alcohol (New York State Education Department, 2001), profound pessimism and contemplation of suicide (Baker, Tandy, & Dixon, 2002).

TBI is a common disability among the civilian population and a rapidly growing disability classification among military personnel returning from Iraq (Operation Iraqi Freedom [OIF], Operation New Dawn [OND]) and Afghanistan (Operation Enduring Freedom [OEF]). Many troops acquire TBI through blast injuries associated with improvised explosive devices (IEDs). It is estimated that 60–80 % of those exposed to an IED blast will incur TBI (Summerall, 2008). The Defense and Veterans Brain Injury Center (2011) reported that during 2010 a total of 31,253 military personnel worldwide incurred TBI as a confirmed medical diagnosis and that the number of troops with TBI has continuously trended upward since the start of military operations in 2001. It is likely that the majority of TBI in OEF, OIF and OND operations go unreported and/or undiagnosed. The BIAA (2011b) estimates that approximately 360,000 OEF/OIF/OND veterans incurred TBI during their service. Throughout this chapter, we use the term veterans to denote individuals who have served in the military and separated from service. The term civilian refers to individuals who have never served in the military.

Community-Based Support Services

Persons with brain injuries in the United States enjoy access to state-of-the-art acute and inpatient care. Greenwald (2010) noted that acute care and inpatient rehabilitation present a coordinated, comprehensive, and multidisciplinary array of services and treatments which may involve a wide range of medical and rehabilitation specialists. Unfortunately, this continuum of care often drops off during the transition to long-term community-based services because health insurance policies often fail to provide long-term care coverage (Starr, Terrill, & King, 2001) and liability insurance claims may require years before final settlement (Bistany, 1994). Further, states struggle to adequately meet the long-term, community-based support needs of persons with brain injuries and their families. As Degeneffe and associates (2008, p. 48) stated: "The delivery of TBI community support services is a fragmented process where significant differences exist among states and local communities. Hence, access to services is largely a matter of circumstance, based on where someone lives when he or she is injured." Utilization of community-based supports is also relevant to veterans with TBI, given factors such as the extended wait time for VA services (e.g., Dao, 2012), reluctance to utilize VA services among some veterans (e.g., United Press International, 2011), being ineligible to receive VA services due to a dishonorable discharge (e.g., United States Department of Veterans Affairs, 2010), and proximity to VA services (Buzza, Ono, Turvey, Wittrock, & Nobel, 2011).

States differ in significant attributes such as the availability of Medicaid Waiver programs for persons with brain injuries, service eligibility criteria, tax-based funds, and monies generated through motor vehicle violations and auto registrations (Degeneffe et al., 2008). For example, in their review of service eligibility criteria for brain injury services in 20 states, Vaughn and King (2001) noted that some states cover persons that incur a brain injury through anoxia due to any cause, while other states only include anoxia as a result of injury or drowning but not from a drug overdose. Overall, the BIAA (2000) concluded that persons with brain injuries often receive fewer benefits from publically funded social welfare programs compared with other disability populations and likewise receive less protection from the Individuals with Disabilities Education and the Americans With Disabilities Acts.

A result of these service provision shortcomings is that families bear the brunt of care-giving responsibilities for their members with brain injuries on a long-term and indefinite basis (Degeneffe, 2001; Kolakowsky-Hayner, Miner, & Kreutzer, 2001). Families face the challenge of meeting their injured family member's physical, emotional, and cognitive needs (Bishop, Degeneffe, & Mast, 2006). This responsibility frequently results in more intense caregiver depression, anxiety, and burden levels which do not diminish over time (Degeneffe, 2001) and can occur irrespective of the level of care-giving provided.

Like civilians, when veterans with TBI return home, their families face substantial care-giving responsibilities. Griffin et al. (2011, p. 1) surveyed 564 family caregivers of veterans with polytrauma injuries which include TBI. Study findings revealed that after a median of 4 years post-injury, 22 % of the veterans still required help with activities of daily living (e.g., bathing, feeding and toileting), and instrumental activities of daily living (e.g., money management, medication management, cooking, cleaning and driving). As in the civilian population, care-giving was primarily provided by parents (62 %) and spouses (32 %); also consistent with the civilian population, most of the caregiving was provided by females (79 %). Approximately 25 % of participants provided more than 40 h per week of care. Of those providing assistance with activities of daily living, 49 % devoted more than 80 h per week of care. A majority of caregivers were balancing other work and/or school responsibilities which only adds to the stress incurred by these families. These findings indicate families require additional help meeting the long-term care needs of injured members. Social support and cultural biases relating to brain injures may further increase family caregiver burden. Phelan et al. (2011) studied 70 family caregivers of veterans with TBI and found that poor caregiver mental outcomes were related to perceived discrimination and stigma directed at both them and their injured family members.

The Brain Injury Association of America

Given the inconsistency of funding and services available to meet the long-term care needs of persons with brain injuries, their families may need to rely on non-profit, non-governmental organizations for information, support, and care coordination. This reflects a long-standing disparity among other disability populations receiving family-based, long-term care including persons with severe mental illness (e.g., National Alliance on Mental Illness), intellectual disabilities (e.g., The Arc), and autism (e.g., The Autism Society of America). Beyond the direct services provided to families and their members with disabilities, these organizations also provide advocacy for increased social awareness, favorable legislation, and increased public spending and service provision.

The BIAA is possibly the most widely-utilized organization providing long-term family support to persons with brain injuries and their families. In existence since 1980, the BIAA (2011a) is the oldest brain injury organization in the United States. The BIAA's website (2011b) indicates it is an organization dedicated to "increasing access to quality health care and raising awareness and understanding of brain injury through advocacy, education, and research."

The BIAA expresses a clear commitment to the needs of family caregivers of persons with brain injuries and devotes considerable funds and staff time to family support, through both the national organization and 43 state affiliate organizations. In 2010, the BIAA national organization (2010) had total revenues of $1,892,198 and expenses of $1,508,660. A total of $105,619 was directly spent on individual and family services, while other expense categories indirectly benefited families through increased public awareness about brain injury, improved government relations and advocacy, and enhanced education, training, and research. In addition, the BIAA (p. 3) maintains the National Brain Injury Information Center (NBIIC), which is a toll-free phone line designed to "…link each caller to the rehabilitation, legal, financial and other support services that are critical to maximizing recovery". Among the 40,000 calls made to the NBIIC in 2010, 50 % were from family and friends.

While the NBIIC can direct families to services and programs available in their local communities and states, direct family assistance services such as support groups are provided through BIAA's network of 43 state affiliate organizations. To highlight its organizational ties to the national organization, each affiliate carries the "Brain Injury Association" identifier before the state name. Links to each of the 43 state affiliates can be found through the national organization's web site (see http://www. biausa.org/state-affiliates.htm). Each state affiliate web site includes information on the unique array of programs and services available in the state.

Focus of the Present Study

Given that families provide extensive care and support to persons with brain injuries and the deleterious outcomes associated with this role, research starting in the early 1980s (e.g., Mathis, 1984; Mauss-Clum & Ryan, 1981) examined the specific needs endorsed by families. Undergirding these studies was a desire to improve professional supports in order to effect better care-giver adaptation to the multiple stresses and strains of care-giving. More recently, family needs research has been conducted using the Family Needs Questionnaire (FNQ) which measures the importance of and degree to which specific needs are met within six factor-analytically determined domains: health information, emotional support, instrumental support, professional support, community support network, and involvement with care (Kreutzer & Marwitz, 1989). In their review of the extant research on family needs following brain injury, Bishop and associates (2006) identified that consistent needs included a desire to; receive accurate information from professionals; be actively involved in the rehabilitation process, and; receive emotional support. Further, family needs were found to change with time and different family needs were associated with family member type (e.g., parent, spouse). Finally, Bishop and associates reviewed several studies finding no relationships among injury characteristics, demographics, and family needs.

Past study of post-brain injury family needs and adjustment has been based largely on the subjective report of family members in quantitatively based survey methods (e.g., Degeneffe, 2009) but also includes such qualitative research approaches as typological content analysis (Chwaliz & Stark-Wroklewski, 1996) and phenomenology (Johnson, 1995). Professional understanding of post-injury family adjustment is limited by a paucity of research studies. The bulk of past studies have been conducted with the assistance of acute care center staff. While books and articles exist that incorporate professional views on service gaps and family adjustment challenges in long-term community rehabilitation, these perspectives are largely anecdotal (e.g., Sachs, 1991).

The present study was designed to provide a comprehensive and empirically-based understanding of long-term community-based adjustment and unmet needs among family caregivers of persons with brain injury from the perspectives of BIAA state affiliate personnel. Our assumption was that such participants possessed unique insights given their involvement with families extends beyond acute-care rehabilitation support and presents a more objective rather than subjective point of view. Accordingly, the study addressed the following questions:

1) What types of supportive services do BIAA affiliates provide to family caregivers of persons with brain injuries?
2) What service gaps exist in long-term, community-based supports provided to families of persons with brain injuries?
3) What are common types of rehabilitation needs faced by family caregivers and to what extent are these needs met?
4) What has been beneficial and what needs improvement in professional services offered to families of persons with brain injuries?

Methods

Target Population

The target population for the study consisted of individuals in leadership positions in each of the 43 BIAA state affiliates. The study authors contacted the BIAA national office in order to solicit their endorsement of the study. The BIAA endorsed the study and provided the authors with contact information for an individual in a leadership position (typically the executive director or the president of the board of directors) at each of the 43 state affiliates. These individuals were contacted by the authors and asked to complete the electronic survey or to identify another individual within the organization who had a thorough understanding of the way the state affiliate supported families to complete the survey. In an effort to assign equal weight to responses from different states, the authors sought to limit survey participation to one response from each of the 43 state affiliates.

Survey Design

Data collection was accomplished through the use of an electronic survey created using a commercially-available, subscription-based survey software package. The survey consisted of four primary components: (a) an informed consent section; (b) a demographic section prompting respondents to describe their role in the organization, the history of their organization and the services offered to families of individuals with brain injury; (c) the FNQ; and (d) a series of open-ended questions prompting respondents to comment upon professional services received by persons with brain injury and their families. Respondents were prompted to share their perspectives of family reactions to brain injury, common challenges, and supports needed after the individual with the brain injury returned home following acute care and hospitalization.

The FNQ (Kreutzer & Marwitz, 1989; Marwitz, 2000) was designed to generate data about family needs following brain injury. The FNQ consists of 40 needs that families may encounter when a loved one experiences brain injury. Respondents are asked to rate the importance of each need (using a four-point scale ranging from "Not Important" to "Very Important") and the extent to which the need has been met (using a three-point scale consisting of "Yes", "Partly", and "No"). The FNQ also includes a "not applicable" (N/A) response option not used in the present study. Survey responses can be used to calculate six subscales derived through factor analysis techniques: Involvement with Care, Community Support Network, Professional Support, Instrumental Support, Emotional Support, and Health Information (Marwitz, 2000). Because the items contained in the FNQ prompt respondents to focus upon their own needs, the instrument was adapted for use with BIAA affiliates who were asked to describe the needs of the range of families that they served. With the permission of the author of the FNQ, Jeffrey Kreutzer, the study authors modified the prompts used in the FNQ to reflect a focus upon state affiliate families (e.g., prompts that began with "I need…" were changed to "My chapter families need…"). We believe that the changes made to the question stems on the FNQ retained the focus upon the five domains of post-injury needs measured by the instrument.

Survey Distribution Methodology

In an effort to maximize the number of responses to the internet survey, the authors utilized elements of Dillman's (2000) tailored design method, which involved soliciting participation in the study using several different messages that were sent to BIAA state affiliates over a period of approximately 18 days. Prior to any contact between the authors and BIAA state affiliates, the BIAA national office distributed a memorandum to the state affiliates informing them of the study and indicating that the BIAA endorsed the study. Approximately 5 days after distribution of the BIAA memorandum, the authors sent e-mail messages to each of the 43 state affiliate representatives introducing the study, informing them that they would be receiving a link to an electronic survey shortly, inviting them to participate, and describing a small token of appreciation that would be sent to them for participating in the study. Two days later the authors sent e-mail messages to each of the 43 state affiliate representatives that contained a link to the survey.

In order to reduce the likelihood that respondents might be identified and to attempt to ensure that only one individual from each state responded to the survey, individuals were not asked to provide their name anywhere in the survey but were provided with a code number to be used when accessing the survey. Approximately 11 days after the link to the electronic survey was sent to each of the 43 state affiliates, affiliates that had not responded to the survey were sent a reminder by e-mail that included a link to the survey. Thank you notes and incentives were then mailed to each of the state affiliates who participated approximately 10 days after the reminder notice.

Data Analysis

Data from the demographic and FNQ sections of the survey were encoded numerically and analyzed using SPSS version 17.0. Descriptive statistics, including response frequencies and means, were computed for individual items as well as for the six subscales associated with the FNQ. Qualitative data generated through responses to open-ended questions posed to respondents at the end of the survey were organized with the assistance of HyperRESEARCH version 2.8 (Depuis, 2007). Working in tandem, the authors commenced with approximately eight pages of single-spaced narrative text provided by survey respondents and engaged in a constant comparative process of analysis (Glaser & Strauss, 1967) using open and axial coding strategies described by Strauss and Corbin (1990). Narrative data was broken down into core elements of meaning. All elements of data were then compared in order to develop codes or categories of conceptually similar data. From these categories and the narrative data associated with each category the researchers extracted and reported themes indicative of ideas or concepts expressed with varying degrees of consensus among respondents.

Results

Representatives from 28 of the 43 state affiliates completed the survey; this response rate corresponds to approximately 65 % of all BIAA state affiliates. Twenty-six of the respondents were paid staff members, while two were members of the board of directors. A majority (n = 17) were executive directors, while others reported being directors of family services (n = 3), service coordinators (n = 3), resource directors (n = 1), secretaries of the board (n = 1), or regional managers (n = 1). Two individuals did not report their titles with the state affiliate.

According to respondents, their organizations had been in existence an average of 24.1 years (SD = 6.9), and had been affiliated with the BIAA an average of 19.8 years (SD = 9.8). The state affiliates employed an average of 6.9 full-time staff (SD = 10.2) and 2.4 part-time staff (SD = 2.8). Respondents were asked to estimate the total number of volunteer hours donated to the state affiliate in 2008 and the mean number of hours was approximately 2,130 (SD = 2,656).

When asked to estimate the composition of state affiliate membership, respondents' estimates indicated that approximately 38.5 % of affiliate members were persons with brain injuries, 26.2 % were family members of persons with brain injuries, 9.5 % were friends of persons with brain injuries, and 28.9 % were professionals. When asked to estimate the race or ethnic composition of family members served by the BIAA, respondents' estimates indicated that approximately 78.0 % of families were White, 10.4 % were African American, 4.3 % were Hispanic/Latino, and 1.4 % were Asian/Pacific Islander.

BIAA state affiliate representatives were asked a series of questions about different ways that family members connect with the state affiliates. Table 16.1 illustrates, in descending order of frequency, the ways that affiliate representatives indicated that families connect with the BIAA state affiliates.

As Table 16.1 indicates, state affiliates indicate that families most frequently establish contact with the state affiliates through referrals from professionals, families, and individuals as well as through the affiliate telephone helpline, web site, and support groups. BIAA state affiliate representatives were asked to indicate the types

Table 16.1 How family members connect to BIAA state chapters

	N	%
Referrals from professionals	28	100.0
Affiliate telephone helpline	27	96.4
Affiliate web site	27	96.4
Referrals from other families	27	96.4
Referrals from family members with brain injuries	26	92.9
Affiliate sponsored support groups	25	89.3
BIAA web site	23	82.1
Fund-raising events	22	78.6
Referrals from the BIAA national office	13	46.4
Membership meetings	3	10.7

Table 16.2 Availability of brain injury services in state

	Not available (%)	Available, not adequate (%)	Available and adequate (%)
Residential care	10.7	85.7	3.6
Legal services	7.1	71.4	21.4
Medicaid waiver	25.0	71.4	3.6
Neuropsychologists	0.0	78.6	21.4
Personal attendant care	10.7	75.0	14.3
Protection and advocacy	0.0	75.0	25.0
Respite care	17.9	78.6	3.6
Sexuality training	70.4	25.9	3.7
Social/interpersonal training	37.0	69.3	3.7
State/Federal vocational rehabilitation	3.6	85.7	10.7
Supported employment	10.7	85.7	3.6
Veterans Affairs	0.0	81.5	18.5

of services that their affiliate provides for family members. Every representative who completed the survey indicated that their affiliate provided families with telephone information and referral, an affiliate web site, and a newsletter. Over 90 % of affiliates provided affiliate families with conferences including information about family needs, written educational materials, and support groups for family members. Informational meetings for family members (provided by 75 % of affiliates) and production and distribution of multimedia content (provided by 50 % of affiliates) were identified much less frequently as services provided to families by state affiliates.

State affiliate representatives were asked to describe the content of their affiliate web site by indicating whether a number of elements appeared on the web site. More than 80 % of state affiliate respondents indicated that their web sites included information on brain injury organizations and professionals, calendars of events, brain injury documents, and information on legislative and policy developments. Fewer respondents indicates that newsletters (75 %) or streaming audio or video (39.3 %) were included on their affiliate web site. None of the respondents indicated that discussion boards or chat rooms were available to families through the affiliate web site.

State affiliates were presented with a list of 12 services pertinent to individuals with brain injury and their families and were asked to describe the extent to which each of the services was available using a three-point scale indicating whether the service was not available, the service was available but insufficient to meet existing needs, or available and adequate to meet existing needs. Table 16.2 summarizes the state affiliate responses to the questions about service availability.

The general pattern of responses to the questions about service availability indicates that respondents believed the majority of brain injury services in their state were available but not at levels that met the existing need. Of note is the proportion of respondents (70.4 %) who indicated that sexuality training was not available in the

Table 16.3 Comparison of importance ratings, BIAA professionals and siblings

	Percent rated important, BIAA (%)	Percent rated important, siblings (%)
Health information	99.2	87.4
Community support network	91.4	81.5
Professional support	94.3	77.2
Instrumental support	92.1	71.4
Involvement with care	79.0	55.2
Emotional support	–	65.8

– Not computed

state at all. Of particular relevance to veterans with brain injuries and their families were services available through the Department of Veterans Affairs. These services were perceived by all BIAA state affiliates to be available, however 81.5 % of respondents indicated that although services were available they were not sufficient to meet the existing needs of veterans.

Family Needs Questionnaire

The family needs reported by BIAA state affiliates were examined by analyzing the FNQ scores with respect to both the mean percentage of need rated as "Important" or "Very Important" and the extent to which needs rated as "Important" or "Very Important" were described as being met. For the purposes of this analysis the percentage of met needs was calculated for only those need rated by respondents as "Important" or "Very Important". The approach to computing the percentage of met needs is consistent with the analytical approach utilized by Serio, Kreutzer, and Gervasio (1995).

Table 16.3 illustrates survey responses to questions about the importance of different family needs according to the six subscales in the FNQ. Included in this table are additional descriptive statistics representing responses to the FNQ of adult siblings of individuals with brain injury from a study of siblings (n = 158) completed by Degeneffe in 2009. The sibling data was drawn from a national data set of 295 adult siblings of persons with TBI, most of who resided in community-based settings. In the 2009 study, the person with the brain injury had been injured approximately 12 years, with a range from approximately 1 to 36 years. These descriptive statistics are included to place the present study in the context of previous studies examining family needs from the perspective of members of the family. For the present study we adapted the question stems on the FNQ to suit the respondent population (i.e., asking BIAA affiliate representatives to identify needs of the families that they served). As a result the questions presented to the two groups were not identical; however we believe that the adapted FNQ retains its focus upon the five domains of post-injury needs measured by the instrument.

Table 16.4 Comparison of percentage of needs identified as met, BIAA professionals and siblings

	Percent rated met, BIAA (%)	Percent rated met, siblings (%)
Health information	10.1	48.4
Community support network	6.3	38.4
Professional support	5.2	36.2
Instrumental support	0.0	56.7
Involvement with care	5.6	40.7
Emotional support	–	31.0

– Not computed

Descriptive statistics for the emotional support subscale are not reported for BIAA state affiliates in Tables 16.3 and 16.4 as one survey item associated with the emotional support subscale was intentionally omitted from the FNQ portion of the survey when the survey questions were adapted for use with BIAA state affiliates. The researchers determined that the question could not be adapted for use with the target population without substantially changing the meaning of the question.

Items associated with the health information scale (which addresses needs related to family members being informed about the course of their family member's medical status and learning how the brain injury has impacted the family member's functional skills) were most frequently identified as important or very important. Following health information needs closely were items in the professional support scale (which addresses needs related to family members being informed about the duration of problems associated with brain injury and needs related to accessing resources for the individual with brain injury), the instrumental support scale (which includes needs such as helping family members to get a break from problems or responsibilities and getting help keeping the house clean), and the community support network scale (which addresses family needs associated with getting others, such as friends and other family members, to understand the problems of the person with brain injury). Survey items associated with the involvement with care scale (which addresses the family's need to be involved in providing input regarding the care, rehabilitation and education of the person with brain injury and being shown that their opinions are used in planning services for the individual with the brain injury) were frequently identified as important or very important by respondents but at a lower rate than items associated with the other scales (Marwitz, 2000).

An examination of sibling responses to the FNQ (Degeneffe, 2009), suggests that BIAA state affiliates identified needs as important or very important more frequently than siblings of persons with brain injury across all five of the FNQ scales where comparisons were made. It should be noted that both respondent groups rated items associated with the health information scale as important or very important most frequently. Items associated with the involvement with care scale were rated as important or very important least frequently by both groups of respondents.

Table 16.4 illustrates survey responses to questions about the extent to which different family needs are met according to the six subscales in the FNQ. Scales with lower percentages of needs rated as met indicate needs where fewer respondents identified items associated with the scale as being met.

Based upon needs rated as important or very important, the BIAA state affiliates did not identify any of the items associated with the instrumental support scale as being fully met. Examination of BIAA state affiliate responses across all of the scales indicates that the state affiliates perceive a great deal of unmet family needs, as all five scales computed for the state affiliates identified the percentage of needs that were met as 10.1 % or less. In contrast, siblings of adults with brain injury studied by Degeneffe (2009) reported higher percentages of needs met than did the BIAA state affiliates. Interestingly, the instrumental support scale, which had the lowest percentage of needs rated as met by BIAA state affiliates (0.0 %), had the highest percentage of needs rated as met by siblings (56.7 %). While the percentage of needs rated as met by siblings was notably higher than the percentage of needs rated as met by BIAA state affiliates, sibling responses to the questions about needs that were met or unmet still resulted in percentages of met needs below 50 % for all scales except instrumental support.

Open-Ended Survey Item

At the conclusion of the survey, state affiliates were presented with an open-ended question that prompted them to describe what has been beneficial and what needs improvement among brain injury professional services received by persons with brain injury and their families. Using a constant comparative process of data analysis (Glaser & Strauss, 1967) open and axial coding processes (Strauss & Corbin, 1990) were employed to identify themes or concepts that emerged with a degree of consensus from the narrative responses provided by state affiliates. In order to enhance the authenticity of the finding, the study authors worked in tandem to sort and code responses, refining categories as new information was uncovered.

Narrative statements provided by respondents could be related to a single conceptual code or could be associated with multiple codes if the statement addressed two or more themes that were developed through the coding approach. Preliminary analysis of narrative responses resulted in 21 data codes. Additional recoding generated the five themes reported in the narrative that appear in Table 16.5 while five additional data codes were dropped from the analysis as a result of low levels of consensus among respondents.

More Funding Is Needed for Community-Based Care

State affiliates made a number of statements describing needs for more community-based care for individuals with brain injury and their families. As one individual put it "We all know that individuals and families need ongoing supports and

Table 16.5 Frequency count and percentages of total responses for most commonly identified themes

	N	%
More funding is needed for community-based care	19	44.2
Medical care coverage needs expansion	10	23.3
Professionals require more brain injury training	6	14.0
Awareness-building campaigns are effective	4	9.3
Quality acute care	4	9.3

services—some, lifelong. These services usually don't exist, due to a lack of funding." Respondents described a lack of services generally as well as varying availability of care across geographic regions. One respondent highlighted the discrepancy between care available during the acute phase of rehabilitation and the care available once the individual returns to his or her community:

> …limited community resources and funding; family is not on radar screen only patient for a limited time and then push on to next level of care; why do we spend so much money on trauma and acute care and provide little quality of life at other end of continuum - why bother????

Medical Care Coverage Needs Expansion

When commenting upon the need to expand medical care coverage, State affiliates focused upon specific services needed by individuals with brain injury (e.g., neuropsychology, occupational therapy, physical therapy and speech therapy) as well as systemic barriers to accessing care, such as time-limited reimbursement for necessary medical services and difficulties families face when attempting to coordinate care. The following statement, offered by one of the state affiliates, summarizes some of the barriers that families encounter:

> …too long to write…health care: too silo-ed, too bureaucratic (red tape and politics), families don't know what they don't know - don't know how to play the game and win; acute care professionals don't have the time or resources to educate or help families…

Professionals Require More Brain Injury Training

Respondents described a variety of needs for training and awareness on the part of professionals who work with individuals with brain injuries and their families. While some state affiliates indicated that general efforts to raise awareness were successful, they highlighted needs for continuing education of professionals and in some statements identified specific categories of professionals (e.g., medical professionals, doctors, case managers, social workers, and attorneys). Comments about the need to provide additional training or increase awareness were often paired with statements about availability of brain injury resources as in the following statement: "…not enough professionals understand brain injury and they don't have the resources if they do".

Awareness-Building Campaigns Are Effective

Statements by respondents indicated that they believed that efforts to increase awareness conducted by BIAA and other entities were productive activities. These efforts were linked to enhancing awareness among family members, professionals, and individuals making career choices in fields related to brain injury. When describing efforts designed to enhance awareness of brain injury, one individual alluded to challenges individuals and families may face once intensive services come to an end and the individual returns home: "Increased outreach and education to service providers including awareness of daily life after services end had been beneficial."

Quality of Acute Care

Comments by respondents indicated that coordination between acute care hospitals, rehabilitation hospitals, and the state affiliates contributed to helping families cope with brain injury. Inpatient and outpatient medical care and rehabilitation services were described by state affiliates as excellent.

Discussion

Through descriptive statistics and qualitative data analyses, we found that the BIAA state affiliates play an important role in meeting long-term community support needs among families of persons with brain injuries. BIAA affiliates provide information, service coordination, and emotional support through a variety of resources such as websites, support groups, and information and referral services. These services are provided free of charge, and for some families, offer the only means of professional assistance. As Table 16.2 documents, participants had extensive involvement in supporting families of persons with brain injury. This proximity gave participants a unique perspective on the nature of family needs following brain injury and existing service gaps in long-term community support for persons with brain injuries and their families.

Clinical Implications

Our findings highlight the need for professional outreach, programs, and funding that extend past acute care rehabilitation. Once family members leave acute care rehabilitation settings, they enter a world with insufficient independent living supports, vocational services, respite, neuropsychological evaluation, sexuality training, protection and advocacy. Professionals they encounter might not have adequate training in brain injury and families may lack the necessary funding to obtain access to the professional services that are available. Our findings support the opinion advanced by policy reviews arguing that insufficient resources are available for long-term care (Degeneffe et al., 2008; Starr et al., 2001; Vaughn, & King, 2001), and are consistent with family care-giving research. For example, Griffin and associates' (2011, p. 5) study of 564 family caregivers of veterans with TBI and other polytrauma injuries found that caregivers needed help with managing their injured family member's pain, aiding with therapies, working with assistive devices, making medical appointments, managing emotional issues, and working with health care, benefits, and legal systems. The similarity of findings to the present study is surprising given the enhanced access veteran families enjoy through the Department of Defense and VA and veteran support agencies compared to the civilian population which the BIAA primarily serves.

Our FNQ results indicate that shortcomings in long-term community-based support of families may be more pervasive than suggested in prior family needs research. Because participants worked with families with various types of caregiving related stresses and strains, they had comprehensive awareness of a wide spectrum of post-injury needs. FNQ ratings for health information, community support network, professional support, instrumental support, and involvement with care needs ranged from 79.0 % to 99.2 % for the importance of these needs, while ratings for the extent to which these needs were met ranged from 0.0 % to 10.1 %. Both sets of outcomes substantially depart from previous FNQ research (Bishop et al., 2006) based on the specific needs of siblings, parents, spouses, and other family members. Previous family needs research found lower ratings of the importance of these needs while giving higher ratings on the extent to which these needs were met.

With regard to needed actions, a first consideration is the need for enhanced professional education and training on brain injury. Our findings support other research which indicates shortcomings in professional skill and understanding of brain injury. For example, Degeneffe and associates (2008) noted that the Council on Rehabilitation Education does not require specific training on brain injury for its accredited Masters in Rehabilitation Counseling university programs. Walker, Boling, and Cobb (1999) surveyed 86 school psychology graduate programs listed with the National Association of School Psychologists regarding the extent to which the programs offered training in neuropsychology/brain injury. Walker and associates found that these programs offered little training in neuropsychology/brain injury and few of the programs' faculty members possessed neuropsychological expertise. Also, Becker, Harrell, and Keller (1993) conducted a national survey of staff training needs among 90 acute, 36 sub-acute, and 110 post-acute brain injury facilities and agencies. A total of 75 % of the participants endorsed a need for specialized TBI training for their professional staff. Also, over 75 % of the programs utilize paraprofessionals, with a rating of 84 % of that group in need of specialized TBI training. Further, Linden and Redpath (2011) assessed attitudes of 90 trainee and 69 qualified nurses in the United Kingdom toward a hypothetical scenario concerning young adult males whose behavior either did (i.e., through drug use) or did not (i.e., through an aneurysm) contribute to their brain injury. Compared to the qualified (i.e., experienced) nurses, trainees held less prejudicial attitudes, were more willing to socially engage, and were more oriented to help the injured persons considered to be responsible for their brain injuries.

Researchers attest to the value of specialized brain injury training through evidence of increased knowledge and skill development. For example, Willer, Button, Willer, and Good (1998) described the outcomes of a 4 day graduate course in Ontario, Canada for 308 professionals, administrators, and paraprofessionals working in a variety of community-based brain injury programs. The curriculum focused on three areas including a) philosophy of rehabilitation; b) knowledge of brain injury, behavior relations and assessment techniques; and c) brain injury rehabilitation interventions. All three groups took a test that measured their knowledge of curriculum content both before and after the course to measure their learning gains. All three groups demonstrated statistically significant gains in their knowledge following the course, with administrators and professionals earning the highest pre- and posttest scores.

With regard to advocacy, professionals need to push for enhanced public policy and funding that expands community-based service options for persons with brain injuries, and thereby reduces care-giving burdens now incurred by families. This point cannot be overstressed given the high numbers of persons incurring brain injuries in the United States annually, along with potentially hundreds of thousands of veterans with TBI returning to their home communities and families. Further, while modern military medicine has focused attention on TBI among veterans of OEF/OIF/OND, significantly less attention has been given to identifying and treating residual TBI among veterans of previous conflicts. It is possible that at least some of the significant health and social burden experienced by veterans of past wars and their families reflects, at least in part, the effects of un-diagnosed TBI. For these reasons, it is important that all state and community providers and programs are knowledgeable about who among the people they serve are veterans and about how to refer veterans with TBI to services available through VA. The BIAA can assume an important role in connecting families with VA. For example, through their websites the BIAA affiliates could provide information and direct links to VA TBI programs and services.

In a statement directed to rehabilitation counselors but which applies to all brain injury professionals, Degeneffe and associates (2008, p. 49) pointed out that, "Overall, rehabilitation counselors need to be part of creating a community-based system of supports that is sufficiently funded, responsive to the needs of injured persons and their families, and based on coordinated efforts among federal, state, and local private and public agencies." Degeneffe and associates noted areas needing particular attention including fully funding TBI programs in the federal agencies addressed by the TBI Act (i.e., Centers for Disease Control, Health Resources and Services Administration, and the NIH), expanding Medicaid waiver programs for persons with TBI, and encouraging the Rehabilitation Services Administration to offer training programs on TBI vocational rehabilitation.

Research Implications

The findings from our study also contain implications for future research. Research is needed to develop evidence-based practices on the most effective approaches to support the long-term needs of persons with brain injuries and their families. The federal government can serve as a funding source for this research through the National Institute on Disability and Rehabilitation Research (NIDDR), NIH, and VA. In particular, research is needed to develop more effective family support interventions along with services for persons with brain injuries including job placement approaches, substance abuse treatment, sexuality training, and psychological adjustment counseling (Degeneffe et al., 2008).

Since 1987, NIDDR has provided funding for a program called "TBI Model Systems of Care." There are currently 16 Model Systems programs located across the United States (Model Systems Knowledge Translation Center, 2011). Many of the goals of the Model Systems program focus on long-term outcomes following TBI (BIAA, 2011c). As an example of this focus, Southeastern Michigan Traumatic Brain Injury Systems (KMRREC, 2006) conducted a project called, "Full Access to Community Life," which focused on peer mentoring, barriers to community integration, and subjective well-being for injured persons and their significant others.

NIH presents an additional federal funding source. As noted, the TBI Act (Degeneffe et al., 2008) charters NIH as one of three federal agencies to fund both applied and basic research on TBI. National Institutes of Health (1999) documented their interest in TBI most notably in their "Consensus Development Conference on the Rehabilitation of Persons with Traumatic Brain Injury," held in October 1998. The conference brought together leading researchers to review research, present research, and suggest future research directions. As part of its discussions, the conference outlined future research needed for enhanced community-based functioning for persons with TBI as well as improved family outcomes following TBI.

With the high number of veterans with TBI returning from OEF, OIF and OND, VA now plays an important role in family support. United States Department of Veterans Affairs (2011b) maintains a specific department devoted to family caregiver support, "VA Caregiver Support Services," which includes such resources as the "Caregiver Support Line," on-line informational resources on various aspects of caregiving (e.g., how to avoid caregiver burnout), and links (2011c) to family support organizations including the BIAA. Families of injured service members and veterans are eligible to receive monetary stipends through the Caregivers and Veterans Omnibus Health Services Act of 2010 (Public Law: 111-163) (Griffin et al., 2011).

Families of service members and veterans with TBI and polytrauma can also receive support from the National Polytrauma System of Care, which includes four Polytrauma Rehabilitation Centers in Richmond, VA, Tampa, FL, Minneapolis, MN, and Palo Alto, CA, and 17 additional Polytrauma Network Sites located across the United States (U.S. Department of Veterans Affairs, 2007a). Upon separation from a Polytrauma Network Center, discharge plans are made that can include the assistance of a Polytrauma Network Site, which in turn helps families utilize local community resources (U.S. Department of Veterans Affairs, 2007b).

VA further demonstrated its attention to family support through funding the Family and Caregiver Experience Survey (FACES), conducted in 2009–2010 by the Center for Chronic Disease Outcomes Research at the Minneapolis VA Medical Center (U.S. Department of Veterans Affairs, 2011a). FACES described caregiver experiences in providing care to their family members with TBI/polytrauma discharged from a Polytrauma Rehabilitation Center between 2001 and 2009. An overall purpose of the study was to help VA determine areas for new program development or improvement. The collective work being done by VA in family support will likely present new insights about how to best support all families (both civilian and service connected) impacted by brain injury.

To further our understanding of family response to brain injury, VA should consider funding future research that compares the experiences of OEF and OIF families of persons with TBI in the general population, given different levels of access to professional services and funding for both groups. Also, VA should consider research that examines ways to partner with civilian entities like the BIAA to address active duty military and veteran family caregiver needs.

Limitations

Several limitations of the present study are noted. First, it is possible that participants overstated the nature of service gaps and family needs given their BIAA affiliate role as advocates for enhanced brain injury services and funding. Also, participant interactions with caregivers were more likely to occur during times when families required more assistance which could have led to overestimations of service gaps and family needs. Also, participant views on family needs were based on interactions with caregivers connected to a BIAA state affiliate. It is possible that family needs among caregivers without this connection might be different.

Conclusions

The national network of BIAA state affiliates play an important role in meeting the long-term, community-based support needs of families of persons with brain injuries. BIAA affiliates provide an extensive array of supports to help manage the demands of care-giving; this proximity informs affiliate views that the current set of long-term, professional supports for persons with brain injuries and their families is insufficient. Given recent attention to the number of veterans returning from OEF, OIF and OND with TBI, there is an historic opportunity to call attention to TBI and its effects on those injured and their family members. This could provide the impetus for developing new levels of community awareness of associated needs and interagency cooperation in meeting them. We hope our findings will motivate professionals and the public to call for enhanced long-term funding, services, and professional training in brain injury.

References

Baker, K. A., Tandy, C. C., & Dixon, D. R. (2002). Traumatic brain injury: A social worker primer with implications for practice [Electronic version]. *Journal of Social Work in Disability & Rehabilitation, 1*(4), 25–42.

Becker, H., Harrell, W. T., & Keller, L. (1993). A survey of professional and paraprofessional training needs for traumatic brain injury rehabilitation. *Journal of Head Trauma Rehabilitation, 8*, 88–101.

Bishop, M., Degeneffe, C. E., & Mast, M. (2006). Family needs after traumatic brain injury: Implications for rehabilitation counseling. *Australian Journal of Rehabilitation Counselling, 12*(2), 73–87.

Bistany, D. V. (1994). Overview of economics of rehabilitation in the United States. In A. Christensen & B. P. Uzzell (Eds.), *Brain injury and neuropsychological rehabilitation: International perspectives* (pp. 245–256). Hillsdale, NJ: Lawrence Erlbaum Associates.

Brain Injury Association of America. (2000). *Issue brief: Traumatic Brain Injury Act of 1996.* Retrieved from http://www.biausa.org/policy_tbiauthorization2.htm

Brain Injury Association of America. (2010). *2010 Annual report.* Retrieved from http://www.biausa.org

Brain Injury Association of America. (2011a). *About us.* Retrieved from http://www.biausa.org/About-Us/about-brain-injury-association.htm

Brain Injury Association of America. (2011b). *Ensure returning service members receive access to effective TBI treatments.* Retrieved from http://www.biausa.org

Brain Injury Association of America. (2011c). *The TBI model systems.* Retrieved from http://www.biausa.org/tbims.htm

Buzza, C., Ono, S., Turvey, C., Wittrock, S., & Nobel, M. (2011). Distance is relative: Unpacking a principle barrier in rural healthcare. *Journal of General Internal Medicine, 26*, 648–654.

Centers for Disease Control and Prevention (CDC), National Center for Injury Prevention and Control. (2003). *Report to Congress on mild traumatic brain injury in the United States: Steps to prevent a serious public health problem.* Atlanta, GA: Centers for Disease Control and Prevention.

Chwaliz, K., & Stark-Wroklewski, K. (1996). The subjective experiences of spouse caregivers on persons with brain injuries: A qualitative analysis. *Applied Neuropsychology, 3*, 28–40.

Dao, J. (2012, September 27). Veterans wait for benefits as claims pile up. *The New York Times.* Retrieved from http://www.nytimes.com/2012/09/28/us/veterans-wait-for-us-aid-amid-growing-backlog-of-claims.html?pagewanted=all&_r=0

Defense and Veterans Brain Injury Center. (2011). *DOD worldwide numbers for traumatic brain injury.* Retrieved from http://www.dvbic.org/TBI-Numbers.aspx

Degeneffe, C. (2001). Family caregiving and traumatic brain injury. *Health and Social Work, 26*(4), 257–268.

Degeneffe, C. E. (2009). The rehabilitation needs of adult siblings of persons with traumatic brain injury: A quantitative investigation. *Australian Journal of Rehabilitation Counselling, 15*(1), 12–27.

Degeneffe, C. E., Boot, D., Kuehne, J., Kuraishi, A., Maristela, F., Noyes, J., et al. (2008). Community-based interventions for persons with traumatic brain injury: A primer for rehabilitation counselors. *Journal of Applied Rehabilitation Counseling, 39*(1), 42–52.

Depuis, P. R. (2007). *HyperResearch (Version 2.8)*. Randolph, MA: Research Ware.

Dillman, D. (2000). *Mail and internet surveys: The tailored design method* (2nd ed.). New York: Wiley.

Faul, M., Xu, L., Wald, M. M., & Coronado, V. G. (2010). *Traumatic brain injury in the United States: Emergency department visits, hospitalizations, and deaths*. Atlanta, GA: Centers for Disease Control and Prevention, National Center for Injury Prevention and Control.

Glaser, B. G., & Strauss, A. L. (1967). *The discovery of grounded theory: Strategies for qualitative research*. Chicago, IL: Aldine.

Greenwald, B. D. (2010). *Traumatic brain injury and acute impatient rehabilitation*. Retrieved from http://www.uab.edu/tbi

Griffin, J. M., Friedemann-Sanchez, G., Jensen, A. C., Taylor, B. C., Gravely, A., Clothier, B., et al. (2011). The invisible side of war: Families caring for US service members with traumatic brain injuries and polytrauma. *Journal of Head Trauma Rehabilitation*. doi:10.1097/HTR.0b013e3182274260.

Johnson, B. P. (1995). One family's experience with head injury: A phenomenological study. *Journal of Neuroscience Nursing, 27*, 113–118.

Kessler Medical Rehabilitation Research and Education Corporation. (2006). *The traumatic brain injury model systems national data center*. Retrieved from http://www.tbindc.org/registry/center.php

Kolakowsky-Hayner, S. A., Miner, K. D., & Kreutzer, J. S. (2001). Long-term life quality and family needs after traumatic brain injury. *Journal of Head Trauma Rehabilitation, 16*(4), 374–385.

Kreutzer, J., & Marwitz, J. (1989). *The family needs questionnaire*. Richmond, VA: The National Resource Center for Traumatic Brain Injury.

Linden, M. A., & Redpath, S. J. (2011). A comparative study of nursing attitudes towards young male survivors of brain injury: A questionnaire survey. *International Journal of Nursing Studies, 48*, 62–69.

Marwitz, J. (2000). *The family needs questionnaire*. Retrieved from http://www.tbims.org/combi/fnq

Mathis, M. (1984). Personal needs of family members of critically ill patients with and without acute brain injury. *Journal of Neurosurgical Nursing, 16*, 36–44.

Mauss-Clum, N., & Ryan, M. (1981). Brain injury and the family. *Journal of Neurosurgical Nursing, 13*, 165–169.

Model Systems Knowledge Translation Center. (2011). *Traumatic brain injury model systems*. Retrieved from http://msktc.washington.edu/tbi/

National Institutes of Health. (1999). *Report of the NIH consensus development conference on the rehabilitation of persons with traumatic brain injury*. Bethesda, MD: U.S. Department of Health and Human Services.

New York State Education Department, Vocational and Educational Services for Individuals with Disabilities. (2001). *Acquired brain injury technical assistance brief*. Retrieved from http://www.vesid.nysed.gov/publications/briefs/braininjury/home.html

Phelan, S. M., Griffin, J. M., Hellerstedt, W. L., Sayer, N. A., Jensen, A. C., Burgess, D. J., et al. (2011). Perceived stigma, strain, and mental health among caregivers of veterans with traumatic brain injury. *Disability and Health Journal, 4*, 177–184.

Sachs, P. R. (1991). *Treating families of brain-injury survivors*. New York: Springer.

Serio, C., Kreutzer, J., & Gervasio, A. (1995). Predicting family needs after traumatic brain injury: Implications for intervention. *Journal of Head Trauma Rehabilitation, 10*(2), 32–45.

Starr, J., Terrill, C. F., & King, M. (2001). *Funding traumatic brain injury services*. Washington, DC: National Conference of State Legislatures.

Strauss, A., & Corbin, J. (1990). *Basics of qualitative research: Techniques and procedures for developing grounded theory*. Thousand Oaks, CA: Sage.

Summerall, E., (2008). *Traumatic brain injury and PTSD fact sheet*. Retrieved from http://www.ncptsd.va.gov

United Press International. (2011, December 26). *Study: Some veterans reluctant to use VA*. Retrieved from http://www.upi.com/Health_News/2011/12/26/Study-Some-veterans-reluctant-to-use-VA/UPI-81901324882663/

United States Department of Veterans Affairs. (2007a). *VA polytrauma system of care*. Retrieved from http://www.polytrauma.va.gov/facility/locations.asp?isFlash=1

United States Department of Veterans Affairs. (2007b). *VA polytrauma system of care frequently asked questions*. Retrieved from http://www.polytrauma.va.govfaq.asp

United States Department of Veterans Affairs. (2010). *Other than honorable discharges: Impact on eligibility for VA health care benefits*. Retrieved October 22, 2012, from http://www.va.gov/healthbenefits/assets/documents/publications/FS16-8.pdf

United States Department of Veterans Affairs. (2011a). *Family and caregiver experience survey*. Retrieved from http://www.hsrd.minneapolis.med.va.gov/FACES/

United States Department of Veterans Affairs. (2011b). *New to caregiving*. Retrieved from http://www.caregiver.va.gov/toolbox_new.asp

United States Department of Veterans Affairs. (2011c). *Useful resources*. Retrieved from http://www.hsrd.minneapolis.med.va.gov/FACES/Resources.asp

Vaughn, S. L., & King, A. (2001). A survey of state programs to finance rehabilitation and community services for individuals with brain injury. *Journal of Head Trauma Rehabilitation, 16*(1), 20–33.

Walker, N. W., Boling, M. S., & Cobb, H. (1999). Training of school psychologists in neuropsychology and brain injury: Results of a national survey of training programs. *Child Neuropsychology, 5*, 137–142.

Willer, B., Button, J., Willer, C., & Good, D. W. (1998). Performance of administrators, professionals, paraprofessionals during community-based brain injury rehabilitation training. *Journal of Head Trauma Rehabilitation, 13*, 82–93.

About the Authors

Ann-Renée Blais, Ph.D., is a Research Psychologist with Defence Research and Development Canada. She obtained a Ph.D. in Quantitative Psychology from the Ohio State University in 2001, and she completed a post-doctoral internship in Experimental Economics at the Centre for Interuniversity Research and Analysis on Organizations, in Montréal, in 2002. Her research focuses on applied statistics and psychological measurement, decision-making under risk, and individual differences in risk-taking attitudes with applications to civilian and military populations.

Adrian Blow, Ph.D., is Associate Professor in the Department of Human Development and Family Studies at Michigan State University where he is the director of the Couple and Family Therapy program. He obtained his doctoral degree from Purdue University. Dr. Blow is involved with several studies related to military deployment including post-deployment adjustment of Michigan National Guard Couples (MING), evaluation of the Buddy-to-Buddy program (a peer to peer support program), and other family based interventions. He and his collaborators work closely with the MING around issues of data collection, service delivery, and reporting to policy makers about issues related to reintegration.

Denise V. Brown, M.S., is a Master's level nationally certified and licensed professional counselor. She is a Research Specialist at the Memphis Veterans Affairs Medical Center. During her time there, she has facilitated telephone support groups focusing on spouses of post deployed service members and facilitated informational webinars for spouses of deployed service members. Previously, she was a therapist at an inpatient mental health facility where she conducted individual, group, and family therapy and served as an evaluator for the state's vocational rehabilitation program. Her interests include chronic mental health disorders, couples therapy, and working with military families.

Emily Hagel Campbell is a Statistician in the Center for Chronic Disease Outcomes Research (CCDOR), a VA Health Services Research & Development Center of Excellence at the Minneapolis VA Health Care System. She provides statistical consulting and analysis services for several research projects within CCDOR including

S. MacDermid Wadsworth and D.S. Riggs (eds.), *Military Deployment and its*
Consequences for Families, Risk and Resilience in Military and Veteran Families,
DOI 10.1007/978-1-4614-8712-8, © Springer Science+Business Media New York 2014

RINGS-2. Since joining CCDORs Statistical and Data Management team in 2009, Emily has focused her interests on applied statistical methods, statistical consulting, and working with complex survey data. She received her Masters of Science in Statistics from the University of Nebraska—Lincoln in 2009.

Kathleen F. Carlson, Ph.D., is an assistant professor in the Department of Public Health and Preventive Medicine, Oregon Health and Science University, and a research investigator at the Portland Center for the Study of Chronic, Comorbid Mental and Physical Disorders, Portland VA Medical Center &, Portland, OR, USA. She was trained as an injury epidemiologist, focusing on behavioral health, risk-taking, and the outcomes of injury, and now studies ways to reduce the risk for re-injury among Veterans with traumatic injuries and enhance their reintegration, participation, and quality of life.

Sherry Dyche Ceperich, Ph.D., is a counseling and rehabilitation psychologist at the Hunter Holmes McGuire Veterans Affairs Medical Center and also in the Department of Psychology, Virginia Commonwealth University School of Medicine in Richmond, VA, USA. Dr. Ceperich has worked with veterans, active duty service members and their families for over 4 years. She currently provides psychotherapy and wellness services for women veterans.

Laurel Davis is a doctoral student in the department of Family Social Science at the University of Minnesota. Her research focuses on family processes that influence social and emotional development in young people. She has worked on projects that include diverse populations of families exposed to adversity, including families experiencing homelessness and military deployment. Laurel is interested in tailoring family-based prevention programs to the needs of diverse families.

Charles Edmund Degeneffe, Ph.D., is coordinator of the master's in rehabilitation counseling program at San Diego State University (SDSU). He also directs the Cognitive Disabilities Certificate Program. Degeneffe's primary research interests focus on adjustment and caregiving for family members of persons with traumatic brain injuries. He completed his doctorate in rehabilitation psychology at the University of Wisconsin-Madison and joined SDSU in 2005. He is credentialed as a certified rehabilitation counselor and by the Academy of Certified Social Workers.

Christopher R. Erbes, Ph.D., is a staff psychologist at the Minneapolis VA Health Care System and a Core Investigator in the Center for Chronic Disease Outcomes Research (CCDOR). He is also an Assistant Professor of Psychiatry at the University of Minnesota Medical School. Dr. Erbes is the co-director of the Readiness and Resilience in National Guard Soldiers (RINGS) Project that studies National Guard Soldiers and their families before, during, and after wartime deployments. His research focuses particularly on interpersonal and environmental predictors of resilience following combat deployments, including intimate relationship and occupational correlates of post-deployment post-traumatic stress symptoms.

Hannah Fairman is a Health Policy Analyst with the Wounded Warrior Project (WWP), a national veterans' service organization dedicated to empowering those wounded in Iraq and Afghanistan. In that capacity, she does research and policy development for WWP's Washington, DC Office of Policy and Government Affairs. Previously, she worked as project coordinator for the Readiness and Resilience in National Guard Soldiers (RINGS) Project at the Minneapolis VA Health Care System in the Center for Chronic Disease Outcomes Research (CCDOR). Ms. Fairman's research interests focus on identifying gaps and barriers to effective mental health care for veterans and their families.

Deniz Fikretoglu, Ph.D., is a clinical psychologist with expertise in military mental health. Currently a Defence Scientist with Defence Research and Development Canada, Dr. Fikretoglu's research focuses on barriers to mental health service use in active military and veteran populations. Dr. Fikretoglu's program of research has been funded by Veterans Affairs Canada, the Department of National Defense, and the Canadian Institutes of Health Research. Her publications have appeared in the *Canadian Journal of Psychiatry*, the *Journal of Traumatic Stress*, and *Medical Care*.

Cathy A. Flynn, Ph.D., is a Senior Program Analyst with the Office of the Secretary of Defense in Military Community & Family Policy. For the past 8 years, Dr. Flynn has worked to bridge research needs and policy development within the Department of Defense (DoD). Her current portfolio includes evaluation development for community and family programs. Prior to coming to the DoD, she was a Senior Research Associate at the Center for Families at Purdue University and research faculty in the Department of Psychology at Loyola University in Chicago. Dr. Flynn received her doctoral degree in Human Development & Social Policy from Northwestern University.

Tanja Frančišković, M.D., Ph.D., has been working in the field of psychotrauma for the last 25 years. Author of numerous scientific articles on traumatic stress she has divided her attention between war veterans and the influence of combat related PTSD on the family. As the head of Department of psychiatry and psychological medicine, School of Medicine, University of Rijeka, she has been involved in educating many generations of future medical and mental health professionals and has authored several textbooks in psychiatry. She is a psychotherapist, educator, and supervisor in group analysis.

Melissa M. Franks, Ph.D., Department of Human Development and Family Studies, Purdue University. Her research on aging families emphasizes marital processes in the day-to-day management of chronic illness. A central feature of Dr. Franks' research on families is her attention to the dyad. Together with her colleagues, she investigates married partners' daily health lifestyle choices and marital interactions, and examines the association of their interactions with their physical health and psychological well-being. Dr. Franks' work demonstrates that exchanges of support between married partners are bidirectional, with each partner attempting to provide aid to promote the health and well-being of the other.

Greta Friedemann-Sánchez, Ph.D., is Associate Professor at the Humphrey School of Public Affairs, University of Minnesota in Minneapolis, MN, USA. She teaches in the International Development Practice and Public Policy programs. A medical and economic anthropologist, Friedemann-Sánchez is interested in women's empowerment and gender equity. Her research aims to understand how and why gender equity or inequity is generated inside of homes through the interlacing of family bargaining dynamics, policy, and cultural norms.

Abigail Gewirtz, Ph.D., L.P., is Associate Professor in the Department of Family Social Science and at the Institute of Child Development at the University of Minnesota. Her primary interests are in trauma, resilience, and promoting children's healthy development with two distinct but interrelated research foci: the impact of exposure to traumatic stressors on parenting and child functioning, and the development, testing, and widespread implementation of family-based interventions. Her studies include a National Institute of Drug Abuse-funded randomized controlled trial to evaluate a web-enhanced parenting program for families with parents returning from deployment to Iraq and Afghanistan (R01DA030114, Gewirtz, PI).

Lisa Gorman, Ph.D., is Program Director of Systems Reform at Michigan Public Health Institute (MPHI). She received her Ph.D. in Family & Child Ecology from Michigan State University. Dr. Gorman works collaboratively with families, public health, universities, policy makers, and other community partners including the National Guard on innovative solutions to improve health outcomes and quality of life for families who face chronic health conditions. Prior to joining MPHI, she worked for Michigan National Guard Family Program office and has been involved in the conceptualization, implementation and evaluation of several programs that promote resilience in military families.

Marshall J. Graney, Ph.D., is a sociologist and statistician with specialty in epidemiology of aging, multiple regression analysis and gerontological caregiving. He is Professor Emeritus, Division of Biostatistics and Epidemiology, Department of Preventive Medicine, at the University of Tennessee Health Science Center and a Statistical Consultant to the Caregiver Center at the Memphis VA Medical Center. Since retirement he has continued to work with the VA Medical Center on their national caregiver programs.

Amy Gravely, M.S., is a statistician in the Center for Chronic Disease Outcomes Research at the Minneapolis Veterans Affairs Health Care System in Minneapolis, MN, USA. Ms. Gravely provides statistical consulting and analysis services for research projects and assists with the interpretation of research findings.

Candice Grayton, M.P.H., is a Senior Research Analyst at the CDM Group; she brings numerous years of experience in health-related research, including performance measurement, evaluation, public health, epidemiological, social sciences and survey research. She works on projects funded by Federal government agencies including DOD, HHS, USDA, and the Department of Education. Most of her research experience has focused on child health and development and she currently manages the daily operations of 7-year longitudinal study of the health behaviors of 2,700 teenagers and young adults. Ms. Grayton is also responsible for creating and delivering the SAS datasets and conducting descriptive analyses.

Joan M. Griffin, Ph.D., is a research investigator in Center for Chronic Disease Outcomes Research at the Minneapolis Veterans Affairs Health Care System and Associate Professor in the Department of Medicine at the University of Minnesota's Medical School, Minneapolis, MN, USA. Dr. Griffin is a social scientist with expertise in using mixed methods to study the impact of paid and unpaid work, including caregiving, on health and family functioning. She also studies how social determinants of health, including health literacy, affect health and health behavior.

Jenny M. Hoobler, Ph.D., is Associate Professor of Management and Director of the Center for Human Resource Management at University of Illinois at Chicago, where she has been on faculty for 8 years. Her research interests focus on gender and diversity in the workplace, leadership behaviors, and work and family. She spent the 2011–2012 academic year on a Fulbright research award, studying women's representation in leadership positions in South African corporations. She currently serves on the editorial boards of four major management journals. She and her husband Ryan live with their dog, Indie, in Chicago's Little Italy.

Linda Hughes-Kirchubel, B.A., is a marketing and communication specialist for the Military Family Research Institute (MFRI) at Purdue University. There, she helps to advance MFRI's mission through development and execution of strategic traditional and digital publications for diverse audiences. Previously, she worked as journalist in California and Indiana, winning state and national recognition for investigative and editorial work. She is currently completing her master's degree Purdue University's Brian Lamb School of Communication, where her research focuses on intersections between organizational narratives, career narratives and the media. She also studies marginalized individuals' resistance of hegemonic forces through use of social media.

Chris Jarman is a doctoral student at Michigan State University's Department of Human Development and Family Studies, where he studies Couple and Family Therapy. He is currently involved in research focusing on resiliency among military soldiers and their family members. Prior to entering MSU, he was involved with research at the United State Department of Veterans Affairs and the University of Michigan. He is a licensed social worker and practices at the MSU Couple and Family Therapy Clinic.

Agnes C. Jensen, B.S., is a Study Coordinator in the Center for Chronic Disease Outcomes Research at the Minneapolis Veterans Affairs Health Care System, Minneapolis, MN, USA. Ms. Jensen is a Veteran, graduating from the US Naval Academy with a degree in economics, and served as a Naval Officer at sea, deploying throughout the Pacific and Indian Oceans.

Alexandria K. Johnson graduated from the University of St. Thomas (St. Paul, MN) with a B.A. in Psychology and Spanish. She then spent 2 years at the Minneapolis

VA Health Care System as a research assistant with the Readiness and Resilience in National Guard Soldiers (RINGS) Project, studying factors that contribute to resilience among National Guard soldiers. She is currently a graduate student in the Clinical Psychology Doctoral Program at the University of Alabama.

Michelle Kees, Ph.D., is a Clinical Assistant Professor in Child and Adolescent Psychiatry in the Department of Psychiatry. She received her PhD in Clinical Psychology at SUNY Stony Brook and completed a postdoctoral fellowship at the Center on Child Abuse & Neglect at the University of Oklahoma Health Sciences Center. Her research interests center on risk and resiliency in military families, parenting during adverse circumstances, intervention development and evaluation, and community dissemination of effective treatments for children and families. Clinically, she specializes in treating childhood anxiety and trauma, parenting guidance, and behavior management in young children.

Miro Klarić, M.D., Ph.D., has graduated from School of Medicine in 1976 and specialized in Neuropsychiatry in 1991. He earned master's degree in 2005, and PhD in 2008 both based on research on psychological consequences of chronic war stress on women. Since 1994 he has been working at Clinical Hospital Mostar, Psychiatric Department where he held the position of Head of the Clinic from 2003 to 2011. Since 2009 he holds the position of assistant professor at the Mostar School of Medicine and is currently assistant director of the Clinical Hospital Mostar.

Meredith Kleykamp, Ph.D., is an Assistant Professor of Sociology at the University of Maryland. Her research examines how institutional memberships, especially military service, pattern labor force outcomes and how these institutional influences vary by racial, ethnic, class, and gender lines. Funded in part by the National Science Foundation, her research investigates how and why military service affects post-military employment over time.

Leanne K. Knobloch, Ph.D., is an associate professor in the Department of Communication at the University of Illinois. Her research addresses how people communicate during transitions, particularly how military families navigate deployment and reintegration. Her scholarship has received the Gerald R. Miller Award Early Career Achievement Award from the International Association for Relationship Research (2008), the Franklin H. Knower Article Award from the Interpersonal Communication Division of the National Communication Association (2011), the Biennial Article Award from the International Association for Relationship Research (2012), and the Golden Anniversary Monograph Award from the National Communication Association (2012).

Mark Kramer, Ph.D., is the project manager for the Readiness and Resilience in National Guard Soldiers (RINGS) Project at the Minneapolis VA Health Care System. Following completion of his PhD in the Clinical Science and Psychopathology Research Program at the University of Minnesota, Dr. Kramer conducted post-doctoral research with Dr. Christopher Patrick. His research interests include the relationship between personality and psychopathology, psychometrics, and dispositional and environmental contributions to the sequelae of trauma.

Mary Jo Larson, Ph.D., M.P.A., is a Senior Scientist in the Institute for Behavioral Health at the Heller School for Social Policy and Management, Brandeis University. She is directing studies funded by the National Institute on Drug Abuse and the Department of Defense related to improving the delivery of behavioral health services for military members and their families and has expertise in topics related to health care utilization and costs, access to care, and outcome measurement. Dr. Larson was a member of the Institute of Medicine committee which issued in 2012 the widely-cited report, *Substance Use Disorders in the U.S. Armed Forces.*

Laura Lorenz, Ph.D., M.Ed., is a Senior Research Associate and Lecturer in the Institute for Behavioral Health, Heller School for Social Policy and Management, Brandeis University. She works on projects funded by the National Institute on Drug Abuse and Department of Defense related to improving the delivery of behavioral health services for military members and their families. Her areas of interest include health policy, harm reduction, lived experience with chronic conditions such as brain injury, and translation of research findings to community interventions and continuing education.

Shelley MacDermid Wadsworth, M.B.A., Ph.D., is a professor of Human Development and Family Studies at Purdue University and an associate dean of the College of Health and Human Sciences. She has more than 10 years of experience studying and working with military family programs and policies across all branches, in active and reserve components. Dr. MacDermid Wadsworth is a fellow of the National Council on Family Relations, a member of the Defense Health Board's Psychological Health External Advisory Committee, and of the Institute of Medicine's Committee on Returning Veterans. She also holds an MBA, and is a certified family life educator.

Jennifer Martindale-Adams, Ed.D., is a counselor, gerontologist and health services researcher at the Memphis VA Medical Center and Assistant Professor, University of Tennessee Health Science Center. She is the Co-Director of the Caregiver Center at the Memphis VA Medical Center. As part of VA's national caregiver program, the Center provides training to VA staff across the country to work with dementia, SCI and TBI caregivers and with spouses of Veterans. She is an investigator for two Army Randomized Clinical Trials to develop supportive interventions for spouse caregivers of deployed and post deployed military personnel.

Donald R. McCreary, Ph.D., is a Defence Scientist with Defence Research and Development Canada, as well as an Adjunct Professor of Psychology at Brock University, an Adjunct Research Professor of Psychology at Carleton University, and a Fellow of the American Psychological Association. His research is in the area of occupational health psychology and focuses on the impact of job-related stress on health and well-being. He has conducted research on psychological resilience, job-related burnout, the stress-health relationship, stress among police officers, and psychological adaptation among people working in High Arctic posts.

Patricia E. Miller, M.A., N.C.C., is a Research Specialist at the Memphis VA Medical Center and the University of Tennessee Preventive Medicine department. She is a nationally certified mental health counselor whose professional experience includes work with traumatic brain injury and post traumatic stress disorder survivors and family members. Patricia has provided group facilitation and research in the areas of dementia, traumatic brain injury, post deployed reintegration and deployment transitions for spouses of Veterans and service members nationwide. She is currently training and coaching VA staff nationwide in the Spouse Telephone Support program as part of the Caregiver Center at the Memphis VAMC.

Beth A. Mohr, M.S., is a Biostatistician in the Institute for Behavioral Health, Heller School for Social Policy and Management, Brandeis University. Her current work includes studying treatment for mental health and substance problems in military service members returning from combat. She also analyzes data for a study about screening for substance abuse problems in primary care. Prior to Brandeis, Ms. Mohr worked as a Biostatistician for a variety of epidemiologic studies and clinical trials. Her interests include military health, mental illness, trauma, and analysis of observational data.

Sidra Montgomery received her B.A. in Sociology from Beloit College. She is currently a doctoral candidate in Sociology at the University of Maryland, College Park. Her primary research interests are military families, military spouses, veterans, and identity. Her master's research focused on an analysis of factors related to military spouses' embracement of the traditional military spouse role. Her dissertation focuses on the rise of "wounded warrior" as a socially constructed category, examining the social meaning of "wounded warrior" and the impact this socially constructed category has on wounded OEF/OIF veterans.

Grady F. Murphy graduated from Purdue University with a degree in Youth, Adult, and Family Services (B.S.) and a minor in Psychology. There, his research centered on the interaction between spousal relationships and health outcomes. Since graduation, he has worked providing humanitarian disaster relief with the American Red Cross. His experience involves several major relief efforts including responses to the 2011 Spring Tornadoes, and more recently, Superstorm Sandy. Grady's current focus is building whole community resiliency by forming partnerships across the private, public, and non-governmental sectors.

Linda Olivia Nichols, Ph.D., a medical anthropologist, is a health services researcher at the Memphis Veterans Affairs Medical Center and Professor, Preventive and Internal Medicine, University of Tennessee Health Science Center. She is the Co-Director of the Caregiver Center at the Memphis VA Medical Center. As part of VA's national caregiver program, the Center provides training to VA staff across the country to work with dementia, SCI and TBI caregivers and with spouses of Veterans.

Ramona Faith Oswald, Ph.D., is professor of Family Studies in the Department of Human and Community Development at the University of Illinois Urbana-Champaign. She has served as Director of Graduate Programs for her department since 2004 and teaches courses on gender, sexuality, and research methods. Her research focuses on how sexual minorities navigate social, legal, and residential contexts and the effects that those contexts have upon their health and well-being. Dr. Oswald has received the *Anselm Strauss Award for Qualitative Research* (twice) as well as the *Jessie Bernard Award for Feminist Research*, both given by the National Council on Family Relations.

Jennifer M. Peach, Ph.D., received her Ph.D. in Social Psychology from the University of Waterloo in 2010 and conducted a post-doctoral fellowship at Defence Research Development Canada's Toronto lab in 2011. She recently joined the Canadian Department of National Defence as a Defence Scientist, and is working in the Organizational Behavior team for Director General Military Personnel Research and Analysis. Her areas of research have included attitudes, automatic thinking, and group influences on behavior. She currently administers the biannual Your-Say survey.

Sean M. Phelan, Ph.D., M.P.H., is an Assistant Professor in the Department of Family Medicine and Community Health at the University of Minnesota's Medical School in Minneapolis, MN, USA. Dr. Phelan's research focuses on the effect of stigma on health and health behavior, and includes how stigma associated with having polytrauma/traumatic brain injury affects patient community integration and how stigma associated with caregiving affects caregiver strain.

Melissa A. Polunsy, Ph.D., is a staff psychologist at the Minneapolis VA Health Care System and Core Investigator in the Center for Chronic Disease Outcomes Research (CCDOR), a VA Health Services Research & Development Center of Excellence. Dr. Polusny holds a joint appointment as Associate Professor in the Department of Psychiatry at the University of Minnesota Medical School. She directs the Readiness and Resilience in National Guard Soldiers (RINGS) Project. Her research interests focus on the longitudinal study of military personnel and their families, including the identification of individual and contextual risk factors associated with PTSD and post-deployment mental health.

David S. Riggs, Ph.D., is the Executive Director of the Center for Deployment Psychology (CDP) and Research Associate Professor at the Uniformed Services University of the Health Sciences (USU). Prior to taking the position with the CDP, Dr. Riggs held clinical research positions at the Center for the Treatment and Study of Anxiety at the University of Pennsylvania and the National Center for PTSD at the Boston VA Medical Center. As a clinical and research psychologist, much of Dr. Riggs' work has focused on trauma, violence, and anxiety with a particular interest in PTSD and its impact on families. As CDP Executive Director, he oversees the development and delivery of training seminars to behavioral health professionals preparing them to provide for the needs of warriors and their families.

Amber J. Seidel, Ph.D., is a research associate with the Center on Aging and the Life at Purdue University. However, she soon will be an assistant professor in the Department of Human Development and Family Studies at Penn State York. Her research focuses on how family experiences, individual characteristics, and health behaviors are linked to couples' experiences and well-being within the context of chronic stressor such as a chronic illness or military deployment. Dr. Seidel is a member of the National Council on Family Relations and is a certified family life educator.

Jim Spira, Ph.D., serves as Director of the Pacific Island Division of the National Center for PTSD. He received his PhD with emphasis in Clinical Health Psychology from UC Berkeley. He completed a Postdoctoral Fellowship in the Department of Psychiatry and Behavioral Sciences at Stanford and a Research Fellowship in Neurology at Scripps in La Jolla. Dr. Spira's research focuses on preventing and treating the wounds of war, including assessment and treatment of mild traumatic brain injury, prevention of PTSD through stress inoculation training, innovative treatments for PTSD including virtual reality exposure therapy and home-based telemental health, and polytrauma treatment.

Martina M. Sternberg, M.Ed., Ph.D., is a nationally certified counselor. She is the assistant director of the Military Family Research Institute at Purdue University and teaches masters level counseling courses at Capella University. She retired from the United States Air Force after serving 20 years and is the mother of a combat veteran. Her interests include GLBT and homeless veteran issues.

Aleksandra Stevanović is a psychology graduate from Faculty of philosophy, University of Rijeka. Clinical work with victims of war-related and civil trauma led her to specialize in clinical psychology. For the last 10 years she devoted herself to several research studies in the field of war related trauma, PTSD, and family, and has published several scientific papers. Apart from her scientific work, she enjoys teaching in the undergraduate programs of School of medicine, University of Rijeka. She is currently involved in gestalt psychotherapy education.

Brent Taylor, Ph.D., is a research investigator and methodologist/biostatistician in the Center for Chronic Disease Outcomes Research at the Minneapolis Veterans Affairs Health Care System and Assistant Professor in the Department of Medicine at University of Minnesota Medical School and in the Division of Epidemiology and Community Health at the University of Minnesota's School of Public Health, Minneapolis, MN, USA. He has extensive experience and expertise in the design and statistical analysis of observation and randomized studies.

Jennifer A. Theiss, Ph.D., is an associate professor in the Department of Communication at Rutgers University. Her research focuses on the role of interpersonal communication in the development and maintenance of romantic relationships, marriages, and families. Her work has advanced the relational turbulence model of romantic relationship development, which she has applied to examine how partners employ interpersonal communication to manage the transition to serious involvement in dating relationships, the transition from deployment to reintegration for military couples, the transition to parenthood for married couples, and the transition to the empty-nest phase of marriage.

Mark Tucker is part-time faculty with the department of Administration, Rehabilitation, and Post-secondary education at San Diego State University (SDSU). He is also a project manager with the Interwork Institute at SDSU where he is engaged in a variety of needs assessment, training and program evaluation activities focused upon disability, education and employment. A certified rehabilitation counselor, he holds a master's degree in rehabilitation counseling from San Diego State University and a doctorate in human rehabilitation from the University of Northern Colorado.

Marcia Valenstein, M.D., is a Professor in the Department of Psychiatry at the University of Michigan and a senior research scientist at the VA Health Services Research and Development service and the Serious Mental Illness Treatment Research and Evaluation Center. She has extensive clinical experience treating veterans in the VA health system. She is a national expert on peer-to-peer programs and was a key member in the collaborative team that conceptualized and implemented the Buddy-to-Buddy program in the Michigan National Guard. Her areas of research focus are medication adherence, depression management strategies, quality of depression care and suicide.

Courtney Harold Van Houtven, Ph.D., is a Research Scientist in Health Services Research and Development in the Center for Health Services Research in Primary Care, Durham VA Medical Center and Associate Professor in the Division of General Internal Medicine, Department of Medicine, Duke University Medical Center, Durham, NC, USA. Dr. Van Houtven's aging and economics research interests encompass how family caregiving affects health care utilization, expenditures, health and wealth outcomes of care recipients and caregivers.

Kathryn Wilder-Schaaf, Ph.D., L.C.P., is a rehabilitation psychologist with the Polytrauma Rehabilitation Center at McGuire Veterans Affairs Medical Center (VAMC) in Richmond, VA, USA. Her research interests include the use of family systems based intervention to both improve patient/caregiver outcomes in rehabilitation settings. She received her M.S. in Marital and Family Therapy from the University of Maryland, PhD in Counseling Psychology from Virginia Commonwealth University (VCU), and completed a postdoctoral fellowship in Neuropsychology and Rehabilitation Psychology at VCU. During her clinical internship at the Minneapolis VAMC, Dr. Wilder Schaaf collaborated with the Family and Caregiver Experiences Study team.

Thomas V. Williams, Ph.D., M.S., is Director, Methods, Measures, Analyses, TRICARE Management Activity. He is responsible for the development of information needed to guide evidence-based decision making and studies that are designed to improve the financing and delivery of healthcare services in the Military Health System. Dr Williams has previously served as an officer in a variety of leadership roles in the U.S. Army Medical Department.

Jeffrey Zuber, M.A., is a Masters level marriage and family counselor. He counseled with adolescents, adults, and families, and performed assessments with caregivers of dementia patients. He is currently a Research Specialist with the University of Tennessee Health Science Center and the Memphis Veterans Affairs Medical Center. He performs data management and analysis for two randomized clinical trials and three caregiver programs that are part of the Caregiver Center at the Memphis VAMC.

Index

S. MacDermid Wadsworth and D.S. Riggs (eds.), *Military Deployment and its
Consequences for Families*, Risk and Resilience in Military and Veteran Families,
DOI 10.1007/978-1-4614-8712-8, © Springer Science+Business Media New York 2014

Printed by Printforce, the Netherlands